HIGH CHURCHMANSHIP IN THE CHURCH OF ENGLAND

HIGH CHURCHMANSHIP IN THE CHURCH OF ENGLAND

From the Sixteenth Century to the late Twentieth Century

Kenneth Hylson-Smith

T&T CLARK
EDINBURGH
1993 ·

T&T CLARK LTD
59 GEORGE STREET
EDINBURGH
EH2 2LQ, SCOTLAND

First Published 1993

ISBN 0 567 09623 8 (HB)
ISBN 0 567 29248 7 (PB)

British Library Cataloguing-in-Publication Data
A Catalogue record for this book is available
from the British Library

Typeset by Trinity Typesetting, Edinburgh
Printed and bound in Great Britain by Bookcraft, Avon

Contents

Preface

Remarkably, there is no book covering the history of the High Church tradition in the Church of England from the Reformation to the late twentieth century; and this is a gap which is widely recognised as needing to be filled. Much work has been done, and much written, especially during the last twenty years, on aspects of High Churchmanship, or on specific, often quite limited, periods of its history, but no attempt has been made to bring together the large number of books, articles and unpublished theses in order to construct a comprehensive chronological account of High Churchmanship in England throughout the last four hundred years, covering beliefs, trends, events, personal biographies, continuities and changes, and relationships with the social, political, constitutional and economic history of the nation.

One of the fruits of undertaking a task such as this is to experience the generosity, kindness and assistance of other people. I wish to make special mention of the library staff of the Bodleian Library and the Oxford Theology Faculty Library; Mrs Patricia Whitehead of the University of Oxford administration; the authors of various unpublished theses (who are acknowledged at the appropriate places in the text), and especially Dr Peter Nockles who, in addition to his magnificent Oxford D.Phil. thesis to which so many authors are indebted and which is shortly to be the basis for a published book, has given the present writer the benefit of his comments on a number of matters in the course of informal conversations; the anonymous publisher's reader who made most useful criticisms and observations about a manuscript which was even more inadequate than the final product; Dr Philip Hillyer, who not only provided a superb index but gave the author greatly appreciated advice and help on other matters; and, finally,

Dr Geoffrey Green and his staff at T & T Clark who have always been courteous and encouraging.

Introduction

It is arguable that there is a continuous, distinguishable High Church tradition in the Church of England throughout the period from the Reformation to the late twentieth century. Such a tradition may be seen in embryo, ill-defined and imprecise, in the Elizabethan era. It was made more explicit by Richard Hooker and Richard Field, and given expression in the life and works of Lancelot Andrewes. It was amplified theologically by the Caroline divines and exemplified in the career and writings of William Laud and the Laudians. It found poetic form with John Donne, Richard Crashaw and George Herbert, and a focus for its spirituality in the life of Nicholas Ferrar and the Little Gidding Community; was continued after the Restoration by conformists like Francis Atterbury and Nonjurors such as Bishop Ken; was perpetuated in the eighteenth century by laymen, including William Law, clerics such as Joseph Butler and Samuel Horsley and groups such as the Hutchinsonians; was reinvigorated by the Hackney Phalanx; sprang into new and energetic life with the Oxford movement; was modified and enlarged in its theological content by the Liberal Catholics, and in its social thinking and concern by the Christian Socialists and the Anglo-Catholic slum priests; attracted much attention and opposition with the so-called ritualists; assumed a new dimension with heroic overseas missionary work and ecumenical initiatives especially in the late nineteenth century and early twentieth century; grappled with the tasks and issues raised by two world wars; burst into new but short-lived life with the inter-World War Anglo-Catholic Congresses, creative theological thinking and movements for social reform; and subsequently experienced six decades of varying fortune but overall decline.

But this identification of an historical thread can be challenged. It may be claimed that all the individuals, groups and movements from the sixteenth century to the present day to which reference has been made, as well as a host of others associated with 'High Churchmanship', were not participating in a continuous process and a single evolving Christian tradition, but were rather responding to the peculiar circumstances confronting them in their day: that they each had their own distinctive beliefs, patterns of behaviour and characteristics, and were not united with other preceding or succeeding individuals, groups and movements by anything more than an identity perceived in hindsight. They may have contained elements upon which later individuals or groups focussed and which they imitated, but this does not necessarily mean that there was a coherent High Church tradition, or any sense of historical continuity among either the participants or observers. Even after the Oxford movement, when such awareness was increased, there were, as we will see, various and sometimes strong currents and cross currents, divisions and antagonisms, which may cause doubt about the identity or oneness of such a tradition.

Certainly, prior to the Restoration, 'High Churchmanship' was largely a response to Puritanism on the one hand and Roman Catholicism on the other. It was, to this extent, a defensive upholding of a *via media*, a sort of Church of England middle ground consensus, without having such a definite form and content as either Puritanism or Roman Catholicism. Puritanism to a certain extent, but more especially Roman Catholicism, had very clear beliefs, codes of practice, systems of authority, structures and organisation. High Churchmanship lacked all of these marks of a fairly clearly defined tradition and school of thought, and was undoubtedly somewhat imprecise, unstructured and unselfconscious. It has in fact been asserted that the term 'High Church Party' 'was not used in an ecclesiastical sense until the last years of the seventeenth century, and the party so described was not sufficiently distinguished from the rest of the Church of

England to require a name until that time'.[1] Although this may be true, those we have already named had in common their stress upon certain selected aspects of the total Christian tradition and they were especially concerned to preserve Catholic continuity. By the end of the seventeenth century, the word 'High' was beginning to acquire a more specific connotation. In a private letter of 1695 it is stated that, 'he is set up for a High Churchman. He bows at going into the Chapel, and at the name of Jesus: he obliges his family to a great strictness in prayers: lets his chaplain say grace: and seems to mind little in his family more than that they strictly conform to the Church services and ceremonies.'[2]

Throughout the latter part of the seventeenth century and into the eighteenth century High Churchmen were characterised by their opposition to Latitudinarianism, and by their alliance with Toryism against Whig and nonconformist assertions. But again, it can be asked if this constituted a definite movement or party within the Church which can be identified as part of a tradition. Likewise, the faith and religious life of Law, Butler, Horsley and others can well be depicted as essentially central Anglicanism and not distinctively High Church; and Hutchinsonianism can be viewed as a rather bizarre and isolated phenomenon – hardly a constituent part of a developing tradition.

It is of note that a more definable, recognisable, continuous, albeit varied High Church tradition can be traced largely from the end of the eighteenth and beginning of the nineteenth

---

[1.] For a discussion of the meaning of the terms, see Peter Nockles, 'Continuity and Change in Anglican High Churchmanship 1792–1850', Oxford University D.Phil thesis, 1982 (a work to which the present comments are greatly indebted, and which has made a major contribution to the study of High Churchmanship in the period it covers), and also G.W.O. Addleshaw, *The High Church Tradition* (1941), George Every, *The High Church Party 1688–1718* (London, 1956), W.R. Fryer, 'The High Churchmen of the Earlier Seventeenth Century' in *Renaissance and Modern Studies* (Nottingham, 1961) and F.L. Cross and E.A. Livingstone (Eds.), *Oxford Dictionary of the Christian Church* (2nd ed., Oxford, 1983), article 'High Churchmen', p. 647.

[2.] William Wake to Arthur Charlett, 15 August 1695, quoted in George Every, *op.cit.*, p.1.

century, just at the time when the Evangelicals started to coalesce into a distinctive body with their own development through to the present day.[3] The Evangelicals had their pre-history in the Reformers of the sixteenth century and the Puritans, but they only emerged as a continuous modern movement in the second quarter of the eighteenth century, and largely remained as scattered individuals until towards the end of that century.

Perhaps there are good historical and sociological reasons why both movements achieved a large measure of identity and continuity at this time. A number of conditions need to be met if a tradition, whether it be 'religious' or 'secular', is to become established and to grow. A considerable number of people need to become aware of distinctive shared beliefs and practices which are of immense importance to them, and which set them apart from others. Outsiders need to identify the group as the special guardian of these particular beliefs and practices. There needs to be some organ for the dissemination of the distinctive beliefs and practices both among those who identify themselves with 'the cause', and among the population in general. By this and other means the enthusiasm of the 'interest group' needs to be sustained at a high level. It is important to have charismatic leaders who focus in themselves the issues at stake, provide an inspired example to the adherents of the tradition concerned, and concentrate in themselves something of the energy and crusading zeal which are indispensable if the tradition is to maintain momentum. If the tradition is to be long-lived, and not to be a movement of enthusiasm which evaporates after a short period, it requires organisational structures and funding. If the 'interest group' is to be more than a temporary phenomenon and to be transformed into a movement, and the movement into a tradition, the matters of central concern need to be perceived not only as of a high order of importance but as of fundamental and permanent significance tied, in

---

[3] See Kenneth Hylson-Smith, *Evangelicals in the Church of England 1734–1984* (Edinburgh, 1989).

the case of religious traditions, into what is regarded as ontologically essential. It adds greatly to the force of a tradition if the participants in that tradition see themselves as the champions of a necessary divine purpose, and the sense of crusading zeal is heightened if there is suffering and even martyrdom. A tradition is gradually reinforced by the noble and heroic lives of some of its chosen members. Sagas of personal and corporate sacrificial service, records of great endeavours and victories won, and a history of cherished ideals upheld in the face of fierce resistance all help to build up a tradition. It is at this point that history is of importance to a tradition, for it serves as a resource. It helps to legitimate the current stance and gives the adherents of the evolving tradition a perspective for understanding their present beliefs and practices. It gives a consciousness of entering into a precious and hardly-earned heritage of which they are stewards in their own day and generation. How does all this apply to the late eighteenth and early nineteenth century High Churchmanship ?

High Churchmanship and Evangelicalism assumed their more definite forms as distinct traditions within the Church of England at the height of the industrial and agricultural revolutions, when urbanisation was rampant, social structures were being transformed, masses of the population were being uprooted, and there was a widespread alienation from religion. In such a prolonged, irreversible process traditional Christianity, which was associated with a stable, largely rural, social order, came under great threat; not necessarily a threat to its survival, although there were those who would gladly have hailed its demise, but rather a threat to the continuance of the Church of England as an institutional expression of Christianity. And in such a situation as this it was those manifestations of the faith which offered a clear set of values and beliefs, and a faith and ideals which were demanding and worth living and dying for, which most appealed, and which most fully met the need of the hour. In desperate times, when so many people were wrestling with traumatic stresses and changes in their personal, family and community lives, and felt vulnerable and threatened, only a faith which

proffered a life-transforming, life-enhancing source of
personal power and strength, and a noble cause worthy of
personal commitment and dedication was of sufficient
attraction to elicit widespread response, and to make its mark
in the community. In secular society there was the teaching
of Locke and the liberty, equality and fraternity of the French
Revolution, the Radicalism of Paine and Bentham, the early
experiments in unionism, the extension of higher education
with the founding of King's College, London, University
College, London and Durham University, and the extension
of political rights, as with the abolition of the Test and
Corporation Acts in 1828, the Catholic Emancipation Act of
1829 and the Reform Act of 1832. In the Church of England
a refuge from the trials and tribulations of the day, and the
offer of salvation and purpose amid the chaos and confusion
was supremely to be found in either Evangelicalism or High
Churchmanship: both groups in their different ways knew
what they believed, what they had to offer and what they
wanted to achieve, and they set clear goals before their
followers. The Evangelicals may have appealed in the main
to the beleagured lower middle and middle classes and the
High Churchmen more to the middle and upper middle class
intellectuals, but both were able to meet deeply felt needs
in a way that was not possible for any other strand of
Churchmanship.

During the late eighteenth and early nineteenth century
both Evangelicals and High Churchmen developed more
effective organisational structures, organs of communication
and means of bonding their followers together than had ever
been achieved by them, or perhaps any other Church of
England groups, in the past. For the Evangelicals the Clapham
Sect, the Church Missionary Society, the British and Foreign
Bible Society, and such newspapers and periodicals as the
Christian Observer and the *Record* were means whereby identity
was firmly established and fellow believers were harnessed and
motivated for action. For the High Church the parallel
development was achieved through the agency of the Hackney
Phalanx, the Society for Promoting Christian Knowledge, the
Society for the Propagation of the Gospel, the *Tracts for the*

Times and such publications as the *British Critic.*

In the Church of England since the Reformation four main strands can be identified: the Evangelicals, represented prior to the eighteenth century by the Puritans, the High Churchmen, the Liberals and Radicals and the Broad Churchmen. There are dangers in any such neat classification, for there have always been many, and often a majority of Churchmen who cannot be clearly assigned to any of these traditions because they combine elements from more than one of them. But such a typology provides one useful model for the interpretation of history. Allowing for the fact that the proportion of Churchmen in each category or combination of categories varies from one time to another, the composition of the Church of England can be represented diagrammatically as follows:

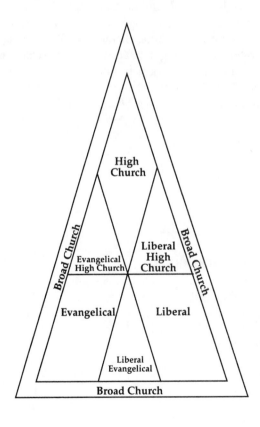

In this model the more pronounced, uncompromising, 'pure' representatives of each tradition can be located in the middle of their particular block. Those who are less clearly identified by themselves and others as belonging solely to one tradition will be located within the block which represents their dominant allegiance but more towards that part of the block which ajoins the other tradition by which they are further influenced. Those who are equally aligned with two of the main traditions, or perhaps more accurately with a tradition of its own which attempts to incorporate the best from two or more of the main traditions, will be located in the block which is appropriately designated.

In presenting such a model the shortcomings, and indeed tendentiousness, of theological geometry are appreciated. And it certainly needs to be recognised that it is difficult in the extreme to define a tradition which changes and grows with its own awareness of itself, and varies both in its character and in its relationship to other traditions from one generation to another. What can be hoped for in such a work as the present history is not so much a precise definition of terms, for this in itself can be somewhat arid, but a voyage of discovery in which diverse and rich treasures are to be found.

PART 1

Reformation to Restoration

1

The Elizabethan and Jacobean Seedbed

By the time of the accession of Elizabeth I in 1558, England had already suffered from thirty years of religious upheaval, change and discord. The nation was still officially a Roman Catholic country in communion with the see of Rome, but there was a long tradition of dissent from Roman Catholicism stretching back to Wyclif and the Lollards. And there were the recent traumatic experiences of the Henrician reforms and acts of state, the short-lived Protestantism under Edward VI and the martyrdoms during the reign of Mary. The 'complex of ideas described by the word "Anglican" did not exist in the Elizabethan church, any more than the word did'.[1] The early Elizabethan church was 'an enforced coalition of contrary religious traditions and tendencies, crudely distinguishable as very protestant, not-so-protestant and crypto-papist'.[2] Even by the end of the sixteenth century England was by no means a thorough-going Protestant country with distinctive Protestant beliefs and a Protestant ethic having been adopted by a majority of the people, let alone the entire population. It is perhaps not surprising that one of the consistent themes in the life and reign of Elizabeth was the

[1] Conrad Russell, *The Causes of the English Civil War* (Oxford, 1990), p.84.
[2] Patrick Collinson, *Archbishop Grindal 1519–1583. The Struggle for a Reformed Church* (London, 1979), p.167.

unremitting search for means whereby the church and the nation could be bound together in unity.[3]

Puritanism,[4] although ill-defined and taking various forms, in general represented that body of people who regarded the Reformation in England as incomplete, and who wished to purify the Church still further in a 'Protestant' direction. Those who worked from within the church looked for reform by constitutional means, 'tarrying for the magistrate'. Among such 'conformists' there was a radical element, headed by Thomas Cartwright and John Field, which demanded the replacement of the episcopate by the presbyterian form of church government. Those who sought reform 'without tarrying for any' included Robert Browne and the Brownists, Henry Barrow, John Greenwood and John Penry. They believed in the right of the individual Christian to interpret the Bible for himself, and the right of Christians to join together as 'the gathered church' in local, autonomous

---

[3] For general histories of the church in the reign of Elizabeth I see Claire Cross, *Church and People 1450–1660. The Triumph of the Laity in the English Church* (1976), A.G. Dickens, *The English Reformation* (1964), Susan Doran and Christopher Durston, *Princes, Pastors and People. The Church and Religion in England 1529–1689* (London and New York, 1991), David L. Edwards, *Christian England* (Vol.2) *From the Reformation to the Eighteenth Century* (1983), W.H. Frere, *The English Church in the Reigns of Elizabeth and James I (1558 – 1625)* (London, 1904), James Gairdner, *A History of the English Church in the Sixteenth Century from the Accession of Henry VIII to the Death of Mary* (London, 1903), John Guy, *Tudor England* (Oxford, 1988), David Loades, *Revolution in Religion: The English Reformation 1530–1570* (Cardiff, 1992), Diarmaid MacCulloch, *The Later Reformation in England 1547–1603* (London, 1990), Maurice Powicke, *The Reformation in England* (London, 1941) and James A. Williamson, *The Tudor Age* (London, 1979). See also Bernard M.G. Reardon, *Religious Thought in the Reformation* (London, 1981) and H.R. McAdoo, *The Spirit of Anglicanism* (1965).

[4] For accounts and comments on Elizabethan Puritanism see especially Patrick Collinson, *The Elizabethan Puritan Movement* (London, 1967), Patrick Collinson, *The Religion of Protestants. The Church in English Society 1559–1625* (Oxford, 1982), Everett H. Emerson, *English Puritanism from John Hooper to John Milton* (Durham North Carolina, 1968), M.M. Knappen, *Tudor Puritanism. A Chapter in the History of Idealism* (1939; Gloucester, Mass, 1963), Patrick McGrath, *Papists and Puritans under Elizabeth I* (London, 1967) and Michael Watts, *The Dissenters. From the Reformation to the French Revolution* (Oxford, 1978).

congregations, unmolested by the magistrate. These Separatists wanted to be free of the Anglican, and indeed Presbyterian, hierarchy, to be rid of conformity, and to exercise what they claimed as their privilege to worship freely according to their own wishes.

But within the Elizabethan church there were also those who challenged the Puritan demand for further reformation, opposed the Calvinism which characterised not only the Puritans but also the English church as a whole, and championed some features of the pre-Reformation 'Catholic' church. Among such were Anthony Corro, William Barrett, Peter Baro, Richard Hooker, Bishops Richard Cheyney of Gloucester and Edmund Guest of Rochester, John Overall of Norwich and Samuel Harsnett, Archbishop of York. To this list may be added two lay members of Parliament, Francis Alford and James Dalton. Although not a very impressive group, with the notable exception of Hooker, they were part of a small, perhaps lonely, submerged band which stressed the sacraments rather than preaching, the authority of the clergy and the belief that religious matters should be settled by the clergy, and which rejected continental forms of Protestantism. They, and others of like mind, were concerned to uphold the notion of continuity in the history of the church, and to maintain all the elements of what they regarded as true Catholicity. They may be reckoned as representatives of a nascent sixteenth century High Church tradition. Perhaps to their number should be added three Archbishops of Canterbury, Matthew Parker, John Whitgift and Richard Bancroft who each, in different ways, tried to retain links with the 'Catholic' past, and strove to preserve the 1559 settlement from further changes.

The Canons of 1604, which incorporated the medieval law of the Church and the advertisements and injunctions issued since 1559, also helped in such preservation. Of the 141 Canons, some regulated worship and the administration of the sacraments, while some dealt with the procedures of ecclesiastical courts or anathematized dissent of various kinds. The clergy were to subscribe without qualification to the royal supremacy, the Thirty-Nine Articles and the Book of Common

Prayer. Parliament refused its assent to the Canons, but the king approved them and Archbishop Bancroft did what he could by dint of admonition and persuasion to obtain the required subscription from the majority of the clergy.

Those in the Church of England who took a 'Catholic' view were hampered not only by the widespread Calvinistic Protestantism in the church but by the increasing unpopularity of Roman Catholicism. Whether the establishment of the Church of England is interpreted as primarily a series of political acts or as a movement in opposition to the abuses, doctrinal accretions and international pretentions of the Roman Church, for most Englishmen of the Elizabethan era Roman Catholicism was a menace. It was a threat to the still immature and vulnerable national church, and in its political and secular form it hazarded the very existence of the country itself. In 1570 Pope Pius V, in the bull *Regnans in Excelsis,* pronounced the Queen to be excommunicated and deposed, and her subjects released from their oaths of allegiance to her. In so doing he not only reinforced the prevailing anti-Roman hostility, but made the position of English Roman Catholics almost intolerable, for they had to choose between loyalty to the English crown and loyalty to the Apostolic See. Romanism as a form of English separatism had begun formally to exist and to be almost inevitably identified with treason.[5] The attempted invasion of the Spanish Armada gave military expression to an aggressive Roman Catholicism, but its rebuff did not finally end the danger, or remove the threat from both within the country and abroad.

No mention has yet been made of John Jewel. Although Jewel (1522–71) was greatly influenced by Peter Martyr, and became one of the intellectual leaders of the reforming party, his teaching may, in certain respects, be considered as

[5] For Roman Catholicism in the reign of Elizabeth I and James I, see especially J.C.H. Aveling, *The Handle and the Axe. The Catholic Recusants in England from Reformation to Emancipation* (1976), John Bossy, *The English Catholic Community 1570–1850* and Patrick McGrath, *op.cit.*

contributing to a 'Catholic' tradition. During the Marian persecution he recanted in terror, and signed an anti-Protestant declaration. Subsequently he fled to Frankfurt in 1555 and confessed his fault before the congregation. His exile brought him into close touch with some of the reformers, and he returned, imbued with their spirit, to participate in the Westminster disputation and assist in the drawing up of a Protestant confession of faith. But, with his scholarship and wide knowledge of antiquity, he maintained his independence of view and, for instance, opposed John Knox and the advanced Calvinists. In 1560 he was appointed Bishop of Salisbury, and he became a strong supporter of the Anglican settlement. He was hostile to Roman Catholicism, and although sympathetic to Geneva he took his stand only on such assertions as could be justified by reference to the double standard of the Scriptures and the doctrine of the primitive Church, as expressed by the authoritative councils and the teaching of the Fathers of the first six centuries.

In 1562 Jewel embodied his beliefs in a defence of the Church of England entitled *Apologia Ecclesiae Anglicanae.* It was a masterpiece of terseness and cogency. In it he endeavoured to prove that general reformation had been necessary. No charge of heresy could be proved against the English Church, as it only made what were considered necessary changes within its competence, which were consistent with a Catholic position. Jewel wrote of the Roman Church: 'We truly have renounced that church wherein we could neither have the word of God sincerely taught nor the sacraments rightly administered, nor the name of God duly called upon.'[6] Nevertheless, he declared that the English church 'would be willing to yield to Rome all the honour Irenaeus gave her if she would return to the doctrine and traditions of the apostles'.[7] He accepted that the Reformers did not labour to

---

[6] Parker Society edition of the works of the English Reformers. III, pp.91f., quoted in Paul Avis, *Anglicanism and the Christian Church. Theological Resources in Historical Perspective* (Edinburgh, 1989), p.23. This chapter is greatly indebted to the work by Avis.

[7] Parker Society, *op.cit.*, I, p.365, quoted in Paul Avis, *op.cit.*, p.25.

create a new church but to reform the old. It was a theme echoed by Whitgift who taught that the church was reformed and not transformed. Jewel emphasised that the Reformers departed from Rome because of its errors and its false doctrine, rather than because of the unholy lives of its leaders. The catholicity of the English Church is secured by virtue of its retention of Catholic doctrine. It was truly catholic and apostolic because it maintained the catholic and apostolic belief at a time when the Roman Church had departed from its true catholicity and apostolicity. Jewel's method of defence was to 'show it plain that God's holy gospel, the ancient bishops, and the primitive Church do make on our side, and that we have not without just cause left these men, or rather have returned to the apostles and old catholic fathers'.[8] He rebutted accusations of sectarianism and antinomianism, attacked the abuses of the Church of Rome and found many of its customs wanting when weighed against the beliefs and practices of antiquity. He asserted that reform by such a body as the Council of Trent was impossible, and that local churches had the right to legislate through provincial synods. *Apologia Ecclesiae Anglicanae* immediately established itself as the best defence of the Anglican claims. It provided 'the first thoroughgoing attempt to prove to the world the catholicity of English doctrine, to demonstrate that the teaching of the English church at no point departed from the church of the apostles and the fathers'.[9]

Divines such as Jewel and Whitgift also maintained a *via media* stance on such matters as episcopacy. Although they vehemently opposed the presbyterian challenge, they would not be provoked into an exaggerated counter claim for the divine right of bishops. They declared 'that, while scripture did not lay down any binding form of church government, episcopacy was an ancient, venerable form and was consonant with the teaching of scripture'. Despite the fact that Whitgift

[8] Quoted in W.H. Frere, *op.cit.*, p.91.

[9] W.M. Southgate, *John Jewel and the Problem of Doctrinal Authority* (Cambridge, Mass., 1962), quoted in Paul Avis, *op.cit.*, p.37.

held episcopacy to be 'apostolical and divine', he retorted, in answer to the taunts of Thomas Cartwright, that 'the notion of biblically prescribed divine-right polity was very popish'. Again, it was belief rather than structures which was important. 'The catholicity of the church for the English Reformers did not reside in the succession of its bishops but in continuity of true doctrine.'[10] The historic episcopate was championed by Jewel, Whitgift and others, but was not regarded as of the essence of the church or as a vital component of her catholicity. It, together with other features of the outward polity of the church, belonged to the sphere of adiaphora, things indifferent.

Richard Hooker and Lancelot Andrewes defined more precisely the shape and doctrine of the Church of England after the initial work of the Reformers and the Elizabethan settlement. It has been claimed that they were 'the founders of High churchmanship and probably its greatest glory',[11] for in the process of expounding the doctrinal basis of the Church of England, and by life as well as word setting forth the essential spirituality of the English Church, they explicitly built upon the apostles, the early Fathers and the whole Catholic inheritance, with Jesus Christ as the corner stone.

Richard Hooker (1554–1600)

Richard Hooker is possibly 'the greatest Anglican theologian',[12] and his name is perhaps 'more widely known than any other English theologian'.[13] It has also been asserted that he was 'the father of Anglo-Catholic theology',[14] and certainly many Anglican Catholics were later to regard him

[10] Paul Avis, *op. cit.*, p.34.

[11] G.W.O. Addleshaw, *The High Church Tradition* (London, 1941), p.24.

[12] Paul Avis, *op. cit.*, p.47.

[13] Francis Paget, *An Introduction to the Fifth Book of Hooker's Treatise of the Laws of Ecclesiastical Polity* (Oxford, 1899), p.1.

[14] L.S. Thornton, *Richard Hooker*, p.101, quoted in Paul Elmer More and Frank Leslie Cross (Eds.), *Anglicanism. The Thought and Practice of the Church of England Illustrated from the Religious Literature of the Seventeenth Century* (London, 1935), p.xix.

as such. He laid the foundation upon which the Caroline divines built, and they in their turn were an important part of the specific Church of England Catholic tradition. This remains true despite the fact that Hooker is a somewhat ambiguous figure, claimed by some Evangelicals as important in the Evangelical tradition, and, for example, by Thomas Arnold as a contributor to the Liberal tradition.

Hooker's reputation rests upon his monumental book of the *Laws of Ecclesiastical Polity*, published in 1594 and 1597. The work holds a conspicuous place in the history of English literature. It is of seminal importance as an apologia for Anglicanism and, from our point of view, of crucial importance as providing one of the foundation texts for the High Church tradition. In it Hooker presented the Church of England with its first systematically argued view of itself as a *via media* between two systems accused by Hooker of betraying traditional catholicity. Both Puritans and Roman Catholics are presented as sinning either by default or excess, and the English Church is portrayed as standing in the middle, preserving the Catholic faith from all corruptions. Although it was written as a defence against submission to Geneva, which, in his view, threatened to reduce the English Reformation to a mere imitation of radical Continental Protestantism, the finished product went far beyond any such intention. Here, for the first time in such an explicit and reasoned way, the Church of England was made aware of its status as a branch of the Church universal, neither Roman nor Calvinist, but at once Catholic and Protestant, with a positive doctrine and discipline of its own.

A brief sketch of the life of Hooker will help to place his work in context as a response to the Puritanism of his day. He was born in 1554, graduated at Corpus Christi College, Oxford, became a Fellow of his College and deputy professor of Hebrew. After a short period as Rector of Drayton Beauchamp, in 1585 he was appointed Master of the Temple, a post which he accepted reluctantly as his country parish, notwithstanding its drawbacks, was more congenial to him than a prominent place in London. Walter Travers, already Reader or afternoon preacher at the Temple, and an ardent

Puritan, had been a contender for the Mastership, and it was almost certain that they would be in conflict. From the start Hooker preached every Sunday morning, and Travers thought it necessary to correct the unsoundness in the Master's sermons when he preached in the afternoon. It was 'pure Canterbury in the morning and Geneva in the afternoon'. After about a year Travers was served with a notice from Whitgift, the Archbishop of Canterbury, forbidding him to preach any more.

Although Travers was silenced, the controversy was not, and it was his experience of controversy at the Temple which led Hooker to write his treatise. He wrote in no aggressive or vindictive spirit. Indeed, he greatly respected the learning and goodness of his opponent, and was puzzled and somewhat disquieted to find that what he profoundly believed and practised was judged by Travers to be corrupt and wrong. It was a challenge to him to re-examine the roots and the basis of his faith. He was not an able and effective preacher, and possibly realised this, but 'he had the knowledge and the power of work and the subtlety and penetration and patience of thought which should avail to make a strong case clear to able men', and 'he had that amplitude of view' which braced him 'for intellectual enterprise on a large scale'.[15]

The work was started while he was at the Temple, and the first four books were completed while he was incumbent of the country living of Boscombe near Salisbury. The fifth Book was finished while he was Rector of Bishopsbourne near Canterbury. He died in 1600, his self-appointed task completed. [16]

The first four books are concerned with the main Puritan principles, and with the principles and conceptions which Hooker set against them. The fifth Book deals with particular allegations of the Puritans against the existing order and ceremonial of the Church.

[15.] Francis Paget, *op.cit.*, p. 111.
[16.] The following summary is greatly indebted to Francis Paget, *op.cit.*

In the Preface Hooker sympathetically and brilliantly surveyed Calvin's work at Geneva, examined why Calvin's discipline was approved by many, including learned men, but pointed to some of its shortcomings and dangers. In the body of the work he declared two opinions 'repugnant unto truth'. On the one hand, the 'schools of Rome' taught 'Scripture to be so insufficient, as if, except traditions were added, it did not contain all revealed and supernatural truth, which absolutely is necessary for the children of men in this life to know that they may in the next be saved'. On the other hand, Puritanism taught that 'Scripture did not only contain all things in that kind necessary, but all things simply, and in such sort that to do any thing according to any other law were not only unnecessary but even opposite unto salvation, unlawful and sinful'.[17]

In the third Book, Hooker defined the unity of the visible body of the Church as consisting of that 'uniformity which all several persons thereunto belonging have by reason of that one Lord whose servants they all profess themselves, that one Faith which they all acknowledge, that one Baptism wherewith they are all initiated'.[18] If they had these marks of recognition they were part of the visible Church even if 'they be impious idolaters, wicked heretics, persons excommunicable, yea, and cast out for notorious improbity'.[19] This was bold and startling language, and some condemned it as making the Church so all-embracing as to lose meaning. But within the Church thus defined, Hooker made an important distinction. The visible Church can only be defined according to the judgement and for the purposes of this life by external, visible marks. However, its membership is divided between, on the one hand, those who are in full communion with the Church, who readily accept her discipline, believing sincerely all the articles of her faith, joining in her worship, nourished with the fullness of

---

[17.] Richard Hooker, *Of the Laws of Ecclesiastical Polity* (Everyman's Library Edition, 1907), Bk. 2, p.281.

[18.] Richard Hooker, *op.cit.*, Bk. 3, p.285.

[19.] Richard Hooker, *op.cit.*, Bk. 3, p.285.

her life and growing continually in her holiness, and, on the other hand, those who are, in varying degrees, unsound, defective and corrupt members.

Hooker then proceeded to the need for 'a difference of persons in the Church'. The clergy are those to whom 'the rest of God's people must be subject as teaching things that appertain to their soul's health'. They are 'necessary for the administration of the word and sacraments, prayers, spiritual censures, and the like'. Furthermore, 'order doth necessarily require that by degrees they be distinguished', and he held that there always had been and always should be at least 'two sorts of ecclesiastical persons, the one subordinate unto the other; as to the Apostles in the beginning and to the Bishop always since'. But while he held episcopacy in high esteem and considered it to have been ordained by God in the period of the church's infancy, he did not infer that it was therefore forever binding on the church, or that churches without episcopacy were invalidated. He maintained that 'the external government of the church is a thing indifferent or "accessory" to the essentials of the Christian faith, an area in which the church has the freedom to make changes to meet fresh circumstances'.[20]

In the fourth Book Hooker addressed himself to the Puritan assertion that the Anglican Church was corrupted with Popish orders, rites and ceremonies which had been banished from certain reformed churches, whose example the Church of England should have followed. Hooker responded with a clear and steady sense of the independence of the Church of England from both the Church of Rome and the reformed churches of the continent. It did not matter if the Church of England used some ceremonies in common with the Roman Church, for both churches shared a common heritage in the ancient Church. The Church of England had also taken its own course of reformation which was more moderate than the sometimes extreme and rigorous course taken elsewhere. Indeed, in this calm and temperate reformation Hooker

---

[20] Paul Avis, *op. cit.*, p.57.

discerned a special sign of God's guiding and restraining hand.

The fifth Book was longer than the Preface and the first four books combined, and it differed in character from them. In the former books Hooker had been concerned with the general tenets of Puritanism and the axioms by which the Puritans would like to see the controversy with the Church of England settled, and over against these he had argued for what he regarded as valid general principles in matters of ecclesiastical polity. In the fifth Book he dealt point by point with specific accusations concerning alleged superstitious Anglican practices, and unacceptable ecclesiastical functions, proceedings and observances. In attempting to meet the various Puritan objections, and in offering an Anglican apologia, Hooker frequently referred to former ages, and especially the early centuries of the Christian Church, but this was done in a pragmatic way, for he made it plain that, in his view, there was no question of antiquity and tradition legislating for all situations for all time. He 'clarifies the Anglican view of prescriptive authority in matters of doctrine and practice. He shows the proper place of scripture, reason and tradition, that famous "threefold cord not quickly broken" which was to become the hall mark of classical Anglicanism.'[21]

Hooker championed the Elizabethan settlement, and provided a theological *raison d'etre* for the Church of England as a whole. His book helped to stabilise the Church and gave it an authority which rested not only upon the Bible, the Prayer Book and the Articles, but upon the practice of the primitive Church. He was not self-consciously in any High Church or other tradition, neither was he perceived as being so by his contemporaries. He can only be 'located' within the Church of England in any 'party' sense in as far as he opposed the Puritan interpretation of Church polity, belief and practice, but he did this as representing mainstream Anglicanism, or Anglican orthodoxy. Much, but not all, of what he taught

[21] Paul Avis, *op.cit.*, p.63.

foreshadowed, or helped to determine the character of later High Church theology, and he was to be regarded by later High Churchmen as an exponent of High Church theology, but it is an unwarranted retrospective interpretation, and reading back into history what was not there at the time, if this is made to imply that either he or his fellow Anglicans in any way thought of themselves as protagonists for a distinctive 'Anglican Catholicism'. Although every book of the *Laws of Ecclesiastical Polity* is directed against some tenet of radical protestantism, it needs to be remembered that Hooker wrote less than forty years after the Elizabethan settlement, when the young Anglican Church was still in the process of seeking , defining and establishing its own identity. He helped to lay the foundations of Anglican ecclesiology, and to give it an explicit theological framework, and in so doing he provided future generations with an apologia for at least some of what were to become treasured High Church beliefs and practices.

But we must not concentrate our focus too narrowly upon the theological significance of Hooker, and loose the wider perspective which places him within the total national, and indeed international political and social scene. To a greater extent than might appear, the teaching of Hooker was, without his awareness of it, moulded by the political, social, economic and religious pre-history and current life of the country. Indeed, in certain respects it can be seen as a product of the historical process out of which it emerged. The whole separation of the English Church from Rome in the sixteenth century was part of the creation of a nation state, and the English reformed Church may be viewed in the first place as national, and an element in the forging of national identity. The English Church sought, like its predecessor, the *Ecclesia Anglicana* of the Middle Ages, to embrace all Christians within its ecclesiastical realm, and this included Christians who were of a very different way of thinking. Such a concept was both an expression and reflection of the nationalism which had been articulated politically in the Henrician acts of defiance against Rome and the Elizabethan stance for independence against Spain or any other foreign intruder. It was likewise an, albeit unconscious, identification with the newly emergent middle class traders, merchants, financiers, business men and other products of growth and prosperity in a country whose social structure was being rapidly and radically changed as a consequence of commercial expansion. Seen from this vantage point, the *Laws of Ecclesiastical Polity* gave to the English reformed Church, for the first time, a clear statement of its religious and philosophical basis, and made evident its status and dignity, within the new nation state, as a 'Church organisation with a type of its own, going its way without slavish submission to Rome, Geneva, or Wittenberg'.[22] In presenting the national state and the national church as identical, Hooker was attempting to create a sense of national unity in the face of what he regarded as one of the perversions of truth perpetrated by the Puritans, who 'separated State and Church as two corporations independent of each other...Hooker's work marks the end of the only period in the history of the nation, when the realisation of this high ideal of a Christian state, whose other name is Church, seemed still possible.'[23] The later High Churchmen who claimed descent from him frequently did not appreciate the historical context in which he wrote, and that his claim for the Church as part of a church-state entity arose out of a grander and more inclusive vision than theirs, and out of a religio-political situation which gave hope for the fulfilment of such a vision. But such a vision, and such potential for its realisation could not be re-created in future ages when the religio-political situation and philosophy was so different from that of the late sixteenth century. All that the later High Churchmen could do was to fit detached fragments of Hooker's building into their structures which rested on less expansive foundations.

In the seventeenth century, as we will see, divine right 'took the place of the constitutional rule to whose hands Hooker

---

[22] Yngve Brilioth, *The Anglican Revival. Studies in the Oxford Movement* (London, 1933), p.2. This paragraph owes much to this insightful and stimulating work.

[23] Yngve Brilioth, *op.cit.*, pp.2, 3.

entrusted the direction of the Church'.[24] The Restoration, with its Act of Uniformity, produced a more constricted Anglicanism than that of Hooker, or even Laud. But there emerged a definite type of Anglican piety which, with its humanistic theology, leaning towards the Church of the Greek Fathers, ascetic ideal of holiness and vein of mysticism, was of a decidedly Catholic temper.

Hooker is therefore not part of a continuous, unbroken, ever-developing and growing or consistent High Church tradition. Rather, he helped to provide, or reinforce, an Anglican consensus which was responsive to particular historical circumstances, and in doing this he provided teaching which has, with varying degrees of legitimacy, been drawn upon by Churchmen of different traditions, as well as by the Church of England as a whole. But given such qualifications, he is of considerable importance as a contributor to the whole corpus of High Church teaching and tradition.

Lancelot Andrewes (1555–1626)

Andrewes was a contemporary of Hooker, and his life thus embraced the same period in the growth of the English Church, when it wrestled with its identity as a *via media* between Rome and Geneva, although he survived until one year after Charles had begun his tragic reign, and thus witnessed the greater intensification of this process. He was born in 1555, the year when the Protestant martyrs suffered in the Marian persecution; he was a schoolboy when Elizabeth was excommunicated; at Cambridge he found himself in the midst of the Puritan ferment, and was involved in the predestination controversy; after his ordination he was engaged in disputation with both recusants and Separatists, and later became the leading apologist against Rome; he was present at the Hampton Court Conference; he was one of the translators

---

[24.] Yngve Brilioth, *op.cit.*, p.4.

of the Authorised Version of the Bible; and he contributed
to the new school of theology which was providing the Church
of England with a firm theological basis. By example and by
teaching he stressed the need for order in public worship,
a high conception of episcopacy and the divine right of kings.[25]

Andrewes entered Pembroke Hall, Cambridge, in 1571, and
there laid the foundation of his renowned great learning, and
especially his knowledge of languages, of which in later life
he was reputed to know Latin, Greek, Hebrew, Chaldee, Syriac,
Arabic and fifteen modern languages. Although he was
influenced by the prevailing strong Puritanism at the
University, the only distinctive Puritan view which he retained
was the doctrine of Sabbatical observance. Conversely, he was
not a pronounced Arminian. He rejected the Calvinist
doctrine of predestination, but he was not concerned to
liberalize the dogma of salvation. Rather, he concentrated
his efforts on vindicating the visible Church, the authority
of episcopacy, and the validity of rites and ceremonies.

In 1576 Andrewes was elected a Fellow of Pembroke. In
1589 he was appointed Vicar of St Giles Cripplegate, an
expanding suburban parish with a population of about four
thousand, and in the same year he succeeded W. Fulke, a
prominent Puritan theologian, as Master of Pembroke Hall.
His incumbency of Cripplegate was attached to a prebend
at St Paul's, where his remarkable preaching abilities first
attracted notice. The main burden of the day-to-day running
of the parish was carried by his curate, but Andrewes was also
actively engaged as chaplain both to Archbishop Whitgift and
to Queen Elizabeth, and, from 1589, he additionally held a
stall at Southwell.

In 1601, at the age of forty-six, he became Dean of
Westminster. In 1605 he was elected Bishop of Chichester,
and from then until the end of the reign of James I he reached
the height of his career as a Court Preacher, preaching at
Court on almost all the Great Festivals. He was the most
popular and admired preacher of the time, and there was

[25.] This paragraph, and indeed the whole section on the life of Andrewes, owes
much to Paul A. Welsby, *Lancelot Andrewes 1555–1626* (1964).

no greater admirer than the king himself. His sermons were well and prayerfully prepared, and thoroughly scriptural. He aimed not merely at the inculcation of morality, but proclaimed the great fundamental facts of the Christian religion and appealed for a response of penitence and faith from his hearers.

During the reign of James I Andrewes was further promoted to the see of Ely in 1609 and Winchester in 1619. In this remaining part of his life he was engaged in various national debates and controversies, sat on the commission which investigated the contentious issue of the Essex nullity suit, accompanied James I to Scotland in an attempt to persuade the Scots to accept episcopacy, and was deeply involved in general in the affairs of the country.

As far as can be ascertained, and judged by the standards of the day, Andrewes was reasonably competent as a diocesan bishop, but he was by no means outstanding. He resided and undertook visitations in his various diocese as often as most and more often than some. As we have seen, he was a brilliant preacher, and he brought to the various offices he held, learning, piety, and distinction as a theological controversialist. He was also a man of prayer, as shown, for instance, in his *Preces Privatae,* which became the most popular and widely read of all Anglican devotional works. S.R. Gardiner presents an attractive picture of him. 'Going in and out as he did amongst the frivolous and grasping courtiers who gathered round the King, he seemed to live in a peculiar atmosphere of holiness.'[26] He combined business acumen with high integrity in financial and other matters. He had a lovable and kind nature, and throughout his life he exhibited both an abstemious and austere manner of life and a great, yet unostentatious, charity and generosity to the poor. Yet, despite these attributes, it is questionable how far he regarded his diocesan work as his main task. Thus, for nineteen consecutive years he spent the two major Festivals of the Church, Christmas

---

[26.] S.R. Gardiner, *History of England, 1603–1644* (1883 edition), II, p.120.

and Easter, in London. He condemned pluralism, yet practised it himself, although he does not appear to have unduly sought preferment. He used Church patronage for the benefit of his family and the advancement of friends, but generally in a way which was to the benefit of the Church. He had a genuine pastoral concern, and yet, when London was beset with the plague he left his parish for a more healthy location. Also, judged by his sermons, it might be expected that he would speak out for truth and justice, and yet, on Commissions, in the Privy Council and the House of Lords, he was largely silent. It is not, however, as a diocesan, or indeed as a preacher that he is chiefly remembered, nor is it therein that his main significance in church history lies, but rather is it to be found in his contribution to the clarification, codifying and exposition of the theological teaching of the Church of England.

'Andrewes was one of the principle influences in the formation of a distinctive Anglican theology, which, in reaction from the rigidity of Puritanism, should be reasonable in outlook and Catholic in tone.'[27] The school of theology of which he was the founder and invigorator followed in the wake of Jewel and Hooker. He and those who laboured with him worked out in detail the application of the foundation principles of the Reformation. They saw, perhaps as the earlier reformers had not been so well able to see, some of the implications of the appeal to Scripture, the relevance of past experience to the life of the Church of their day, and, more especially, what was involved in the precedents set by the primitive and undivided Church. They recovered a more Catholic theology, and united that with the recovery of decency and order in public worship, and some approximation to the standard of external ceremonial and ornament which had been set up at the beginning of Elizabeth's reign but had never been attained.

[27.] F.L. Cross and E.A. Livingstone (Eds.), *Oxford Dictionary of the Christian Church* (2nd ed., Oxford, 1983), p.52, to which the account of the life of Andrewes is greatly indebted.

Andrewes built his theology on sound learning. In addition to his remarkable proficiency in languages, he had an encyclopaedic knowledge of the Greek and Latin classics, of the Fathers – both Eastern and Western – of the ancient Church and of the Canonists and the Schoolmen. It was a learning which was not primarily original, but it gave him a wide frame of reference in considering theological matters, and a deep appreciation of tradition in the interpretation of the Scriptures. He had a high view of episcopacy, regarding bishops as successors of the Apostles, and of the ordained ministry in general, holding, for example, that the power of absolution was left not to the whole body of Christians, but to the Apostles as ministers, priests and preachers, 'and consequently to those that in that office and function do succeed them, to whom and by whom the commission is still continued'.[28] Nevertheless, despite his belief that bishops were of divine right, he taught that this did not entail any condemnation of those churches which because of necessity have no bishops.

He had a high doctrine of the Eucharist, emphasising the real presence of Christ in the sacrament, and stressing that in the sacrament we receive the true body and blood of Christ. He constantly used sacrificial language to describe the rite, and declared that the Church of England held fast to the essential Catholic conception of the Eucharist as a sacrifice. He wanted the Church of England to express its worship in decent and ordered ceremonial, and in his own chapel he used the mixed chalice, incense and altar lights. It seemed natural to Andrewes and others of his reverent type of mind, that the three low bows with which the courtier approached the king should be used by the celebrant, aware as he was of the presence of God at the Holy Table. Other ceremonial enhancements were taken from the practice of the early Church or from the customs of the East, and were regarded at the time as less open to misunderstanding than old English

[28.] *Sermons*, V, pp.82ff., quoted in Paul A. Welsby, *op.cit.*, p.69.

or Western ceremonies. Thus there began the practice of turning to the East for the creed at the daily prayer and Eucharist and the use of the credence table. But, despite various innovations, old customs were not neglected: the use of copes and wafer-bread, the washing of the priest's hands before he prepared the elements, the mingling of water with wine in the chalice, and the use of incense were among the customs which were resuscitated or carefully preserved. It does not appear that with any of these matters Andrewes was a zealous introducer and propagator of high ceremonial, but the practices which he adopted in his own chapel more and more commended themselves to others and became the model for other cathedrals besides Winchester, and his modest and unobtrusive example exercised a great and widespread influence.

Andrewes has been described as 'the first great preacher of the English Catholic Church'.[29] What is most striking in his theology as depicted in his sermons is the extremely important place occupied by the Incarnation. To him it was the central, most revolutionary event in human history, for it inaugurated a new relationship between man and God. Andrewes consistently proclaimed the possibility that anyone could find eternal salvation, but only in and through the person of Christ, the God-man. In Christ this life can and should be experienced in the here and now. It is a foretaste of what is to come. Any human activity, private or public, should reflect the new reality inaugurated by the Incarnation, the union of humanity and divinity in Christ. Andrewes was spremely concerned with soteriology: his theology and preaching was Christocentric. But he also stressed the importance of the Holy Spirit as the one who authenticates the redemptive action of Christ. The Holy Spirit is a divine Person in the fullest sense, in total equality with the Father and the Son. And 'by conversion of heart, man is incorporated into the Body of Christ, which is the Church, and thus partakes

---

[29] Nicholas Lossky, *Lancelot Andrewes the Preacher (1555–1626). The Origins of the Mystical Theology of the Church of England* (Oxford, 1991), p. 326.

of the blessing of the divine-human union realised in Christ'.[30] For Andrewes, 'the revealed truths, the Holy Scriptures in particular, can only be interpreted in the Church, that is to say within the unity of the same Spirit who is the same throughout the ages, in accordance with all the confessors of the Catholic and Apostolic Faith'.[31] To the *via media* of the English Church, Andrewes, together, one must say, with others, and especially with Hooker, 'brought theological and historical enrichment, investing it with a positive apologia based on Scripture and the Fathers and delivering it from a predominantly negative defence against Rome or a too close alliance with Calvinism. He demonstrated the fact that Anglicanism had its own body of theology and its own historical continuity, and thus established its claim to be a true and real part of the Church Catholic of all ages.'[32] In doing so both Hooker and Andrewes helped to build something which was to endure. They provided future High Churchmen with a conceptual framework and point of reference which were to help in the construction of a tradition as yet in its infancy.

[30.] Nicholas Lossky, *op.cit.*, p.331.
[31.] Nicholas Lossky, *op.cit.*, p.334.
[32.] Paul A. Welsby, *op.cit.*, p.275.

2

Laud and Laudianism

The issues which dominated the thoughts, actions and writings of Jewel, Whitgift, Hooker and Andrewes in their opposition to Puritanism, took on a polarized political form in the years from 1625 to 1662. It was a time of crisis, in many ways as serious and significant as the Reformation in the history of the English Church, and at the eye of the storm was William Laud. This was the period of climacteric confrontation, in which 'the divergence between historic, traditional Christianity, with its creeds and its Episcopal system, and the new dogmas and disciplines which had been elaborated in Germany and Switzerland, and which were echoed from many English pulpits, was one which must eventually lead to open conflict'.[1] Laud championed the position which had been emphatically asserted by Andrewes. He believed in the essential Catholicity of the English Church, and in the divine right of episcopacy. He was able through the offices he held, and willing because of his belief in using power and authority to achieve his goals, to adopt a course of action which had not been possible for his predecessors. Laud, and Laudianism, united with the insensitive, assertive and single minded ambitions of Charles I, inevitably resulted in conflict, although few would have anticipated such a fearful and devastating outcome as the violence, divisiveness and trauma of the Civil War, the execution of Charles and Laud, the Protectorate, the Commonwealth and the Restoration.

[1.] William Holden Hutton, *The English Church from the Accession of Charles I to the Death of Anne (1625–1714)* (London, 1903), p.1.

William Laud was born at Reading in 1573, the only son of a Reading clothier. He matriculated as a Commoner of St John's College, Oxford, in 1589. As an undergraduate under the learned and devout tutorship of John Buckeridge, he established his academic work on the foundation of the fathers and councils, and boldly opposed the dominant Calvinism of the University. Together with Buckeridge and William Juxon, he helped to spread High Church doctrines, first in the college, which was somewhat liberal in its tradition, then in Oxford, and ultimately throughout England.

Laud was made a deacon in 1600, held a divinity lecturership in 1602 and in 1603 became a proctor and was appointed chaplain to the Earl of Devon. In that year he showed himself a strenuous opponent of the Millenary Petition presented to the new king by his Puritan subjects. In 1607 he was presented to the living of Stanford in Northamptonshire, to which was added in the following year the advowson of North Kilworth – exchanged for West Tilbury in 1609 and Cuckson in 1610. In 1608 he proceeded to his Doctorate of Divinity. He secured the patronage of Dr Richard Neile, Bishop of Rochester, who was to prove of immense help in his career. From Neile Laud received several of his preferments, and it was also through Neile that he came to the attention of the king.

In 1611 Laud was elected President of St John's. He was promptly plunged into theological controversy. His Catholic and anti-Puritan views aroused the ire of many, and especially Robert Abbott, Master of Balliol, the elder brother of the Archbishop of Canterbury and, from 1612 onwards, Regius Professor of Divinity. But by his force of character, his determination and his persistence he reinforced the College as the stronghold of Arminianism in Oxford. His wider influence was enhanced by his appointment as one of the king's chaplains. The period of Laud's connection with St John's also 'marks the rise of the college from a poor and struggling foundation, owing its presidents to the favour of Christ Church and its continued existence to almost chance benefactions, to a position of prominence, if not preponderance, in the University'.[2]

[2.] William Holden Hutton, *William Laud* (London, 1895), p.14, a book to which this chapter owes much.

Laud publicly demonstrated his ecclesiastical convictions and determination to introduce ecclesiastical, liturgical and disciplinary reform in his capacity as Dean of Gloucester, to which post he was appointed in 1616. He signalled his arrival by having the communion table removed from its former place in the body of the cathedral and fixed altarwise in the chancel, and by ordering those who entered the cathedral to bow to it. Such action was symptomatic of doctrinal belief: that the table was an altar, and the elements the body and blood of Christ, transmuted by the divine power delegated to the priest. The changes outraged the Bishop and caused a storm at the beginning of his deanery. But he remained Dean until he received the bishopric of St David's in 1621.

It was at this time that Laud was increasingly drawn into the political arena and into a web of politico-religious activity which was to characterise Laudianism with its emphasis upon what was considered to be the rightful coalition of church and state. For a few years George Abbot, as Archbishop of Canterbury, had largely directed the ecclesiastical policy of the government, but as his fortune waned, that of Laud rose. Abbot was being eclipsed by the rising of a new star, George Villiers, first Duke of Buckingham. As Laud gained his favour, he found the door to the highest positions in church and state open to him, and stepped in. 'If he sought power, it was not because he loved it for itself or any of the privileges, but because he wished to impose his ideal in church government, an ideal to which all else was with him subservient.'[3] Personal ambition was not important to him, wealth, splendour and status did not count, he did not delight in lavish pomp, and personal extravagance was anathema to him. He rather found beauty in austerity and rigorously regulated personal indulgence. He was, in certain respects, 'a fit minister for the austere pietist Charles I'.[4] King James distrusted Laud, but he was in decline, discredited by the

[3] H.R. Trevor-Roper, *Archbishop Laud 1573–1645* (2nd ed. London, 1965), p.53, a book to which this chapter is greatly indebted.

[4] H.R. Trevor-Roper, *op.cit.*, p.54.

failure of the Spanish match and the attempt to recover the Palatinate without recourse to war. Laud's arch enemy John Williams, Bishop of Lincoln and then Archbishop of York, had backed the king rather than Buckingham and Prince Charles, and in doing so had invested in the present rather than in the future. Laud pressed home his advantage and undermined his rival. In 1625 James I died. Buckingham applied to Laud for a list of clergy most eligible for promotion, and Laud responded with a list of names divided into two categories, headed respectively 'O' for orthodox or Arminian, and 'P' for Puritan or heterodox. Laud had started on that part of his career where he was embroiled in the political, social and economic, as well as the religious, life of the country. He was a prominent member of the court of a new king who had distinctive and strong political and religious opinions, and on whose favour he was to depend for his continued power and influence.

Charles I was prepared to defend the English church, as he viewed it, against Puritanism, and increasingly against a predominantly Puritan Parliament. His court continued to be crowded with Papists or crypto-Papists, while Puritans were distrusted and feared. Laud did not approve of all of the king's ideals, nor admire and approve of the many time-servers who surrounded the monarch. But it was essential that he should preserve his influence with the king and Buckingham if he was to retain and increase his authority, and his power to promote High Church beliefs and practices. If he was to be deprived of court favour he had no power of his own to fall back upon.

Laud was concerned to make the Church a great social institution, having independent power based on such 'material wealth as would make it an estate in the realm'.[5] He sought to recover the property of the Church which had been alienated during the reign of Henry VIII, and 'to secure it against a second dissolution by an emphatic declaration of its sacred character'.[6] He had a high view of the relationship

    [5] H.R. Trevor-Roper, *op.cit.*, p.95.
    [6] H.R. Trevor-Roper, *op.cit.*, p.96.

of church and state, and of the place of the Church in society. He wished to restore social harmony, social justice, social stability and communal responsibility by a restoration of the former rights of the Crown, of the people and of the Church even at the expense of material and intellectual progress. Such a grand design, such a stupendous task of reconstruction, was frequently carried out in a narrow, intolerant spirit and gradually gave way to destructive conservatism, but the ideal remained. It was a vision held by Laud and Lord Wentworth, but ranged against them were the strongest forces in the country, the pioneers of the remarkable Elizabethan and Jacobean material and intellectual revolution who united their zeal for progress and the achievement of personal ambition and wealth with a ruthless attack on the establishment and the rights and privileges of the Church, and who found in Puritanism a sanctification for their aims, and an ally in their cause. It was a clash of giants, and a titanic struggle was inevitable. In such a confrontation, the king frequently hindered Laud and Wentworth 'by his dilettantism, his selfishness, and his dependence on an irresponsible court'.[7]

In order to accomplish his master plan Laud saw the reformation of the Church as a top priority: it must be purified in doctrine, in discipline, in worship and in practice. His translation to the bishopric of London in 1628, and to the Archbishopric of Canterbury in 1633 gave him new and elevated platforms for influence and action, as did his election as Chancellor of Oxford University in 1629. Machinery already existed which merely needed to be re-activated. There were episcopal courts, the Star Chamber, the Council of the North and the Court of High Commission, and Laud revivified these, much to the annoyance of his opponents who, inarticulate at national level because of the dissolution of Parliament, could only proceed with local acts of sabotage such as churchwardens thwarting their vicars. From his seats of ecclesiastical and secular power, Laud so profoundly influenced church, state and education that their character

---

[7] H.R. Trevor-Roper, *op.cit.*, p.101.

was changed not only for the duration of his life, but for the rest of the century, despite the Puritan interlude, and indeed for centuries to come.

In church affairs, he first addressed himself to the reform of worship. He set forth the essence of his philosophy in the *Epistle Dedicatory* to his conference with the Jesuit, John Fisher:

> It is true, the inward worship of the heart is the great service of God, and no service acceptable without it; but the external worship of God in His Church is the great witness to the world, that our heart stands right in that service of God. Take this away, or bring it into contempt, and what light is there left 'to shine before men that they may see our devotion, and glorify our Father which is in Heaven'? And... these thoughts are they, and no other, which have made me labour so much as I have done for decency and an orderly settlement of the external worship of God in the Church; for of that which is inward there can be no witness among men nor no example for men. Now, no external action in the world can be uniform without some ceremonies; and these in religion, the ancienter they be the better, so they may fit time and place. Too many overburden the service of God, and too few leave it naked. And scarce anything hath hurt religion more in these broken times than an opinion in too many men, that because Rome hath thrust some unnecessary and many superstitious ceremonies upon the Church, therefore the Reformation must have none at all; not considering therewhile, that ceremonies are the hedge that fence the substance of religion from all the indignities which profaneness and sacrilege too commonly put upon it. And a great weakness it is, not to see the strength which ceremonies – things weak enough in themselves, God knows – add even to religion itself. [8]

[8.] William Laud, *Epistle Dedicatory* to his conference with Fisher, quoted in William Holden Hutton, *William Laud, op.cit.*, pp.69, 70.

It was in this spirit, and animated by a keen desire to restore the Church to its high estate, that Laud took steps, which he thought were urgently needed, to reinstate order and reverence in public worship. He organised the removal of altars to permanent positions at the east end of churches and cathedrals, not, at least primarily, because of a particular belief in the doctrine of the Real Presence and the Eucharistic Sacrifice, which he, like Andrewes, undoubtedly held, but practically because the permanent placing of the altar in the middle of the church tended to irreverence. In crowded churches the thoughtless laid their hats and coats on it, and it shared in the general neglect which a prevailing idea of the opposition between spiritual and external worship had engendered. Uniformity, and obedience to Church order also promoted reverence. Laud therefore insisted that all should receive the Holy Sacrament kneeling, and he enforced the custom in royal chapels and cathedrals, that worshippers should bow 'towards' the altar, but not 'to' the altar.

'To men who felt as the Puritans did, Laud's emphasis on ritual and ceremony, on 'the beauty of holiness', seemed little better than Popery.'[9] Throughout the 1630s Laud was acutely conscious of the popular accusation of popery levelled against him and his fellow 'High Church' bishops. But he spoke out more vociferously than any other councillor against conversions to Rome at court and within London, and even begged the king on his knees to expel the main proselytizers. Such opposition did not stem from personal anti-popery so much as a concern that such conversions would imply that the Anglican Church was seriously deficient as a true Church. He was anxious to show that the Church of England was a purer expression of catholicity than Rome.[10]

---

[9] Christopher Hill, *The Century of Revolution 1603–1714* (London, 1961), pp.79, 80. Julian Davies, *The Caroline Captivity of the Church. Charles I and the Remoulding of Anglicanism 1625–1641* (Oxford, 1992), pp.205-214, 218, 232, 245, 250, questions the extent to which Laud championed the re-siting of communion tables, and, more widely, the extent to which Charles rather than Laud promoted 'Laudianism'.

[10] These comments are based on Julian Davies, *op.cit.*, p.257.

Laud instituted visitations in all diocese of his province to help bring order, regularity and greater decorum to the worship and life of the parishes. He justified his encouragement of the use of the surplice, the cope at communions and consecrations, and other vestments in church services, as in keeping with the practices of historic Christianity. It was all part of his passion for a truly worshipping Church.

With this emphasis on the Church there was an accompanying higher evaluation of the two indelible marks of the visible church, the bishops and those whom they ordained. Also, as a consequence of the increased importance attached to the succession of grace, functions related to benediction received greater prominence: 'the consecration of the elements, the sign of the cross at baptism, the consecration of church structures and objects, the blessing after marriage and at the end of the service, the confirmation of the young, churching after childbirth, and hearing confession, and of course the ordination of priests and deacons'.[11]

Laud and the Puritans who were at loggerheads over his liturgical and other church reforms, were also at odds over his attitude to the lay use of Sunday. Charles I reissued his father's *Book of Sports,* and Laud was at one with him in denouncing sabbatarianism, and in commending such recreations as dancing, maypoles, ales and archery. The Puritans found this obnoxious, impious and unacceptable, for they wished to enforce strict restrictions on what was permissable on Sundays. The difference did not stem from disagreement about the need for the Church to be an aesthetic and austere body, but from a definition of the Church. To Laud and other High Churchmen it was a separate, visible body represented by the clergy who were a class quite distinct from the laity whom they guided and directed; whereas, to the Puritan, minister and congregation were all one, and the

---

[11.] Julian Davies, *op.cit.*, p.54.

aestheticism which the Catholic Anglican confined to the clergy, was, by the Puritan, demanded of all the godly.[12]

In his conflict with the Puritans Laud used the full rigour of the law and its accompanying punishments againts such Puritan nonconformists as William Prynne, Henry Burton and John Bastwick. These and others suffered the indignity of the pillory, the agony of having their ears cropped or removed, and the extended suffering of imprisonment in the foul prisons of that age. They were to exact their full retribution with the execution of both Charles I and Laud. Laud has been especially criticised for the way he used the Star Chamber, but he viewed actions by that daunting body as a means of penalising expressions of opinion which were subversive of the social order; his attitude towards those who were judged offenders was not personal or vindictive. It was all of one piece with his conservatism, and with his consistent policy in church and state of upholding tradition and order, and fostering religious and social stability.

Laud had a deep love of learning and longed to see learned clergy in the parishes of the land. He advanced learning largely by his lifelong support of Oxford University, and St John's College in particular. He was a most generous benefactor to his own college, and provided innumerable books and manuscripts for its library, including some magnificent, rare, beautifully bound folios, valuable copies of the classical authors, and exquisite Oriental works. He also donated over one thousand three hundred manuscripts in twelve languages, and five cabinets of coins, to the Bodleian Library. Despite all the pressures and demands made upon him, and in the midst of mutifarious interests and activities, he always retained his close connection with Oxford. As Chancellor, he was responsible for much new building which transformed St John's College, including the completion of Canterbury Quadrangle, perhaps the most beautiful quadrangle in Oxford, was an active and effective patron of learning and

---

[12.] This analysis is based on H.R. Trevor-Roper, *op.cit.*, pp.155, 156.

culture, codified the statutes, and established the lasting influence of the Church in the life of the University.

By 1636 Laud was at the zenith of his career. He had monopolised moral and spiritual authority in church and state, and had developed an impressive power base. But his position was at best precarious, and at worse untenable. In general, he had the backing of Charles I, of Wentworth, and later of Stafford, but there were few others who offered support. His political base was not as sound, and he did not have the reserves of power which were available to the opposition. He was also the victim of a political dilemma: he could only thrive, and indeed survive, as long as the unquestioned rule by the sovereign was in force, and yet 'the more precarious this rule became, the more deeply was Laud committed to its defence, even when it openly violated the principles which he was proclaiming'. [13] It was at the root of Laud's political creed to accept the constitution as he found it, and to serve the monarch with unreserved loyalty and devotion, but this did not make him blind to the failings of the government or the personal weaknesses of the king.

Laud's life and work, especially as Archbishop, was entwined in the tumultuous and fraught political history of his day, the details of which are too complex to describe and analyse in such a work as this. As his fate was bound up with that of Charles I, so the decline of the king meant the decline of the Archbishop. As the power struggle intensified and more and more embittered the feelings of the combatants, and as his enemies and detractors gained the ascendency, his defeat became almost inevitable. But he continued to conduct himself with dignity, and remained true to his principles. 'To the end, amid the wildest terrors of alarmed Protestantism, and when, between the intrigues of the court, the weakness of the King, and the fierce attacks of his adversaries, it was difficult indeed to keep a clear head and a brave heart, he steered an even course. Rome could not lure nor could Geneva affright him. His heart stood fast, for he believed in the Divine

---

[13] H.R. Trevor-Roper, *op.cit.*, pp.297, 298.

mission which God had given to the English Church.'[14] His trial was his triumph, for he displayed a self-control which was worthy of a Christian about to die; and he met his death with an impressive calmness and fortitude. On the scaffold he knelt down and prayed:

> Lord, I am coming as fast as I can: I know I must pass through the shadow of death before I can come to Thee; but it is but *umbra mortis,* a mere shadow of death, a little darkness upon nature: but Thou, by Thy merits and passion, hast broken through the jaws of death. The Lord receive my soul, and have mercy upon me, and bless this kingdom with peace and plenty, and with brotherly love and charity, that there may not be this effusion of Christian blood among them, for Jesus Christ His sake, if it be Thy will.

There followed a moment more in silent prayer, and then he said, 'Lord receive my soul',[15] and all was over.

'I die as I have lived', Laud declared, 'in the true orthodox profession of the Catholic faith of Christ, foreshadowed by the prophets and preached to the world by Christ Himself, His blessed Apostles and their successors; and a true member of His Catholic Church, within the communion of a living part thereof, the present Church of England, as it stands established by law.'[16]

The Church of England in general, and Anglican Catholicism in particular, has for two hundred and fifty years looked back to Laud as an example in faith and conduct of that Churchmanship which emphasises catholicity: continuity with and descent from Christ and his Apostles; the central importance in the life of the Church of episcopacy; a deep concern that the worship of the Church should be of prime importance in the life of the Church, and should be conducted

---

[14.] William Holden Hutton, *William Laud, op. cit.,* p.160.

[15.] Quoted in William Holden Hutton, *William Laud, op.cit.,* p.223.

[16.] Quoted in William Holden Hutton, *William Laud, op.cit.,* p.236.

with reverence and awe; a focus on the altar, in churches furnished and adorned in such a way as to enhance the beauty of holiness and stimulate worship; the centrality of the sacraments, and a doctrine of the Eucharist which stresses the presence of Christ, but which admits of neither the transubstantiation of Roman theology nor of the consubstantiation of Luther; and an affirmation of the English Church as part of the historic Church, joined still, in spite of outward division, by the one Catholic faith.

English Arminianism

Laud's significance may also be seen in the context of the rise of English Arminianism. By the end of the sixteenth century Calvinism was the dominant theology of the Church of England. The Arminians were a very small minority. There were some clerical dissidents who did not accept predestinarian theology. Indeed it was their disputes in Cambridge in the 1590s which led Whitgift to draft the Lambeth Articles. And there were those who had begun to give a new emphasis to the sacraments as a counter-balance to the quite widespread stress on sermons in the Church's worship. There were also a few erudite clergy, and most notably Richard Bancroft, the future Archbishop of Canterbury, who elaborated the theory that episcopacy had been ordained by God and constituted for all time a necessary requriement for a true church. The first public, national, challenge to Calvinism came at the Hampton Court Conference of 1604; and by the second decade of the seventeenth century there were sufficient Arminian clergy to make up a party, with Richard Neile at its head, and including Andrewes, John Overall and John Buckeridge. They did not consider the time was ripe for their views to be fully expressed in print, but they did show their beliefs in action, as when Neile went as Bishop of Durham in 1617 and promptly converted the holy table in the Cathedral into an altar. The Synod of Dort, 1618-19, helped to deepen the divisions and polarise the parties within the Church of England, and thereby also helped to weaken the consensus which had characterised the Elizabethan and Jacobean Church.[17]

By the time Charles I came to the throne in 1625 the Arminian influence was pronounced at court, in the Church and in the universities. Charles made no attempt to disguise his religious preferences. For example, contrary to the advice of Archbishop Abbot against furthering the ambition and career of Richard Montagu, in 1625 Charles created him a royal chaplain. In 1624 Montagu had published *A New Gag for an Old Goose* which was followed by *Appello Caesarem*. They seemed to minimize the differences between the Church of England and Roman Catholicism. They caused such alarm that two Calvinist peers, the earl of Warwick and Viscount Saye and Sele, called a theological debate at York House, the London residence of the Duke of Buckingham, in 1626. At this Conference Charles reaffirmed his preferences by very explicitly endorcing the Arminians who themselves went to fresh lengths to show that the Prayer Book could be used to modify the Calvinism which had, for generations, been assumed to be contained in the Articles. Buckingham, who had previously been all things to all men theologically, seeing the way the wind from the throne was blowing, began to lean decisively against the Calvinists.

By 1628 leading Arminians were holding some of the key English bishoprics. Neile had gone from Durham to Winchester and was translated to York in 1632. Montagu was Bishop of Chichester and Francis White was at Norwich. By the 1630s Matthew Wren succeeded White and then in 1635 moved to Ely, Walter Curle became Bishop of Winchester and Augustine Lindsell Bishop of Peterborough. Yet the Laudians never achieved an absolute dominance over the episcopate.

But it was the decision of Charles to dispense with parliament in 1629 which ushered in a decade when 'the anti-

---

[17.] For the Synod of Dort and its relevance to the English theological and Church scene, see Nicholas Tyacke, *Anti-Calvinists. The Rise of English Arminianism c1590–1640* (Oxford, 1987), ch.4.

Calvinist party became considerable both for power and for number'.[18] The term Arminian has commonly been used to describe this body of anti-Calvinist opinion, but it does not mean that the Dutch theologian Jacobus Arminius was normally the source of the ideas so labelled. 'Arminianism itself can plausibly be understood as part of a more widespread philosophical scepticism, engendered by way of reaction to the dogmatic certainties of the sixteenth-century Reformation.'[19] There was a coherent body of anti-Calvinist religious thought which was gaining ground in various regions of early seventeenth-century Europe. In England, although the Arminians asserted the orthodoxy of free will and universal grace, they also stressed the hierarchical nature of both church and state against the incipient egalitarianism of Calvinism. With all their concern to purvey a gospel of hope, in which salvation was the potential lot of everyone, 'the English Arminian mode, as it emerged during the 1630s, was that of communal and ritualized worship rather than an individual response to preaching or Bible reading'.[20] The basis of this was the English Prayer Book, and the English Arminians built on the Prayer Book in their elaboration of a pattern of church life.

Laud's policy tied him, and the Laudianism of which he was the prime author and executive, to a particular political system, partly by accident and partly by design. Laudianism was in fact 'Arminianism as part of the new Caroline synthesis of religion and politics',[21] and it alarmed the political classes to such an extent that it drove them, ultimately, to revolt. It was under Charles I that Arminianism became monarchical, and the initiative for this came from Charles himself. Charles was somewhat quixotic, with a cavalier attitude to canonical authority. He was unpredictable and, although he in general

---

[18] Peter Heylyn, *Historia Quinqa-Articularis*, iii, p.110, quoted in Nicholas Tyacke, *op.cit.*, p.181.

[19] Nicholas Tyacke, *op.cit.*, p.245. See also H.R. Trevor-Roper, *Religion, the Reformation and Social Change* (1967), pp.193-236.

[20] Nicholas Tyacke, *op.cit.*, p.246.

[21] H.R. Trevor-Roper, *Catholics, Anglicans and Puritanss* (1987) p.114.

supported Laud, such support was not dependable, and on occasions he gave only lukewarm endorsement to Laud's policies. The Royal Instructions of 1629 reveal something of his attitude to ecclesiastical matters. They constituted a radical, if rather disorganised programme to subordinate the pulpit to the liturgy and to uproot nonconformity within the Church. They also indicate his decision to resort to more authoritarian modes of control after the dissolution of Parliament, and they reveal his dictatorial tendency. He wanted the restoration of strong, conciliar government under the law, and his 'sense of order and decorum, his aestheticism, his whole concept of culture, led him naturally towards the Arminian clergy, and from the beginning he gave them his patronage'.[22] It is understandable that the Arminians seized their chance. It was both their opportunity, a major source of their power, and their downfall. It was possibly not Laudianism which ruined Charles I, but Charles I who ruined Laudianism; but it re-emerged in 1660 freed from its political association to form part of a new Anglican synthesis.

The Restoration Church

'The identification of the Church of England with the Royalist cause was apparent throughout the Rebellion and the Interregnum and the Laudian defence of Anglican formularies prepared the way, not only for the Restoration of monarchy, but also for the re-establishment of the Church on the foundation of the Book of Common Prayer.'[23] Charles II initially had in mind the remodelling of the Church in the interests of comprehensiveness – a compromise settlement to accommodate various interests – but the plans which he and others contemplated were, to a large extent, frustrated.[24]

[22.] H.R. Trevor-Roper, *Catholics, Anglicans and Puritans, op.cit.*, p.114.

[23.] John W. Packer, *The Transformation of Anglicanism 1643–1660, with special reference to Henry Hammond* (Manchester, 1969), p.146.

[24.] See Robert S. Bosher, *The Making of the Restoration Settlement. The Influence of the Laudians 1649–1662*, and I.M. Green, *The Re-Establishment of the Church of England 1660–1663* (Oxford, 1978).

There were of course competing bodies of opinion. To the right there were the more extreme supporters of episcopacy who resisted any reduction in episcopal power. And to the left there were the Independents and covenanting Presbyterians who opposed the re-appearance of episcopacy in any shape or form, and they posed the most serious challenge to a compromise church settlement, especially as they had considerable and active support in all three kingdoms. The more zealous Cavaliers opposed a moderate solution, while the 'submission of the Cromwellian army to the Restoration did not mean that it had suddenly become a strong supporter of the monarchy, let alone episcopacy'.[25] Amid all the strongly held partisan views it appears that it was in the Privy Council alone that a majority could be found in favour of a compromise.

The exact 'party' composition of the Restoration Church which finally emerged in the period 1660 to 1662 has been a matter of debate, but the influence of Laudianism has generally been acknowledged as considerable. R.S. Bosher maintains that 'the second year of the Restoration saw the triumph of a militant High Anglicanism in the Establishment, and the final exclusion of the nonconforming clergy ... At the Restoration the Laudian party emerged as the dominant force on the religious scene.'[26] And he makes it clear that the 'Laudian party' were mostly not, in his definition, personal disciples of Laud, nor did they constitute what in a more recent sense would be seen as an ecclesiastical party within the Church of England. 'They were High Churchmen who shared the religious viewpoint of Laud, and who were in wholehearted agreement in their method of defending the Church's interests both before and after the Restoration.'[27] They had a common attitude to fundamental issues and their policy in dealing with Puritans distinguished them from other groups of Anglicans. They were, however, not conscious of being one party among several, but regarded themselves as

---

[25.] I.M. Green, *op.cit.*, p.11.
[26.] Robert S. Bosher, *op.cit.*, pp.xiii, xiv.
[27.] Robert S. Bosher, *op.cit.*, p.xv.

'the faithful remnant of a persecuted Church, from which all others had fallen away'.[28]

Bosher claims that by 1662, 'the Church for which Laud died was re-established on firmer foundations than it had ever known in his lifetime'.[29] But even he concedes that there were important limitations to the victory, for the resurgent Laudianism was a creed shorn of Laud's political and economic aims. The Church at the Restoration surrendered any pretensions to political independence.

That the restored English Church after 1660 had to some extent a Laudian hue was in part due to the great and lasting impact which Laud and Laudianism had made on the religious life of the country, and to the deposit of respect and even affection for 'decency and order' which he had inculcated, despite his own unpopularity. It was partly a result of a reaction to Puritanism and partly a consequence of the glow which martyrdom cast upon Laud himself and the system for which he lived and died. But the 1660 restoration of a largely Laudian Church also 'owed something to the survival, throughout the revolutionary period, of the original intellectual movement which had inspired it, before it had been diverted into the political synthesis; and that survival was aided by the group of men who, during the personal rule of Charles I, met together at the country house of Lord Falkland at Great Tew'.[30]

The Great Tew circle consisted mainly of young men who formed a kind of continuing seminar or reading party at the Oxfordshire house of Lucius Cary, second Viscount Falkland, in the 1630s, in the halcyon years before the disruption of the civil wars and revolution. The house was within twelve miles of Oxford, and the company of Oxford intellectuals and eminent men from London included Dr Gilbert Sheldon, later Archbishop of Canterbury, Dr George Morley, Bishop of Winchester, Dr Henry Hammond, who has been described as the 'father of English biblical criticism', Dr John Earle, Bishop of Salisbury, and William Chillingworth, the

---

[28.] Robert S. Bosher, *op.cit.*, p.xv.

[29.] Robert S. Bosher, *op.cit.*, pp.1, 2.

[30.] H.R. Trevor-Roper, *Catholics, Anglicans and Puritans*, *op.cit.*, p.x.

philosopher. There was a freedom of debate which ensured
that opinions were various and that no orthodoxy reigned.
Indeed it has been described as a liberal rather than a High
Church group. It was Arminian in tone and overall doctrine,
rational in method, ecumenical, conciliatory, non-
authoritarian and respectful of lay opinion and interests. The
members of the circle were royalist, but critical of the personal
rule of Charles I. They were ambivalent about Laud. Although
they were Arminians they were opposed to his clericalism,
and they looked back from the political Arminianism of the
Laudians to what was more attractive to them, the intellectual
Arminianism of Andrewes. They united their Arminianism
with an acceptance of critical reason and humanist
scholarship.

Special mention should be made of Henry Hammond
(1605–60) He was an outstanding member of the Laudian
party. During the Cromwellian years he, as much as any other
person, strove for the continued existence of the Church of
England. He was regarded by many of his contemporaries,
and later by Tractarians, as the embodiment of Anglicanism
in the seventeenth century. In the course of a short life he
suffered ejection as a parish priest and as a university divine.
He was one of the chaplains who attended Charles I when
permitted during the last tense and alarming years of that
monarch's life, and he was greatly regarded by the king. He
was a teacher of great learning and foresight, and a man of
high personal devotion and integrity. He is acknowledged as
a most important, if not the principal, architect of the
reconstruction of the Anglican Church. He was inflexible in
his High Church principles. He was uncompromising in his
belief about episcopacy, claiming it to be of divine right, and
of apostolical institution; and his rigidity on this point represented a hardening of the Anglican doctrine of ministry, which
was put into effect with divisive results in 1662. He died before
parliament was convened to welcome back king Charles II.

Whatever may have contributed to its survival and re-
emergence after 1660, there was a depth and profundity in
the quality of the Restoration Laudianism which was
impressive. 'The churchmanship of the restored Laudian

school was characterised by its wealth of patristic scholarship and learning, and by its interest in the Eastern Orthodox Church.'[31] There were constant appeals to the practice of the primitive, undivided Church. There was reliance upon the inerrancy of Scripture tested and interpreted in its tenor by the traditions of the ecumenical decrees. There was a careful study of Orthodox history and traditions, a revived zeal for Greek patristic literature, and a resolve to cultivate close and friendly relations with the Orthodox Church which was regarded as a venerable and apostolic communion, and one which uncompromisingly rejected the Papal supremacy. As a corollary to this, the episcopal character of the the English Church was given greater emphasis, and stress was laid on what separated, rather than what united, the English Church and Protestant Dissenters. Initiatives were also taken to establish communication with the Latin Gallican Church. In their ecumenical endeavours the Laudians sensed an affinity with Catholic forms of piety and devotion: their devotional life was governed by same Catholic traditions, and was marked by disciplined austerity; their modes of public worship were characterised by the prolific use of symbol and ceremony; and celibacy was highly esteemed.

As we move away from 1660, so the theological temper of the age becomes increasingly determined by the Cambridge Platonists, and then by the men of Latitude. The High Church fortunes wavered markedly, but overall were in decline. The Laudian tradition withered. For 'the space of a century from the Restoration, the men of Latitude enjoyed a popularity and vogue of astonishing proportions'.[32]

The Achilles' heel of Laudianism in the post 1660 period was perhaps its fervid upholding of the political principles of divine right, passive obedience and the sinfulness of revolution. It was an understandable reaction to the horrific memory of regicide and of Republican rule, but it foundered on the secret Romanism of Charles II and the avowed Papalism of James II.

---

[31] Norman Sykes, *Church and State in England in the Eighteenth Century* (Cambridge, 1934), p.17.
[32] Norman Sykes, *op.cit.*, p.23.

3

Seventeenth Century High Church Spirituality

A good insight into certain facets of seventeenth century High Church spirituality is provided by the life and work of two remarkable men, Nicholas Ferrar and George Herbert.

Nicholas Ferrar (1592–1637) and Little Gidding

Nicholas Ferrar was born in London in 1592, the son of a merchant.[1] His parents were devout Church people and he was educated in a school which not only stimulated his bright intellect, but nurtured his early and vivid awareness of God. From school he went up to Clare Hall, Cambridge. He took his BA in 1610, and was elected to a fellowship. At Cambridge he revealed powers of effortless leadership, and although he was in no way assertive, he was able to inspire and bring out the best in others. These were qualities which were to serve him well in his secular and religious careers.

In 1613 he accompanied Elizabeth of Bohemia on her journey to her new home in the Palatinate. It was the start of a five year period of foreign travel, mainly in Italy, and largely for the sake of his seriously bad health. He returned in 1618, and in the following year took his father's place in

---

[1] For the life of Nicholas Ferrar, and for details of the Little Gidding Community, see A.L. Maycock, *Nicholas Ferrar of Little Gidding* (London, 1938). This is a work to which the present chapter owes much.

the Virginia Company. His brother was Deputy Treasurer, and in 1622 Nicholas was likewise elected Deputy. About a year later he was elected Member of Parliament for Lymington. His parliamentary career was brief. He was offered the choice of two important posts in Government service: either a clerkship of the Privy Council or the British embassy in Savoy. He refused both because of his determination to enter upon a life of religious retirement as soon as his duties permitted. It was a decision shared by all the members of the family, and also by members of the Collett family, who were united to the Ferrars by marriage – they decided to dedicate themselves fully to God as a united family in a single community.

From now onwards Nicholas was the unquestioned head of the family. He discovered that the Lordship of the Manor of Little Gidding, a hamlet on the Huntingdonshire border, was coming vacant, and he was convinced that this was the right place to which the family should go. He arranged for his mother to purchase it in 1624 from her share of her deceased husband's estate. The large manor house was in a shocking condition, and about thirty yards away was a little church which had been converted into a hay barn. The isolated buildings stood on a low ridge with a fine view. The parish was depopulated but for a few shepherds, and was not sufficiently important to be marked on any maps.

Unknown to anyone in the family, even, apparently, his mother, Nicholas was preparing for his ordination as a deacon. To only one person, his dear friend and tutor Augustine Lindsell, had Nicholas confided his intention. So, when he left the London family home early on the morning of Trinity Sunday 1626 before anyone was about, and walked through the empty streets to Westminster Abbey, it was Lindsell who met him, and accompanied him to King Henry VII's chapel, where William Laud, then Bishop of St Davids, awaited them. 'Believe me', Lindsell said to Laud afterwards, 'you have never ordained such a man and probably never will again.'[2]

---

[2] A.L. Maycock, *op.cit.*, p.119.

Immediately after this, Nicholas was offered two lucrative livings, but he now had a set purpose, and a week later the family took their final leave of their London home, and moved to Little Gidding.

For at least the first three or four years the energies of the family were mainly absorbed in what amounted to little short of a complete rebuilding project. The task was gradually and laboriously accomplished. The reconstruction of the buildings, their furnishing and adornment, and such work as the fashioning of altar hangings, of curtains, carpets and cushions for the seats – all was carried out on the spot by members of the two families. Nicholas obtained the consent of Williams, Bishop of Lincoln, their diocesan, that the church should be used once more for common worship, and that the Litany should be recited daily as a special act of intercession for the people of London who had just experienced an appalling plague.

The number of those living at Little Gidding varied from time to time, as there was a constant coming and going of relatives and friends, some of whom stayed for considerable periods. Some children were sent to Little Gidding as part of their education. Members of the family community might be away on private visits, and Nicholas was usually absent at least once a year on family business, including, for example, one period of six weeks in London on a Royal Commission to consider the condition of Virginia. Nevertheless, the core community was about thirty. The permanent nucleus consisted of old Mrs Ferrar, her two elder children, John and Susanna, with their respective families, and Nicholas. There were always small children at Little Gidding, for as the younger Collett daughters, Elizabeth, Joyce and Judith, began to grow up, the young Mapletofts, the children of the marriage of Joshua Mapletoft to Susanna Ferrar, were received into the family on the death of their father. A school was started, and manned by three resident masters who worked under Nicholas' general direction and shared fully in the life of the community.

In such a tightly-knit group all was not placid and harmonious. John Ferrar was devoted to his brother Nicholas and readily accepted his leadership, but his wife Bathsheba regarded this as ridiculous and contemptible subservience. Also, she did not have the same vocation to the religious life, and it is therefore understandable that she found the Little Gidding fraternity and its ways irksome. The resulting tension and conflict was intense, awkward to handle and protracted.

At the other extreme, Mary and Anna Collett regarded themselves as irrevocably pledged to the single life, and their commitment may even have been ratified and consecrated by the authority of the Church in the person of Bishop Williams. But the rule of Little Gidding was in no sense monastic. There is no evidence that Nicholas intended to restore the monastic life in England. Some members of the community were married, and, as we have seen, the community included children; all members of the community maintained active contact with the outside world; none of them took vows, with the possible exception of Mary and Anna Collett; and Nicholas was always quick to correct anyone who referred to Little Gidding as a nunnery. The uniqueness of Little Gidding was simply that it was a special way of life adopted by a family.

The influence of Nicholas was paramount. 'Every feature of the life at Little Gidding bore the stamp of his personality; it was he who inspired, directed and sustained all the activities, both temporal and spiritual. To describe Little Gidding is to describe the mind and the ideals of Nicholas Ferrar.'[3] What appealed to him was simplicity and order in worship and life, and this was central to the ethos and conduct of the community.

Underlying all aspects of the life of the community was a profound reverence for the Scriptures, and especially the Gospels and the Psalter; a veneration for the lives and writings of the Christian Fathers; a concern for prayer and worship to be central to all activity, and a constant striving for greater holiness; love of the Anglican liturgy; hatred of idleness in any form; and a concern to be of service by means of various

---

[3] A.L. Maycock, *op.cit.*, p.189.

and far-reaching works of charity. Each day, from 6 a.m. onwards until 8 p.m., a short office was said at each hour, which lasted a quarter of an hour and consisted of a hymn, a portion of the Psalter and a reading from the Gospels. In addition, there were entirely voluntary night watches, so that there should be ceaseless watching and praying. The worship, if the antithesis is not a false one, was essentially Biblical rather than sacramental. On the first Sunday in each month there was a Communion, and every Sunday people in the surrounding area were invited to join in the worship. Nicholas made it known in the neighbouring parishes that any child who was prepared to study the Psalms and memorize them under his direction should come to Little Gidding at 9.30 on Sunday mornings. They were then asked to remain for the 10.30 service in the church, and given lunch in the home. It appears that there were often forty or fifty of these 'Psalm children'.

Every day was full of activity, but it was well ordered and unhurried, and, in keeping with one of Nicholas' guiding principles, long periods of sustained work on any one occupation were avoided. By these means much was achieved, but freshness and serenity were preserved. The range of activities was considerable.

In the early years, with so much practical work to be undertaken, there was little spare time for recreation or for intellectual pursuits, yet the Ferrars were an extremely talented and cultured family. They were extraordinarily well-read, and they had a high sense of the dignity of learning and of its place in a full Christian life. Out of this came the idea of the 'Little Academy': a study circle in which they told stories, examined historical matters and present problems, and generally sought to stimulate each other academically and spiritually. Some record of the 'Little Academy' has been preserved in five neatly bound gilt folio volumes by Mary Collett under the collective title of *Lives, Characters, Histories and Tales for moral and religious Instruction.* It was also in keeping with this reflective approach to their faith that Nicholas translated the *Divine Considerations* of Juan Valdez, a work which recalled its readers to a life of simplicity and purity of heart, and protested against the belief that the devout life was the vocation of a chosen few. Yet another illustration of this feature of the Little Gidding life was the compilation of *Concordances* or *Harmonies of the Scriptures* which became, even in Nicholas' lifetime, famous throughout England. They 'count amongst the most remarkable feats of book production ever carried out in this country'.[4]

For many years the countless visitors to Little Gidding were confronted on arrival by a framed announcement which reflected something of the philosophy and aspirations of the fraternity:

He who (by reproof of our errors and remonstrance of that which is more perfect) seeks to make us better is welcome as an angel of God – but – He who any ways goes about to disturb us in that which is and ought to be among Christians (Tho' it be not usual in the world) is a burden whilst he stays and shall bear his judgement, whosoever he be.

He who (by a cheerful participation and approbation of that which is good) confirms us in the same, is welcome as a Christian friend – but – He who faults us in absence for that which in presence he makes show to approve of, doth by a double guilt of flattery and slander violate the bands both of friendship and charity.

Many clergy came to Little Gidding to stay a week or more, to join in the devotions, and to assist in the night watches. Bishop Lindsell of Peterborough and Bishop Williams of Lincoln were visitors who were greatly influenced by the community. After Nicholas' death, King Charles spent a refreshing day at the house. The poet and scholar Richard Crashaw was a good friend of the community and a frequent visitor, and although it seems that Nicholas and George Herbert, the saintly parish priest and poet, only met once after their acquaintance as undergraduates at Cambridge, there grew up between them a beautiful relationship of

---

[4] A.L. Maycock, *op.cit.*, pp.148, 149.

sympathy, understanding and uninterrupted friendship which arose spontaneously out of a complete spiritual harmony. It was of such a depth and profundity that it has been said that it 'set its mark upon English spirituality for a hundred years and more'.[5]

'In some sense Little Gidding may be regarded as the spiritual focus of all that was best and holiest in the Caroline Church.'[6] In an age of much strife and turbulance it was like an oasis of sanctity, sanity and inspiration. Its essential nature was perhaps best exemplified in the wider world in the life, work and teaching of the poet just mentioned, George Herbert.

George Herbert (1593–1633)

George Herbert was born in 1593. Both his father and mother were members of quite distinquished, public-spirited, families, but his mother was the most creative influence in his early life. He grew up 'in an atmosphere where beauty and holiness, poetry and devotion, were living esteemed treasures'.[7] He was educated privately, then at Westminster School, from where he went to Trinity College, Cambridge. He graduated in 1611, and was elected to a fellowship in 1615. In 1619 he was chosen as University Orator, an appointment he held for eight years. He hoped that like his predecessor in that post he might go on to be Secretary of State, especially as he was at that time high in the king's favour. But this was not to be. He lost two prominent patrons in the fourteen months before the king himself died in 1625. After much reflection, he resolved to be ordained, and within the year he was made deacon. He was appointed incumbent of the village of Leighton Ecclesia and a Prebendary of Lincoln. The church was derelict, and the incumbency was a sinecure which was supposed to involve

---

[5] A.L. Maycock, *op.cit.*, p.234.

[6] A.L. Maycock, *op.cit.*, p.233.

[7] Margaret Cropper, *Flame Touches Flame* (London, 1949), p.3. A work to which this account of George Herbert owes much.

no duties except one sermon each year in the cathedral. Herbert did not receive it in that spirit, but planned to collect sufficient money to rebuild the church. But his health was poor and he lacked confidence that he would fulfil his vocation as a priest. He regarded himself as ineffective, with no fruit to show for his sacrifice, and he expressed his dejection, and the spiritual conflict which raged within him, in such poems as *The Collar*:

> But as I rav'd and grew more fierce and wild
> At every word
> Methought I heard one calling, 'Child,'
> And I replied, 'My Lord.'

He was in anguish for two years, at the end of which he found himself in smoother water; his health improved, and he slowly regained confidence. This recovery was aided by the mutual love of Herbert and Jane Danvers, their wholehearted, swift courtship, and their marriage.

After a year of marriage he was offered the rectory of Fugglestone with Bemerton. It was to be the scene of the rest of a life of saintliness, worship, service, and an outpouring of poetry.

Herbert had a high view of the calling and life of an Anglican clergyman in general and of a country priest in particular. 'A Pastor', he wrote, 'is the Deputy of Christ for the reclaiming of Man to the obedience of God.'[8] On the night of his induction he said, 'I will now use all my endeavours to bring my relations and dependents to a love and reliance on him, who never fails those that trust him. But above all, I will be sure to live well, because the virtuous life of a clergyman is the most powerful eloquance to persuade all that see it to reverence and love, and at least to desire to live like him. And this I will do, because I know we live in an age that hath more need of good examples than precepts.' He spoke reverentially of the God who 'hath honoured me so much

---

[8.] George Herbert, *The Country Parson*, quoted in Margaret Cropper, *op.cit.*, p.14.

as to call me to serve him at his altar'.[9] The prayer and worship, which was at the very centre of his personal life, and of the life of the parish, had a powerful and persuasive effect in the lives of people in the neighbourhood. Twice each day he, his wife and the whole family, went to the church and joined with other parishioners in prayer: 'and some of the meaner sort of his parish did so love and reverence Mr. Herbert, that they would let their plough rest when Mr. Herbert's Saints'-bell rung to prayers, that they might also offer their devotions to God with him; and would then return back to their plough'. Isaak Walton, who draws upon this testimony, adds that 'his most holy life was such, that it begat such reverence to God, and to him, that they thought themselves the happier when they carried Mr. Herbert's blessing back with them to their labour. Thus powerful was his reason and example to persuade others to a practical piety and devotion.'[10]

As he lay dying in 1633, George Herbert handed to a friend a book to be delivered to Nicholas Ferrar, in which Herbert said Ferrar would find 'a picture of the many spiritual conflicts that have passed between God and my soul, before I could subject mine to the will of Jesus my master; in whose service I have found perfect freedom'. He asked that Ferrar should read it and then, 'if he can think it may turn to the advantage of any dejected poor soul, let it be made public; if not let him burn it'.[11] Nicholas was deeply moved when he received the precious gift a few days after his friend's death. He read and re-read it, and was seen to embrace and kiss the little volume again and again, declaring that it was a rich jewel. He would not allow any tampering with the text, and it appeared with a short preface by him. Thus was published the volume of poems called *The Temple* – a work that was to exert as profound an influence upon religious thought and poetry in England as, perhaps, any other book written during the seventeenth century. In the thirty years after its publication

---

[9] Izaak Walton, *The Lives of Dr. John Donne, Sir Henry Wotton, Mr. Richard Hooker, Mr. George Herbert and Dr. Robert Sanderson* (new edition, London, 1847), p.247.

[10] Izaak Walton, *op.cit.*, p.259.

[11] Izaak Walton, *op.cit.*, p.271.

20,000 copies were sold. It was the dying legacy of a man who had served his own and future generations well by his acts of charity, his poetic works and his quiet, unobtrusive but profoundly potent influence as a man of God.

'In the field of spirituality and poetry, John Donne, Lancelot Andrewes, George Herbert, Henry Vaughan and Nicholas Ferrar represent the flower of a Church of England spirituality distinct from that of the Counter-Reformation Catholicism – or of continental Protestantism.'[12] We have taken three of these to illustrate the essence of this spirituality which later High Churchmen claimed as part of their heritage; a claim which may with considerable qualifications be conceded, as long as it is recognised that they each had their own distinctiveness, did not regard themselves as belonging to any party or grouping, and are in fact part of the spiritual inheritance not only of the High Church, or indeed the Church of England, but of the whole Church in England.

Doctrinal principles – the seventeenth century divines

It is impossible within the confines of the present work to give an adequate account of the many and varied contributions to the High Church tradition made by the divines of the seventeenth-century, additional to those already mentioned, but a few extracts from some of their writings will at least give a flavour of what they taught.[13] This is important as future generations of High Churchmen, especially some in the nineteenth and twentieth centuries, were to regard these divines as of particular significance.

John Cosin (1594–1672) sets out in a letter to the Countess of Peterborough the main points in his view of the Church. In so doing he gives a good insight into the foundations of

---

[12.] E.G. Rupp, *Religion in England 1688–1791* (Oxford, 1986), p.53.

[13.] The quotations which follow are taken mostly from Paul Elmer More and Frank Leslie Cross (Eds.), *Anglicanism. The Thought and Practice of the Church of England, Illustrated from the Religious Literature of the Seventeenth Century* (London, 1935). See also John Chandos (Ed.), *In God's Name. Examples of Preaching in England 1534–1662* (London, 1971).

seventeenth century High Church belief and practice, allowing for the fact that there was not complete uniformity of belief among High Churchmen, and many of them might well have dissented from Cosin in certain particulars of what he enumerates:

> We that profess the Catholic Faith and Religion in the Church of England do not agree with the Roman Catholics in any thing whereunto they now endeavour to convert us... If the Roman Catholics would make the essence of their Church (as we do ours) to consist in these following points, we are at accord with them in the reception and believing of:
>
> 1. All the two and twenty canonical books of the Old Testament, and the twenty-seven of the New, as the only foundation and perfect rule of our faith.
>
> 2. All the apostolical and ancient Creeds, especially those which are commonly called the Apostles' Creed, the Nicene Creed, and the Creed of St. Athanasius; all which are clearly deduced out of the Scriptures.
>
> 3. All the decrees of faith and doctrine set forth, as well in the first four General Councils, as in all other Councils, which those first four approved and confirmed, and in the fifth and sixth General Councils besides (than which we find no more to be General), and in all the following Councils that be thereunto agreeable, and in all the anathemas and condemnations given out by those Councils against heretics, for the defence of the Catholic Faith.
>
> 4. The unanimous and general consent of the ancient Catholic Fathers and the universal Church of Christ in the interpretation of the Holy Scriptures, and the collection of all necessary matters of Faith from them during the first six hundred years, and downwards to our own days.
>
> 5. In acknowledgement of the Bishop of Rome, if he

would rule and be ruled by the ancient canons of the Church, to be the Patriarch of the West, by right of ecclesiastical and imperial constitution, in such places where the kings and governors of those places had received him, and found it behooveful for them to make use of his jurisdiction, without any necessary dependence upon him by divine right.

6. In the reception and use of the two blessed Sacraments of our Saviour; in the Confirmation of those persons that are to be strengthened in their Christian Faith, by prayer and imposition of hands, according to the the examples of the holy Apostles and ancient Bishops of the Catholic Church; in the public and solemn benediction of persons that are to be joined together in Holy Matrimony; in public or private absolution of penitent sinners; in the consecrating of Bishops, and the ordaining of Priests and Deacons, for the service of God in His Church by a lawful succession; and in visiting the sick, by praying for them, and administering the Blessed Sacrament to them, together with a final absolution of them from their repented sins.

7. In commemorating at the Eucharist the Sacrifice of Christ's Body and Blood once truly offered for us.

8. In acknowledging His sacramental, spiritual, true, and real Presence there to the souls of all them that come faithfully and devoutly to receive Him according to His own institution in that Holy Sacrament.

9. In giving thanks to God for them that are departed out of this life in the true Faith of Christ's Catholic Church; and in praying to God, that they may have a joyful resurrection, and a perfect consummation of bliss, both in their bodies and souls, in His eternal kingdom of glory.

10. In the historical and moderate use of painted and true stories, either for memory or ornament, where there is no danger to have them abused or worshipped with religious honour.

11. In the use of indulgences, or abating the rigour of the canons imposed upon offenders, according to their repentance, and their want of ability to undergo them.

12. In the administration of the two Sacraments, and other rites of the Church, with ceremonies of decency and order, according to the precept of the Apostle, and the free practice of the ancient Christians.

13. In observing such Holy days and times of fasting as were in use in the first ages of the Church, or afterwards received upon just grounds, by public or lawful authority.

14. Finally, in the reception of all ecclesiastical consititutions and canons made for the ordering of our Church; or others which are not repugnant either to the Word of God, or the power of kings, or the laws established by right authority in any nation.[14]

John Overall (1560–1619), in common with the other divines we are considering, placed a high value on apostolic succession. He wrote:

Furthermore, it is most apparent by the testimonies of all Antiquity, Fathers, and Ecclesiastical Histories, that all the Churches in Christendom that were planted and governed by the Apostles, and by such their coadjutors, apostolical persons, as unto whom the Apostles had to that end fully communicated their apostolical authority, did think that after the death, either of any of the Apostles, which ruled amongst them, or of any other the said Bishops ordained by them, it was the meaning of the Holy Ghost, testified sufficiently by the practice of the Apostles, that the same order and form of ecclesiastical government should continue in the Church for ever. And therefore upon the death of any of them, either Apostles or Bishops, they, the said Churches, did always supply their places with others the most worthy

---

[14.] Paul Elmer More and Frank Leslie Cross (Eds.), *op.cit.*, pp. 53–56.

and eminent persons amongst them; who, with the like power and authority that their predecessors had, did ever succeed them. Insomuch as in every city and episcopal see, where there were divers priests and ministers of the Word and Sacraments and but one Bishop only, the catalogues of the names, not of their Priests but of their Bishops, were very carefully kept from time to time, together with the names of the Apostles or Apostolical persons, the Bishops their predecessors, from whom they derived their succession. Of which succession of Bishops, whilst the succession of truth continued with it, the ancient Fathers made great account and use when any false teachers did broach new doctrine, as if they had received the same from the Apostles; choking them with this, that they were not able to shew any Apostolical Church that ever taught as they did.[15]

John Bramhall (1594–1663) stressed the continuity of the English Church, before, during and after the Reformation: 'the Church of England before the Reformation and the Church of England after the Reformation are as much the same church, as a garden, before it is weeded and after it is weeded, is the same garden'.[16] He was an ardent member of the English Church but was not fanatical about conformity to its doctrines. He wrote:

We do not suffer any man 'to reject' the Thirty-Nine Articles of the Church of England 'at his pleasure'; yet neither do we look upon them as essentials of saving faith or 'legacies of Christ and of His Apostles'; but in a mean, as pious opinions fitted for the preservation of unity. Neither do we oblige any man to believe them, but only not to contradict them.[17]

[15.] Paul Elmer More and Frank Leslie Cross (Eds.), *op.cit.*, p.371.

[16.] John Bramhall, *A Just Vindication of the Church of England from the unjust aspersion of criminal schism* (1654), 1, p.113, quoted in Paul Avis, *Anglicanism and the Christian Church*, *op.cit.*, p.117.

[17.] Paul Elmer More and Frank Leslie Cross (Eds.), *op.cit.*, p.186.

Bramhall, like Overall and his contemporary Caroline divines, believed that the perfection of a church and its glory were incomplete without episcopacy, but he declared his belief that the lack of episcopacy in a church did not invalidate it as a church:

> Episcopal Divines will readily subscribe to the determination of the learned Bishop of Winchester [Andrewes], in his Answer to the Second Epistle of Molinaeus – 'Neverthless, if our form [*viz.*, Episcopacy] be of Divine right, it doth not follow from thence that there is no salvation without it, or that a Church cannot consist without it. He is blind who does not see Churches consisting without it; he is hard-hearted who denieth them salvation. We are none of those hard-hearted persons; we put a great difference between these things. There may be something absent in the exterior regiment, which is of Divine right, and yet salvation be to be had.' This mistake proceedeth from not distinguishing between the true nature and essence of the Church, which we do readily grant them, and the integrity or perfection of a Church, which we cannot grant them without swerving from the judgement of the Catholic Church.[18]

Bramhall extended this measure of tolerence to his view about baptism:

> If infants which die unbaptized be excluded from all hope of salvation, then it is by reason of that original corruption which they derive by propagation from their parents, because 'no polluted thing can enter into Heaven'; for we know, that infants are not capable of any actual sins. But this reason is not sufficient; for the Jewish infants were as subject to original sin and had a remedy appointed for it by God, as well as Christians, that is, the Sacrament of Circumcision; which though

---

[18.] Paul Elmer More and Frank Leslie Cross (Eds.), *op.cit.*, p.403.

it should be admitted that it did not causally produce grace, yet it is confessed by the Romanists that it did certainly procure grace, and was as strictly enjoined to them as Baptism is to us. *The uncircumcised male child...shall be cut off from his people.* But this notwithstanding, the Jewish infants, dying without Circumcision, might be saved. Neither is God more propitious to the Jewish infants than to the Christian, for *He hath loved the tents of Sion above all the tabernacles of Jacob.* Therefore Christian infants may be saved likewise without Baptism. That the Jewish children might be saved without Circumcision is thus proved by the institution of God. Circumcision was not celebrated till the eighth day after the nativity; but many thousand Jewish infants died before the eighth day, and consequently without Circumcision; to exclude all those from hope of salvation for want of Circumcision, which by God's own ordinance they might not have, intrencheth too much upon the goodness of God. More particularly, David's child died upon the seventh day, and yet David doubted not to say, I *shall go to him, but he shall not return to me.*[19]

Regarding the Eucharist, Bramhall wrote:

The Holy Eucharist is a commemoration, a representation, an application of the all-sufficient propitiatory Sacrifice of the Cross. If his Sacrifice of the Mass have any other propitiatory power or virtue in it than to commemorate, represent, and apply the merit of the Sacrifice of the Cross, let him speak plainly what it is...

We acknowledge an Eucharistical Sacrifice of praise and thanksgiving; a commemorative Sacrifice or a memorial of the Sacrifice of the Cross; a representative Sacrifice, or a representation of the Passion of Christ before the

---

[19.] Paul Elmer More and Frank Leslie Cross (Eds.), *op.cit.*, p.439.

eyes of His Heavenly Father; an impetrative Sacrifice, or an impetation of the fruit and benefit of His Passion by way of real prayer; and, lastly, an applicative Sacrifice, or an application of His Merits unto our souls. Let him that dare go one step further than we do; and say that it is a suppletory Sacrifice, to supply the defects of the Sacrifice of the Cross. Or else let them hold their peace and speak no more against us in this point of sacrifice for ever.[20]

Herbert Thorndike (1598–1672) was one of a small group of truly systematic Anglican theologians, which includes Richard Hooker and Henry Hammond, and a great High Church divine, but 'his views were challenged by members of his own school, as well as by those of a more liberal outlook'.[21] In common with other seventeenth century High Churchmen we are considering, while asserting episcopacy to be of divine right he refused to impugn the reformed churches of the continent for their lack of it, and certainly refused to unchurch them.

Jeremy Taylor (1613–67) accepted the general catholic approach to the sacramental life, the threefold ministry and orthodoxy of doctrine, and he found his inspiration in the primitive Church, but he was also continually critical of inherited dogma. He upheld the centrality of episcopacy, which, he argued, was indirectly but intentionally instituted by Christ in his appointment of the Apostles as an order distinct from presbyters, 'with the power of confirmation and ordination and a mandate to appoint successors'.[22] He accepted it as not less than 'an apostolic ordinance, and delivered to us by the same authority that the observation of the Lord's day is'.[23] But, like Bramhall and Cosin, he does

---

[20] Paul Elmer More and Frank Leslie Cross (Eds.), *op.cit.*, p.496.

[21] Paul Avis, *op.cit.*, p.147.

[22] Paul Avis, *op.cit.*, p.122.

[23] Jeremy Taylor, *Of the Sacred Order and Offices of Episcopacy by Divine Institution, Apostolical Tradition and Catholic Practice*, VII, p.74, quoted in Paul Avis, *op.cit.*, p.122.

not thereby imply any condemnation of the reformed churches whose ordinations always had been without bishops: they stood or fell as judged by their own Master.

Taylor exposed what he regarded as the inadequacy of tradition, councils, Fathers and popes, in that all of them were fallible. He declared as certain that 'the Scripture is a full and sufficient rule to Christians in faith and manners, a full and perfect declaration of the Will of God'.[24] But even the Scriptures, except in 'things plain, necessary and fundamental', require interpretation, for unaided they are not a clear guide. For Taylor, reason was the best guide and judge, although he presupposed a received catholicism which preserved him from the perhaps more pronounced and unqualified rationalism of William Chillingworth and some other members of the Great Tew circle. 'In questioning aspects of the substance of the catholicism to which he was undoubtedly committed he followed the leading of his conscience and his own compassionate nature.'[25]

After showing early, somewhat extreme, radical views, Edward Stillingfleet (1635–99) backed off and followed the consensus of the seventeenth century High Church divines we have briefly considered. He attempted to show that no one form of church government is of divine origin, permanently right and binding on all ages, not even episcopacy. Episcopacy was good, but it was not essential. He personally recommended a modified episcopacy whereby there would no longer be grand prelates, and the office of bishop would become more pastoral, with smaller diocese where the bishop would be assisted by a synod of presbyters with the involvement of the enfranchised laity.

William Beveridge (1637–1708) was a convinced Church of England man with cautionary advice for any who might contemplate membership of any 'sect'. He wrote:

But if you leave the Communion or fellowship of our Church, and join yourselves to any of the sects which

---

[24] Paul Elmer More and Frank Leslie Cross (Eds.), *op.cit.*, p.91.
[25] Paul Avis, *op.cit.*, p.127.

are risen up amongst us, as you will be certain to want many of the means of grace which you here enjoy, you will be uncertain whether you shall enjoy any of them, so as to attain the end for which they are appointed, even the salvation of your souls; for you will be uncertain whether they who administer them be lawfully called and sent by Christ to do it, as be sure many of them are not. You will be uncertain whether you can join with them in prayer; for in some places they know not what they say, in other places they themselves know not what they intend to say, until they have said it, and how then can you know it ? You will be uncertain whether you shall ever receive any benefit from the Sacrament of the Lord's Supper; for some never administer it at all, others do it either so imperfectly or so irregularly, that the virtue and efficacy of it is very much impaired, if not quite destroyed; you will be uncertain, whether they preach the true doctrine of the Gospel, for they never subscribe to it, or solemnly promise to preach that and no other; neither are they ever called to account for any thing they say or teach, be it never so false or contrary to what Christ and His Apostles taught, so that they may lead you blindfold whithersoever they please, without control; and after all, you will be uncertain whether they seek you or yours, for they have no more obligation upon them to take care of your souls than you have to take care of theirs; and therefore the most favourable and the most charitable construction that can be put upon the separation from our Church, is, that it is leaving a certainty for an uncertainty, which no wise man would do in any thing, much less in a matter upon which his eternal happiness and salvation depends; from whence you may easily observe, that it is your wisdom and interest, as well as duty, to be steadfast as in the doctrine, so likewise in fellowship or communion with the Church, as the first Disciples were.[26]

[26.] Paul Elmer More and Frank Leslie Cross (Eds.), *op. cit.*, p.82.

His strong belief in the Church of England was accompanied and reinforced by a firm commitment to the doctrine of apostolical succession:

> Hence the Apostles, being thus ordained and instructed by Our Lord, took special care to transfer the same Spirit to others which they had received from Him. But this they could not do after the same manner as Christ had done it to them, even by breathing upon them: for that way was peculiar to Christ, from Whom the Spirit proceedeth. Wherefore, they being doubtless directed thereto by the same Spirit, transmitted it to others by laying their hands upon them, which was the old way that had been used in the Church before: for so Moses communicated the Spirit of Wisdom to Joshua, thereby constituting him his successor in the government of Israel, even by laying his hands upon him, Deut. xxxiv, 9...
>
> Thus therefore it is that the Apostolical Office hath been handed down from one to another ever since the Apostles' days to our time...
>
> And so it is to this day. All the efficacy that there is or can be in the administration of any ecclesiastical office depends altogether upon the Spirit of God going along with the office, and assisting at the execution of it. Without which, the Sacraments we administer would be but empty signs and our preaching no more than beating of the air...
>
> As for schism, they certainly hazard their salvation at a strange rate, who separate themselves from such a Church as ours is, wherein the Apostolical Succession, the root of all Christian Communion, hath been so entirely preserved, and the Word and Sacraments are so effectually administered... And therefore, to speak modestly, they must needs run a very great hazard who cut themselves off from ours, and by consequence from the Catholic Church...[27]

[27] Paul Elmer More and Frank Leslie Cross (Eds.), *op.cit.*, pp.372-374.

In summary, if one can generalise, the Caroline divines wished to restore the grandeur of Christian truth which, they thought, had been lost in the confusion and turmoil of the sixteenth century. It consisted of an acceptance of the supremacy of the Scriptures, and of doctrine as set forth in the Creeds, a veneration for the Fathers, a concern to exalt the Church and the ministry, and a wholeness of life which found its centre in the incarnation; and all this supported by a massive learning. They did not attempt to construct a systematic body of doctrine on the lines of Calvin, but did take seriously what they regarded as the profound concern of the English Reformers to return to antiquity.

Liturgical concerns

The concern of the Caroline divines for true doctrine was paralleled by a widespread seventeenth century High Church liturgical concern. It has been said that the 'Roman Catholics attacked the Church of England for substituting a vernacular liturgy in place of the historic Latin rite; the Puritans were opposed to the whole idea of liturgy. Worship to them was a matter of metrical psalms chosen by the minister, extemporary prayer, and above all sermons.'[28] In contrast, the Caroline divines sought for a Catholic Liturgy, more in keeping with ancient piety.

There were many seventeenth century writers on liturgy, most of whom can be identified with the High Church tradition. Although not exhaustive, it included Richard Hooker, Lancelot Andrewes, John Cosin, Henry Thorndike, Jeremy Taylor, Anthony Sparrow, Hamon L'Estrange, John Durel, Thomas Comber, William Beveridge, William Nicholls and Charles Wheatly.[29]

Hooker laid the foundation by distinguishing clearly between the prayer of the individual and that of the Church

---

[28] G.W.O. Addleshaw, *The High Church Tradition*, p.20.
[29] G.W.O. Addleshaw, *op.cit.*, pp.30, 31.

in the liturgy. Andrewes and Cosin contributed to liturgical thought as much by their lives, and their liturgical example as by their writings. Thorndike provided the first systematic Anglican exploration of early liturgies, and a study in the theory of liturgy. He attempted to attach a meaning to the words uniformity and edification, and emphasised the importance of giving its rightful place in liturgical thought to the Eucharistic sacrifice. He viewed the Eucharist as the climax of the liturgy, and thought that until it became the chief Sunday service the ideals of the Reformers would not be fully realised.

All the liturgists mentioned never tired of proclaiming the superiority of the Book of Common Prayer as a liturgy to that of Rome, because all the faithful can take part. Such participation is achieved by the responses of the congregation and not the choir only; the shortness of the prayers; the fact that the prayers are simple and usually contain only one thought; and by the use of the vernacular. Bishop Bull roundly declared that in the Roman Church there was no common prayer for 'the priests say and do all; the people being left to gaze about, or to whisper one to another, or to look upon their private manuals of devotion, according as their private inclination leads them'.[30]

The seventeenth century liturgists were also of one accord in finding the centre of the liturgy in the Eucharist. They gave great reverence to the altar, bowing to it when they went up to make their communion. They emphasised the greater spiritual value and acceptability to God of corporate prayer as represented by the Anglican liturgy, compared with private prayer, but in so doing they tended to undervalue the importance of private prayer in the life of the individual. Jeremy Taylor, Denis Granville and Thomas Ken were almost the only liturgists who showed any knowledge or sympathy with contemplative prayer: the majority of them were seemingly content with discursive meditations.

---

[30] George Bull, *Works*, ed. 1846, II, p.300, quoted in G.W.O. Addleshaw, *op. cit.*, p.43.

The seventeenth century liturgists loved to worship. They had grasped the principles and meaning of liturgy, and to a remarkable extent were able to communicate their beliefs, understanding and spirit in order to make their age liturgically minded. 'They interpreted the Prayer Book and gave it form and meaning; under their hands a Protestant service was transformed into a Catholic liturgy; they discovered its beauties; they lived it and were ready to die for it.'[31] They interpreted the Prayer Book not as an Anglican counterpart to the Protestant Church Orders of the continent, but in the context of a Catholic inheritance.

The liturgists did a thorough and painstaking work of revision on the Prayer Book, removing anomalies and inconsistencies, and giving it additional polish and form. They provided, for example, the now familiar names of the prayers in the Communion Service, such as the Collect for Purity, the Collect of Humble Access, the Prayer of Consecration, the Prayer of Oblation and the Collect of Thanksgiving.

Three features were in their view essential in any liturgy, and were exhibited to a high degree of excellence in the Anglican rite: edification, order and uniformity. The Prayer Book services and the ceremonial of the Church of England provided an ideal vehicle for the full edification of the worshippers in that they allowed for the use of speech, visual stimulus, bodily actions, gestures, symbolism and congregational involvement in such combination as to produce an overall sense of awe and wonder. This in its turn promoted spiritual growth, the upbuilding of faith and holiness and a true spirit of adoration. The danger of an over elaborate ceremonial being a distraction was recognised. A liturgy was reckoned as edifying when it led the worshippers to forget themselves in the glory of Catholic worship. The Prayer Book also inculcated order. All its parts cohered in such an excellent way that they influenced and affected each other. Nothing could be omitted either by the minister or the people without injury to the whole, and without spoiling

---

[31] G.W.O. Addleshaw, *op.cit.*, p.63.

its total efficacy. Such ceremonial accompaniments as vestments, the mixed chalice, the lavabo and incense were commonly used by High Churchmen in a scheme of ceremonial which was intended to reinforce this Prayer Book order, while keeping it distinct from the Latin rite. In such worship the cross was typically the focus rather than the resurrection. They gloried in the Eucharist because they gloried in Calvary and in the cross.

Uniformity, which was provided by the Prayer Book, was important for pastoral and devotional reasons as it avoided dependence on the variable qualities and provisions of those ministers who led unstructured, extempore worship. Worship led in an extempore way consisted essentially of a congregation entering into the private thoughts and devotion of one person, the minister, with all his propensity for self-glorification, and with all his inadequacies, with the congregation wondering what would come next, rather than being caught up in an age-long, universal form of worship, the product of age-long spiritual wisdom, which allowed a self-forgetfulness in adoration. The seventeenth century liturgists saw in the liturgy a visible sign and means of creating that inner unity which should mark the life of the Church. 'By it we are formed in the mind of the Church; in using it daily we are linked not only with each other but with the Church down the ages; gradually we grow up into the mind and outlook of the Church and loose that individualism which cuts us asunder from our fellow Christians. The meeting of the faithful in the liturgy makes the worship of the Church on earth an analogue of that offered in the heavenly sanctuary where the Church is truly one.'[32] George Herbert likened a Christian congregation praying 'with one heart and one voice, and in one reverent posture' to the beauty of that Jerusalem which is at peace with itself. Uniformity of worship was also seen as an expression of the unity of Church and State, of the country as a single nation, of the potential identity of nation and Church, and of the wholeness of Christianity.

[32] G.W.O. Addleshaw, *op.cit.*, p.60.

PART 2

From the Nonjurors to the Hackney Phalanx

4

The Nonjurors and the Conforming High Churchmen

The Laudian tradition quickly lost its influence in the Established Church after the Revolution, largely because the change of dynasty led to schism. The so-called Nonjurors were those members of the Church of England who, at this time, 'scrupled to take the Oaths of Allegiance and Supremacy to William and Mary on the grounds that by so doing they would break their previous oaths to James II and his successors'.[1] There were nine bishops and some four hundred priests who were deprived of their livings, as well as a number of prominent laymen. As the bishops were deprived by Act of Parliament and their successors similarly appointed, with no attempt to comply with canonical procedure, the Nonjuring clergy continued to regard them as their lawful bishops, and many

---

[1.] F.L. Cross and E.A. Livingstone (Eds.), *Oxford Dictionary of the Christian Church* (2nd ed., Oxford, 1983) p.979, an account to which the present summary is indebted. For the general history of this period see especially Christopher Hill, *The Century of Revolution 1603–1714* (1961). For the Nonjurors and the conforming High Churchmen, in addition to the works previously cited or to which reference is made below, see S.C. Carpenter, *Eighteenth Century Church and People* (1959), W.K. Lowther Clarke, *Eighteenth Century Piety* (1944), F.L. Cross, *The Oxford Movement and the Seventeenth Century* (London, 1933), V.H.H. Green, *Religion at Oxford and Cambridge. A History c.1160–1960* (1964), A. Tindal Hart, *The Life and Times of John Sharp Archbishop of York* (1949), Stephen Neill, *Anglicanism* (1958), John H. Overton, *The Nonjurors* (1902), John H. Overton, *Life in the English Church (1660–1714)* (London, 1885), James H. Rigg, *Oxford High Anglicanism and its Chief Leaders* (1895), E.G. Rupp, *Religion in England 1688–1791* (1986), and J.W.C. Wand, *The High Church Schism. Four Lectures on the Non-Jurors* (1951).

of the conforming clergy considered that their sees had been irregularly vacated. To ensure the succession of Nonjuring Bishops, the leading Nonjuror, Archbishop Sancroft, delegated his archiepiscopal powers to Bishop W. Lloyd of Norwich in 1692; and in 1694 G. Hickes and T. Wagstaffe were secretly consecrated Bishops, with the respective titles of Thetford and Ipswich after the *congé d'élire* had been received from the exiled James II.

The Nonjurors were divided over key issues, including the question of the lawfulness of worshipping in their parish church, with the majority opting for their own, illegal, services. There was particularly fierce difference of opinion among them in the period 1719 to 1732, between the Usagers and the Non-Usagers over the acceptance or non-acceptance of a specially devised Communion Service based partly on primitive Christian liturgies and partly on the 1549 Book of Common Prayer; the Usagers being so named from four 'usages' which the new rite contained – the mixed chalice, prayers for the dead, a prayer for the descent of the Holy Ghost on the elements and an Oblatory prayer. The Nonjurors position was complicated by the possibility of a restoration of the Stuarts, especially in the early Hanoverian period. The regular line of Nonjuring bishops ended with the death of Richard Gordon in 1779, and an irregular line finished in 1805 with the death of Charles Booth. But long before this the Nonjurors had virtually disappeared through absorbtion into the Established Church.

Those 'who went out because their consciences forbade them to break their oaths to the apostate son of the martyr-king'[2] were the foremost representatives of the High Anglican school. By their schism, these Nonjurors fatally weakened the Laudian party within the Church. It was in effect such Nonjurors as Sancroft, Ken, Dodwell and Robert Nelson, together with a circle of conforming churchmen who were allied to them, despite taking the oath to William III and afterwards to the Hanoverian dynasty, men like Bishop

---

[2] Yngve Brilioth, *The Anglican Revival. Studies in the Oxford Movement* (London, 1933), pp.16f.

Atterbury, Bishop George Bull, Bishop William Beveridge and Bishop Thomas Wilson, who represented a definite Catholic conception of the Church at the turn of the century.They referred to the authority of the early Church as the highest standard next to the Bible; emphasised the importance of the priestly office; had an institutional conception of the Church; showed a preference for the first Prayer Book of Edward VI with its somewhat richer liturgy compared with that used officially in the English Church; stressed the four usages to which reference has just been made; and had a view of the Eucharist which at least approximated closely to the Sacrifice of the Mass.

The Nonjurors belief in the crucial importance of episcopacy, even to the extent 'that non-episcopal churches were no churches, their ministers were laymen and their sacraments no sacraments',[3] helped to further the Anglican sense of distance from and reserve towards the continental churches of the Reformation and the Nonconformist churches in England. 'But for all their suspicion of the continental protestants, the nonjurors were no friends of Rome.'[4] They constructed a doctrine of the church as a separate entity – as Law did with Hoadly in the Bangorian controversy – and it was this doctrine which was adopted by the Oxford movement.

The Nonjurors were the supreme upholders of the Anglican doctrine of the Divine Right of Kings and the duty of passive obedience. Their high conception of the Church as a spiritual society with its own laws, their stress on the external forms of worship, and the other characteristics we have noted, linked them with the Caroline divines, and led the Tractarians to look back to them as part of the tradition they saw themselves as perpetuating. As a group they were powerful exemplars of 'catholic' principles. But, because this was so, and because they were 'outsiders', with few, and, as time progressed, a diminishing number, of conformist sympathisers or equivalents, and because of the opposition their Jacobite

[3] Paul Avis, *Anglicanism and the Christian Church*, p.90.
[4] Paul Avis, *op.cit.*, p.91.

connections aroused, the very principles for which they stood were, for most of the eighteenth century, poorly represented within the Church of England.

It is not contradictory to concur with historians, and especially High Church historians of the nineteenth century, in their estimate of the Nonjurors as heralds of the Oxford movement, at least in a certain quite narrowly defined way, while, at the same time agreeing that their protest was political in principle. For the Nonjurors did not compartmentalise their beliefs and actions, and for them the root of the matter was a crisis of Christian conscience, grounded in a Christian view of church and society, and in this they foreshadowed the Tractarians. Nonetheless, in their loyalty to the Reformation, and in their refusal to accept doctrines such as Transubstantiation and the Real Presence, they looked backwards to Laud rather than forward to Hurrell Froude.

Thomas Ken (1637–1711)

Thomas Ken was a leading Nonjuror, and he has always been regarded and honoured as a shining light among them. He was also seen by later High Churchmen as perhaps the most significant Nonjuring contributor to the High Church tradition. It is therefore appropriate to consider his life and work in some detail.

He was the youngest son of an attorney in the Court of Common Pleas, a member of an ancient Somerset family. His mother died when he was only four years of age, but Anne, a step-sister by a previous marriage of Thomas's father, devoted herself to his upbringing. Five years later she married no less a person than Izaac Walton, who, upon the death of Thomas's father in 1651, became the boy's guardian.

Ken was educated at Winchester and Hart Hall, Oxford. He graduated at New College, Oxford, in 1661 and was elected a Fellow of the College. He immersed himself in the study of the Fathers of the Primitive Church, in an Oxford which was by then no longer under Puritan control. After several pastoral cures and a time as chaplain to the Bishop of

Winchester, from 1672 he taught at Winchester College, and was Prebendary of the Cathedral. During this time he wrote a *Manual of Prayers* for boys, and also possibly his two famous morning and evening hymns, 'Awake, my soul, and with the sun', and 'Glory to Thee, my God, this night'. In 1679 Charles II appointed him chaplain to Princess Mary at The Hague, and in the same year Oxford honoured him with a Doctorate in Divinity. In 1685 he was consecrated Bishop of Bath and Wells. Two years later appeared his *Exposition of Divine Love;* or the *Practice of Divine Love,* which is a classic expression of Laudian doctrine, and clearly reveals his Catholicism, 'firmly Anglican and non-Roman'.[5]

In his diocesan work Ken demonstrated his pastoral and charitable instincts in a variety of ways: by the organisation of relief for the persecuted Huguenot refugees; by his establishment of schools for poor children; and by his personal actions, such as having twelve poor men or women to dine with him on Sundays. But while he was conscientiously discharging his duties, storm clouds were gathering over the national scene which were to profoundly disrupt his life.

By his overt Roman Catholicism; his merciless suppression of the Monmouth uprising; his attempts to override Parliament and parliamentary processes; and his despotic repealing and setting aside of laws without reference to the elected assembly, James II alienated many, including the English bishops. Finally, his Declarations of Indulgence of 1687 and 1689, and his demand that they should be read in all the churches, provoked seven bishops, led by Archbishop Sancroft, and including Ken, to write him a letter of protest. The seven bishops were imprisoned, put on trial in Westminster Hall amid scenes of great public excitment, and acquitted to the accompaniment of widespread intense and prolonged jubilation: they immediately became public heroes, acclaimed throughout the land. Yet they 'had come through

---

[5] Hugh A.L. Rice, *Thomas Ken Bishop and Non-Juror* (London, 1958), p.84, a work which has been of considerable help in the present account of Ken's life. See also E.H. Plumptre, *The Life of Thomas Ken Bishop of Bath and Wells,* 2 vols. (1890).

victorious at the cost of immeasurable grief and heaviness of heart'[6] because they had found themselves opposed to the wishes of their king. Their purpose had not been defiance of him they regarded as the Lord's annointed, but the defence of the laws of England and the rights of the Church. They had simply done what they regarded as the duty of the Church. At the time of the 1688/89 Revolution Ken remained unflinchingly loyal to the king who had given him so little cause for such loyalty. Together with the other Nonjurors, he stood firmly by his understanding of the divine right of kings and passive obedience, determined to resist any deposition of the king or election of any other king, or to assent to any breaking of the link in the royal chain. When James had succeeded to the throne, Ken and all his fellow bishops and priests had solemnly sworn allegiance to him and his lawful heirs and successors, in what was to them not just a requirement by Act of Parliament, but a religious oath, 'a solemn promise and vow made, as it were, in the presence and name of God. Parliament could compel them to take it, but Parliament could not dispense them from keeping it.'[7] The Nonjurors had taken the Oath of Allegiance to a king who, in their opinion, had neither abdicated nor been legally deposed, and they considered it incompatible with their sense of loyalty to take a further oath to what they regarded as that king's supplanter. For some, like Sancroft, their course was immediately clear, while others weighed the issues carefully, listened to counter arguments, and wrestled with their own consciences. But in either case the Nonjurors were resolute, and in no spirit of harsh, unbending rigorism, arrogance or self-complacency, but rather with sadness yet conviction, made their costly decision, and went out into the wilderness. In 1691, the nine bishops and four hundred priests were formally deprived.

For the rest of his life Ken lived in retirement. In 1703 Kidder, who had held the see since Ken's deposition, died, but Ken refused the offer of reinstatement. He was a moderate

---

6. Hugh A.L. Rice, *op.cit.*, p.134.
7. Hugh A.L. Rice, *op.cit.*, p.159.

among the Nonjurors. At the extreme there were those who considered themselves to be the only legitimate holders of the sees from which they were ejected, and, consequently, thought that they were entitled to the obedience of the clergy of those diocese. They regarded themselves as 'the true Catholic Church of the country, the faithful remnant who alone had not bowed the knee to the usurping Baal',[8] and those who had replaced them were seen as intruders and schismatics. As we have seen, in order to maintain what they saw as true, Nonjuring, apostolic succession, the Nonjurors consecrated their own bishops. The action caused division within the Nonjuring ranks, and Ken, who disliked what had been done, merely tolerated what he could not approve. The clandestine consecrations helped to place the Nonjurors under suspicion as plotters with known Jacobites to overthrow the regime; and it drove an even greater wedge between moderates such as Ken, and the extremists, whose attitude he and others such as Frampton, Kettlewell, Dodwell and Robert Nelson found increasingly distasteful.

Ken was the last survivor of the original Nonjuring bishops. He died on 19 March 1711. In his will, he wrote, 'I die in the Holy Catholic and Apostolic Faith, professed by the whole Church, before the division of East and West; more particularly I die in the Communion of the Church of England, as it stands distinguished from all Papal and Puritan Innovations, and as it adheres to the doctrine of the Cross.'[9] It was a declaration of the faith by which he had tried to live, and in which he had died, and it was true to the Laudian tradition into which he had entered. But, even so, he, like William Law, is difficult to categorise as a typical Nonjuror, or indeed as a 'type' at all, unless it be that he was part of that tradition of holiness to which George Herbert belonged, and should be regarded as taking his place with those whose hearts lay not in polemic, but in 'practical divinity'.

Although Ken and his fellow Nonjurors were among the most distinguished of the Catholic-minded clergy and laymen

---

8. Hugh A.L. Rice, *op.cit.*, p.185.
9. Quoted in Hugh A.L. Rice, *op.cit.*, pp.216, 217.

of their generation, they left a sprinkling of such Churchmen within the Established Church; but it was a divided and troubled Church.

'In the generation after the Revolution of 1688 the Church of England had to face the harsh fact that its status and authority had been severely diminished.'[10] At the Restoration, and after the traumatic experience of the previous two decades, the clergy had become committed to a high religious theory of kingship, and the Revolution was a shattering blow to the whole Anglican alliance of church and state. It resulted in a radical re-appraisal of the role of the national Church in English society. With the crisis of 1688/89 and the replacement of the Stuart dynasty, the majority of the clergy took the oaths of allegiance, usually on the casuistical argument that they would obey William as *de facto* king, but continue to honour James as their *de jure* prince, but most did so with deeply uneasy consciences. Many Churchmen were prepared to campaign vigorously for a return to a past when church and state had conjoined in a single authoritarian regime. During much of the time around the turn of the century, when these were still very much live issues, for a period of thirty years, Francis Atterbury was 'the prime mover and champion of the High Church cause'.[11]

Francis Atterbury (1662–1732)

Atterbury was educated at Westminster School and Christ Church, Oxford, where he became a tutor. He was ordained deacon in 1687. In 1691 he became Lecturer at St Bride's, Fleet Street, where he was an instant success, and almost immediately established his reputation in Court circles as an excellent preacher. In 1693 he was elected minister of the ancient Hospitals of Bridewell and Bethlehem, promptly

---

[10.] G.V. Bennett, *The Tory Crisis in Church and State 1688–1730. The career of Francis Atterbury Bishop of Rochester* (Oxford, 1975), p.vii. A work to which this chapter owes much.

[11.] G.V. Bennett, *op.cit.*, p.viii.

attracted crowds to his preaching, and was soon chosen as a Chaplain-in-Ordinary to the King and Queen. He was only thirty, but he had secured a place of some prominence in the London scene. In his preaching he laid stress on personal religion and on the free and mysterious gift of salvation to individuals. He also emphasised the need for prayer, the sacraments and times of quiet for the attainment of a true knowledge of God. It was at this stage of his career that he was drawn more deeply into some of the key political issues of the day.

In the last decade of the century, the discontents, anxieties and confusion among the clergy became grist to the political mill. From about 1697 there is evidence of the formation of a new High Church party as one aspect of the new Tory party which remorselessly attacked the Ministers of King William. In this alliance, clerical propagandists were recruited systematically under the supervision of the Earl of Rochester, who was aided by three survivors of the pre-Revolution regime, Bishops Compton of London, Trelawny of Exeter and Sprat of Rochester. Dean Aldrich of Christ Church recruited a number of energetic, emminently literate young divines in the Tory crusade, and it was by means of this old Tory connection that Atterbury became so committed and active in the political conflict. He quickly emerged as the stormy petrel of the High Church revolt, and, for some years, 'at every step the story of Anglican Toryism marches parallel'[12] with his career.

In 1696 Atterbury displayed his journalistic flair most effectively in his pamphlet, *A Letter to a Convocation Man,* which began the famous Convocation controversy. It rehearsed all the grievances of the Church, and demanded as the sole remedy an active, effective Convocation. William Wake, Canon of Christ Church and Rector of St James's, Picadilly, replied, at the request of Archbishop Tenison, in a work which, much to the disappointment of the Archbishop, was long and tedious, and in the event disastrous for the case it presented, for it seemed like a completely Erastian argument, and it

---

[12.] G.V. Bennett, *op.cit.*, p.viii.

aroused widespread anger. It also provoked Atterbury to a rejoinder; a book entitled *The Rights, Powers and Privileges of an English Convocation* (1700), which it took him two years of study and research to produce. It was a tour de force which, together with his previous work on this subject, helped to establish him as the champion of Convocation against the Crown, and of the clergy against the bishops. He wished to make Convocation a means whereby 'urgently needed measures could be taken to restore the authority and status of the Church'.[13]

In 1709 Dr Sacheverell, a High Church divine, electrified an already tense and volatile religious and political atmosphere by preaching the most famous, or notorious, sermon of the century. He vigorously upheld the doctrine of non-resistance, and declared in violent language the perils facing the Church from Dissenters and the Whig government's policy of toleration and allowance of occasional conformity. His views were condemned by the Commons, and he was impeached. The resulting trial was in effect a grand parliamentary inquest on the Revolution of 1688, and the sentence of three years suspension from preaching was so light as to be a triumph for the accused, who became a popular hero. He had delivered a High Church and Tory party blow to the Whigs, who fell from power in 1710 largely as a result of this affair. It was a further demonstration of the interplay between High Churchmanship and Tory party politics in an age of religious and political instability. Nevertheless a long period of Whig domination and comparative tranquility was about to be inaugurated.

The death of Queen Anne in 1714, and the establishment in power of the Whigs, were two major reverses for the High Church Tories. By then Atterbury was Bishop of Rochester, and he despaired that the Tory party would ever be able to re-assert itself sufficiently to restore the Church to its ancient standing and authority. Church and state seemed to him to have fallen into bondage to the Whig oligarchy. As with others

---

[13] G.V. Bennett, *op.cit.*, p.57.

at this time, in his despondency he looked, for the first time, to a Jacobite military intervention to break the Whig hegemony and re-establish the Church in its rightful place in the life of the nation. It was a tragedy, and the cause of his downfall, that he thought that the well-being of the Church of England was dependent on the political regime, and was best promoted by political agitation. He was drawn into Jacobite intrigue, but the various schemes in which he was involved utterly failed, and in 1722 he was arrested and remanded to the Tower of London on a charge of high treason. He was deprived of all his preferments and banished for ever from the Kingdom. All subjects of the Crown were forbidden to communicate with him by speech or in writing except under licence of the Privy Seal. Exiled to the continent, he still championed the Stuart cause and plotted for the re-instatement of the Stuarts, not as an end in itself, but as a means to the re-establishment of what he regarded as the uniquely English version of the alliance of church and state. His understanding in this, as in many other matters, was moulded to a great extent by the teaching and practice of Laud, and by Sheldon and Sancroft in the post–1660 era.

He died in exile in 1732 with his hopes unfulfilled. His body was returned to England and laid to rest beside his wife and two daughters.

Atterbury represented an extreme example of hitching the High Church star to the Tory, and even Jacobite, waggon, even as Laud had hitched his to that of Charles I. To varying degrees, many of the late seventeenth and early eighteenth century High Churchmen did the same. It was a religio-political identity which was to contribute to their diminished influence during the next half century and more. For although the extent of High Church aridity during the eighteenth century has frequently been exaggerated, it was not a period of particular fruitfulness for their cause. 'Atterbury, for all his brilliance was an ecclesiastical comet, and there was something bogus about Sacheverell.'[14] The real strength and quality of the High Church at the time

---

[14] E.G. Rupp, *Religion in England 1688–1791* (Oxford, 1986), p.70.

was represented by the less flamboyant, less publicly prominent John Sharp, Archbishop of York. His whole ministry had its deepest roots in practical theology, in devotion and in a profound and attractive spirituality. Such qualities as these, he shared with fellow clergy like George Bull, Bishop of St Davids, and laymen such as Robert Nelson.

5

A Patchy Century

Although the century and more from the time of the Nonjurors to the Oxford movement was not a high point in High Church life, no period which included Bishop Joseph Butler, Bishop Samuel Horsley, High Church clergy such as Daniel Waterland and Samuel Wesley, the father of John and Charles Wesley, William Law, the Hutchinsonians and the Hackney Phalanx can be disregarded without doing grave injustice to all those concerned, and without depriving the High Church tradition of an important part of its inheritance.

Undoubtedly High Churchmen faced many difficulties in the 1730s.[1] They had been weakened by the Nonjuring deprivations. They felt politically threatened by ministerial indifference or hostility. They, in company with all orthodox Churchmen, had to contend with the deistical controversy which reached its height at about that time; and under the influence of such men as William Whiston and Samuel Clarke, it seemed that Arian heresy had gained alarming ground. Such protagonists as Dr Thomas Rundle and Benjamin Hoadly attacked the authenticity of an apostolic episcopate. The Church's claim to exercise judgement in matters of faith had come under renewed assault, as when the High Churchman Dr Thomas Coney had been vigorously opposed by James Foster, a dissenting minister, for his action in refusing communion to a man suspected of Arian sympathies. And

[1] This whole section owes much to Richard Sharpe, 'The Historical Background 1730 to 1780', in Geoffrey Rowell (Ed.), *Tradition Renewed: The Oxford Movement Conference Papers* (London, 1986), pp.4ff.

High Churchmen, like all Churchmen of that period, were confronted by a high level of immorality and decadence in society at large. High Churchmen played their part in responding to these various challenges. Joseph Butler was foremost in defending orthodox Christianity against deism, and Thomas Sherlock, Bishop of Salisbury, wrote with distinction in the controversy; Richard Smalbroke, Bishop of Lichfield, was a consistent defender of the spiritual and material privileges of the Church against Hoadly and the Dissenting Deputies; Dr Henry Stebbing upheld the Church's claim to a divine, not human, commission, and refuted the argument that the arbitrary criteria of 'happiness', 'virtue' or 'sincerity' were appropriate or adequate for assessing the integrity of the faith; and, finally, Daniel Waterland provided a body of teaching which was of great service to the Church not only in his day, but in generations to come.

Daniel Waterland (1683–1740)

Daniel Waterland took an active part in the theological controversies of his time. If Francis Atterbury symbolised extreme High Church views in the first decades of the eighteenth century, Waterland 'was a high church protestant theologian in the days when such a combination was still possible, indeed the norm, and an orthodox Whig...when the high theological ground was assumed to lie with the Tories'.[2] He delighted to defend the orthodox Church of England theology against Deism, Latitudinarianism and certain of the Nonjuring doctrines. He continued the High Church tradition of treading a middle path between the continental Protestant developments and what were seen as the errors of Rome; he maintained a balance between reform and the preservation of Catholicity. 'When our pious Reformers, about two hundred years ago, went about restoring religion to its ancient purity,' he declared, 'they did it in a regular and

---

[2] Paul Avis, *Anglicanism and the Christian Church*, p.150, a work to which this chapter is indebted.

orderly way, under the direction and countenance of the ruling powers and with due regard to such a regular ministry as Christ had appointed in the church.'[3]

Waterland was a typical High Church Anglican exponent of the synthesis between Scripture, antiquity and reason. He upheld the paramount authority of Scripture and looked for guidance to the early Church on occasions where Scripture itself was unclear. He adopted such an approach in his influential exposition of eucharistic theology.

Two principal schools of thought guided the understanding of the Eucharist for eighteenth century High Churchmen. The first derived from Andrewes, Overall, Heylyn, Thorndike and Mede and from the late seventeenth century revived awareness of the liturgies of the early Eastern Church, and found expression in such works as *The Unbloody Sacrifice* (1714) by John Johnson of Cranbrook. This tradition stressed the continuity of the Eucharist with the Old Testament sacrifices, and asserted that Christ was offered in every Eucharist, not hypostatically, as supposed by the Tridentine Church of Rome, but representatively and really, 'in mystery and effect'. Such beliefs were associated with the four usages, which, as we have previously noted, the Nonjurors incorporated in their liturgy of 1718. The second school of thought was derived from Cranmer, Laud, Taylor and Cudworth, and was expounded in Waterland's *Review of the Doctrine of the Eucharist* (1737).

Waterland defended the Protestant doctrine of forensic justification, and would not yield to any belief which derogated from the importance of such a belief, or the sacrifice of Christ as making such justification possible. 'The Eucharist was a commemorative and representative service, which possessed a sacrificial aspect from the remembrance of Christ's death, and the sacramental Presence was to be understood as the virtue and grace of the Lord's Body and Blood communicated to the worthy receiver.'[4] His rejection of any expiatory

[3] R.T. Holtby, *Daniel Waterland 1683–1740* (Carlisle, 1966), p.207, quoted in Paul Avis, *op.cit.*, p.150.

[4] F.L. Cross and E.A. Livingstone (Eds.), *Oxford Dictionary of the Christian Church*, (2nd ed., Oxford, 1983) p.1462.

connotation in the doctrine of the Eucharist was even more strongly stressed in another passage. 'To imagine any expiatory sacrifice now to stand between us and the great sacrifice of Christ', he wrote, 'is to keep us still at a distance when we are allowed to draw near: it is dishonouring the grace of the gospel; and, in short, is a flat contradiction to both Testaments.'[5] Waterland sought to steer a middle course between the high views of the Real Presence represented by some of the Nonjurors, and the minimizing opinions of Socinians and Deists.

In his defence of Christian fundamentals, and in his balanced approach to Scripture, antiquity and reason, Waterland probably did more than any other theologian of his day to check the advance of unorthodox doctrine in the Church of England, and he contributed significantly to the corpus of High Church teaching.

Joseph Butler (1692–1752)

Joseph Butler was a philosopher of the first rank. His *Analogy of Religion* (1736) transcended in importance and influence what it achieved in his own day and its place in the debate which provoked it; it was a work of major permanent significance both philosophicaly and theologicaly. Indeed, Butler 'ranks among the greatest exponents of natural theology and ethics in England since the Reformation'.[6] By his writing he immensely influenced some leading High Churchmen throughout the succeeding centuries.

Butler was both a product of and a key creator of the Age of Reason. His *Analogy of Religion* makes clear the central place he accorded to reason in his philosophy: reason is 'the only faculty we have wherewith to judge concerning anything, even revelation itself', he declared. 'First. It is the province of reason to judge of the morality of the scripture...whether it contains things plainly contradictory to wisdom, justice or

[5] Quoted in Paul Avis, *op.cit.*, p.151.
[6] F.L. Cross and E.A. Livingstone (Eds.), *op.cit.*, p.214.

goodness; to what the light of nature teaches us of God... Secondly. Reason is able to judge, and must, of the evidence of revelation, and of the objections urged against that evidence.'[7]

Although he elevated the faculty of reason to such a high level, Butler was insistent on its limitations, on its function to serve an overriding moral purpose, and on its supreme purpose as a means whereby we apprehend transcendent truth. In this his view contrasted with the secularised notion of reason propagated by Locke and his devotees.

In his argument with the Deists, Butler developed the idea of probability. It was a concept by means of which he attempted to hold together the rational and the moral. He came to see probability as the guide to the interpretation of life, and the way of providing at least limited assurance in our earthly state of moral probation. It was received by many as expressing the essential ethos of Anglicanism with its restraint, its steady and cautious approach and its determination to continue quietly and humbly serving others and doing good, but not prying into myteries too deep for us.

The most redoubtable defenders and expositors of the Butlerian doctrine in the nineteenth century were John Keble and William Gladstone. In his 1880 sermon on Butler, R.W. Church judged that, 'this great book [*the Analogy of Religion*], with the sermons which illustrate it, has had perhaps, directly or indirectly, more to do with the shaping of the strongest religious and moral thought in England, in the generation which is now passing away, than the writings of anyone who can be named'.[8]

William Wake (1657–1737)

Another prominent High Churchman of the period, and one who had particularly great breadth of charity and liberality,

---

[7] J. Butler, *The Analogy of Religion, Natural and Revealed* (London 1889 edition), p.229, quoted in Paul Avis, *op.cit.*, p.281.

[8] Quoted in Paul Avis, *op.cit.*, p.284.

was William Wake. He was outstanding in his strenuous work for unity both with the reformed churches of the continent and with the Roman Catholic Gallican Church in France, as well as with the Eastern churches. Nonetheless, despite his wide and deep ecumenical sympathies, 'Wake stood in the authentic tradition of Caroline high churchmanship.'[9] For instance, he commended sacramental confession as a practice recommended by the Church of England; he wished that penance was more fully used in the English Church; he rejected extreme Lutheran and extreme Calvinist tenets of salvation by faith alone without works, and the doctrine of double predestination; he refused offices vacated by the Nonjurors; he insisted on the apostolicity of episcopacy, and on episcopacy as the only basis for the union of protestants, but refused to unchurch non-episcopal ministries. 'It is Wake's unfailing liberality and his willingness to tolerate differences over non-fundamentals that sets him in the liberal catholic tradition, along with Taylor, Stillingfleet and Burnet.'[10]

Parish witness

The High Church tradition was kept alive not only by a few prominent individuals. In the mid-eighteenth century it was perpetuated through the ministry and life of important parishes including, in London, St Andrew's, Holborn, St Clement Dane's, St Giles, Cripplegate and St Mary-le-Bow. The tradition was also kept alive in the quiet of the countryside by countless High Church clergy, as is well demonstrated with the Wesley family. For it was as the children of a High Church rector, the Rev. Samuel Wesley, and his remarkable wife, Susannah, at Epworth in the county of Lincolnshire, that John and Charles Wesley were nurtured in beliefs and practices which they never wholly cast off, and which were much in evidence in the Oxford circle of earnest, devout, and scholarly

---

[9] W. Wake, *An Exposition of the Doctrine of the Church of England* (London 1686), p.32, quoted in Paul Avis, *op.cit.*, p.131.

[10] Paul Avis, *op.cit.*, p.132.

Christians they gathered around them in what became known as the 'Holy Club'. In addition to visiting the Oxford prison, teaching children, rising at five every morning, praying for each other and for their friends, and observing weekly communion, this dedicated band of High Churchmen tenaciously held not only to all the doctrines of the Church of England, but also to all its discipline, with a strict observance of the rubrics and canons. And the High Church principles of the rector of Epworth and his wife were preserved in the nineteenth century through the illustrious offspring of Charles Wesley. Such a pattern of transmitted tradition was repeated time and time again and was of incalculable importance.

John Hutchinson (1675–1737) and the Hutchinsonians

It was in the mid-eighteenth century that the Hutchinsonians appeared on the scene and took over the High Church aesthetic spiritual mantle from the Oxford Methodists. They are a little known, and inadequately acknowledged group, for they played an important part in the evolving High Church tradition. John Hutchinson was born in 1675, the son of a yeoman of Wensley Dale in the North Riding. He passed many of his early years as steward to the Earl of Scarborough and the Duke of Somerset, with responsibility for work in collieries. His interest in natural science seems to have been stimulated by his observations of rock formations and other phenomena in the bowels of the earth. At the same time he studied the Hebrew language, and he claimed to have found meanings in some of the primary words which neither the Jewish Rabbis nor Christian scholars had discerned. He founded a school of philosophy and theology which held that God had revealed to mankind from the beginning a means of understanding the created world, and this was embodied in the writings of Moses. Hutchinson died in 1737, and soon after that his works, which consisted of an extensive exposition of his beliefs, were published collectively. In his main work, *Moses's Principia* (1724), he

predicated that Hebrew was the primitive language of
mankind which, if correctly interpreted, gave the key to all
knowledge whether secular or religious.

There were elements of the teaching of Hutchinson, and
likewise of his followers for decades to come, which were
somewhat bizarre, but the core of it was acceptable to a wide
range of orthodox Christians:

> The dominating characteristic of Hutchinson's thought
> was its God-centredness. Certainty came not from the
> perceptions of the individual, which give knowledge only
> of the merely material, but by the gracious initiative of
> the Trinity. Fallen mankind could recognise spiritual
> truth only because God chose to reveal it...the human
> intellect was created to enable mankind to contemplate
> the self-revelation of God...[The Hutchinsonians]
> condemned Natural Religion from their conviction that
> salvation depended wholly on acceptance of God's
> revealed will. Hutchinsonians had no patience with the
> Enlightenment's Pelagianising concern for 'undogmatic
> moralism'...Obedience to God was the one necessary
> virtue.[11]

The early Hutchinsonians were not conspicuously Anglican
in their loyalties. It was later that two Anglican recruits, George
Horne and William Jones (of Nayland), who were both drawn
to the cause while students at Oxford, imparted to the
movement a strong High Church and anti-Dissenting tone.
Even with such influence, Hutchinsonianism never
completely lost the obscurantist cosmogony imprinted upon
it by its founder. But increasingly the apostles of the movement
found a more credible function in defending traditional
church order against continuing erosion. The goal of
Hutchinsonians was Christian godliness combined with
Christian order, and they breathed a genuine spirit of religious

---

[11.] E.A. Varley, *The Last of the Prince Bishops. William Van Mildert and the High
Church Movement of the early nineteenth century* (Cambridge, 1992), p.41.

revival. Indeed, George Horne and the Rev. George Berkeley so preached that they were accused of being Methodists, whereas they were in fact both Catholic and sacramental High Churchmen. George Horne moulded his spirituality on William Law's aesthetic example and teaching. He displayed a devotional warmth and intensity which was reminiscent of George Herbert, Thomas Ken and Robert Nelson, but which was alien to the prevailing Georgian High Anglicanism. His habits of fasting were strict, especially at such times as the commemoration of the Royal Martyr on 30 January, and he shared with Law and the later Tractarians, a high regard for celibacy as a spiritual ideal. Horne's Hutchinsonian friends, Jones of Nayland and William Stevens adopted the same spirituality and life style; and it was through them and others that the link was forged between Hutchinsonianism, the Hackney Phalanx and the Oxford movement.

By the the beginning of the reign of George III in 1760 there had emerged a distinctively Anglican, and largely High Church, Hutchinsonianism. But not all Hutchinsonians shared the affinity with Evangelicalism which Horne, for example, displayed, and the broad evolution was away from it. 'The entente between High Churchmanship and Calvinism, exemplified by Horne's defence of the six Calvinistic Methodists expelled from St Edmund Hall in 1768 for praying and preaching in private houses and his collaboration with Evangelicals like Toplady to resist alterations in the liturgy and Articles in 1772-3 lasted until the late 1790s, when Daubeny's attack on Wilberforce's *Practical View* sparked off two decades of controversy.'[12] Hutchinsonians were the nearest thing to a coherent body on the High Church side of the eighteenth-century Church of England. They were linked by ties of friendship and blood and they formed a compact coterie, whose members corresponded and tried to help one another whenever possible. Their numbers remained small but they exerted a large and growing influence during the first half of George III's reign. The advance of

---

[12.] F.C. Mather, *High Church Prophet. Bishop Samuel Horsley (1733-1806) and the Caroline Tradition in the later Georgian Church* (Oxford, 1992), p.13, a book to which this section of the present work is greatly indebted.

the brotherhood was to a great extent due to the capacity and willingness of its members to tread the lesser corridors of power for their own and their friends' advantage. They never lacked powerful connections.

Indeed, far from according with the usual caricature of eighteenth century High Churchmen, not only the Hutchinsonians, but subsequently the Hackney Phalanx and some other pre-Tractarian High Churchmen, were accused in their day of being enthusiasts, just as the leaders of the Oxford movement were to be in their day. Much of eighteenth and early nineteenth century High Churchmanship certainly was formal, without vision, and spiritually moribund or dead, but there was also an aliveness and vitality in parts of it, especially during the early part of the nineteenth century, which must not be overlooked, and Hutchinsonianism made some direct or indirect contribution to this.

The Hutchinsonians were mainly ordained men. The time had not yet dawned when laymen were to play a leading role in the life of the church. But, from our point of view, there were two High Church laymen of the period who are worthy of mention: William Law and Samuel Johnson.

William Law (1686–1761)

William Law was arguably the greatest High Church moralist of the mid-eighteenth century. In his *Three Letters to the Bishop of Bangor* (1717) he provided a welcomed, competent and convincing reply to Bishop Hoadly's attack on High Church principles. He defended the authority of tradition and the power and authenticity of the church's temporal jurisdiction against Hoadly's spiritualising of the text, 'My kingdom is not of this world'. Such was the abiding value of these famous but little read letters that Charles Gore issued a reprint of them in 1893. But Law's reputation, and his more weighty long term influence, was achieved through his two works on the Christian life: *On Christian Perfection* (1726), and, more especially, *A Serious Call to a Devout and Holy Life* (1728). The latter was inspired by the teaching of Johann Tauler, Jan van

Ruysbroeck, Thomas à Kempis, and other orthodox spiritual writers. It was 'a forceful exhortation to embrace the Christian life in its moral and aesthetical fulness'.[13] Law insisted on the need for the practice in everyday life of temperance, humility and self-control, all animated by the supreme intention of glorifying God, to which every human activity should be directed. The work was characterised by simplicity of teaching and a vigorous style, and it was soon established as a classic, probably having more influence than any other post-Reformation spiritual book other than *The Pilgrims Progress.* Out of reverence for it John Keble kept a copy of *The Serious Call* in a drawer. Law was later to come under the influence of the German Protestant mystic Jakob Boehme, and to emphasise the indwelling of Christ in the soul to such an extent that he verged on the Quaker conception of the 'Inner Light'. This was to estrange him from many of his former admirers, such as John Wesley, but he had already done sufficient to make his mark on Church teaching in general, and on that of the Anglican High Church in particular.

Samuel Johnson (1709–84)

Samuel Johnson, the author, lexicographer and conversationalist, who, through the classic biography of James Boswell, has become a symbol of the fundamental characteristics, ethos and standards of the eighteenth century, ascribed his conversion as a young man to his reading of Law's *Serious Call.* Unlike Law, he was not a Nonjuror, but he was a strong High Churchman, regular and sincere in his religious duties, and very generous to his friends and to the poor. He sometimes caused surprise by his marked tolerance of Roman Catholics. Although he was on friendly terms with individual Nonconformists, he did not conceal his dislike of Presbyterianism and Nonconformity as a whole.

[13.] F.L. Cross and E.A. Livingstone (Eds.), *Oxford Dictionary of the Christian Church,* (2nd ed., Oxford, 1983), p.805.

'Two-bottle' High Churchmanship

The Oxford Methodists, the Hutchinsonians and William Law represented an aesthetic ideal at one pole of the High Church tradition. But from the late 1730s there was a reaction from the other extreme within High Churchmanship.[14] For in 1739, Joseph Trapp, a Tory High Churchman, who had assisted Dr Sacheverell at his trial in 1709 and had sided with William Law in the Bangorian controversy, assailed not only the Oxford Methodists who were abandoning their aesthetic High Churchmanship for illuminist evangelicalism, but William Law himself, on grounds of enthusiasm and fanaticism. In reaction to the aesthetic severity of Law, Trapp set forth an ideal of spiritual life which, with its reasonableness, avoidance of excess and utilitarian overtones, recalled the teaching of John Tillotson and William Warburton and the spiritual tone of Latitudinarianism. During much of the eighteenth century it was this form of 'two-bottle' High Churchmanship, rather than the aesthetic form, which asserted itself and was more widely accepted. And it was this form which gave to eighteenth century High Churchmanship the reputation of worldliness, self-indulgence and spiritual deadness; a reputation which was largely accepted by the Tractarians as deserved, and which provoked them to introduce a more dynamic and vibrant spirituality.

Enduring theological concerns

Nonetheless, as we have seen, throughout the middle and second half of the eighteenth century High Churchmanship was not dead: it upheld High Church ideals, and, more than that, it added new elements to the body of High Church teaching. In its task of preservation, special importance was attached to Church discipline, the Eucharist, the Book of Common Prayer and the liturgy.

[14.] The following comments are based on Peter Nockles, 'Continuity and Change in Anglican High Churchmanship 1792–1850' (Oxford University D. Phil thesis, 1982).

The quarrel with the Methodists over breaches of parish order and the holding of irregular services, which was associated with a more general opposition to 'enthusiasm' and the moderate Calvinism of the Church of England Evangelicals, helped High Churchmen to refine their views on church discipline.

The Eucharist

Then there was the continuing High Church reaffirmation of Catholic teaching concerning the sacrament of the Lord's Supper against reductionist views. There were three identifiable High Church theories, and High Churchmen often combined one or more of them. The most extreme conceived of the Eucharist as a proper and propitiatory sacrifice, in which the bread and wine were themselves offered to God as symbols of Christ's oblation, begun not on the cross but when the rite was instituted at the Last Supper. This had been a Nonjuring tenet, but it was upheld throughout the mid-eighteenth century period by a small minority of obscure divines in the Church of England, but including the eminent High Church controversialist Archdeacon Charles Daubeny.

A broader band of High Church opinion affirmed that the Eucharist was a commemorative or memorial sacrifice: one by which, in the words of Prebendary George Berkeley, Christians do not 'barely commemorate their Saviour's death', but also 'powerfully plead in the court of heaven the merits of his vicarious sufferings'.[15] This teaching was in line with the theology of the moderate Caroline divines of the seventeenth century such as Jeremy Taylor, and it was expounded in the mid and later eighteenth century by Gloster Ridley and the leading Hutchinsonians.

Thirdly, there were many eighteenth century divines who were anxious to uphold the sacrificial character of the Lord's

---

[15.] Elize Berkeley (Ed.), *Sermons by the late Rev. George Berkeley* (1799), pp.89-105, quoted in F.C. Mather, *op.cit.*, p.18.

Supper, but who took special pains to guard against any suggestion that the Holy Communion service possessed any virtue of its own distinct from the one, sufficient sacrifice once offered on Calvary. They regarded the Eucharist as a feast upon that sacrifice: a banquet in which the faithful communicant made a covenant with his God by doing symbolically what Jewish and pagan sacrificers had effected literally, namely consuming a portion of the victim slain. This was in accord with antecedents which lay outside the High Church tradition, being traceable to the seventeenth century Cambridge Platonist, Ralph Cudworth.

Wheatley expressed the common view of High Churchmen of that age when he asserted that the greatest duty of Christian people was participation in the Eucharist, 'wherein we intercede on earth, in conjunction with the great intercession of our high Priest in heaven, and plead in the virtue and merits of the same sacrifice here, which he is continually urging for us there'. Although throughout the eighteenth century the Eucharist was sparingly administered, with a frequency of above five or six times a year being unusual in rural areas, High Churchmen were conspicuous for their efforts to raise the standards of eucharistic observance.

The Book of Common Prayer

The High Church stress upon the Eucharist was accompanied by a constant attachment to the Book of Common Prayer as 'the most primitive and complete collection of public Devotion in the World'. Its excellence, Wheatley declared, was 'deservedly admired by the eastern churches, and by the most eminent Protestants beyond the seas...[and] in short, honoured by all but the Romanists, whose interest it opposeth, and the Dissenters, whose prejudices will not let them see its lustre'.[16] High Churchmen considered that to depart from it was unjustifiable and a breach of necessary Church unity.

[16.] Richard Sharpe, *op.cit.*, p.19, a paper on which the following comments are based.

They were careful to adhere to the rubrics. They were ready to subordinate private preferences to the greater needs of unity; a view which distinguished them from some of their nineteenth-century successors. This pragmatic approach was also evident in Charles Wheatley's *Rational Illustration of the Book of Common Prayer*,[17] which may legitimately be claimed as the definitive liturgical commentary of the age. He defended the claims of the Church to a spiritual commission independent of any reliance on the state; he taught that divine service should be conducted with regularity and dignity; he insisted on the duty of daily public prayer, and the need for fixed places of worship formally dedicated and treated with scrupulous reverence; and he expressed appreciation of the value of external gestures such as facing east for the creed and bowing at the name of Jesus, which he said were useful aids to devotion, although he considered that the alb, cope and pastoral staff were obsolete.

High Churchmen helped to re-establish their commitment to the Prayer Book in a prolonged controversy over Prayer Book revision. High Churchmen such as Henry Stebbing and Gloster Ridley defended a conservative view against such radical proposals as the entire omission of the Athanasian and Nicene Creeds and the rephrasing of all specifically Trinitarian formulas.

Towards the end of the century High Churchmen led the Anglican counter attack against Dissenters who assailed the fundamental doctrines of the Church of England, and then attacked its privileged position as an establishment; the latter assault not infrequently being merged with the secular struggle for political liberties and civil rights which radicals conducted in England before and during the French Revolution.

During this difficult period from the late 1780s to the first decade of the new century Samuel Horsley did much to provide a new role-definition of High Churchmanship.

[17.] Charles Wheatley, *Rational Illustration of the Book of Common Prayer*, 8th edn., 1759.
[18.] Richard Sharpe, *op. cit.*, p.11

Samuel Horsley (1733–1806)

Horsley [19] was trained as a scientist, edited the works of Isaac
Newton and helped to plan the Royal Society's voyages of
exploration. He was Bishop first of St Davids, then of
Rochester and finally of St Asaph. He was assiduous in the
attention he gave to the business of the House of Lords during
a critical period, and he was forthright in his stand on the
great moral issues of the day, on religious toleration, the
abolition of the slave trade and the impeachment of Warren
Hastings.

Horsley was drawn into a dogmatic and distinct High
Churchmanship partly as a consequence of his friendship with,
and respect for Dr Samuel Johnson, and his attraction to
Johnson's loyal old-fashioned Tory Anglicanism, but mostly
as a result of his own much-publicised Trinitarian controversy
with Joseph Priestley between 1783 and 1790. The controversy
helped to revive a positive High Church theology and, more
specifically, provided Horsley with the opportunity to
proclaim his attachment to the High Church doctrine of the
apostolic succession of the ministry.

Horsley was a staunch Church of England man, and he
fought Lord Stanhope's bill for general religious liberty. He
'was the hammer of the Protestant Dissenters in their efforts
to remove the Test and Corporation Acts'. [20] He believed that
the Church of England was in danger. But he was vigorous
in his efforts to promote the relief of Roman Catholics, for
he saw them as allies against revolution and unbelief. Indeed,
he was a true friend of Roman Catholics. His favour towards
them was rooted in a sincere belief in toleration as understood
by conservative Churchmen of the time. It was additionally
based on a sense of shared theological conviction which
extended to many parts, though not to the whole, of the
Roman system. The endorsement he gave in the House of

---

[19] For the life and work of Samuel Horsley, see especially F. C. Mather, *High Church
Prophet. Bishop Samuel Horsley (1733–1806) and the Caroline Tradition in the later Georgian
Church* (Oxford, 1992), a book to which the present account owes much.

[20] F.C. Mather, *op.cit.*, p.18.

Lords to the Ultramontane position on canonical obedience, and John Milner's public recognition from the Roman Catholic side that there were two different types of Anglicanism, were features of the co-operation which helped to define 'orthodox' High Churchmanship and to fix its position in the Church of England in the decade around the turn of the century.

Certain key, distinctively High Church, convictions largely determined Horsley's outlook. First, he held strongly to belief in the divine origin of the ministerial commission and that episcopacy was the means whereby, from apostolic times to the present, spiritual authority had been transmitted to the clergy. While remaining a thoroughgoing exponent of the union of church and state, his stress on the independent spiritual authority of the Church's episcopal ministry, to which the will and acts of the prince must give civil effect, helped to fashion a concept which was later adopted by the Tractarians.

Samuel Horsley's High Churchmanship was indicated secondly by a leaning towards the Catholic view of the Eucharist. In common with many other Churchmen of the eighteenth century he had a preference for the Communion service in the first Prayer Book of King Edward VI, over the amended version of 1552 which divided the central eucharistic prayer, and removed those features of the ancient order most strongly suggestive of the sacrifice of the Mass and the real presence of Christ in the sacrament.

Thirdly, he emphasised the mysterious quality of religion in contrast to the rationalism and cult of plainness which had been propagated by such Latitudinarian divines as Archbishop Herring and Bishop Hoadly.

Lastly, as a mark of his High Churchmanship, Horsley assigned great importance to tradition as a mentor of church doctrine and practice.

When Samuel Horsley died in 1806 there was only a loosely compacted High Church party, but it had established a momentum. His death was an irreparable loss to this High Church group as it deprived the High Church reform movement of its figurehead and statesman. He had achieved much, and the renewal of High Churchmanship was about to enter a more advanced phase. The High Church influence was perhaps at its height in the inner councils of both church and state during the twenty years or so prior to the Oxford movement. High Churchmen dominated the episcopate and many were Archdeacons, Deans, royal chaplains or Heads of Houses at Oxford and Cambridge. It was a dominance which was exemplified by the fact that, as we will see, under the administration of Lord Liverpool in particular, Henry Handley Norris, a leading member of the Hackney Phalanx, was popularly known as the 'bishop-maker'. High Churchmanship had been kept in a sufficiently good state of health during the period since the 1730s to allow it to burst out afresh in the form first of the Hackney Phalanx and then of the Oxford movement.

6

The Hackney Phalanx

The Hackney Phalanx has suffered at the hands of historians, and not least of all historians of the Oxford movement who, in most cases, have given it little attention let alone sympathetic treatment. It has often been denigrated as a dull and inconsequential propagator of mere ecclesiasticism. It has frequently been perceived as a group of unimaginative 'High and Dry' Tories who displayed little warmth or depth of spirituality. It has been eclipsed in historical description and analysis, almost to the extent of being ignored, by the focus upon the Evangelical Clapham Sect, which has been viewed as a more prominent and significant contemporary group, and by concentration upon the Oxford movement, which has been portrayed as the true reviver of authentic traditional High Churchmanship. This general judgement at the bar of history is unfortunate, inaccurate and inadequate. The Hackney Phalanx, or Clapton Sect, should not be dismissed as but the inheritor of a High and Dry churchmanship which it perpetuated until the Oxford movement rightly assumed the mantle of the lost seventeenth century High Churchmanship. As we have seen, High Churchmanship continued, albeit for a few decades of the eighteenth century in a somewhat disjointed and sparodic way, and the Hackney Phalanx was an honourable and worthy representative of that tradition, making its own distinctive contribution to it. It was an important movement in the evolution of Anglican Catholicism, and played a vital part in the history of the Church of England as a whole. 'Historians, in commenting on the sober temperament which prevented them from manifesting the piety of the Tractarians have overlooked the fact that they had an enthusiasm of their own which gave their utterances a zeal unmatched by the Orthodox Establishment in the years of the French Revolution and Wars. For them the *status quo* was no matter of mere utility; it was sacred. The preservation of order was a divine commandment, not a human expedient.'[1] What they wrote and said was not animated by a concern for personal piety, although this was of central importance to them, but by passion for the preservation of existing authority at a time when such authority was under severe threat, in an age of iconoclasm, and with pressures for reform or revolution in all and every aspect of national life. This unyielding determination to remain faithful to what they perceived as a God given purpose gave them their own brand of intensity, which bears comparison with the differently based and motivated intensity of the Evangelicals at the time. They were engaged in a crusade, assured, in the face of the French Revolution and French Wars and stirrings of discontent at home, that they were right in their view of church, state and salvation. And they generally communicated their convictions in a way which was far more virile, and far less in the style of eighteenth century decorum, moderation or dry formality, than has commonly been acknowledged.

Joshua Watson (1771–1855)

The history of the Hackney Phalanx is bound up with the personal history of Joshua Watson.[2] He was born on 9 May 1771 in London, the son of a wealthy wine merchant and

[1] Nancy Uhlar Murray, 'The Influence of the French Revolution on the Church of England and its Rivals, 1789–1802.' Oxford University D. Phil., 1975. A work to which this chapter is much indebted.

[2] The following account of the life and work of Joshua Watson, and the Hackney Phalanx, is greatly indebted to A.B. Webster, *Joshua Watson: the Story of a Layman, 1771–1855* (London, 1954). For the life of Joshua Watson see also E. Churton, *Memoir of Joshua Watson*, 2 vols. (Oxford, 1861).

government contractor. After attending a commercial school, he became his father's partner, and in 1797 married Mary Sikes, the daughter of a banker, and a niece of Watson's close friend, Thomas Sikes, the vicar of Guilsborough.

His father had taught him to combine a firm and resolute belief and trust in God with business diligence, and he tried in various ways to help promote the well being of his workers. It also appears that over the course of his life he gave away over half his possessions. And that represented considerable charity, for not only did he inherit riches, but during the Napoleonic era he made a fortune. As he became increasingly prosperous, he became more and more convinced 'that he was entangled and ensnared in business when the divine command and the needs of men required him to use his abilities and his wealth in the service of God and his fellows'.[3]

Watson did not experience any sudden conversion. His whole upbringing had implanted in him an immovable conviction that happiness in this world and the next depended on a righteous life. He was by nature reticent, and he abhored introspection, sermonising and drama or ostentation in religious matters. His momentous decision to abandon his business life and give himself to new tasks was therefore seen by him not as a climacteric event, but had 'all the inevitability of a duty gladly accepted'.[4] It was a decision to which the teaching of the Church, the example of some of his friends and the example of philanthropic and humanitarian work undertaken by the Evangelicals all contributed. In 1814 he gave sufficient notice to his partners to allow them to find another merchant with adequate capital to take his place, and retired from the City. During the remainder of his life, and especially during the following twenty years, he made a contribution to the life of the Church of England which places him among a select band of laymen of all time. He was instrumental in shaping and executing the policy of the Church of England and, like his contemporary William

[3.] A.B. Webster, *op.cit.*
[4.] A.B. Webster, *op.cit.*

Wilberforce, he demonstrated what a wealthy man, dedicated to the service of God, could achieve. Unlike Wilberforce, he was not a charismatic leader, able to arouse the enthusiasm of a crowd. He was more at home on a committee than in the vanguard of a crusade; but it was committees which were needed then, and Watson was highly regarded for his ability, tirelessness, dedication, clear headedness and integrity. Unfortunately, neither he nor the Phalanx as a whole attracted the young, and this was to prove a major problem when the young enthusiasts of the Oxford movement were not sympathetic to what they saw as the ponderous old men of Hackney who were lacking in vision. But this was all in the distant future. From the battle of Trafalgar to the Reform Bill, much of the creative work in the Church was inspired and organised by Watson and his friends.

After his retirement from business, Watson spent much of his time in his Westminster house conveniently close to the Parliament buildings, the government offices and Lambeth Palace. But his real home and base was in what was then the village of Hackney, a community which, like the neighbouring village of Clapton, was detached from the sprawling city.

A tightly knit group

The Hackney Phalanx, like the Clapham Sect, was a tightly knit group of friends which combined scope for individuality with brotherhood and a common purpose. Many of them were related by blood or marriage. Joshua Watson's wife was the niece of both the Rev. Thomas Sikes, the 'Pope' of Guilsborough, and the Rev. Charles Daubeny, the unpaid curate of the church at which Hackney Phalanx members worshipped. Henry Handley Norris was Watson's brother-in-law, and he in turn was a relative of Edward Churton, Archdeacon of Cleveland, and Watson's biographer. These family ties were strengthened by an intense interest in one anothers children, shown in the mass of letters about births, marriages, deaths and achievements, and by frequently shared holidays. There was also a useful variety and complementarity of talents among the fraternity, so that each member was able to make his or her distinctive contribution to the collective work of the Phalanx.

The members of the Phalanx were united by a common religious and political outlook and a high degree of agreement on most of the religious and political issues of the day. All the members were Tories as well as High Churchmen, all were middle-class and all read the same devotional books.

Joshua's brother, Archdeacon Watson (1770–1839) was Vicar of Hackney for more than forty years and a strong supporter of the Phalanx, despite the fact that he was prevented by poor health from taking a leading part in its affairs, so that the clerical leadership of the fraternity was taken by his curate, Henry Handley Norris (1771–1850).

Norris was an intimate friend and confidant of Joshua Watson, and for much of their lives they rejoiced in taking 'sweet counsel together'. Norris shared in all Joshua's work, and was also thought to be Lord Liverpool's confidential adviser on matters of ecclesiastical appointments. Lord Liverpool favoured moderate High Churchmanship, and he was also a man of unquestioned integrity. He was looked upon by the Phalanx as an ideal Prime Minister, whose help was sought when the church particularly needed the assistance of the state.

Charles Daubeny (1745–1827)

Charles Daubeny was the leading writer on theological matters among the Phalanx members, and much that he wrote became High Church orthodoxy. He was the son of a Bristol merchant. He attended New College, Oxford, where he became a Hutchinsonian. He was the non-resident incumbent of North Bradley, Wiltshire, but used his private fortune to restore the church. In 1798 he opened a 'free church' for the poor in Bath, and became its first minister. He was later made Archdeacon of Salisbury. He, like other members of the Hackney Phalanx, has been portrayed as having a somewhat formal and arid spiritual life, and indeed as being an archetypal 'High and Dry' churchman of his generation, but on closer examination he is seen to have had a rich spiritual life.[5] He kept his own spiritual diaries and manuals of devotion, chanted a morning hymn in his garden on rising and spent whole days locked in his study deep in devotion. He translated Lancelot Andrewes' *Morning Prayer* for daily use, and as aids to his devotions he drew fully on the richest treasures of Caroline and Nonjuring spirituality. He also appreciated the fervent piety of such moderate Evangelicals of his day as William Wilberforce.

Of particular importance was his celebrated *Guide to the Church* which came out in 1798. It was as rigid in its teaching as any latter-day Anglo-Catholic work. He was dogmatic in his insistence that the true Church must have a duly commissioned ministry deriving its authority in direct line from the apostles. The priesthood is a divine institution. Sacraments are the 'seals of the divine covenant'.[6] The sacraments of the Dissenters are mere human ordinances and without effect, because the Dissenters lack a properly constituted ministry. He reserved a milder censure for the Roman Catholic Church, for he claimed that Canterbury and Rome were agreed on essentials.

William Stevens (1732–1807)

Among the laymen, William Stevens was in the forefront. He had been sent to the same commercial school as Watson and was engaged in commerce. Together with William Jones, Vicar of Nayland, he published a series of pamphlets during the period of the French revolutionary crisis, attacking the English supporters of the Revolution and especially Tom Paine and

---

[5] The comments in this section owe much to Peter Nockles, 'Continuity and Change in Anglican High Churchmanship 1792–1850' (Oxford University D.Phil. thesis, 1982).

[6] C. Daubeny, *Guide to the Church* (ed. 1829), p.6, quoted in Bernard M. G. Reardon, *Religious Thought in the Victorian Age. A Survey from Coleridge to Gore* (London, 1971), p.34.

Dr Priestley. Like the earlier prominent eighteenth century High Churchman, Dr Samuel Johnson, Stevens was a firm supporter of the Prayer Book services. He was Treasurer of Queen Anne's Bounty, a member of several church and charitable societies, and one of the founders of the gathering of friends named Nobodys Club.

Other notable members

There were between fifty and one hundred laymen and clergymen who either counted themselves part of the Phalanx or worked in close association with its members to achieve its objectives. Prominent among these were various members of the Wordsworth family, including Dr Christopher Wordsworth (1774–1846) who became Master of Trinity College, Cambridge, and was the author of an exposition on the doctrine of the Church, *Theophilus Anglicanus* (1843). He persuaded Archbishop Manners-Sutton to accept Watson as his principal lay adviser, and he also introduced Watson to his brother, the poet William Wordsworth (1770–1850). There was also the Tory propagandist John Gifford, who edited *The Anti-Jacobean Review;* two judges, Sir John Richardson and Sir James Alan Park; the magistrate John Bowler, and the Bowdler family, who had supported the last of the Nonjurors; the barrister who organised the Loyal Association, John Reeves; the authoress and pamphleteer Sarah Trimmer; Robert Southey, the Poet Laureate; Sir T.D. Acland, a prominent Tory Member of Parliament; and Professor Baden Powell, although he ultimately abandoned the Hackney standpoint.

Special mention should perhaps be made of Alexander Knox (1757–1831) who, in much of his teaching, anticipated the Oxford movement. He affirmed that the Church of England was a reformed branch of the Church Catholic, and not a 'protestant' Church. He emphasised the need for Apostolic Succession, the Book of Common Prayer and the Thirty-Nine Articles. He occasionally corresponded with John Wesley, whom he greatly admired, and he was 'fully in accord with the spiritual ideals of Methodism, if not with its express theology. What his own party needed, he was convinced, was an infusion of the Methodists' fervour.'[7]

Episcopal support

Unlike the Clapham Sect, the Hackney Phalanx, far from being estranged from the highest echelons of the Church, was well represented in the hierarchy.[8] At least eight men who either were bishops in the late eighteenth century or were raised to the bench in the early nineteenth century, reckoned themselves as friends of the Phalanx. The English bishops who gave support were George Horne, William Van Mildert, Samuel Horsley, John Douglas, Herbert Marsh, Charles Manners-Sutton, and John Randolph; and there was also Thomas Middleton, the first Bishop of Calcutta. Of these, George Horne, the Hutchinsonian, was a pivotal figure. As President of Magdalen College, he united with three other Heads of Colleges, Dr Wetherell of University College, Dr Hodges of Oriel, and his successor at Magdalen, Dr Martin Routh, to form a powerful focus for High Church life at Oxford. He was Bishop of Norwich from 1790 until his death in 1792, having William Jones as his Chaplain and William Stevens, his cousin, as an intimate friend. The ranks of the Phalanx also included Dean Thomas Rennell, whom Pitt called 'the Demosthenes of the pulpit', Dean Nathaniel Wetherell of Hereford, George Berkeley, Vice-Dean of Canterbury, and Archdeacon Joseph Holden Pott.

As we have previously noted, Bishop Horsley was especially notable. And Bishop William Van Mildert was influential in the councils of the Phalanx. He was very much aware of the need for the Church to be salt and light in the world by its involvement in the affairs of the country locally and nationally. He dreamed of the Church of England 'as the soul of the State, as the servant of every citizen, as the custodian of true

---

[7.] Bernard M.G. Reardon, *op.cit.*, p.37.
[8.] See Peter Nockles, *op.cit.*

learning and wisdom, as an act of loving homage offered to God in the consciousness of unworthiness but with a confidence founded on Divine Grace'.[9]

The *British Critic*

The Phalanx also had an important vehicle for communication in the *British Critic*. That influential magazine had been founded by a group of High Churchmen who had been appalled at the spread of revolutionary principles. About 1812 it was acquired by Joshua Watson and H.H. Norris, and edited by some of their ablest theological friends, William Van Mildert, Thomas Fanshawe Middleton and Thomas Rennell. All contributions to the magazine reflected the same High Church point of view, and even bishops were on occasions rebuked if they appeared to infringe High Church principles. Attacks on the Church were vigorously opposed, while actions such as the sending of bishops to India were applauded. Voluntary organisations and societies, including the Church Missionary Society, which did not have the official sanction of the Church leaders and the state, were treated with suspicion. The journal appealed to those who valued serious, well written theological articles, but it also included consideration of literature, foreign affairs and other topical matters. With this wide coverage it displayed a breadth of perspective and a degree of animation far removed from the dryness normally associated with eighteenth century High Churchmanship.

Theology and politics

The Phalanx looked back especially to Laud and the Caroline divines, with Jeremy Taylor as a particular source of teaching

---

[9.] E.A. Varley, *The Last of the Prince Bishops. William Van Mildert and the High Church Movement of the early nineteenth century*, p.106.

and inspiration. The theological focus of the members was more on the incarnation than on the atonement. They accepted natural theology in that they looked for evidence of God in nature. They exalted the place of the visible Church as an essential part of God's scheme of redemption, and some of them distrusted the Nonconformists, even on occasions succumbing to lurid language, as when William Jones of Nayland damned free church chapels as 'synagogues of Satan'. They believed that there was no salvation outside the true Church and that dissenters were in a state of schism. The high view of church and state common among the Hackney Phalanx members led them to believe that all Christian citizens were in a relationship of children to their mother the Church of England, even if they belonged to Nonconformist churches. This absorbing interest in the Church, rather than individual conversion, with all its consequential ramifications in terms of Christian belief and political activity, was fundamental in the whole ordering of their affairs.

They shared with High Churchmen in general, and in contrast to the Evangelicals, a conviction that the efficacy of communion depended on its administration by a properly commissioned clergyman, with the service conducted within a true branch of the Catholic Church, and of course this included the Church of England. God did not need to make his presence known and felt through special effusions of his Spirit, as in Apostolic times, but was fully able to accomplish what he wanted through the regular services and ordinances of his Church, administered by his ordained clergy and bishops. It followed that there was an emphasis on liturgy and the sacraments rather than on preaching, which was considered an appendage to the Church service.

As we have previously had cause to mention in passing, members of the Hackney Phalanx were acutely wary of 'enthusiasm'. They were strongly opposed to introspection, self-examination and the uninhibited expression of religious feelings, even in the intimacy of their own diaries. 'For my part', said William Wordsworth, 'I have been averse to frequent mention of the mysteries of the Christian faith; not from a want of a due sense of their momentous nature, but the contrary. I felt it far too deeply to venture on handling the subject as many scruple not to do.'[10] The Phalanx members would have readily endorsed this attitude. Much of their strength lay in their restraint, and in the firmness of their convictions. Nonetheless, although in many ways commendable, their apprehension about any undue expression of feelings in religious matters probably cost them dearly. It was a hindrance to the greater enrichment of their own lives and it diminished the attractiveness of their cause to others. It was perhaps due to an over-defensive reaction to the Evangelicals, whom they too readily dismissed, as they did the more intensely pious Tractarians, as excessively emotional, and to an over-concern to remain rational, calm and placid in matters religious as in all things. And yet even they could be roused by causes in which they passionately believed, and, as we have seen, they were not without sensitivity in their own spiritual lives.

Politically, the Hackney Phalanx were loyal supporters of the cautious new reforming Toryism which was led successively by William Pitt, Spencer Perceval, Lord Liverpool and Robert Peel. They greatly distrusted the radical movement, and were horrified by the 1832 Reform Act extension of the franchise. They were stalwart and resolute establishment men. In all that they did they were concerned to work through the established structures of the Church and the state.

In a quiet, largely unsung way the Phalanx accomplished a great deal, especially in education, in the provision of new churches, in the regeneration of the old Church societies, in supplying additional staff for parishes, in promoting relief for a devastated German people and in supporting the Church overseas.

Educational reform and the National Society

The Clapton fraternity first addressed itself to educational

---

[10] A.F. Potts, *Ecclesiastical Sonnets of William Wordsworth* (Yale U.P., 1922), p.17, quoted in A.B. Webster, *op.cit.*, p.21.

reform, for elementary education seemed to them to be one of the greatest needs of the age. Many thousands of children in London and the rapidly expanding new industrial towns were growing up to be ignorant and illiterate. In the eighteenth century Grammar Schools, Dissenting Academies, Charity Schools and Dames' Schools had done magnificent work, but they were wholly inadequate for the new, rapid increase in the population and the ever more complex industrial society of the early nineteenth century. There were too few schools, and there was active opposition to the extension of educational provision by those in society who considered that education would make workers insolent and restless. There was also the rivalry for educational control between the Church, the Nonconformists and the state. Two self-taught enthusiasts, Dr Andrew Bell and Joseph Lancaster had already founded schools, the former accepting and the latter rejecting Church control. There was almost universal recognition that Christianity should be part of the education provided under any scheme, but in practice the Church of England and the Nonconformists vied for the right to superintend whatever system was devised. And of course anything on a scale which even remotely measured up to the need would be massively expensive.

An inner group of the Phalanx, headed by Joshua Watson, H.H. Norris and John Bowles, set to work on a project which resulted in the inauguration in 1811 of The National Society for Promoting the Education of the Poor in the Principles of the Established Church, more commonly known as The National Society. The Prince Regent was the Patron, the Archbishop of Canterbury was President, and the other bishops were Vice-Presidents, thus making clear that this was the Church acting in its corporate capacity rather than a mere private society run by a group of self-appointed zealots. Watson was elected Treasurer and Norris temporary Secretary; and by their initiative and energetic leadership property and funds were acquired within a few months for a school in London. A vigorous campaign was started to encourage the formation of local parish schools throughout the land, and requests for schoolmasters, books and advice were received not only from parishes but also from overseas dioceses, the Army and Navy and others who wanted to run classes or organise schools. By 1815 every diocese in England was consulting the Society, and one hundred thousand children were in its schools – a number that rose to almost one million twenty years later. But with the repeal of the Test and Corporation Acts and the Catholic Emancipation Act, there was an increased tendency towards disestablishment, and with the introduction after 1833 of state assistance for education, the Society became less effective. Henceforth, as Watson and the Society attempted to cope with a Whig reforming government, so they became increasingly conservative and opposed to change. Nonetheless, Watson and his friends had successfully conducted an impressive mass literacy campaign. They had pioneered popular elementary education, ensured that education in England would be Christian and not secular for the foreseeable future, and enabled the national Church to control directly at least some of the schools as a prelude to the dual system introduced in 1870. They were not mean achievements.

Strengthening the Church in industrial areas

The members of the Phalanx were acutely aware of the condition of the Church in the newly emergent industrial areas. This was perhaps the thing which most heavily weighed on their minds. Christian schools, Christian missions and Christian charity were of secondary importance if England was becoming increasingly pagan. The Church needed to be strengthened, especially in the new industrial towns. It was John Bowdler who originated a High Church scheme for Church-building. Again, as with education, the concern was for the Church to act in its corporate capacity rather than for action to be taken by a private society. Spencer Percival, the Prime Minister, was approached; and then a petition was sent to his successor Lord Liverpool, signed by both High Churchmen and Evangelicals. An Incorporated Church Building Society was founded, and its considerable success was mainly due to the drive, vigour and hard work of Bowdler, George Bramwell, William Davis and Joshua Watson. All the effort bore fruit. In 1818 the House of Commons voted £1,000,000 for Church-building, to be administered by a Commission on which Watson served, and this was supplemented in 1824 by a further £500,000, to which was added over £200,000 in subscriptions. It was a central tenet of the Commission's strategy that the churches built should help to meet the existing pressing needs, and they were constructed with this in mind rather than being refined and of intricate design. Watson was a key figure in the wise management of the Government grants and in raising large voluntary donations during the next twenty years: and it taxed all his abilities. 'The building programme depended upon him more than any other single man.'[11]

After having done a gigantic work on the provision of new churches Watson and a small group of colleagues turned to the equally urgent need for extra curates to assist the desperately hard pressed urban clergy. The Evangelical Church Pastoral-Aid Society had already been established in 1836, but the High Churchmen found similar difficulties in supporting this new body as they had experienced with the Church Missionary Society. The CPAS laid down doctrinal requirements and was not prepared to leave the licensing of curates to the bishops, and it also employed lay workers, arousing High Church fears that this was the prelude to unacceptable lay preachers. An unsuccessful attempt was made to pursuade the sponsors of the CPAS to modify their rules, so Watson, Sir Robert Inglis, MP, and Benjamin Harrison founded the Additional Curates Society in 1837, which was pledged to work through the bishops. Watson gave a lump sum of £500 and £100 each year for the rest of his life, as well as drawing up the society's constitution, and serving as joint Hon. Treasurer.

[11] A.B. Webster, *op.cit.*, ch.5.

Wider interests and dwindling influence

Watson was a superb administrator and diplomat, and he used his skills to help in a further, unromantic, unsensational, hidden but immensely valuable service: the removal of some of the 'anomalies and anachronisms in the Churches administrative machinery and the transformation of its relations with the State, an inevitable consequence of the entrance of Free Churchmen and Roman Catholics into Parliament'. [12]

Watson and his fellow-workers did not confine their interests and activities to national issues. They had an international view of human affairs, and this was exceptional in an age when, in general, High Churchmen were somewhat insular and inward-looking. They were especially concerned about the Napoleonic devastation of Germany, and anxious that aid should be given to assist German recovery. As a consequence of their prompting, the Archbishop of Canterbury issued an Appeal, the Government made a grant and a letter was distributed to churches throughout the land requiring a collection in every church.

By 1832 Watson was over sixty and beginning to feel the effect of many years of strenuous labour and responsibility. He was less able constantly to attend committees or persistently provide guidance to ecclesiastics and politicians. He continued to exert considerable influence, especially as the close friend and confidant of Bishop Blomfield, but his halcyon days were passed. In the 1830s the Phalanx continued its work, but at a lower key, and in a less forthright manner. It was particularly concerned to encourage Church reform, with three priorities: 'appointments to be made according to merit, translations of bishops to be greatly restricted, and ecclesiastical property to be redistributed'.[13]

The Phalanx and its leader were not only worn out; they were somewhat fearful about what the future held in store

---

[12.] A.B. Webster, *op.cit.*, ch.6.
[13.] A.B. Webster, *op.cit.*, ch.6.

for the Church of England. Despite their remarkably impressive achievements they had not been attracting many new, and especially young, recruits. They had no theologians who could speak out boldly and authoritatively on behalf of a Church which was assailed by liberals and reformers, and was undergoing a crisis of confidence as severe as any in its history. The so-called High Church revival which was about to dawn was clerical and academic, rather than lay and practical; and it was reformist and adventurous rather than conservative and reticent. In brief, the movement centred on Oxford differed in certain fundamental ways from the movement centred on Hackney. Watson was to remain in contact with the new movement as a friendly critic, but he and others knew that he and his Hackney friends had been superseded.

Relations with the Tractarians

The divide between the 'establishment men', or Zs, as Hurrell Froude contemptuously called them, and the Tractarians became evident at an early stage. It first appeared at the Hadleigh Conference in July 1833. Hugh James Rose, who hosted the Conference, was a close friend of Watson and a sympathiser with his principles and aims, and others at the Conference were likewise sympathetic, so the Zs got their way. But the split between the two wings of High Churchmanship which was manifest at Hadleigh, widened considerably from 1835 onwards. In that year Pusey's *Tract on Baptism* appeared to so emphasise the grievousness of post-baptismal sin that, in the view of Rose and others, it allowed for no remission of sin after baptism, and Rose protested at such teaching. It was one of the first indications of a doctrinal breach between the two groups. In 1838 the publication of Froude's *Remains* further, and much more seriously, offended the old High Churchmen, because of the hostility to the Reformation and the contempt for the Reformers which it revealed, and because of the exhuberant, unrestrained spirituality of its author which was so at variance with the sober reverence of the Phalanx members. The old High Churchmen were also uneasy about some implicit, or even explicit, criticisms of the Church of England, especially when this was accompanied by a favourable view of Romanism; but Watson remained unwilling to sanction any public condemnation. *Tract 90*, with its attempt to justify a non-Protestant interpretation of the Thirty-Nine Articles, was a further shock.

In his old age Watson viewed the Oxford movement with mixed feelings. He acknowledged that it had greatly helped to defeat the enemies of Christianity and the Church in an age of revolution and liberalism; it had reminded the Church of England that it was heir to a Catholic past as well as the Reformation; it had made the Church more aware than it had been of its innate authority; and it had made the Church more capable of initiating new ventures at home and overseas. But there was loss as well as gain. A number of men had seceded to Rome, and a focus for Romeward tendencies had been provided within the Church of England for those so inclined. Also the eager young Tractarians had alienated many friends of the Church, and caused needless divisions within it. The movement, Watson felt, had become a party within the Church, instead of a group of men with a new devotion to the Gospel who were intent on binding together Church and nation in a common allegiance. If they would only have had more patience, and gone more slowly, if they would only have submitted their work to some wise and cautious committee, if they would only have considered more carefully the consequences of their acts, then they might have united the Church and made the movement a greater, more telling force in the national life. So much of what they had done and said and written seemed to him to have been unnecessary.

But in many ways his reflections and comments were not unfriendly for, despite their differences, both he and the Tractarians believed that they were promoting a common cause. Amid the abuse aroused by the departure of Newman, Pusey wrote to Watson:

One had become so much the object of suspicion, that I cannot say how cheering it was to be recognised by you as carrying on the same torch which we had received from yourself and those of your generation who had remained faithful to the old teaching. We seemed no longer separated by a chasm from the old times and old paths, to which we wished to lead people back; the links which united us to those of old seemed to be restored. It seems hard to wish to keep you from your greater rest; yet I trust that you will be for some time spared to us, finding rest in defusing peace amidst our troubled waters, and a witness yet further to the principles you have brought down to us.'[14]

Watson received this as a great compliment. 'He could not be sure, but as he reflected on the Movement, and balanced the gain and the loss, his judgement as well as his affection and loyalty told him that the gain was greater than the loss.'[15]

World mission

An account of the Hackney Phalanx would be incomplete without testimony to their contribution to world mission. For many years members of the Phalanx played a leading part in the old established Church of England missionary societies, the Society for Promoting Christian Knowledge and the Society for the Propagation of the Gospel. On the initiative of the Phalanx, a committee was set up in 1810 to help revitalise the SPCK, largely by means of organising local diocesan committees, with the sanction and under the direction of the bishops. In 1814 Watson became Treasurer of the SPCK. He also laboured energetically for the SPG, and strove to link the two societies together as closely as possible. Like the SPCK,

[14] E. Churton, *Memoir of Joshua Watson*, 2 vols. (Oxford, 1861), Vol. II, pp. 82, 83, quoted in A.B. Webster, *op.cit.*, p.112.

[15] A.B. Webster, *op.cit.*, p.113. For a discussion of the relationship between the Tractarians and the old High Churchmen see David Forrester, *Young Dr. Pusey. A Study in Development* (1989), Peter Nockles, *op.cit.*, and Geoffrey Rowell (Ed.), *Tradition Renewed: the Oxford Movement Conference Papers* (London, 1986).

the SPG was in urgent need of new men and new ideas: it had degenerated into a board for holding various trust funds. Its total income was only about £8,000 of which less than £500 came from donations or subscriptions. By the time of Watson's death in 1855 this had increased to more than £82,000, mainly due to an enormous increase in subscriptions, and to frequent collections in churches.[16]

Phalanx members kept themselves fully informed about the Church overseas, so that they were well placed to respond to varied calls for personnel or money. They recognised the need to provide assistance to overseas diocese while at the same time encouraging and fostering the independence of those diocese.

It is well to note that it was in the sphere of world mission that the extent of common ground between the Clapham and the Clapton Sects was perhaps most clearly demonstrated.[17] William Wilberforce had been particularly attracted by the National Society, had given generously to its funds and had attended a number of its public meetings. This shared concern for educational matters inspired Wilberforce to seek Phalanx support for a scheme to promote the evangelisation of India. A public campaign was mounted and pressure put on the Lords and the Commons. The Evangelicals took the lead, but High Churchmen were involved. As a consequence of their united efforts Parliament authorised the admission of missionaries to India and created a small establishment of one bishop and three archdeacons. The Evangelicals accepted gracefully, albeit with disappointment, the appointment of T.F. Middleton, one of the most able and energetic members of the Phalanx, as the first bishop. And despite the forthright High Churchmanship of Middleton in India the spirit of co-operation between the Evangelicals and the High Churchmen was not quenched. The Saints and the Phalanx also maintained a measure of co-operation despite an abortive attempt, instigated by Christopher Wordsworth and Reginald

[16.] See F. Pascoe, *Two Hundred Years of the SPG*, pp.831, 832, referred to in A.B. Webster, *op.cit.*, p.115.

[17.] The following comments owe much to E.A. Varley, *op.cit.*

Heber, to bring about the union of the CMS and the SPG. Watson and his associates, probably to a large extent influenced by the social disturbances of the immediate post-Napoleonic Wars era and their fear, for it was little if anything less than fear, of any taint of enthusiasm, decided that further collaboration with the Evangelicals and their dissenting friends was incompatible with their own understanding of Anglican responsibility, for they were resolutely committed to the principle that responsibility for missionary work, as indeed for social and other work, should be assumed by the whole of the Church of England. But they were instrumental in placing mission and social issues on the agenda of every bishop, and also every aspiring and would-be bishop, and this achievement was complementary to the somewhat different approach adopted by the Evangelicals.

PART 3

The Oxford Movement

7

The Causes, Origins and Context of the Oxford Movement

Within the wider political, social, economic and constitutional history of England, the Oxford movement may be seen both as a product of the age in which it arose, and as a determined effort to turn back the tide of history. The process of industrialisation, urbanisation, massive and accelerating population growth, erosion of traditional social norms and undermining of social structures had reached a peak by the second quarter of the nineteenth century.[1] It produced a radicalism which was expressed in working class Corresponding Societies and early attempts at trade unionism; in such demonstrations and fierce repressive responses as the Peterloo Massacre of 1819; in Luddite revolts; in the establishment of the 'godless college of Gower Street' as the embryo of the University of London; in Tom Paine's *Rights of Man;* in Jeremy Bentham's Utilitarian ethics; in the establishment of Mechanics' Institutes as organs of popular education; in the dissemination of handbooks of popular

---

[1] For a description of this process of industrialisation and urbanisation see especially Asa Briggs, *The Age of Improvement* (London, 1959), Alan D. Gilbert, *Religion and Society in Industrial England: Church, Chapel and Social Change 1740–1914* (1976), E. Halévy, *A History of the English People in the Nineteenth Century,* Vol. I, *England in 1815,* Vol. II, *The Liberal Awakening,* E. Hobsbawm, *The Age of Revolution* (1962), E.P. Thompson, *The Making of the English Working Class* (Harmondsworth, 1968), J. Steven Watson, *The Reign of George III. 1760–1815* (Oxford, 1960) and E.L. Woodward, *The Age of Reform, 1815–1870* (Oxford, 1938).

science through the Society for the Diffusion of Useful Knowledge; in the emancipation of slavery movement; in the abolition of the Test and Corporation Acts in 1828, and in the granting of Catholic Emancipation in 1829; and in the Reform Act of 1832. So great and irrevocable was the process of change that it can justifiably be called a revolution, or, indeed, a series of revolutions; and in the wake of such turmoil and transformation, the relationship of church and state and of the Church with the people was unavoidably and fundamentally altered for ever. There was an almost total transmutation of the whole fabric of society, creating new and powerful social classes, new and serious social problems and an irretrievable undermining of long established social relationships. It was an era of the most rapid and most radical change in the history of the country, and yet it was met for the most part by intransigence, conservatism, inflexibility and lack of understanding in the Church of England. The structure and organisation of the Church were archaic, its social and political ideology was outmoded and there was a lamentable absence of insight and vision.

Confronted by the pressures from a growing proletariate and a newly emergent middle class for religious toleration, extended franchise, and social justice, the Church, with the exception of a few notable individuals, clung tenaciously to its long established rights and entrenched privileges. Clerical sympathies were with the Tories, and the long Tory rule had created a bench of bishops of the same hue. When conservative statesmen at the end of the twenties and in the thirties were obliged to carry out some of the most vociferously demanded reforms, their motives and actions were seen by almost all Christian leaders as hostile to the Church and religion, and were energetically fought at every point. Once again, the Church saw itself in danger and reacted accordingly. The Church had become accustomed to a large measure of harmony between itself and the State and could view Parliament as a kind of lay synod. The reforms of 1828, 1829 and 1832 'banished Hooker's Church ideal for ever to the fairy regions of the theoretic ideal, and gave a new actuality to the Puritan conception of the Church, though in a new form'.[2] It meant

---

[2.] Yngve Brilioth, *The Anglican Revival. Studies in the Oxford Movement* (London, 1933), p.95.

that Parliament was no longer an exclusively Anglican body. The Church of England was no longer in quite the same way the church of the nation. Non-Anglicans were now given access to political power, and that power could be used to legislate in a way which was antipathetic to the Church of England.[3] What had recently come to pass in France could be enacted in England. All this was but a pinnacle in a process which had been going on for a century and more and was to continue afterwards through to the present day; what modern sociologists have dubbed the process of secularisation.[4]

Within the comprehensive context just outlined the Oxford movement can be considered as a clarion call to the Church to rally round former conservative, traditional values in determined opposition to the blatant, corrosive forces of radicalism and liberalism in their various guises. It can be seen as a crusade to resist the prevailing secular trends in a desperate rearguard action to restore the beleaguered Church to its, perhaps to some extent imagined, former status, authority and power. Such an interpretation does not lessen the validity of the religious beliefs and values which were enshrined in the movement. Considered from a purely religious and ecclesiastical point of view, the defence of the authority, dignity and independence of the Church as a divine institution; the assertion of the Apostolic succession and of

[3.] See Geoffrey Rowell, *The Vision Glorious. Themes and Personalities of the Catholic Renewal in Anglicanism* (Oxford, 1983), p.1.

For the history of the church in the eighteenth century and early nineteenth century, in addition to the works already cited, or cited below, see W.J. Baker, 'The Attitudes of English Churchmen, 1800–1850, towards the Reformation' (Cambridge University Ph.D. thesis, 1966), S.C. Carpenter, *Church and People, 1789–1889* (1933), Owen Chadwick (Ed.), *The Mind of the Oxford Movement* (1960), Owen Chadwick, *The Victorian Church*, 2 vols. (1966, 1970), F. Warre Cornish, *The English Church in the Nineteenth Century*, 2 vols. (1910).

[4.] For a discussion of the concept and process of secularisation see Peter L. Berger, *The Sacred Canopy* (New York, 1967), Peter L. Berger, *A Rumour of Angels* (New York, 1969), Michael Hill, *A Sociology of Religion* (1973), Ch. 11, Thomas Luckmann, *The Invisible Religion: The Transformation of Symbols in Industrial Society* (New York, 1967), David Martin, *The Religious and the Secular* (1969), Bryan Wilson, *Religion in Secular Society* (Harmondsworth, 1966) and Bryan Wilson, *Contemporary Transformations of Religion* (Oxford, 1976).

the supreme importance and divine nature of the ministry and of episcopacy in particular; the authority given to tradition, and especially to the early Fathers and councils; the re-assertion of the centrality in the life of the Church of the sacraments; and the call to a life of holiness, with a renewed sense of the numinous in both worship and daily life: all these are in no way denigrated if, at the same time, the movement can, with hindsight, be seen, at least in its church-state aspect, as an attempt to resist irresistable change, and an heroic defence of an ideal which belonged to a former age and to circumstances which had passed, never to return. The whole movement tended to look backwards, and to gain its inspiration from the early Church or the Middle Ages, and there was an almost unconscious reaching out after a lost, coherent, authoritarian ecclesiastical order which was alien to their contemporary world of factories, railways, new social classes, agitation and anti-authoritarianism.

The philosophical objections of the Tractarian leaders to liberalism and Utilitarian radical politics need to be appreciated for an understanding of their reactions to the historical situation which confronted them. The prevailing spirit of rationalism, liberalism, erastianism and Utilitarianism was anathema to Keble, Froude and Newman. All three conceived of the Church's mission to society in essentially spiritual terms. They were severe critics of the society in which they lived. 'They portrayed the Benthamite school of philosophers as unfeeling and rational, the Whig aristocracy as insensitive and mercenary. This was the atomised society built on self-interest, laissez-faire and Utilitarianism.'[5]

Keble's understanding of society was diametrically opposed to that of the political economists. His 'Anglicanism in its social manifestations accorded well with the poetic, pre-industrial, anti-commercialist spirit about which he wrote, spoke, preached and prayed with such intensity, vehemence and commitment. Within its confines, the rich and the poor had

---

[5] John Henry Lewis Rowlands, *Church, State and Society. The Attitudes of John Keble, Richard Hurrell Froude and John Henry Newman, 1827–1845* (Worthing, 1989), p.223, a book to which the following section is much indebted.

their appointed destinies, and destinations. Keble's concern was that Tradition was being replaced by Utilitarianism.'[6] Order and decency were, to him, of prime importance in all spheres of life, political, social and commercial as well as religious. 'The vision which Keble had of the ideal society was hierarchical, authoritatively structured and scrupulously ordered along traditional lines.'[7] Order in society required men to be content with their position and status. Insubordination and rebellion were wicked, and indeed blasphemous. Better than individual striving was concern for the peace of society and of the Church. 'In Keble's society the corporateness, homogeneity and totality of things took precedence over all that was individualistic, personal and subjective.' Far sounder than the discontent encouraged by the social philosophers of the age was the contentment of his congregation; a Christian society nurtured by Tradition, 'which encouraged that perfect resignation, that humility of character which was conducive to sanctification'.[8]

For Froude the emphasis was similar. He looked to the restoration of the Church to its medieval splendour at the centre of society, and he shared with Keble and Newman a hatred of the Whigs and every appearance of liberalism.

Newman saw Benthamite philosophy as being only concerned with expedients. It was preoccupied with facts which made an instant appeal to the intellect and attempted to turn man into a person of calculus only. The pursuit of truth was regarded only as a syllogistic process. Logic ruled, and imagination and feeling was at a discount. Society was inebriated with the attractions of the Utilitarian spirit, and Newman made clear his detestation of it and his opposition to liberalism in its various semblances. He was especially concerned about the liberal Anglicans and all they represented. Whigs with their adulation of progress, knowledge, civilisation and the march of the mind wished

[6] John Henry Lewis Rowlands, *op.cit.*, p.58
[7] John Henry Lewis Rowlands, *op.cit.*, pp.63, 64.
[8] John Henry Lewis Rowlands, *op.cit.*, p.66.

to rid Christianity of its supernatural element.[9] To Newman there was an unequivocal choice between the liberal way and the dogmatic principle, which alone had strength. The liberal Anglicans believed that statements about Christian truth could and should be modified to suit the spirit of the age in which they were made, whereas Newman believed that the revealed message was given once and for all by God, to be more and more fully comprehended as time went on. To Newman, the task of the Church was to 'sanctify individuals, spiritualise society and redeem the times. Let her be associated with movements which have mere political ends, the result is always the same. Her life is imperilled.'[10]

Although in retrospect much of what was said and undertaken by the Tractarians may be analysed as a mistaken reaction to irreversable historical developments, what they taught and demonstrated in their lives provided a well and truly laid foundation which was to stand firm in the testing times ahead. The movement undoubtedly harnessed a genuine religious commitment and produced new spiritual life and energy. Indeed, it can be considered as an inheritor of the century-long Evangelical movement which, by 1833, was to some extent in decline. The Oxford movement was, in certain respects, a manifestation of a religious renaissance, or at least the continuation of a spiritual revival, but in a different form. The Evangelical roots of many of the Tractarians were, perhaps, an indication of the roots of the all-embracing movement as a whole, for Evangelicals and Tractarians shared such fundamental hallmarks as the stress on holiness, firm commitment to dogmatic statements in opposition to the anti-dogmatic stance of liberalism, acceptance of the supreme authority of the Bible in matters of faith and practice, the need for personal faith and a life of Christian dedication and service.

Those involved in the movement in its first twelve years were largely unaware of the real nature and significance of the political, social and economic forces which helped both

---

[9.] John Henry Lewis Rowlands, *op.cit.*, p.186.
[10.] John Henry Lewis Rowlands, *op.cit.*, p.228.

to produce the movement and to mould its character; but they were far more aware of the debt to the prevailing literary and philosophical climate. Of special significance may be mentioned the Romantic reawakening of the historical sense, particularly in the work of Sir Walter Scott, but also in the writings of the members of the Lake School. The Romantics were likewise important in the profundity of their observation and appreciation of nature. They may, in certain of their pre-suppositions and teaching, have been unsympathetic to the teaching of the Oxford movement, but in general they aroused large sections of the population to that which *The Christian Year* expressed so poignantly, 'the mystic communion, the correspondence, between the message of the external world and the doctrines of revealed religion'.[11] The Oxford movement also owed much to the complex, ever evolving philosophy of Samuel Taylor Coleridge, and in particular to his ideal of the supernatural Church.

As a purely religious phenomenon, seen in terms of the wider life of the Church of England, it is important to appreciate that the Tractarians were not, as has too often been portrayed, the sole inheritors of older High Churchmanship. As we have already indicated, by 1833 there were a number of strands of High Churchmanship.[12] In addition to the Hackney Phalanx High Churchmanship included the 'High and Drys' such as Godfrey Faussett, and moderate or orthodox churchmen such as C.S. Bird. Then there were the High Churchmen especially identified and labelled as Zs by the Tractarians themselves, prominent among whom were Hugh James Rose, Edward Churton, W.F. Hook, William Palmer of Worcester College, William Sewell, Benjamin Harrison, William Gresley, George Ayliffe Poole and Richard Jelf. All of these groups and individuals, in propagating their own notions of 'church principles' and 'reformed catholicism', regarded themselves as true heirs of the Catholic tradition.

[11] Yngve Brilioth, *op.cit.*, p.72.
[12] For a full discussion of the complex facets of High Churchmanship in this period see Peter Nockles, 'Continuity and Change in Anglican High Churchmanship 1792–1850' (Oxford University, D.Phil. thesis, 1982).

Although they were not united in any clearly recognised school or movement, as were the Tractarians, these various High Churchmen were not mere isolated individuals. They attained a large measure of coherence as a result of close ties of family and, above all, personal allegiance and friendship. Their geographical concentration, especially in London, helped to unite them. Moreover, the old High Churchmen were drawn together by their common membership of clubs and church organisations such as the SPCK, SPG and National Society. Of special importance in instilling such a sense of unity was the Club of Nobody's Friends, founded in 1800, which we have already encountered. The elected membership of the Club between 1800 and 1850 fully represented the leadership of the old High Churchmanship, as distinct from those who came to be tagged Tractarian. Indeed, after 1841, the Club became something of a focal point for those Zs who were opposed to what they considered were the excesses of the Oxford movement. In contrast to the more innovative, progressive nature of the Oxford movement, the Club had an essentially establishment character, with many of its High Church members being archdeacons, deans and bishops, or, among the laity, lawyers. It strove to retain and enhance the independence, authority and influence of the Church.

8

The Leaders

John Keble (1792–1866)

Of the three Oxford movement giants, Keble, Newman and Pusey, Keble has received the least attention and the least acknowledgement for his contribution not only to the movement but to the history of the Church. This is partly due to the fact that his life was not 'before the world' to the extent that Newman's and Pusey's were, and none can tell the impact he had on people and the course of events far and wide in a quiet, unobtrusive and unostentatious way.[1] His contemporaries were quick to recognise his importance, and indeed within the movement he was, in certain respects, seen as pre-eminent. Newman especially, and Pusey to a lesser extent, unintentionally attracted the limelight to themselves. Nonetheless, of these three Keble was the oldest 'and, in a sense, the first in the field'.[2] His book of poems, *The Christian Year,* was published six years before the accepted date for the beginning of the movement, and it rapidly established itself not only as the foundation devotional text of the movement, but as a work of lasting value which was to have an almost

---

[1] See Georgina Battiscombe, *John Keble. A Study in Limitations* (London, 1963), p.ix. This is a work to which our account of Keble owes much.

For the life, work and thought of Keble see also J.T. Coleridge, *A Memoir of the Rev. John Keble M.A. Late vicar of Hursley* (Oxford and London, 1874), and Walter Lock, *John Keble. A Biography* (1893).

[2] Georgina Battiscombe, *op.cit.,* p.xvi.

incalculable effect on English religious life in the nineteenth century. It was Keble, with his roots in the High Church Tory tradition, who exercised such a great influence on the Oxford of his day that he helped to prepare the ground for the impending movement. It was Keble who preached the Assize Sermon in 1833 which inaugurated the movement; and it was Keble who, by his saintly life, 'blessed and fructified'[3] the movement. It was Keble also who initially took the movement out to the world beyond Oxford, yet remained its most respected adviser and elder statesman.

He was born in 1792. His father was a clergyman, like so many of his family, being parish priest of Coln St Aldwyn near Fairford in Gloucestershire, and in his childhood he was surrounded by relations in a close-knit family. He appears to have had few if any playmates beyond this family circle. His father reversed the usual custom by entirely educating his sons himself, while sending his three daughters away for short periods to a boarding school. The education he imparted was most thorough and effective. The two boys learnt four languages and the girls Latin as well as the more conventional French and Italian, and all of them were remarkably well-read in English literature and history. Thus John avoided the brutalities of a public school, but by missing such schooling also did not benefit from the opportunity of mixing with other boys. The home life he enjoyed provided him with the character forming environment of books, animals, flowers, family affection, the Cotswold countryside and the 'reticent, reverent and practical'[4] High Churchmanship of his father.

In 1807 he won a scholarship and went up to Corpus Christi, Oxford. He flourished in the congenial loveliness of an Oxford which was then small and homogeneous, and dedicated to providing a literary education almost exclusively for Anglican gentlemen. Nearly every Fellow was in Orders and the Oxford of Keble's undergraduate days was 'comfortably reminiscent of a cathedral close'.[5] It was expected that Keble would achieve

---

[3]. Georgina Battiscombe, *op.cit.*, p.xviii.

[4]. Charlotte Yonge, quoted in Georgina Battiscombe, *op.cit.*, p.11.

[5]. Georgina Battiscombe, *op.cit.*, p.18.

a brilliant examination result and the expectation was not disappointed: in company with a fellow student named Bathurst, he repeated the feat which Robert Peel alone had previously achieved, and was awarded a Double First. He had attained to the highest Oxford Honours at the age of entry to the University for most young men. Whereas Peel was twenty when he won his Double First, and William Gladstone twenty-two, Keble was only eighteen. Four days before his nineteenth birthday, he was elected to an Oriel Fellowship, a prize which was then regarded as the crown and seal of a successful University career. Then his depth of character was revealed. Amid the mighty men of argument who constituted the Oriel Common Room, he remained true to the reverent, conservative High Church ideals of his home, and was untouched by the free-ranging and sceptical temper of the College society around him. Indeed, 'far from Oriel influencing John Keble it was John Keble who influenced Oriel'.[6]

In 1815 he was ordained deacon and later in the year priest. He then promptly became curate of Eastleach, a neighbouring parish to Fairford, and retained the post for eight years. For a few months in 1817 he left Oxford and gave himself entirely to the parochial work, but by the beginning of 1818 he was once more installed at Oriel, this time as College Tutor, an appointment which was viewed as part of his work as an ordained clergyman. So he combined parish and College roles.

In Oxford he was increasingly venerated. He grew steadily and undramatically in his own devotional and spiritual life, for he never experienced any sudden conversion or radical change. He had a deep belief in sacramental religion, but a reticence which meant that his religious and moral influence over others was largely the influence of example; and it was especially powerful in the lives of Newman, Froude and Pusey. But there was to be another break in his Oxford career, for in 1823 he resigned his Oriel Fellowship to become curate

---

[6.] Georgina Battiscombe, *op.cit.*, pp.29, 30.

of Southrop, a few miles from Fairford. It was there that he sowed the first seeds of the Oxford movement, for he held vacation reading-parties for Oxford students and attracted Hurrell Froude, Robert Wilberforce, one of the four sons of the Evangelical leader of the Clapham Sect, William Wilberforce, and William Williams.

In 1827 he published *The Christian Year*. By its tone as much as by its content, it advocated a sober, even sombre, godliness which was somewhat lacking in emotion and music. It did not aspire to being great literature: it was written as a commentary on the Book of Common Prayer and as a guide to devotion, and as such it was to be of immense help and comfort to thousands. It also contained poems which were to win permanent fame, including the Whitsun hymn, 'When God of old came down from Heaven', and the evening hymn 'Sun of my soul'. There is little in it which can be regarded as specifically Tractarian or High Church, although it has always been regarded as a central work in the life of the Oxford movement. It was probably its ethos, its close identity with the teaching of the Prayer Book, and its encouragement to a restrained, but profound and deep holiness which appealed to Tractarians and High Churchmen in general, as well as to a much wider readership.

One of the immediate results of the publication of *The Christian Year* and its rapid and widespread popularity, was to bring Keble into a new prominence, and his leap to fame made him an obvious choice for an appropriate important University post. In this same year the Provostship of Oriel fell vacant, and the only candidates worthy of serious consideration were the Vice-Provost, Edward Hawkins, and Keble. Perhaps much to his regret in later life, Newman voted for Hawkins, defending his choice with the remark 'You know we are not electing an angel but a Provost.' Pusey voted likewise, convinced of Keble's lack of business ability and worldly acumen. Keble's natural distaste for a struggle, and his genuine Christian humility made him resolve to avoid a contested election, and he quickly withdrew in favour of Hawkins.

In 1829 Keble for the first time expressed his Tory principles in a political campaign when he joined with Newman and Froude to attack Peel because of his reversal of policy in declaring his support for Catholic Emancipation. It marked the first public concerted action of the triumverate who were to combine as leaders of the Oxford movement. His attitude to Catholic Emancipation was somewhat blinkered, for he seemed unable even to contemplate the injustice done to Roman Catholics in withholding emancipation in his passionate concern to protect the interests of the Church of England. Importantly, he responded to the Catholic Emancipation Act as a challenge to the Church of England to re-consider and re-define the basis of its authority since it could no longer shelter behind the authority of a Parliament which might soon admit men of all Christian traditions or no religion at all. It was his response to this challenge which motivated and formed the substance of his 1833 Assize Sermon. His heart was full of foreboding for the future. England appeared to be drifting from its Christian heritage, and the call of Christians was to resist the national apostasy.

In his private life there were two matters of note at this time. He was engaged in editing the works of Richard Hooker, and in 1831 he was elected Professor of Poetry at Oxford.

In 1835 he was offered, and accepted, that which he had long desired, the living of Hursley, and within a few months he had married Charlotte Clarke. In January 1836 he was inducted as Vicar and settled down to his cherished life of devotion, counsel, writing and service, for his lot was now permanently fixed.

Hursley was a community of about thirteen hundred people located between the high Hampshire chalk downs and the heavily wooded country bordering the New Forest, in which the generous and devout Churchman, Sir William Heathcote, ruled as squire and worked in close and happy partnership with the parson for the betterment of the parish. For thirty years Keble attempted to put the principles of the Oxford movement into practice. He laid great stress on the duty of church-going as a 'service' due to God rather than as primarily a means of edification. Comparatively little emphasis was laid on the sermon, although teaching was regarded as of paramount importance. Thus, at Sunday Evensong there was no sermon, but Keble catechised the children, boys on one Sunday, girls the next, and after the catechising he summed up questions and answers in a brief, practical manner for the benefit of the listening adults. Daily Mattins and Evensong was introduced, there was an increase in the number of celebrations of Holy Communion, and a rise in the number of communicants. In contrast to most parishes where confirmation candidates were given little or no preparation beforehand, Keble attached great importance to confirmation and took the utmost pains with his candidates, giving them instruction every week for a period of six months to a year before the actual confirmation. An especially interesting candidate was Charlotte Yonge who lived nearby. The friendship which Keble and Charlotte developed was to be a source of great joy to them both, and she brought her best-selling story books to him for approval and criticism before publication.

Keble's care of his parishioners became proverbial, and it was not all gentleness, for he was stern where necessary. The children were his special concern and delight, and no matter what the pressures of work might be, he spent one hour each morning and afternoon teaching in the village school. He controversially adopted the practice of private confession, because he regarded it as an essential part of his pastoral ministry, in order to really know the minds and souls of his parishioners, and also vital for the enforcement of discipline. In the matter of morality he was, however, not severely and harshly restrictive. He did not try to enforce a repressive piety. Indeed, he attracted some criticism for allowing penny-readings throughout the solemn season of Lent, and introduced certain Sunday games such as cricket after Evensong, for he wished Sunday to be a cheerful day. His critics were ever ready to comment, and when he opened a parish reading room, despite great care in the choice of books, he found that even the works of Scott were not sufficiently innocuous, and he had to withdraw *Old Mortality* from circulation.

During his time at Hursley Keble continued his literary

activities. He joined with Pusey and Newman in editing the *Library of the Fathers,* a series of translations of the works of the early Fathers of the Church. He also published a metrical version of the psalms. His cooperation with Pusey deepened and enriched their already intimate friendship, and this was one of the most important aspects of his later life. In 1846 he issued a volume of poems about children under the title *Lyra Innocentium,* which was much valued by the devout, but never attained to the worldwide popularity of *The Christian Year.* Other works included the writing and editing of the *Life and Works of Bishop Wilson of Sodor and Man* and a pamphlet on *Eucharistic Adoration.*

In September 1865 the aged trio, Newman, Pusey and Keble met at Hursley. It was an encounter which brought as much pain as pleasure to each of them, yet they were happy to feel that at last they were at peace with each other. Keble died very peacefully less than a year later, in the early hours of Maundy Thursday, 29 March 1866, and on 11 May Charlotte followed him. So many people wanted to do him honour that the necessary money was soon subscribed for a very considerable memorial, Keble College, Oxford. It was a response to the memory of a man who had a brilliant intellect, but who was most loved for his wisdom, wholesomeness, idiosyncracies, limitations and holiness.

John Henry Newman (1801–90)

Of the writing of books on John Henry Newman there seems to be no end.[7] His own masterpiece of literary style and religious autobiography, *Apologia Pro Vita Sua,* is universally acclaimed. 'No autobiography in the English language has

---

[7.] For the life and work of Newman the main sources are his *Apologia Pro Vita Sua,* first published 1864, but for which we quote from the Everyman Edition, London, 1912, reprinted 1946; Sheridan Gilley, *Newman and his Age* (London, 1990), Ian Ker, *John Henry Newman. A Biography* (Oxford, 1990) and Wilfred Ward, *The Life of John Henry Cardinal Newman,* 2 vols. (London, 1912).

been more read; to the nineteenth century it bears a relation not less characteristic than Boswell's *"Johnson"* to the eighteenth.'[8] In the *Apologia* 'the stages of Newman's pilgrimage are related with a grace and sincerity of style that have hardly been equalled in English or in any northern tongue'. It is 'one of the noblest pieces of spiritual history the world possesses'.[9] To this have been added a large number of readily available works giving a comprehensive coverage of Newman's life, work and thought, so we will confine ourselves to those aspects which are most significant in placing him within the context of the events of his day and within the stream of the High Church tradition.

Newman was born on 21 February 1801 in the City of London. Both his parents had a trading background, his father being a banker, the son of a grocer, and his mother the daughter of a paper-maker. Although not Evangelical, they laid great stress on having the Bible read in Church, in the family and in private. From our point of view, the most relevant features of his childhood and adolescent years were his sense of the numinous and his conversion. He wrote of his childhood 'I used to wish the Arabian Tales were true: my imagination ran on unknown influences, on magical powers, and talismans...I thought life might be a dream, or I an Angel, and all the world a deception, my fellow-angels by a playful device concealing themselves from me, and deceiving me with the semblance of a material world...I was superstitious, and for some time previous to my conversion used constantly to cross myself on going into the dark.'[10] He describes his conversion in equally memorable words. 'When I was fifteen (in the autumn of 1816) a great change of thought took place in me. I fell under the influence of a definite creed, and received into my intellect impressions of dogma, which, through God's mercy, have never been effaced or obscured...I...believed that the inward conversion of which

---

[8.] W. Barry, quoted in the Everyman Edition of *Apologia Pro Vita Sua* (London, 1946), p.vii.

[9.] Introduction to the Everyman Edition of *Apologia Pro Vita Sua*, pp. viii, ix.

[10.] John Henry Newman, *Apologia Pro Vita Sua, op.cit.*, pp.29, 30.

I was conscious (and of which I still am more certain than that I have hands and feet) would last into the next life, and that I was elected to eternal glory.'[11] He speaks of the influence of a work of William Romaine, the Evangelical clergyman, 'in the direction of those childish imaginations which I have already mentioned, viz. in isolating me from the objects which surrounded me, confirming me in my mistrust of the reality of material phenomena, and in making me rest in the thought of two and two only supreme and luminously self-evident beings, myself and my Creator'.[12] Indeed, the religious influences in his pre-University years mainly came from Evangelical sources: from Thomas Scott, 'the writer who made a deeper impression on my mind than any other, and to whom (humanly speaking) I almost owe my soul';[13] Daniel Wilson whose lips he 'hung upon'; Joseph Milner, whose *Church History* he read, and 'was nothing short of enamoured of the long extracts from St. Augustine and the other Fathers...as being the religion of the primitive Christians'; and John Newton, whose work on the prophecies convinced him that 'the Pope was the Antichrist predicted by Daniel, St. Paul and St. John'. 'The main Catholic doctrine of the warfare between the city of God and the powers of darkness was also deeply impressed upon my mind', he wrote, by William Law's *Serious Call.*

Newman went up to Trinity College, Oxford, in 1816, obtained a scholarship, worked intensely for as much as thirteen or fourteen hours a day, but over-reached himself and obtained a very poor degree, not even attaining second class honours. This was intensely disappointing, especially as much had been expected of him, but he boldly and audaciously entered for an Oriel Fellowship: and he was successful, being elected Fellow on 12 April 1822.

The years of Edward Copleston's provostship, from 1814 to 1826, 'were the golden age of Oriel, when it made its contribution to the late Georgian "Oxford renaissance" of

[11] John Henry Newman, *Apologia Pro Vita Sua, op.cit.,* p.31.

[12] John Henry Newman, *Apologia Pro Vita Sua, op.cit.,* p.31.

[13] John Henry Newman, *Apologia Pro Vita Sua, op.cit.,* p.32.

scholarly study. It was said of the common room that it "stank of Logic", and the Senior Fellows were collectively known as the "Noetics", because of their devotion to knowledge'.[14] Newman encountered at first hand in that common room men who in various ways changed his religious outlook.

Richard Whately, afterwards Archbishop of Dublin, taught him to think for himself, to rely upon himself. Edward Hawkins, later Provost of Oriel, taught him to weigh his words and be cautious in his statements. His teaching was the primary dissolvent of Newman's Evangelicalism: in it he opposed any notion of the division of the Christian world into those who are all darkness and those who are all light, claiming that religious and moral excellence is a matter of degree. It was Hawkins who taught Newman about the value of tradition, and who gave him a copy of John Bird Sumner's *Treatise on Apostolic Preaching*, whereby Newman learnt to give up his remaining Calvinism and received the doctrine of baptismal regeneration. Among the lesser known Fellows of Oriel, the Rev. William James convinced Newman of the truth of the doctrine of apostolic succession.

It was at about this time, around 1823, that Newman read Bishop Joseph Butler's *Analogy of Religion*. From Butler he learnt of 'the existence of the Church, as a substantive body or corporation'; and Butler fixed in his mind 'those anti-Erastian views of church polity, which were one of the most prominent features of the Tractarian Movement'.[15]

Despite all these influences and impulses towards a transfer from Evangelicalism to High Churchmanship, Newman also experienced the siren call of liberalism as he pondered the works of Conyers Middleton and David Hume.

In May 1824 he accepted the curacy of St Clement's, 'a growing working-class parish with a population of about two thousand, situated just beyond Magdalen Bridge'.[16] In September 1824 his father died. In the following month he was elected junior treasurer at Oriel. In 1825 he became Vice-

---

[14] Sheridan Gilley, *op. cit.*, p.42.

[15] John Henry Newman, *Apologia Pro Vita Sua*, *op. cit.*, p.37.

[16] Ian Ker, *op. cit.*, p.20.

Principal of Alban Hall, a college with only about twelve undergraduates in residence. In 1826 he was appointed as a tutor at Oriel, but later in the year, perhaps as a consequence of the combined effect of the prospect of examining in the Schools, intense preparation for this, the emotional stress of changing theological views, the death of his father and the financial turmoil within the family, as well as the disturbance of adjusting to a new Provost, he experienced a nervous collapse. This disruption of his life helped to awake him somewhat rudely from his preference for intellectual rather than moral excellence. Also, there was the injection of a new religious dynamism into the life of Oriel with the election in 1826 of two new Fellows, Robert Wilberforce, the son of the great Evangelical leader, who was to become one of the leading High Church theologians of his day before becoming a Roman Catholic, and Hurrell Froude. By 1828 Newman was fully recovered and was appointed Vicar of St Mary's, the University Church, in succession to Edward Hawkins. Also in 1828 Froude and Wilberforce were appointed tutors. Although this meant that Newman was no longer alone in his pastoral interpretation of the role and duties of a tutor, a year later he was eased out of his tutorship because such a conception was not acceptable to the Provost, Hawkins. In 1829 he was elected to the post of joint secretary of the Oxford branch of the largely Evangelical Church Missionary Society.

These were the outward circumstances of his life up to the time when, with increasing momentum, national events helped to precipitate Newman, Keble and Froude into the Oxford movement; events which we will follow in some detail later. For, from then onwards, the life and work of Newman became inextricably bound up with the movement whose character, course and outcome were to be so much determined by his actions, beliefs and personality.

Edward Bouverie Pusey (1800–82)

The life of Pusey, 'although profoundly influential, was singularly uneventful. It was a continuous stream of lectures, sermons, letters, interviews.'[17] It was in spite of his own natural inclinations that he became involved so deeply in the Oxford movement, and in the post-1845 developments to which his name was attached, but he is undoubtedly a central figure in the Church life of his period and an important part of the High Church tradition.

Pusey was born at Pusey House in Berkshire on 22 August 1800. His father was the Honourable Philip Bouverie, youngest son of Jacob, first Viscount Folkestone, and an inflexible Tory, devout and bounteous in his unostentatious charity, and a domestic autocrat. His mother, Lady Lucy Sherard, exercised great influence upon her children because of her dignity and humility, her high religious and moral standards and conduct, her charity and conscientiousness. Edward was the second of four children, all boys. He was educated at Eton. Just before going up to Christ Church, Oxford, he met Maria Barker and immediately felt a deep affection for her. His father opposed the relationship and for a long time forbade all social intercourse between them, so that Edward had to experience nine years of alternating hope and disappointment, with serious adverse effects upon his character, before they eventually married.

At Christ Church he does not appear to have had many intimate friends, possibly because of his poor health, his shyness, his preoccupation with his attachment to Maria Barker and his industriousness. After obtaining his expected first class, he went on to achieve the distinction of an Oriel Fellowship.

In 1825 Pusey decided to spend some time studying in Germany. This was partly because first hand experience of agnosticism, if not atheism, in a friend of his had left him with unanswered questions. It was also partly because he was aware of the importance of German theological writing and

[17.] Henry Parry Liddon, *The Life of Edward Bouverie Pusey,* 4 vols. (London, 1893), vol.1, p.vii. This is the standard work on the life of Pusey and, although many of its interpretations of issues relating to the life of Pusey have subsequently been questioned, it remains the most important source for the biography of Pusey.

thought, and how few scholars in England knew the language or had experienced anything of German theological learning in its country of origin. In a period of intense study under J.G. Eichhorn, and D.J. Pott at Göttingen, an acquaintance with Friedrich Schleiermacher and Augustus Neander and a friendship with D.F. Strauss in Berlin, he 'whetted without satisfying his appetite for the studies which were now more and more identified with the central purpose of his life'.[18] He had already been working for some time at Hebrew, and thought that a real knowledge of that language required a background of Arabic and the other cognate languages. In addition, he was seriously reflecting on questions concerning the authority and trustworthiness of the scriptures; and he considered that a knowledge of the Oriental tongues was ancillary to such a quest. He decided that a second visit to Germany was necessary, and this he undertook in 1826. On that visit he plunged into Syriac and Chaldee, set to work on Arabic, drew up a comprehensive anotated list of the modern German commentators on St Paul and studied various subsidiary subjects. When he returned to England the following year he was a Semitic scholar of note and familiar with the history of modern Protestant speculation on religious topics.[19]

A succession of personal events of significance followed. He became engaged to Maria; his father died suddenly and unexpectedly; he had a complete break down of health and had to leave Oxford for four months; he was ordained deacon; and on 12 June 1828 he married Maria.[20]

A few days before his ordination as deacon in 1828, his book on the *Theology of Germany* was published. It was a response to a work by Hugh James Rose of Cambridge. Rose

[18.] Henry Parry Liddon, *op.cit.*, p.94.

[19.] For a discussion of some aspects of Pusey's intellectual development and academic work, see David Forrester, *Young Dr. Pusey. A Study in Development* (1989), David Jasper, 'Pusey's Lectures on Types and Prophecies of the Old Testament', and Alan Livesley, 'Regius Professor of Hebrew' in Perry Butler (Ed.), *Pusey Rediscovered* (London, 1983).

[20.] For comments on his married life see David W.F. Forrester, 'Dr. Pusey's Marriage', in Perry Butler (Ed.), *op.cit.*

had issued a warning that German theology had succumbed
to rationalism and had largely repudiated the substance and
heart of the Christian creed, because there were inadequate
or non-existent controls such as subscription to confessions
of faith, the use of a settled form of public worship and clear
ecclesiastical guidance and discipline. Much as he later
regretted it, Pusey countered this with a less dark and
forbidding picture of German theology and a more sanguine
forecast for the religious future of the country. In his will he
asked that his book should not be reprinted, for he thought
he had not been sufficiently alive to the character and extent
of the concessions which German theologians had made to
the enemies of faith. It was an error of judgement which cost
him much agony, for he wished to safeguard people against
forces hostile to their faith, and his miscalculation tended
to make him more cautious and conservative ever afterwards.

In the same year, 1828, Pusey was offered and accepted
the Regius Professorship of Hebrew. It was an appointment
which determined his house and work for the remaining fifty-
four years of his life. For the next five years his most serious
work was the completion of the *Catalogue of Arabic Manuscripts*
in the Bodleian Library, although much of his time was taken
up with the varied duties of his post. He continued to exert
himself to the utmost, so that at one stage he was overcome
with illness and took some months to recover.

This brings us up to 1833 and to the dawn of the events
which are detailed in the next chapter. By that date Pusey
was still very young, but he was a man of oustanding erudition,
with an established reputation, occupying an important and
prestigious Oxford Chair, and of such standing that he was
to be a key figure in determining the course and nature of
events during the crucial years 1833 to 1845, and beyond.[21]

[21.] The course of the mental and spiritual development of Pusey which eventually
brought him into the Tractarian movement has been variously interpreted by
Liddon in his *Life*, David Forrester, in *Young Dr.Pusey*, *op. cit.*, H.C.G. Matthew,
'Edward Bouverie Pusey: from Scholar to Tractarian', *Journal of Theological Studies*
n.s. 32 (1981), pp. 101-124, and Leighton Frappell, '"Science" in the Service
of Orthodoxy: The Early Intellectual Development of E.B. Pusey', in Perry Butler
(Ed.), *op.cit.*

Richard Hurrell Froude (1803–36)

A fourth pioneer of the movement, Richard Hurrell Froude, also deserves special mention. He was born in 1803, and educated at Eton and Oriel College, Oxford, where he was a pupil of Keble, and where he was elected a Fellow, along with Robert Wilberforce, in 1826. From 1827 to 1830 he was a College Tutor, with Newman and Wilberforce as colleagues. In 1831 his poor health greatly deteriorated and he was away from Oxford for long periods. He died in 1836.

By all accounts he was a remarkable man, who had a dynamic and lasting influence upon many, and especially Keble and Newman. During his short life he dazzled his contemporaries. No one, with the possible exception of Keble, was more responsible for the impulse which led to the movement. He had outstanding powers of intellect and character and was a brilliant conversationalist. He was a mathematician of stature, and an enthusiast for the mechanical, hydrostatic and astronomical sciences. He displayed an originality of thought about architecture which was uncommon at that time, and he was a poet. He had a well developed ability to grapple with abstract thought, was quick to see inferences, and had a sensitive, acute imagination with an exquisite sense of beauty. And yet he had an adventurous and bold spirit which was manifested in a love for sports and games, a passion for the sea and sailing with a delight in the rigours of rough weather, and a consuming interest in adventurous cross country horse riding. In his own religious life he submitted himself to a merciless self-discipline which astounded his close friends when it was revealed by the publication of his *Remains*. Indeed, in his inner life as well as in his lifestyle, he tended to extremes, doing all things with perhaps an over-commitment and excess of enthusiasm. Politically he was a Tory of the Tories in a day of radical reform, and he was a fastidious, high-tempered English gentleman. 'He hated conventional phrases and religious commonplaces, and anything in religion that seemed unreal.'[22] Nevertheless, despite this crusade against cant and

[22.] C.P.S. Clarke, *The Oxford Movement and After* (London, 1932), pp.43, 44.

hypocrisy, and although he was severe with himself, the impression he left with his contemporaries was one of tenderness and gentleness rather than severity.

So varied, complex and forceful was he, that it is difficult to portray his qualities adequately. His antagonism to the Reformation, his scorn for the maxim, 'The Bible and the Bible only is the religion of Protestantism', his glorification in Tradition as a main source of teaching, his exaltation of virginity, and the Blessed Virgin as its great pattern, his belief in the Real Presence in the Blessed Sacrament, in medieval miracles and in self-mortification and penance: and all these things communicated to others through the most effective medium of his charm, wit and energetic personality, ensured that he was a potent force in Oxford, and an inspiration to many. One of his abiding great acts was to bring Newman and Keble together. In his *Remains*, he wrote, 'Do you know the story of the murderer who had done one good thing in his life? Well, if I was ever asked what good deed I had ever done, I should say that I had brought Keble and Newman to understand each other.'[23]

Others there were who played their lesser but important parts, of whom three will be briefly considered: Charles Marriott, Isaac Williams and James Mozley.

Charles Marriott (1811–58)

'Charles Marriott was a man who was drawn into the movement, almost in spite of himself, attracted by the character of the leaders, the greatness of its object, and the purity and nobleness of the motives which prompted it.'[24] He was by disposition an eclectic, recognising the validity of the views of opposing schools or theories, and he was averse to party allegiances or action. He was a fellow of Oriel, a man of profound and deep learning who nevertheless found great difficulty in communicating his thoughts either in public, or

---

23. John Henry Newman, *Apologia Pro Vita Sua, op.cit.*, p.42.
24. R.W. Church, *The Oxford Movement 1833-1845* (London, 1892), p.79.

in private conversation. He had an absorbing, humble devotion to holiness and an unswerving and touching fidelity to the movement, of which he remained a leader, with Pusey, after the secession of Newman to the Roman Catholic Church. From 1839 to 1841 he was the first principal of Chichester Theological College, and from 1850 to 1855 he was vicar of the University Church at Oxford. From 1841 onwards he collaborated with Pusey and Keble in producing the *Library of the Fathers,* but he was largely confined to the correcting of translations, collating of manuscripts and editing of texts. 'Marriott's great contribution to the movement was his solid, simple goodness, his immovable hope, his confidence that things would come right.'[25]

Isaac Williams (1802–65)

Isaac Williams was the son of a well-to-do Welsh barrister who practised in London. He was born in Wales, and 'the mountains and the poetry and the passionate romanticism of his native land were in his blood'.[26] He won a scholarship to Trinity College, Oxford, but went there 'devoted to cricket and Latin, dances and country visits, and quite indifferent to religion'.[27] The great transformation in his life came when he attended Keble's Southrop reading party. The force of Keble's life, example and teaching was irresistible to the young, impressionable Williams. He became a devoted Christian, a disciple of Keble and a close companion of Froude. He was elected Fellow and Tutor of Trinity and for a short time was Newman's curate at St Mary's. He was one of the poets of the movement, and it is somewhat ironic that this modest, reformist rather than revolutionary man, was the cause, as we will see, of two great storms which broke over the movement: one as a consequence of the publication in

---

[25] R.W. Church, *op.cit.,* pp.88-89.

[26] Geoffrey Faber, *Oxford Apostles. A Character Study of the Oxford Movement* (Harmondsworth, 1954), p.198.

[27] Geoffrey Faber, *op.cit.,* p.199.

1839 of his Tract 80, under the title, *On Reserve in Communicating Religious Knowledge,* and the other when he stood for the Oxford Professorship of Poetry. In 1842, distrustful of Romeward trends within the movement, he left Oxford, married and lived in Gloucestershire until his death in 1865. He remained a firm and rather old-fashioned High Church Anglican.

James Bowling Mozley (1813–78)

James Mozley was the author of learned and solid theological works on predestination, baptismal regeneration and miracles, but his most polemical and brilliant writing is to be found in his essays. These included devastating criticisms of Luther, and the consequences of Lutheran teaching, comments on rationalism and romanticism, and observations on the contemporary champions of Luther, Thomas Arnold and Thomas Carlyle. Mozley continued to be loyal to the Oxford movement after the secession of Newman and was indeed one of its foremost members in Oxford, although his views changed in his later years.

9

The Course of Events

The Assize Sermon

In his Assize Sermon on 14 July 1833 Keble encapsulated and made public thoughts which had been agitating many High Churchmen and others for years past. It was probably one of the half dozen most noteworthy sermons in the whole history of the Church of England. In it Keble expressed the fear that England was wilfully rejecting her ancient belief that 'as a Christian nation she is also a part of the Christian Church, and in all her legislation and policy bound by the fundamental rules of that Church'.[1] The British nation wished to free itself from religious restraints. Keble saw evidence of this 'apostate mind' not so much in the Irish Bishoprics Bill as in the widespread spirit of religious indifference, a notable increase in perjury and disregard for the sanctity of an oath, and a growing disrespect towards 'the successors of the Apostles', that is, the bishops. The bishops themselves had little belief in the sacred nature of their own authority. The sermon expressed alarm at the Erastian principles of subjection to the state, on which the Church of England was to all appearances to be governed. So long as full civic rights could only be enjoyed by members of the Church so long could church and state be

---

[1.] Quoted in Georgina Battiscombe, *John Keble. A Study in Limitations* (London, 1963), pp. 152, 153.

fairly described as two aspects of the same entity.[2] It was intolerable that the state legislature, the members of which were not even bound to express their belief in the Atonement, had virtually usurped the commission of the Church to make ecclesiastical laws in matters wholly or partly spiritual. It was likewise an affront that the state legislature had ratified the principle that the Apostolic Church was only to stand, in the eyes of the state, as one sect among many, depending for any pre-eminence she might still appear to retain merely upon the accident of having at the time a strong party in the country.[3] Keble proclaimed a high view of the Anglican Church as the representative in England of the whole Church Catholic and Apostolic, a society 'built upon the Apostles and prophets, Jesus Christ Himself being the chief corner-stone'. It was a Church which possessed the authority of Christ, handed on by Him to the Apostles, and descending from them via their successors. The Church of England was a true part of the Catholic and Apostolic Church to which all people's loyalty was ultimately due. This Church was in danger of betrayal into the hands of libertines. But even if it succumbed and disappeared, as other Churches such as those of Byzantium and Ephesus had done in the past, still the Church Catholic and Apostolic would live on. The gates of Hell could not prevail against it. The Churchman has an unfailing, certain hope that victory will finally be complete, universal and eternal.

Such a magnificent vision of the Church 'burst upon the stagnant waters of contemporary Anglicanism with all the dynamic forces of something new and surprising'.[4] But to the

[2] See Georgina Battiscombe, *op.cit.*, p.154.

[3] See Georgina Battiscombe, *op.cit.*, p.154.

[4] Georgina Battiscombe, *op.cit.*, p.156.

In addition to the works previously quoted or to which reference is made below, special attention is drawn to the following as helpful for an understanding of the Oxford movement 1833–1845: H. Clegg, 'Evangelicals and Tractarians. An investigation of the connecting links between the two movements in the Church of England in the earlier part of last century and a consideration of how, and how far these links came to be broken' (Bristol University M.A. thesis, 1965), E.R. Fairweather (Ed.), *The Oxford Movement* (New York and Oxford, 1964), R.H. Greenfield, 'The Attitude of the Tractarians to the Roman Catholic Church 1833–

High Churchman Keble it was but the expression of the traditional beliefs which he inherited from the Caroline divines, which were as familiar as the Lord's Prayer or the Apostles' Creed. And so it was as the Oxford movement developed; for to him it was the defence of doctrines dear and long cherished in the intimacy of the family circle, whereas, to the other Tractarians, and especially to Froude, Isaac Williams and more particularly Newman, it was more like the spreading of a new revelation.

Eleven days after the sermon, four clergymen met in conference at the rectory of the Rev. Hugh James Rose at Hadleigh: besides Rose, there was Richard Hurrell Froude, William Palmer and Arthur Perceval. At this small gathering, ideas and anxieties which had been filling the minds of a number of earnest Churchmen for some time, which had brought them into communication with one another, and which had so recently been publicly declared by Keble, were intensely debated. William Palmer of Worcester College, Oxford, later Sir William Palmer, 'who next to Rose carried most weight, was very shy, very sedate, very correct, very learned'[5] and was described modestly by Newman as 'the only really learned man among us'. The Rev. the Hon. Arthur Philip Perceval was Rector of East Horsley, Surrey, a Royal Chaplain, and a son of a peer. Froude, as we have seen, was one of the Oriel circle which was to pioneer the Oxford movement. Lastly, Rose was a distinguished Cambridge man who, as previously noted, had crossed swords with Pusey over the interpretation of German theological trends, was a trusted chaplain of Archbishop Howley, was later in the same year appointed Divinity Professor at the new University of Durham and was subsequently to become Principal of King's College, London. In 1832 he had founded the *British Magazine* as an organ for the proclamation of High Church principles. The

---

1850', (Oxford University D.Phil. thesis, 1956), Elizabeth Jay (Ed.), *The Evangelical and Oxford Movements* (Cambridge, 1983), Shane Leslie, *The Oxford Movement* (1933), W.R.W. Stephens, *The Life and Letters of Walter Farquhar Hook*, 2 vols. (1880), N.P. Williams and C. Harris (Eds.), *Northern Catholicism* (1933).

5. C.P.S. Clarke, *The Oxford Movement and After* (London, 1932), p.57.

only apparent result of the meeting was an abortive project to form an association for the defence of the Church. In place of this scheme, an address was presented to the Archbishop which was signed by some seven thousand clergymen, and this was followed by a Lay Address from two hundred and thirty thousand heads of families.

Tracts for the Times

On 9 September 1833 the first of the Tracts was issued. It brought the movement to the attention of a wide audience, and gave it a name. Newman was the author, and it was entitled *Thoughts on the Ministerial Commission, respectfully addressed to the Clergy*. It was a short, four-page, leaflet, issued at 1d, and written in a clear, excellent English form which arrested attention at once. He wrote it in a mood of intense exhuberance and joyous energy which he never experienced before or after. He was employed in a work which he had been dreaming about, and he undertook it with supreme confidence in the cause to which he and his fellow crusaders were committing themselves. They were, he said, 'upholding that primitive Christianity which was delivered for all time by the early teachers of the Church and which was registered and attested in the Anglican formularies and by the Anglican divines'.[6] He was concerned to restore an ancient religion which, he was convinced, had well nigh faded out of the land through changes over the previous one hundred and fifty years. It would, he asserted, be a second Reformation, but better, for it would return not to the sixteenth but to the seventeenth century. The Whigs had come to do their worse, bishoprics were being suppressed, property confiscated, and sees would soon receive unsuitable occupants. The Church was in danger. There was no time to be lost.

Tracts had been a traditional Evangelical product for fifty years, but they had become hackneyed and emotional appeals, perhaps appropriate for the uneducated to whom they were

---

[6] R.W. Church, *The Oxford Movement 1833–1845* (London, 1892), p.111.

addressed, but discredited in more literate circles and ridiculed by Thackeray and Dickens. Newman and his fellow authors changed them into something quite different from that, or indeed from anything of the kind known in England prior to their day. The new tracts were clear, brief, stern appeals to conscience and reason, challenging and calculated to startle and even offend or annoy, and intense in purpose. They had a common tone of energy and urgency, as written by men with a set determination to utter a cry of alarm and a call for response in the face of a dire emergency. The appeal they made was not a popular one to the many, but a demanding one to the few, to the teachers rather than to the taught. The early tracts set forth no new doctrine. They pointed to what was obvious, old-fashioned and commonplace, but neglected and unfamiliar, and therefore novel to that age. They taught people to think less of preaching than of the sacraments and services of the Church; discouraged all that was showy and ostentatious, and stressed the value of inner and unseen self-discipline, and the cultivation of industry, humility, self-distrust, obedience and, above all else, holiness. 'These, then, were the first public utterances of the Movement as a whole, and they rang out like pistol shots.'[7]

A campaign had begun, and in the Long Vacation of 1833 Newman and his friends rode round to country vicarages carrying parcels of the Tracts and begging the clergy to read them. Newman advocated the Oxford views in a series of letters to the *Record* newspaper. Recruits began to be gained, including William Gladstone and Dr Pusey. Pusey introduced changes, not only in that he produced a Tract which was initialled rather than anonymous, as previously, longer, more erudite, weighty and elaborate than the earlier Tracts, but because of who he was. 'He gave us a position and a name...Dr Pusey was a Professor and a Canon of Christ Church; he had a vast influence in consequence of his deep religious seriousness, the munificence of his charities, his professorship, his family connections, and his easy relations with the University authorities...Dr Pusey was, to use a common expression, a host

---

[7] S.L. Ollard, *A Short History of the Oxford Movement* (1915; London, 1933), p.43.

in himself; he was able to give a name, a form, and a personality to what was without him a sort of mob.'[8]

Differences with the old High Churchmen

The publication of the Tracts brought to a head the differences between the rising Oxford crusaders and the old High Churchmen. The latter, represented by William Palmer and Joshua Watson, wished to offend no one, to include Evangelicals if they would co-operate, and to present to the world the spectacle of a body united to defend the 'Establishment' against any further encroachments of the state. They 'feared anything that would divide the men of goodwill, or alienate the rulers of the Church'.[9] They wanted the Archbishops to feel that when they confronted the enemies of the Church they had the solid backing of the great majority of the clergy. The old High Churchmen were reticent and feared for the consequences of what they regarded as the excessively forward actions and dangerous outspokenness of the young men in Oxford. The zealous leaders of the new movement appeared to the old High Churchmen to be preaching on the house-tops what the old guard had been breathing almost in spirit, and they feared lest this should cause unnecessary offence. The belief of Froude in 'making a row in the world', and of Newman that 'one gains nothing by sitting still' was alien to the Zs. They did not sympathise with Newman who asserted that 'the Apostles did not sit still, and agitation is the order of the day'.

Meanwhile there was another force at work which made a contribution of inestimable worth to the propagation of the ideals of the movement – as great, if not greater than the Tracts and Pusey's adhesion – Newman's sermons at the University Church of St Mary, of which he was the Vicar. The impression they made can in a small measure be gauged from two testimonies, both of which came from men who did not share

---

[8.] John Henry Newman, *Apologia Pro Vita Sua* (Everyman edition, 1912), p.77.
[9.] C.P.S. Clarke, *op.cit.*, p.65.

Newman's convictions. The Presbyterian J.C. Sharp wrote of the remarkable impact of Newman's preaching, and concluded that 'after hearing these sermons you might come away still not believing the tenets peculiar to the High Church system, but you would be harder than most men if you did not feel more than ever ashamed of coarseness, selfishness, worldliness, if you did not feel the things of faith brought closer to the soul'.[10] Matthew Arnold never had any sympathy with the objects of the movement, yet he was captivated by Newman's preaching. 'Who could resist the charm of that spiritual apparition, gliding in the dim afternoon light of the aisles of St. Mary's, rising into the pulpit, and then in the most entrancing of voices breaking the silence with words and thoughts which were a religious music – subtle, sweet, mournful. Happy the man who in that susceptible season of youth hears such voices. They are a possession to him for ever.'[11]

The movement was increasingly gaining public awareness and support, but even in the early days there was external strife and internal tension. The first pitched battle with the Liberals was over the appointment of Dr Hampden as Regius Professor of Divinity. Dr Hampden was orthodox in that he accepted the doctrines of the Church of England and of the Creeds, but he considered that there were 'formularies which may be only the interpretations of doctrine and inferences from Scripture of a particular time or set of men; and he was desirous of putting into their proper place the authority of such formularies'.[12] Whether or not his views were misinterpreted, they outraged the feelings of many Tractarians, Evangelicals and 'High and Dry' Churchmen as being an assault on subscription. In the climate of the day, which was disturbed and fraught with suspicion, protest was inevitable, and Newman took a leading part in the agitation. Dr Hampden was appointed, but convocation resolved that he should be deprived of his vote in the choice of University preachers.

[10] J.C. Sharp, *Studies in Poetry and Philosophy* (1868), pp. 275, 278, quoted in S.L. Ollard, *op.cit.*, p.50.

[11] M. Arnold, *Discourses in America*, p.139, quoted in S.L. Ollard, *op.cit.*, pp.50, 51.

[12] R.W. Church, *op.cit.*, pp.164, 165.

The size of the majority in reaching this decision, four hundred and seventy-four to ninety-four, shows that the victory was due to widespread support and to a combination of groups, not just the Tractarians, but it also shows how organised and powerful the Tractarians were a mere three years after the inauguration of the movement. And their evident influence produced a public and furious response from the redoubtable Dr Thomas Arnold. He forthrightly condemned them and all that they stood for in an article under the title, 'Dr Hampden and the Oxford Malignants', denouncing them as 'formalist, judaizing fanatics who have ever been the peculiar disgrace of the Church of England'.[13] So immoderate were his comments that even his favourite disciple, A.P. Stanley, thought the article 'a most sad thing'.

Evangelical opposition

At about the time of Arnold's fulmination, there were the first signs of serious Evangelical opposition. In the initial stages of the Oxford movement there had been no great reaction from the Evangelicals, and there was no serious controversy between the two groups for about three years.[14] Indeed, they had found common cause in opposition to the removal of subscription to the Thirty-Nine Articles at matriculation, and, as we have seen, in the campaign against the appointment of Dr Hampden. More fundamentally, there was a fairly general recognition in both camps in the early stages of the movement that the passion for social, political and ecclesiastical reform could be viewed as an assault on the Church, that it heralded a battle between the Church and the state, and that Christians as a whole needed to meet the challenge in institutional terms. The zeal of the Tractarians was attractive to many Evangelicals. It was not clear in those formative years of the movement that

[13.] See the *Edinburgh Review,* No. cxxvii, April 1836, 'Dr Hampden and the Oxford Malignants'.

[14.] For works on the relationship of the Evangelical and Tractarian movements see note 1. above.

sacramentalism, and all that flowed from high sacramental teaching, might cause division, especially as the Evangelicals had been instrumental in re-awakening Churchmen to the importance of frequent communion. But it was the common pursuit of holiness which most tightly bound Evangelicals and Tractarians. Even when the Evangelicals developed a distaste for the teaching and principles of the Tractarians, they continued to have a profound appreciation of the religious poetry of Keble and they greatly admired the sermons of Newman. They retained a sense of oneness with the Tractarians in urging the virtues and duties of holiness in what seemed to both groups to be an increasingly secular age.

The *Christian Observer* attacked the Oxford movement in 1837, but the first concerted and intense Evangelical opposition came in 1838 with the publication of Tract 80 on *Reserve in Religious Teaching* and, more especially, with the appearance of the first two volumes of Froude's *Remains*. It was not Evangelicals alone who were gravely shocked and offended by this latter work, for it raised a widespread storm of protest which battered the still young movement. The issuing of the book for general circulation was a major and disastrous indiscretion, because it revealed the personal history and intimate diary of a devout man who expressed himself with characteristic frankness, boldness and honesty in the intimacy of his own private reflections and self-examination, and it would have been wiser to have left it as a private manuscript. The work presented to the public not only contained the innermost communings of his stern, disciplined spiritual life, but set forth his slashing and devastating criticisms of the leaders of the English sixteenth century Reformation. A determination to be faithful to the Protestant Reformation was a powerful trait in the English religious life of the time, and it was a profound shock for Englishmen to read the published letters of an English clergyman, a Fellow and Tutor of an Oxford College, which included such sentences as these – 'I am becoming less and less a loyal son of the Reformation'[15]; or, 'Really, I hate the

---

[15.] *Remains of the late Rev Richard Hurrell Froude, M.A.* (London, 1838), vol. 1, p.336, quoted in S.L. Ollard, *op.cit.*, p.58.

Reformation and the Reformers more and more'[16]; or again, 'Why do you praise Ridley? Do you know sufficient good about him to counterbalance the fact that he was the associate of Cranmer, Peter Martyr, and Bucer?'[17]; or, perhaps most strongly of all, 'The Reformation was a limb badly set; it must be broken again to be righted.'[18] From the date of its publication onwards, Froude's *Remains* 'have been the quarry to which every Protestant controversialist has gone for stones to throw at the Oxford Movement'.[19] In Oxford, the immediate and most public expression of the horror and disgust felt was a plan to embarass the Tractarian leaders, and at the same time declare loyalty to the Reformation, by means of a monument to Cranmer, Ridley and Latimer. The Martyrs Memorial was erected largely as a result of the efforts of C. P. Golightly.

Internal changes

But all of this made little difference to the progress of the movement. By now it had spread to London, where Margaret Chapel, the predecessor of All Saints', Margaret Street, became a Tractarian centre with Frederick Oakeley, Fellow of Balliol, as its incumbent. In 1838 the movement had become the owner of a review, the *British Critic*, and, with Newman as editor, it published a succession of brilliant articles. Despite the opposition and the trials and distractions of the time, Newman could still say in retrospect that in 'the spring of 1839 my position in the Anglican Church was at its height. I had supreme confidence in my controversial status. I had a great and still growing success in recommending it to others.'[20]

But changes were imminent which were to be fatal to the movement in its first phase. Newman himself experienced

---

[16] *Remains, op.cit.*, p.389.

[17] *Remains, op.cit.*, pp. 393, 394.

[18] *Remains, op.cit.*, pp. 433, 434.

[19] S.L. Ollard, *op.cit.*, p.58.

[20] John Henry Newman, *Apologia Pro Vita Sua, op.cit.*, p.102, quoted in S.L. Ollard, *op.cit.*, pp.60, 61.

doubts and difficulties which undermined his faith in the Church of England and set him on the path to Rome and, more generally, the movement itself started to show a tendency to bifurcate, 'one fork still pointing to antiquity and the Caroline divines, the other to Rome'.[21]

The first significant cause of decline was the erosion of Newman's confidence and belief in the Church of England. In the summer of 1839 he had been studying the Monophysite controversy and, for the first time, a doubt entered his mind regarding the tenableness of Anglicanism. 'I had', he said, 'seen the shadow of a hand on the wall. He who has seen a ghost cannot be as if he had never seen it. The heavens had opened and closed again...The thought for the moment had been, The Church of Rome will be found right after all; and then it had vanished. My old convictions remained as before.'[22] But two more blows came soon after this. In an article on the Donatists, Dr Nicholas Wiseman compared Anglicans to the Donatists who separated from the Church in the fourth century on a point of discipline. The article may not have made much of an impression on Newman, but a friend pointed out the words of St Augustine, 'Securus iudicat orbis terrarum' – 'The whole world judges right'. That is to say, the final test of any disputed question is the judgement of the whole Church, which must be right as against the single opinion of any isolated individual or body. It pierced him like a sword. 'The ghost had come a second time.' It was a 'most uncomfortable article', he wrote in his letters; 'the first real hit from Romanism which has happened to me'; it gave him, as he says, 'a stomach-ache'.[23] Nonetheless, he still believed that the Church of England was part of the Catholic Church, with its roots in antiquity, and he set out to prove this in the fateful Tract 90. In the meantime, divisions were appearing in the movements membership, which, in his view, made Tract 90 even more necessary.

[21.] C.P.S. Clarke, *op.cit.*, p.88.
[22.] John Henry Newman, *Apologia Pro Vita Sua, op.cit.*, p.121, quoted in R.W. Church, *op.cit.*, p.226.
[23.] Quoted in R.W. Church, *op.cit.*, p.226.

As the movement had developed, men joined it who did not fully share that passionate love and zeal for the English Church which characterised the pioneers. Nor did they have 'that acquaintance with its historical theology, and that temper of discipline, sobriety, and self-distrust, which marked its first representatives'.[24] These younger adherents were caught up in the dynamic of the movement and the prospect of a new world in contrast to the worn-out old one. Some of them were men of considerable intellectual ability, such as Frederick Faber, J.D. Dalgairns, Frederick Oakeley, J.R. Bloxam and W.G. Ward. They were united in being 'keenly religious men',[25] as Newman described them, but they also shared Romanward inclinations. F.W. Faber (1824–63), Fellow of University College, had been an Evangelical. He joined the Oxford movement in 1836, and is chiefly remembered as the author of some very popular hymns. By 1843, as a result of a visit to Rome, he could say with lyrical enthusiasm that Rome 'is quite different from any place I have ever been at; I bless God that there is such a place upon the face of this sinful earth...I feel as if I should like to satisfy my feelings by walking barefoot and bareheaded in the streets.' Dalgairns was attracted to the movement by its affinities with all that was deep in idea and earnest in life, and by its resistance to what was unreal and shallow; but he was eventually repelled by what he saw as its insularity, compromise and want of completeness. Oakeley was an accomplished musician and, as the incumbent of Margaret Chapel in London, a forerunner in the movement 'to realise the capacities of the Anglican ritual for impressive devotional use'.[26] Bloxam, a Fellow of Magdalen, who was Newman's curate at Littlemore from 1837 to 1840, considered it was his duty to remain in the Church of England but to work for the reunion and restoration of the English Church to Catholic unity. He was the go-between in such correspondence as there was between the advanced wing of the Tractarians and Rome. Ward, a Fellow and Tutor of Balliol,

---

24. R.W. Church, *op.cit.*, p.235.
25. Quoted in C.P.S. Clarke, *op.cit.*, pp. 92, 93.
26. R.W. Church, *op.cit.*, p.371.

was the most fiery, dedicated and well known of the Romeward group in Oxford. We will meet him later when we consider the disturbing effect of his publication in 1844 of *The Ideal of a Christian Church*. Such were the core of the group. 'Both the theory and the actual system of Rome, as far as they understood it, had attractions for them which nothing else had.'[27] It was a great reversal of the original intentions of the movement and the motivations of its founders in its early days. For them the claims and merits of the Church of England as a true branch of Catholic Christendom had been paramount, and none of the Tractarians had seriously thought at that time of Rome, except as a corrupt system containing some good and Catholic elements.

Of course the new Romeward trend caused concern to those such as Robert Wilberforce, Charles Marriott, Frederic Rogers, R.W. Church, Isaac Williams, William Copeland and James Mozley, who remained steadfast in their loyalty to the original aims of the movement, and others like Dr W.F. Hook, who were old-fashioned High Churchmen and friends of the movement before it assumed its Romeward aspect. We have already met and briefly considered Wilberforce, Marriott, Williams and Mozley. Rogers, afterward Sir Frederic Rogers, and then Lord Blachford, was a devoted and intimate friend of Newman, and became a distinguished civil servant. Church was to become the historian of the movement. William J. Copeland, was a Fellow of Trinity, and one of the best Latin scholars in Oxford, when he threw in his lot with the Tractarians and took his share in work on the *Library of the Fathers*. He was also one of Newman's curates, chiefly at Littlemore, where he was long remembered and loved.

By 1839 Dr Hook had become alarmed. 'I do wish', he wrote to Pusey, 'you and Newman would just point out to us what is your standing-point – the position you have decided to take. At present the whole system seems so nearly that of attacking the Church of England and palliating the Church of Rome.'[28] 'Among the younger men', he wrote to Pusey two years later,

[27] R.W. Church, *op. cit.*, p.239.
[28] Pusey House MSS, quoted in C.P.S. Clarke, *op. cit.*, p.96.

in 1841, 'there is a growing attachment to Romanism, as now distinguished from Catholicism – quite a hatred of Catholic practice, which they are pleased to call merely Anglican.'[29]

'Tract 90'

The formation of a strong Romanising section within the Tractarian body was clearly damaging to the movement as a whole, and dangerous to the Church. By 1841 the problem was acute. Newman then wrote Tract 90 to assure the Romanisers, and incidentally himself, that it was possible to hold all Catholic doctrine while assenting to the Articles. He asserted that the Articles, 'the offspring of an uncatholic age, are, through God's good providence, at least not uncatholic, and may be subscribed by those who aim at being Catholic in heart and doctrine'. He claimed that those who subscribed to the Articles might take them in their plain, literal sense, and were not bound to interpret them according to the opinion of those who drew them up. He distinguished between the Romish doctrine condemned in the Articles, which he took to be the received doctrine of the day when the articles were written, the Roman doctrine subsequently promulgated by the Council of Trent, the primitive doctrine and the Greek doctrine. Thus, while Article xxii condemned the 'Romish doctrine concerning purgatory, pardons, worshipping, and adoration as well of images and relics and also invocation of saints, as a fond thing, vainly invented', it did not 'necessarily condemn either the primitive doctrine concerning purgatory, or that maintained by the Greeks at the Council of Florence'.[30]

The effect of the Tract was immediate, widespread, violent and decisive. It set the whole University and much of the country ablaze with heated debate and forthright condemnation. It changed the whole character and fortune of the movement. It was the single most potent cause of the final

---

[29.] *Ibid.*
[30.] C.P.S. Clarke, *op.cit.*, pp. 100, 101.

decline of the movement in its first formative phase, and the response to it was climacteric in the spiritual life and the career of Newman. The Tract deeply offended a multitude of people who were accustomed to interpreting the Articles on traditional Protestant lines as a barrier against Roman teaching. Four Oxford Tutors, among them A.C. Tait of Balliol, later Archbishop of Canterbury, printed a joint memorial protesting against the teaching of the Tract, and the Heads of Houses, preferring not to wait for any explanation from Newman, though one was known to be coming, solemnly denounced the Tract, branded it as dishonest, and posted their condemnation around the colleges. Newman considered that his place in the movement was lost, and public confidence in him at an end. 'In every part of the country and every class of society, in newspapers,...in pulpits, at dinner tables, in coffee rooms, in railway carriages, I was denounced as a traitor,'[31] he lamented. It was a public declaration of war by the Oxford authorities against the movement and its leaders. 'The suspicions, alarms, antipathies, jealousies, which had long been smouldering among those in power, had at last taken shape in a definite act.'[32] On the one hand Newman had seriously miscalculated the possible reaction. On the other the Heads entirely failed to recognise the elevated moral and religious purpose of those they opposed, and did not fully grasp the Tractarian theology.

In deference to the Bishop of Oxford, Newman agreed to stop the series of Tracts, provided the bishops would not condemn Tract 90. Newman felt betrayed when, after a short period, the bishops, one after another, began to attack both the Tract and its author.

Further developments

Towards the end of 1841 two further blows were struck, which wounded both Newman and other Tractarians, although they

---

[31.] John Henry Newman, *Apologia Pro Vita Sua,* quoted in S.L. Ollard, *op.cit.,* p.84.
[32.] R.W. Church, *op.cit.,* p.296.

were only indirectly connected with the theological controversy at Oxford. The one was the contest for the Poetry Professorship vacated by Keble, which degenerated into an issue of theological association, rather than academic and literary suitability, between Isaac Williams representing the Tractarians, and James Garbett who successfully opposed him. The other matter was the scheme for the establishment of a Protestant Bishopric in Jerusalem as a joint venture of the English Church and the State Church of Prussia, which Newman said, 'was one of the blows which broke me'. With all these internal tensions and doubts and external events to reinforce them, Newman was on his death bed as regards his membership of the Anglican Church.

In hindsight it is clear that by the end of 1841 the writing was on the wall, for those with eyes to read it, indicating that the end of the 'Oxford' phase of the Oxford movement was in sight. In February 1843 Newman preached his last sermon before the University, and in October of the same year he celebrated his last Eucharist at the altar of St Mary's. From then onwards he rarely performed any ministerial act. It was also in 1843 that Pusey, who occupied such a prominent place in the University, was accused of preaching in a University sermon doctrine which was contrary to that of the Church of England and, without a hearing or formal trial, was pronounced guilty and forbidden by the Vice-Chancellor to preach in the University for two years. Fuel was added to the already raging fire of controversy with the publication in 1844 of W.G. Ward's *The Ideal of a Christian Church*, the sting of which was the claim that the author could keep his place in the English Church while holding and teaching all Roman doctrine. The University formally condemned the book and deprived Ward of all his degrees.

The course of events was moving to its climax. In September 1843 Newman took leave as it were of the Church of England with his Littlemore sermon on the Parting of Friends. The end came for him, and effectively for the first phase of the movement, in 1845. On an evening of wind and rain on 8 October, a remarkable-looking man, Father Dominic Barberi, who was evidently a foreigner and shabbily dressed in black, found his way to Littlemore, and the following day received Newman into the Roman Catholic Church. The blow had fallen, and Newman was gone. But under the leadership of Pusey, Keble, Church, Marriott and Mozley the movement went on, and widened its geographical spread. New tasks were undertaken and the leaders wrestled with differences of belief and practice in a renewed search for identity. It was to be a period of continuity and change.

PART 4

1845 to 1914

10

Continuity and Change

Within the broad historical sweep of the High Church tradition 1833 was important, but it can too readily be over emphasised as a turning-point. The novelty of the Tractarian teaching should not be overstated. There was High Church continuity as well as change in the history of that tradition before, during and after the 1833–1845 period, and some would consider that the continuity was more significant than the change.

The Oxford movement leaders did not set out to innovate but to restore. Nonetheless, in appealing to the example of their seventeenth century predecessors they tended to give scant regard to all that had been contributed to the High Church tradition in the years between what they regarded as a lost golden age, and the decadent times in which they reckoned that they themselves lived. They appreciated the importance of Joseph Butler, and to a lesser extent William Law, but otherwise their gaze was cast back beyond the eighteenth century to their beloved seventeenth century divines. They viewed the eighteenth century and early nineteenth century to a large extent as a High Church tradition wilderness. And this is an interpretation, or rather a misinterpretation, which has been widely accepted ever since. As we have indicated, the Tractarians were particularly prone to undervalue the clear, loyal and consistent High Church teaching of the Hackney Phalanx and the generation of High Churchmen immediately preceding their own. There was more continuity than they were prepared to acknowledge.

There was a measure of discontinuity in that the Tractarians responded to past High Church teaching in a distinctive way:

> The great difference between them and the older men
> was that they had come to see the past in a more dramatic
> light. It was not enough simply to accept traditional
> doctrines as things always taught; rather their truth was
> to be felt, to be taken to the heart...On their lips the
> term 'catholic' acquired a fresh, almost revolutionary,
> significance. The doctrine of the apostolic succession
> reappeared as a principle to be striven for and with full
> recognition of its practical implications. What in short
> the Oxford leaders did for the old High Church theology
> was to make it into a cause, so that endorsement of their
> opinions became the equivalent of loyalty to the Church
> itself.[1]

The young men of Oxford displayed all the missionary
energy which typified a genuine spiritual revival. However,
in doing so a fundamental difference became evident. The
'older high churchmen took as their standard of catholicity

---

[1] Bernard M.G. Reardon, *Religious Thought in the Victorian Age. A Survey from Coleridge to Gore* (London, 1971), p.33. Among many works covering the history of the Church in the period 1845 to 1914 to which reference has not so far been made, the following are especially relevant to the themes explored in this chapter: A.M. Allchin, *The Silent Rebellion: Anglican religious communities, 1845–1900* (1958), Peter F. Anson, *The Call of the Cloister. Religious Communities and Kindred Bodies in the Anglican Communion* (1955), M.A. Crowther, *Church Embattled: Religious Controversy in Mid-Victorian England* (1970), Marcus Donovan, *After the Tractarians* (1933), Charles Gore (Ed.), *Lux Mundi. A Series of Studies in the Religion of the Incarnation* (1889), George William Herring, 'Tractarianism to Ritualism. A Study of some aspects of Tractarianism outside Oxford, from the time of Newman's conversion in 1845, until the first ritual commission in 1867' (Oxford University D.Phil. thesis, Oxford, 1984), Kenneth Leech and Rowan Williams (Eds.), *Essays Catholic and Radical. A Jubilee Group Symposium for the 150th Anniversary of the beginning of the Oxford Movement 1833–1983* (London, 1983), David Newsome, *The Parting of Friends: a study of the Wilberforces and Henry Manning* (1960), G.L. Prestige, *The Life of Charles Gore. A Great Englishman* (1935), B.A. Smith, *Dean Church. The Anglican Response to Newman* (1958), John Tulloch, *Movements of Religious Thought in Britain during the Nineteenth Century* (1885), N.P. Williams and C. Harris (Eds.), *Northern Catholicism. Centenary Studies in the Oxford and Parallel Movements* (1933).

the Anglican formularies, and supported them from Scripture and antiquity, whereas the later Tractarians used the appeal to antiquity to correct and supplement the Anglican formularies'.[2] W. F. Hook as an old High Churchman made clear the contrast between his view of the Church and that of the later Tractarians:

> When I was called a High Churchman, we meant by the word one who, having ascertained that the Church of England was reformed on the right principle, cordially accepted the Reformers. We meant by a High Churchman one who, thinking the Church wiser than himself, observed her regulations and obeyed her laws, whether we understood them or not.[3]

But what of the period after 1845 ? 'In so far as there is a traditional interpretation of the years from 1845 to the 1860's it runs briefly as follows:- the loss of Newman, and those who followed him to Rome, was a shattering blow to the Movement. In the years that followed, E.B. Pusey, John Keble and a few others rallied the fragments of Tractarianism and, against all the odds including further blows such as the Gorham Judgement, held it together. Having survived these years of trial the Movement then developed, quite naturally, in the direction of increased ceremonial usage in the 1860's, which once more brought it to the forefront of public attention, and heaped upon it further attacks.'[4]

However accurate or imprecise this description may be it raises the whole, much debated question of what is the correct balance between continuity and change in the transition from the Oxford based Tractarianism of the years 1833 to 1845 to an undoubtedly different situation four decades later. The very fact that 'the Movement' is so often confined to the years 1833 to 1845, and is then seen to end, and to be superceded

---

[2] Reginald H. Fuller, 'The Classical High Church Reaction to the Tractarians', in Geoffrey Rowell (Ed.), *Tradition Renewed*, p.53.

[3] Reginald H. Fuller, *op.cit.*, p.54.

[4] George William Herring, *op.cit.*, Abstract.

after a space of time by a new breed of Catholic Anglicans, the so-called ritualists and the slum priests of the Christian Socialism era, tends to give credence to a discontinuity interpretation, and to discount the elements of continuity. This is reinforced by the contrast frequently drawn between the theology and presuppositions of the Tractarians compared with those of Charles Gore, the Holy Club and Liberal Catholicism.

Perhaps the extent of continuity is greater than is often depicted, and the 1845 divide somewhat over stated. The departure of Newman in 1845 was a shattering blow to those most intimately associated with him, hardly lessened by its predictability in the preceding months, but it may have been less traumatic for the movement as a whole than has commonly been assumed, and especially for the many outside the small inner circle of Tractarians in Oxford. In some ways it was a relief that Newman and the Romanisers within the movement had gone, and in certain respects it gave a new lease of life to a movement which had attracted severe criticism and opposition largely because of the evidence of its Romeward tendencies, not least of all in some of its foremost leaders. Most of the Tractarian clergy in the late forties and throughout the following decade were moderate men. They differed little from their contemporaries, except in that they spearheaded such changes as the removal of pews and the introduction of daily services; issues which were soon to be taken up as church-wide campaigns. In the main the post-1845 heirs of the Tractarians were characterised by moderation rather than fanaticism in their attitude to such controversial matters as the re-introduction of disused ceremonies and private confession, although there were exceptions such as Littledale and Neale who could hardly be described as moderates. Anyhow, as we will see later, some of these practices were known and approved by Tractarians prior to 1845, so that there was a measure of continuity here, as well as change.

But if there was continuity as well as change in the period after 1845, the balance was strongly tipped in the direction of change from the 1860s onwards. It was then that ritualistic practices became more widespread and adventurous, and new, 'liberal', theological thinking became more prominant among High Churchmen. The more extreme ritualists in a number of ways profoundly shifted the emphasis of the Oxford movement, and the Liberal Catholics adopted views which were anathema to some of the surviving Tractarians of the 1833 to 1845 period. As the pioneer Tractarians differed from the older High Churchmen of their day and the preceding half century, in seeing themselves and being seen as more progressive and radical, so the Anglican Catholic ritualists and liberals, whilst they had much in common with the earlier Tractarians, perceived themselves and were seen, as differing from them in tone and method as well as in belief and practice.

The elements of continuity and change are well depicted, and can perhaps be best understood, in the lives and work of two of the dominant High Churchmen of the age: R.W. Church and Charles Gore.

Richard William Church (1815–90)

It has been claimed that the importance of the life and work of R.W. Church, and indeed 'his unique place among the nursing fathers of modern Anglicanism', lies in what his subtle, largely unsung influence was able to effect in the interval between the Oxford movement of the period 1833–1845 and the 'new genius of the *Lux Mundi* school rising, apparently like a phoenix out of the ashes, forty-five years afterwards'.[5]

He was born in 1815 and was admitted to Wadham College, Oxford, in 1832. His Oxford life covered the period of the Oxford movement, for after graduating with a first he was elected Fellow of Oriel. Initially, he had no part in the movement, but at Oriel he came under the immediate and powerful influence of Keble, Newman and Froude and supported the Tractarians.

[5.] B.A. Smith, *Dean Church. The Anglican Response to Newman* (London, 1958), p.vii. A work to which this section owes much.

With the dramatic departure of Newman in 1845, there developed among some High Churchmen 'a sort of stoical conservatism', in which those concerned were 'led along the path of saintliness by the honourable figure of Pusey, and encouraged by the old-fashioned sweetness of John Keble and Isaac Williams'.[6] These Churchmen were forerunners of Henry Parry Liddon, and a strand of Anglo-Catholicism which was to extend to the present day. But there was another strand represented by Church, James Mozley and Frederic Rogers, whose adherents particularly wrestled with the question of Anglican identity in the wake of issues raised by Newman in his secession to Rome. They attempted to re-establish what they regarded as the lost but true nature of the English Church, acknowledging that Anglican assumptions needed to be 'tested...in the light of fact and history'.[7] Two convictions, which superficially might have appeared incompatible, characterised Church's outlook: he was orthodox to the point of seeming old-fashioned, yet he welcomed the attempt to rethink and restate the Christian faith.[8] Some thought him a Tractarian, some a trimmer. For forty-five years and more, especially for the eighteen years from 1871 to 1890 while he was much in the public eye as Dean of St Paul's, he trod this uneasy path. As a Catholic Anglican, he strove to preserve those Catholic elements which he thought were vital to the orthodoxy of any Church. He did not endorse that sort of 'Catholicism' which attempted, as a kind of fifth column, to bring about the day when the whole Anglican Church would be captured, and purged of all traces of Protestantism. He was a loyal Churchman all his days until, on 9 December 1890, 'very quietly (to use the words of Lord Blachford) he slipped cable, and, as one belonging to another country, was "off to the South" '.[9]

---

6. B.A. Smith, *op.cit.*, p.51.
7. B.A. Smith, *op.cit.*, p.51.
8. B.A. Smith, *op.cit.*, p.143.
9. B.A. Smith, *op.cit.*, p.301.

Charles Gore (1853–1932)

For fifty years and more Charles Gore played a prominent part in the life of the English Church in general, and within the ranks of High Churchmen in particular. He was born at Wimbledon on 22 January 1853, the fourth child and youngest son of parents who both derived their ancestry directly from an Irish peerage. He appears to have had a happy childhood in a household which set before itself the twin ideals of Christian devotion and hard work. He was educated at a fashionable school at Malvern Wells and then at Harrow, where he was shy, scholarly and argumentative. He edited the school magazine and was a leading light in the school debating society. Although Harrow during his time was definitely Evangelical, Gore and his friends formed a small but distinguished group who were High Church, with social and political views which were much more radical than the prevailing Liberalism of the Whig aristocracy. He was profoundly influenced by B.F. Westcott, an assistant master who afterwards acquired fame as a Biblical scholar and Bishop of Durham. Gore made expeditions to London where he was especially attracted by the worship at St Alban's, Holborn, and the teaching of Arthur Henry Stanton. From Stanton, he learnt 'to make his confession, to love the Mass, and to fast on Fridays'.[10] In 1870 he was elected to a Balliol scholarship, and went up to Oxford the following year, taking with him a considerable reputation from Harrow.

Throughout his brilliant University career Gore combined deep and ever maturing Christian convictions with an acute sense of the need for personal and social righteousness. His mind 'was fundamentally and by now incurably religious. Theology and, by consequence for a person of his intellectual constitution, philosophy also, formed his predominant interests. His concern for the maintenance of the Christian

---

[10] G.L. Prestige, *The Life of Charles Gore. A Great Englishman* (London, 1935), p.11. Inevitably the present account of the life and work of Gore is heavily indebted to this splendid biography.

moral standard, his interest in programmes of personal and social conduct, and his passion for the redress of social grievances, were all subsidiary to the religious motive...He was a reformer because he was a Christian.'[11] His circle of friends and those who exercised most influence upon him included George Russell, H.P. Liddon, R.M. Benson and Henry Scott Holland. Holland had been a neighbour at Wimbledon from many years past and, until his death in 1918, Gore enjoyed a close and precious friendship with him, for they were bound together by an almost identical outlook on social and religious matters, and were both motivated by the same Christian dedication. On Holland's death Gore paid a tribute to his friend which shows this community of thought and feeling. 'For the last forty years and more, there was no question, speculative or practical, which has presented itself to my mind, on which I have not found myself asking "What will Holland say?" and been disposed to feel that I must be wrong, if I turned out to be thinking differently from him.'[12] Later Edward Talbot was admitted into this intimacy, to form a remarkable trio.

In 1875 Gore obtained his expected double first in Greats, and there soon followed a fellowship at Trinity. The following year he was ordained deacon. He acknowledged himself to be a High Churchman, loved the kind of ceremonial which some called ritualistic, but had grave reservations about the Ritualists whom he considered injudicious and even offensive and arrogant. From the outset of his Trinity career, largely through his association with Scott Holland, he was drawn into a circle of older men, among whom Holland, Talbot and the religious philosopher J.R. Illingworth were prominent. They were all dons in holy orders, and they were united in loyalty to the Catholic creeds and the constitution of the Church. But they also emphasised the importance of reason in religious matters. Holland ironically dubbed them 'The Holy Party'.

[11.] G.L. Prestige, *op.cit.*, pp.14, 15.
[12.] G.L. Prestige, *op.cit.*, p.18.

Much as he loved academic life, Gore longed for pastoral work to complement it. Consequently, after he was ordained priest in 1878, he undertook an assistant curacy at Christ Church, Bootle, and shortly after that moved to St Margaret's, Prince's Road, Liverpool. But in 1879 he accepted the office of Vice-Principal of Cuddesdon Theological College. He was attracted back to Oxford by the prospect of a post which would be almost entirely theological, and which would have as its main purpose the forming of men's minds and characters for that very pastoral work on which he had set his heart. He thoroughly enjoyed his new appointment. His vitality, massive learning, friendliness, humour, originality and holiness were greatly appreciated by the students.

It was at this time that the differences in outlook and method became apparent between Gore and Holland on the one hand and H.P. Liddon on the other. Liddon was the mouthpiece of Dr Pusey, who by now dwelt apart, never appeared in public and was soon to die. He represented Pusey's essential conservatism, whereas Gore and Holland were the leaders of progressive radicalism, and were animated by a prophetic ardour and fervency of spirit. It was a cleavage which was to become more severe within a short time, and which was to bequeth to Anglo-Catholicism a continuing division of belief and ethos.

Pusey died in September 1882, and as a substantial and lasting memorial to him his admirers purchased the whole of his library and bought a house in St Giles' to house both the books and the custodians. The new centre was also established in order to provide for Biblical and liturgical research, and 'a re-statement of portions of the evidences of Christianity as shall meet the needs of the modern world of thought'; in order permanently to 'secure to the Church of England some accomplished teachers of theology in Oxford'; and in order to provide pastors who should 'as opportunity may serve, act as friends and advisers of the Church of England undergraduates'.[13] The priests attached to it were called

---

[13.] Extracts from a statement by H.P. Liddon in *The Times* during November 1882, quoted in G.L. Prestige, *op.cit.*, pp.49, 50.

Librarians, and Gore was appointed Principal Librarian despite his candid admission that he did not adhere in every point to the teaching of Dr Pusey. He left Cuddesdon, and after a few months assisting the Oxford Mission in Calcutta, he took up his new appointment.

Under Gore the new enterprise flourished, with undergraduates flocking to him as they had done at Cuddesdon. He 'rapidly became the most potent religious force in Oxford'.[14] He perpetuated at Pusey House the spirit and temper of the Holy Party. In the years 1887 to 1889 he was instrumental in three momentous initiatives: the inauguration of the Society of the Resurrection, out of which within a few years grew a new religious order; the foundation of the Christian Social Union; and the publication of a volume of essays under the title of *Lux Mundi,* which shook the religious world. So significant were each of these that we will but note them in this sketch of Gore's life, and consider them more fully elsewhere.

In 1891 Gore delivered the Bampton Lectures, which were published the following year and ran quickly through a series of reprints. The book further established his reputation as a theologian of eminence, and as a public figure. But by now he was committed more fully to the Community of the Resurrection, and he yearned for a parish with a sort of institute attached where he and fellow members of the Community could combine parochial service with writing and lecturing, having the needs of working men directly in view. As a result, in 1893 he was inducted to the benefice of Radley, five miles from Oxford. During his eight months there he took his parish duties very seriously, but he found that he was not suited to a country living. It was for him a crushing, but, perhaps for that reason, a very useful experience of first hand contact with 'ordinary' working men and women and their families. It was with relief that after this short period he was made a canon of Westminster.

[14.] G.L. Prestige, *op.cit.*, p.76.

In London his preaching was attractive to many. The force with which his convictions were presented astonished people accustomed to formal or academic expositions of the Christian religion. It has been claimed that 'he inspired the mind and touched the conscience to a degree surpassing any other Churchman of his generation'.[15] His teaching was based on Scripture, and he sought to make the Bible a powerful source of practical righteousness. He advocated the fullest possible freedom in matters of ceremonial, demanded votes for women in the Church, and remained a radical even in his ecclesiasticism.

In 1902 Gore was consecrated Bishop of Worcester after a forthright protest by the Church Association. The diocese was, in the view of Gore and others, of unmanageable size. It was divided into two parts, the old Worcester diocese and the massive connurbation of Birmingham, in a somewhat uneasy marriage. With his reforming zeal and concern for social righteousness, it was Birmingham which really appealed to him, and he strove to constitute it as an independent diocese, with an undertaking that he would donate the whole of the fortune due to him on the death of his mother, about £10,000, towards the costs involved. The new diocese was created, and Gore was enthroned in 1905 as its first bishop. For his residence he took a house in Edgbaston, which he declared to be the ugliest villa in western Europe, he kept no carriage or car of his own but used public transport or received help from volunteers, and he continued the accustomed simplicity of his domestic life. His generosity was prodigious, with endless anonymous gifts to poor priests and others and donations to a multitude of causes. His pastoral care was appreciated by clergy of varying Churchmanship, but he was stern and unbending to the scandalous or careless priest. Administratively he was less at ease. He intensely disliked organisation and was frustrated by the mechanisms of ecclesiastical government. He was active in social agitation, especially in the fields of housing, gambling, industrial

---

15. G.L. Prestige, *op.cit.*, p.166.

relations, education and where matters of working class welfare were at stake, and he frequently spoke up on these or related issues in local authority bodies or the House of Lords. He was an avid supporter of the Workers' Educational Association and showed the keenest interest in Birmingham University. He earnestly advocated Church reform, whereby the Church would be allowed to govern itself through its own bishops, supported by representatives of the clergy and laity, and the ecclesiastical courts would be reconstituted in order to provide tribunals which Churchmen would respect and obey.

In 1911 Gore accepted the bishopric of Oxford. It was to prove a bewildering new experience of isolated leadership. He found that he was at odds with the wealthy laity of Oxford and the establishment in the countryside because of his 'Socialism', his support in 1913 for the Welsh Disestablishment Bill, and his proposal to create two new dioceses for Berkshire and Buckinghamshire. He also had conflicts with clergy in his diocese because he attempted to restrict the practice of reserving the sacrament, and to curb what he declared to be irresponsible or excessive ritualistic practices. His health suffered under the pressure of work and responsibility, and the strain of these various controversies. During the 1914–18 war, as we will see, although he resolutely opposed German militarism, and thought that it should be smashed, he also warned against self-righteousness. Wearied by a multitude of pressures, and somewhat disheartened by tendencies and actions of the Church, such as the nomination of Hensley Henson as Bishop of Hereford, and the decision of the Representative Church Council in 1919 that the franchise of the future Church Assembly should be thrown open to the unconfirmed, which he thought was treating the spiritual obligations of Church membership with something like contempt, he decided to resign his office in July 1919.

Retirement gave Gore ample opportunity to reflect, to speak at meetings, and to write, the result of which was that his reputation and influence were immeasurably enhanced at home and abroad. He chaired the concluding session of the first Anglo-Catholic Congress held in London in 1920, and was received with such enthusiasm, no doubt because of his personality rather than for his principles, that he had to restrain the capacity audience at the Albert Hall as he delivered his address; and he spoke at the second Congress in 1923. In the early years of his retirement he was largely occupied with the writing of a trilogy of theological works, *Belief in God* (1921), *Belief in Christ* (1922) and *The Holy Spirit and the Church* (1924), the three volumes bearing a common subsidiary title, *The Reconstruction of Belief.* The intention in these books was in keeping with his lifelong purpose, to provide a rational re-assertion of primitive Christianity, taking modern thinking into account. In them as well as by other means, he sought to examine the whole subject of the existence and dispensation of God in a spirit of free enquiry, unfettered either by the pre-emptions of authority or by the *a priori* preconceptions of anti-supernaturalists. It was an approach which he viewed as characteristic of Liberal Catholicism, but which was anathema to some Anglo-Catholics.

For Gore, Liberal Catholicism was a Catholicism which was restrained in its expression of 'authority', and, within the limits of the creeds and decrees of the Councils, left as much room to move as possible. He was persistent and severe in his criticism of Anglo-Catholicism in its modern development. He never was a leader of Anglo-Catholicism as a section of the Church of England, and by the time of his retirement he was almost completely alienated from those who inspired and governed the policy of the younger Anglo-Catholics. He was especially alarmed at their admiration for the Roman Church and their devotion to Roman ideals. They in their turn were revolted by what he stood for. All his life he had been independent and uncompromising, with views which were not acceptable to traditional and conservative Anglo-Catholics, and his aim had always been to influence the Church in general rather than to support or captain a party.

Gore remained active and outspoken in his last years. He did all he could to help secure the passage of the Revised Prayer Book into law, despite the Anglo-Catholic opposition. In 1927 he produced a volume of essays under the title, *Christ and Society,* in which he briefly reviewed the social implications of the Gospel and the social teaching of Christendom. He presided over a large group of Anglican scholars in an ambitious undertaking which resulted in 1928 in *A New Commentary on Holy Scripture.* As a sequel to his Gifford Lectures in 1929–30, he composed the last of his important books, *The Philosophy of the Good Life,* which was a final tribute to his powers of mind and character, especially as it entailed a new line of study for him when he was over seventy-five years of age. He remained remarkably active to the end. He made an extended visit to India, returning in May 1931. In January 1932, he visited London on a cold and rainy day in order to participate in a farewell for the newly consecrated Bishop of Labuan and Sarawak. But within a few days he was ill and obviously dying. When Archbishop Davidson visited him he was weak and twice lapsed into a semi-conscious state, and each time the Archbishop heard him say quite clearly the words 'Transcendent Glory'. On the morning of Sunday 17 January 1932, he died.

Gore's theology, and the theology of his circle of close associates, demonstrates the nature of the High Church theological continuity and change in the post-1845 era. It belonged to the Oxford movement tradition, but it was not simply the successor of Tractarianism. And some of the survivors of the movement, notably H.P. Liddon, reckoned that it blatantly contradicted and undermined all that Newman, Keble and Pusey had striven for.

Henry Parry Liddon (1829–90)

Henry Parry Liddon had been one of W.J. Butler's curates at Wantage (1852–4), first vice-principal of Cuddesdon Theological College (1854–9), and vice-principal of St Edmund Hall, Oxford (1859–62). In the sixties he was a stalwart opponent of the post-Tractarian Oxford liberalism. He was appointed prebendary of Salisbury in 1864 and Canon of St Paul's in 1870, in which post he attracted large congregations to his powerful preaching. In 1870 he was appointed Dean Ireland Professor of Exegesis at Oxford, and he used his enhanced status and influence chiefly in the extension of Catholic principles. In his Bampton Lectures on *The Divinity of Our Lord,* published in 1867, he sought to maintain the strictest standard of orthodoxy without making any concessions to the difficulties then being raised by biblical criticism. He was the indefatigable chronicler of the *Life of Pusey* in four substantial volumes – a token of his admiration for a friend with whom he shared so many of his strongly held beliefs. He saw the Church already 'on an inclined plane, leading swiftly and certainly towards Socinianism tempered by indifference'.[16] His writings and teaching were dedicated to the preservation of an orthodox Anglican Catholicism and were destitute of originality, for to him originality could only mean novelty, and novelty could only mean heresy.

Liddon had a high regard for Charles Gore, and indeed he had been largely responsible for securing Gore's appointment as principal of Pusey House. It was therefore a devastating blow to the older man when Gore went so far as to propagate opinions which Pusey would have judged a betrayal of the orthodox faith. Liddon deplored the new outlook which the heirs of the Tractarians believed was demanded by the changing times and the advance of knowledge. The appearance of *Lux Mundi,* which encapsulated the new teaching, was so traumatic to Liddon that it may well have hastened his death some months later.

Lux Mundi and Kenotic Christology

The Preface to the book made its genesis and purpose very clear. 'The writers', it tells us, 'found themselves at Oxford together between the years 1875–1885, engaged in the common work of University education; and compelled for their own sake, no less than that of others, to attempt to put the Catholic faith into its right relation to modern intellectual

---

[16.] H.P. Liddon, *The Divinity of Our Lord* (1867), quoted in Bernard M.G. Reardon, *op. cit.,* p.430.

and moral problems.' As a consequence of their same Churchmanship and frequent meetings, 'a common body of thought and sentiment, and a common method of commending the faith to the acceptance of others, tended to form itself'. They shared the conviction that Jesus Christ was still and would continue to be the Light of the world. They were sure that if people could rid themselves of prejudices and mistaken notions, and if they would look afresh at what the Christian faith really means, they would find it as adequate as ever to interpret life and the whole range of human knowledge, and to give intellectual as well as moral freedom. But they were conscious also that if the true meaning of the faith was to be made sufficiently plain and evident it needed to be disencumbered, reinterpreted and explained. The great mysteries of Christianity needed to be communicated anew to each age.

They wrote not as 'guessers at truth', but 'as servants of the Catholic Creed and Church', aiming only at interpreting the faith they had received. But they also wrote with the conviction that they lived in an epoch of 'profound transformation, intellectual and social, abounding in new needs, new points of view, new questions; and certain therefore to involve great changes in the outlying departments of theology, where it is linked on to other sciences, and to necessitate some general restatement of its claim and meaning'.

They thought that theology should undergo a new development. They would not apply the term development to anything which failed to preserve the 'type of the Christian Creed and the Christian Church', because development did not mean innovation or heresy; but, on the other hand they did not mean a mere 'intensification of a current tendency from within, a narrowing and hardening of theology by simply giving it greater definiteness or multiplying its dogmas'. The real development of theology was, to them, a 'process in which the Church, standing firm in her old truths, enters into the apprehension of the social and intellectual movements of each age: and because "the truth makes her free" is able to assimilate all new knowledge, to throw herself into the sanctification of each new social order, bringing forth out of her treasures things new and old, and shewing again and again her power of witnessing under changed conditions to the catholic capacity of her faith and life'. The collection of essays was an attempt to contribute to such a development. It was not intended to be a complete theological treatise, or a controversial defence of religious truths, but rather a positive presentation of 'the central ideas and principles of religion in the light of contemporary thought and current problems'.

Although want of space meant certain omissions, including a separate and specific consideration of such subjects as sin, historical evidences and miracles, it was hoped that the teaching on other matters gave sufficient indication of at least the general views of the writers on the missing topics.

The Preface finally made clear that the contributors wrote 'not as mere individuals, but as ministers, under common conditions, of a common faith'. They wanted the work 'to be the expression of a common mind and a common hope'.

Lux Mundi made very explicit and public the change in High Church theological thinking since the time of the Tractarians. The general aims, as just outlined, and the essays which applied these aims to particular, and sometimes controversial, subjects, caused various, and often quite strong, reactions. To some, like the Broad Churchman Gordon Cosmo Lang, the publication of the book was a momentous and thrilling event, for 'the firm sacramental teaching which was the kernel of the Oxford movement' combined with 'the candour, freedom and breadth of view which marked Maurice, Kingsley and Robertson of Brighton' was exactly what was needed.[17] It was, to such Churchmen, a coalescence of Broad and High Churchmanship. Many High Churchmen also welcomed the attempt to remain faithful to historic High Church theology while engaging with the demands of modern thought. But, as already noted, to many conservative High Churchmen it was a bitter shock, and a betrayal of High Church beliefs by those who should have been guardians of

---

[17.] J.G. Lockhart, *Cosmo Gordon Lang* (London, 1949), p.84.

the faith delivered to them, and for which they were accredited teachers.

Lux Mundi was subtitled '*A series of studies in the Religion of the Incarnation*', 'and this declared interest was in keeping with the already settled trend of English theology, associated alike with the Tractarian teaching and with Coleridge, Maurice and the Cambridge theologians, towards readjusting the balance between the incarnation and the atonement'. The authors were concerned to stress 'both the intrinsic importance and the ramifying implications of the claim that in Christ the Son of God had assumed human nature'.[18] Their willingness to seek new aids for the communication of this doctrine and other tenets of the old faith is indicated by their readiness to turn for intellectual guidance to the philosopher T.H. Green, a far from orthodox believer, and to adopt a measure of neo-idealism.

The contribution which aroused most interest and gave the most offence was that by the editor, Charles Gore, on 'The Holy Spirit and Inspiration'. Gore confronted the by then inescapable issue of the implications of biblical criticism for the historic faith. He concluded that although it was impossible to maintain the historicity of the Old Testament at all points, and although Jesus himself spoke as a Jew of his own century, with the limitations that implied, yet it was inadmissible to represent the New Testament history as 'idealized', and therefore to some extent falsified, 'without results disastrous to the Christian Creed'. There was an absolute coincidence of idea and fact. Gore was adamant throughout his life that the church must insist that although the New Testament may contain errors of detail, in a general sense the history is entirely trustworthy.

Such concession to modern criticism caused some consternation, but it was his aside in his essay on the problem of Christ's human knowledge which especially distressed Liddon and others, for whom the gospel history implied without a doubt that 'the knowledge infused into the human

---

[18] Bernard M.G. Reardon, *op.cit.*, p.433.

soul of Jesus was ordinarily and practically equivalent to omniscience'.[19] Gore insisted that Christ revealed God 'but through, and under conditions of, a true human nature. Thus He used human nature, its relation to God, its conditions of experience, its growth in knowledge, its limitation of knowledge...He shews no signs at all of transcending the science of His age. Equally He shews no signs of transcending the history of His age. He does not reveal His eternity by statements as to what happened in the past, or was to happen in the future, outside the ken of existing history.' Gore adds a footnote to this in which he states that Christ 'never exhibits the omniscience of bare Godhead in the realm of natural knowledge; such as would be required to anticipate the results of modern science or criticism. This "self-emptying" of God in the Incarnation is, we must always remember, no failure of power, but a continuous act of Self-sacrifice: cf. 2 Cor. viii.9 and Phil. ii.7. Indeed God "declares His almighty power most chiefly" in this condescension, whereby He "beggared Himself" of Divine prerogatives, to put Himself in our place.'[20]

Gore elaborated this theory of kenosis in the *Dissertations*. He considered that New Testament criticism had raised the whole issue of the gospel's historicity and that a modern theologian was bound to view Christ's manhood in a historical perspective. In this regard 'much of the patristic and all of the medieval theology was inadequate'.[21] He held that the Church, while preserving continuity in doctrine, should be free to 're-express its theological mind, as it has so often already done, in view of fresh developments in the intellectual, moral and social life of man'.[22] He wanted to make plain his belief that under the conditions of the mortal incarnate life the divine Son 'did, and as it would appear habitually – doubtless by a voluntary action of his own self-limiting and self-

---

[19] Charles Gore (Ed.), *Lux Mundi*, quoted in Bernard M.G. Reardon, *op.cit.*, p.449. This is a book to which the following comments are greatly indebted.

[20] Charles Gore (Ed.), *Lux Mundi* (London, 1889), p.360, n.

[21] *Dissertations on subjects connected with the Incarnation* (London, 1895), p.9, quoted in Bernard M.G. Reardon, *op.cit.*, pp. 449, 450.

[22] Dissertations, *op.cit.*, p.213, quoted in Bernard M.G. Reardon, *op.cit.*, p.450.

restraining love – cease from the exercise of those functions and powers, including the divine omniscience, which would have been incompatible with a truly human experience'.[23] He was concerned with the moral force of the kenotic principle, and although he was fully aware of the metaphysical difficulties raised by the concept, he was prepared to let these go unanswered, as constituting a problem which was essentially unanswerable.

Kenotic Christology remained in the forefront of theological discussion until well into the twentieth century, and attracted opposition from such eminent theologians as Hastings Rashdall, William Sanday and William Temple.

The Body of Christ

A further major contribution of Gore's to theological debate at the turn of the century was his study of eucharistic doctrine in *The Body of Christ* (1901). It is a masterpiece, and one of the best works on this subject by an English divine. He claimed that the perception of the Eucharist as 'the extension of the incarnation' was not solely confined to the Tractarians but was patristic, and he gladly concurred with it. Indeed it is consonant with his whole turn of thought to apply the expression to the Church itself, or to the sacraments in general, with the Eucharist as the special medium or focus of the divine presence. Gore considered that in communion it is the whole Christ who is received, but he denied that as a sacrifice it was in any way a repetition of Calvary. Its true meaning is to be found in its relation to the offering of the glorified Christ in heaven:

The sacrifice of the Son of Man once offered in death has been accepted in glory. In the power of that sacrifice Christ ever lives, our high priest and perpetual

---

[23.] Dissertations, *op.cit.*, p.95, quoted in Bernard M.G. Reardon, *op.cit.*, p.450.

intercessor, the continually accepted propitiation of our sins unto the end of time. All that we need to do and can do is to make thankful commemoration, in His way and by His Spirit, of His redemptive sufferings, and to unite ourselves to His perpetual intercession when He presents Himself for us in the heavenly places, or as He makes Himself present among us in our eucharistic worship.[24]

Liberal Catholicism

Gore was the chief proponent of what he called Liberal Catholicism. He identified Liberal Catholicism with Anglicanism. The Church of England was Catholicism reformed and preserved in accordance with the teaching of Scripture. He believed that Liberal Catholicism was precisely embodied in the Anglican appeal to Scripture, antiquity and reason, it did not denote a party or peculiar dogmas. It meant that the constant appeal to Scripture as the standard of doctrine and moral judgement went hand in hand with concern for the intellectual integrity of the individual. He was implacably hostile to any type of liberalism which tampered with the Catholic creeds. To some Catholic Anglicans of more Ultramontane sympathies, such as Lord Halifax, he seemed to be too much a Protestant, if not a 'modernist'. But he was intransigent towards modernism, was indeed foremost as a protagonist in the modernist controversy, and hammered them unmercifully. He was resolutely opposed to any undermining of belief in the substantial historicity of the events in which Christianity originated, and to the end he made the historical claims of Christianity the foundation of his apologetic method. Among such claims were the literal truth of Christ's virgin birth and bodily resurrection, to which he believed that express assent should be required at least from the clergy. These doctrines could not, in his opinion,

---

[24.] Charles Gore, *The Body of Christ*, p.183, quoted in Bernard M.G. Reardon, *op.cit.*, p.452.

be taken in any merely figurative sense, although he did concede that the idea of Christ's upward motion in the ascension could be interpreted symbolically. But the virgin birth and the resurrection were actual historical events. Nature is not a closed system which excludes all possibility of intrusion from without. Gore acknowledged the reign of law but postulated a higher and lower order of things in which, in the interest of the higher, the divine action may fittingly abrogate the lower.

Far from being liberal in any way as defined by the Modern Churchmen's Union, he appeared a conservative as measured by the standards of a later, younger, school of High Churchmen who were more open to the influences of what he regarded as a dangerously radical type of New Testament criticism, and who adopted a religious philosophy, accordingly, which was based on the pragmatic value of Christian experience rather than on the assumed authenticity of Christ's historical claims.

For about forty years Gore exercised an influence upon Anglican opinion which was probably greater than any other living divine. But by the 1920s other more radical High Churchmen were to play their part in the High Churchmanship of their day, and, as we will see, they were to make yet another distinctive contribution to the High Church tradition. It was to be one more phase in the process of continuity and change in the hundred years after the initial Oxford movement.

The doctrine of the Church

There was also High Church continuity and change from pre-Tractarianism through Tractarianism to later Anglican Catholicism in the understanding of the nature and characteristics of the church, the ordained ministry and the sacraments, church-state relations and the relationship between the Church of England the Roman Catholic Church and Nonconformity.

Some contemporary observers of the Oxford movement

detected close links between Evangelicalism and Tractarianism, but where they commented on the differences between the two movements they often focused on the doctrine of the Church. Gladstone acknowledged that 'the Evangelical clergy were the heralds of a real and profound revival, the revival of spiritual life'. But he judged that spiritual life to be conceived largely in terms of individual conversion. 'There was', he said, 'no corresponding recognition of the perpetual, indistructible existence of the Church of God.' Gladstone suggested that the idea of the Church was frequently reduced to little more than language about 'our venerable Establishment'.[25] During the time of the movement, in 1842, he wrote of 'those great Catholic principles which distinguish our Church from many other Protestant bodies: such, for instance, as the doctrines of grace in Baptism, of the real sacramental Presence in the Eucharist, of absolution, of universal or Catholic consent, of the Apostolic foundation of the Episcopate, and of its being the source of lawful Church power, and of a valid ministry'.[26]

The old High Churchmanship of the eighteenth century was characterised by social conservatism expressed as political Toryism, and consistent suspicion of Roman Catholicism and Protestant dissent. As we have seen, the Hackney Phalanx, as representative of this tradition, ensured that their works were undertaken within or with the blessing of the Church of England. They were antipathetic to interdenominational or non-denominational organisations. Nevertheless they were generally irenic and avoided a hostile or aggressive attitude either to Roman Catholicism or to Nonconformity.

But the nineteenth century churches generally were far more denominationally conscious and sectarian. There was a massive expansion of Nonconformity after about 1790. The Church of England's position was weakened as the Industrial Revolution created the unchurched cities of the north. There was a Roman

---

[25] D.C. Lathbury, *Correspondence on Church and Religion of William Ewart Gladstone* (1960), 1, pp.7, 8, quoted in Geoffrey Rowell, *The Vision Glorious*, p.7.

[26] D.C. Lathbury, *op.cit.*, 1, p.240, quoted in Geoffrey Rowell, *op.cit.*, p.7.

Catholic population explosion in Ireland, with an overflow into the industrial towns of mainland Britain. All this increased the Church of England's sense of fierce defensiveness. On the other hand both Nonconformists and Roman Catholics saw in their growing numbers and influence an opportunity to exert themselves, and to right some of the wrongs which they had endured for so long at the hand of what they regarded as a repressive and oppressive Establishment. And the Oxford movement contributed greatly to the rapid widening of the gulf between the Church Establishment and both Nonconformity and Roman Catholicism. The 'movement precipitated a new bitterness in inter-church polemic, in which all the churches expanded on the basis of a fiercer hatred for one another'.[27] Some High Church attitudes were extremely crude. The learned and otherwise noble-hearted John Mason Neale articulated this belligerence when he declared of 'the brave old Church of England':

> Dissenters are like mushrooms,
>   That flourish but a day;
> Twelve hundred years through smiles and tears
> She hath lasted on alway!...
>
> The true old Church of England
> She alone hath pow'r to teach;
> 'Tis presumption in Dissenters
> When they pretend to preach... [28]

The church as a school for saints, built up by apostolic creeds, ministry and sacraments, was a vision Newman had derived from his study of the Fathers. It was the appeal to the undivided church of the first four centuries which seemed to him characteristic of Anglicanism. As the Church of England strove to remain faithful to that tradition, in

---

[27.] S.W. Sykes and S.W. Gilley, 'No Bishop, No Church! The Tractarian Impact on Anglicanism', in Geoffrey Rowell (Ed.), *Tradition Renewed*, p.135.

[28.] Quoted in S.W. Sykes and S.W. Gilley, *op.cit.*, p.128.

distinction from the over-systematisation of Roman theology and the idiosyncratic individualism of Protestantism, she witnessed to a *via media*.

The Tractarians fought for the protection of the rights of the church as a divinely ordained, divinely established and divinely sustained institution, but they differed from some former High Churchmen in their view of the right relationship between church and state. The old High Church attitude to the union of church and state and to the ideal of a religious establishment rested on a deep conviction of the divine origin of all political power and authority, and on a sacral notion of monarchy which committed the sovereign to positive religious doctrines as the 'nursing father' of the church.[29] It was a view which could be traced back to the full and detailed exposition of Richard Hooker, the partnership of Laud with the Martyr King and the teaching of the Caroline divines. But in contrast to this tradition, the Tractarians increasingly resisted the concept of any political alliance by the church and any interference by the state in the affairs of the church, even if this was in a defensive capacity. It was essentially a practical response to changing political circumstances, with theoretical justification coming later. The later Anglo-Catholics tended to concur with these views and condemn any close alliance of church and state as Erastian. But there was also discontinuity of view in that there was an element of attachment to sacral monarchy in early Tractarianism, despite their fear of Erastianism, which was absent in late Anglo-Catholicism.

There was a powerful trend in the Oxford movement from an early date, especially marked in Newman, which questioned the rights and status of national churches. This was again in contrast to the old High Church teaching and caused the old High Churchmen great concern as they were wedded to all that was entailed in the Church of England as an established national church. This attitude of the Tractarians was seen by

---

[29] Many of the comments on the Tractarian view of church-state relations and on other matters discussed in this chapter owe much to Peter Nockles, 'Continuity and Change in Anglican High Churchmanship 1792–1850' (1982).

the old High Churchmen as demonstrating the essentially party, extraneous and sectarian character of the Oxford movement. In the old High Church teaching the royal supremacy was seen positively as a reflection of the monarch's sacral and quasi-religious character as 'Defender of the Faith'. Yet the difference of view on this whole question of the church and state between the Tractarians and the old High Churchmanship can be overstated. For all their strictures on the Zs attitudes the early Tractarians were remarkably in accord with the more political beliefs of old High Churchmanship. Almost to a man they were high Tories and ardent royalists, and anyhow 'it was the interdependence of church and state, and not the dependence of the church upon the state'[30] that underlay the old High Church attitude.

The dissatisfaction with the church and the consequent questionings about church-state relations was part of an innovative, restless, revolutionary and indeterminate quality in the Oxford movement, in which its leaders never acknowledged a definite *terminus loci*. In this, as in other matters which we have discussed, it is arguable that the Zs were left isolated as the more faithful representatives in their day of the old High Church tradition, even if it is considered that that tradition with regard to church and state relations had been overtaken by political and constitutional developments and was in urgent need of modification. Whether justified or not, the Zs felt betrayed and abandoned on this and other issues as old High Churchmanship was assailed on all sides and fell from the dominant and influential position in the church which it had enjoyed in the decades prior to the Oxford movement. The Tractarians shared with the old High Churchmen a veneration for the church, and a determination to exalt it as of divine origin and of central importance in the economy of God, but they bequeathed to posterity a new Anglican Catholic view of the place of the

---

[30.] Peter Nockles, 'The Oxford Movement: historical background 1780–1833', in Geoffrey Rowell (Ed.), *Tradition Renewed*, p.30, referring to E.R. Norman, *Church and Society in England, 1770–1970: an historical study* (London, 1976), p.22.

church in society, and more especially of its relations with the state.

The Tractarians also made a distinctive contribution to the doctrine of the church in their 'restoration to the church of a sense of sacramental instrumentality'. Of particular significance was Newman's idea of the church as a community. The model of the church which Newman set forth was 'a personal, familial, yet structured communion'.[31] And this concept influenced the thinking and action of post-1845 Anglican Catholics.

From the time of the early Tracts, the Oxford movement vehemently upheld the doctrine of apostolic succession, although, as we have seen, this was not novel. It was a belief which had been precious to most of the High Churchmen whose history we have recounted, and had been presented in a coherent form by, amongst others, many of the Caroline divines and Nonjurors such as Charles Leslie, Henry Dodwell and George Hickes, by William Law, the Hutchinsonians, Charles Daubeny, and Thomas Sikes. Later, however, the Oxford movement diverged in its teaching on this subject from the old Anglican Catholicism. The Tractarians were perhaps more rigid in the exposition of their view of episcopacy than, for example, seventeenth century High Church teaching would have given precedence: but this helped to restore 'to the Church of England a consciousness of her place in the Catholic Church of Christ, as a great episcopal communion and not just a national church. Indeed the movement's stress on the necessity of the episcopal office undergirded the nineteenth-century development of an international Anglican communion in Africa, Asia, the Americas and the Pacific, which occurred despite the Church's loss of its traditional role in the life of the English nation.'[32]

[31.] See Louis Weil, 'The Tractarian Liturgical Inheritance Re-assessed', in Geoffrey Rowell (Ed.), *Tradition Renewed*, p.116.

[32.] S.W. Sykes and S.W. Gilley, *op.cit.*, p.134.

The sacraments and holiness

The sacraments, like the church and its ministry, were of crucial importance to Tractarians, as they had been to their High Church forebears. They believed that what they signify is 'the unity of the mystical body, head and members, that is, our unity as the people of God in Christ. From our baptism into the body, we are involved in the corporate experience of a common faith. Every Eucharist is a celebration of a realisation of that unity established through baptism. It is not a sacrament of individual or private salvation; it is salvation through incorporation into the redeemed community.'[33]

The new life of baptism, its regenerating power and its place within the whole life of the church were key themes of the Tractarians. Pusey expressed this belief, which he and the other Tractarians regarded as the teaching of the ancient Church and of the Anglican Church of the past, when he said that baptism means that we are 'engrafted into Christ, and thereby receive a full principle of life, afterwards to be developed and enlarged by the fuller influences of His grace; so that neither is baptism looked upon as an infusion of grace distinct from incorporation into Christ, nor is that incorporation conceived as separate from its attendant blessings'.[34] By the time of the Oxford movement the question of baptismal regeneration had become a subject of lively, if not to say heated, discussion. In former times both High Church Anglicans and others in general had been able to express their beliefs in the words of the Articles and the Prayer Book, but in the first decades of the nineteenth century baptism was expounded more fully by Bishop R. Mant and others as the vehicle of justification. For Newman and some of his fellow Tractarians the acceptance of this doctrine was decisive in their personal development, and was one of the strongest indicators of their defection from Evangelicalism.

[33.] Louis Weil, *op.cit.*, pp.116, 117.
[34.] Quoted in Geoffrey Rowell, *The Vision Glorious*, p.17.

As with baptism the Tractarian view of the Eucharist had its roots in the old Anglican tradition. Even on the threshold of the Caroline High-Anglicanism Bishop Andrewes in his sermons showed how the thought of the divine indwelling was united to a quasi-physical conception of grace, and closely connected with the idea of the incarnation. The Eucharist was to Andrewes a means of participating in the divine nature, whereby He might dwell in us, and we in Him; He taking our flesh, and we receiving His Spirit. Throughout the seventeenth and eighteenth centuries High Churchmen varied in their views. As we have previously noted, some further accentuated the stress on the Real Presence, some gave emphasis to the Eucharist as a commemorative sacrifice, as for example in the teaching of Cosin, while others tended towards a receptionist view. There was a dualism in the Eucharistic teaching of the Oxford movement. On the one hand the doctrine of the Real Presence, on the other a deepening of the mystical content of the Eucharist as a means of the inflowing of the divine grace into man, and the taking up of the individual into the divine.

One of the most significant incidents in the mid-nineteenth century period of continuity and change involving the High Church doctrine of the Real Presence was the action taken against Archdeacon George Anthony Denison in the Exeter diocese. He was not only prosecuted for teaching the doctrine of the Real Presence in the Eucharist, but in 1855 he was accused of unwarrentedly requiring of ordination candidates that they should confess that the inward reality of the sacrament was received by all, wicked as well as faithful. The case assumed a national dimension and importance because behind the local accuser, a neighbouring clergyman, Joseph Ditcher, was the zealous Evangelical Archdeacon Henry Law, and behind Law stood the Evangelical Alliance and Lord Shaftesbury. It was a muddled affair in which, after a commission of enquiry, the Evangelical Archbishop of Canterbury, J.B. Sumner, conducted the trial. Judgement was given against Denison with sentence of deprivation, but on appeal the case was dismissed by both the Court of Arches and the Judicial Committee of the Privy Council on technical and not doctrinal grounds. The failure of the prosecution made Denison into something of a minor martyr; he achieved a popularity which he had not previously enjoyed, and with this there was a measure of gain for the High Church cause which he was championing. But not all High Churchmen were in agreement with what he was upholding and the case highlighted differences in High Church theological opinion, as well as giving the Evangelicals an unfortunate taste for legal persecution.

But whatever their differences of theological understanding, there was for all Tractarians and their successors an intimate link between their reverence for the Eucharist and the overarching concern for holiness, which was, for example, demonstrated in the life and teaching of Pusey. 'Pusey's sermons are shot throught with a sense of awe, reverence, and wonder before the grace, mercy, and holiness of God. The adoration of the contemplative before the mystery of the God who, coming down to the lowest part of our need, takes us to Himself, and exalts us in Christ to the heavenly places – that is the temper and disposition which he sought to share... The mystery of the Incarnation prepares us for the mystery of the Eucharistic presence.'[35] This sense of the numinous, and of man's response in worship to God's grace, and especially to the wonder of the Incarnation, must, he declared, be joined inseparably with service to the poor and needy or the worship of God becomes a blasphemy. Theology and practice must be united. At the very heart of the Eucharist was the cross, and the cross should be at the very heart of Christians in their daily lives. 'Our life', Pusey declared, 'from Baptism to our death should be a practice of the Cross, a learning to be crucified, a crucifixion of our passions, appetites, desires, wills, until, one by one, they be all nailed, and we have no will, but the will of our Father which is in Heaven.'[36] Fasting, self-denial, our acceptance of apparently

---

[35] Geoffrey Rowell, *The Vision Glorious*, pp.81, 82.

[36] E.B. Pusey, *Parochial Sermons*, III (revd. ed., 1878), quoted in Geoffrey Rowell, *The Vision Glorious*, p.84.

undeserved suffering; these are the ways we take and bear the cross. Holiness of life was considered by the Tractarians as a visible means of authenticating if not proving the truth of Christianity in the eyes of the unbelieving. Austerity and a disciplined style of living were signs of commitment, and indeed they were even a test of whether we are Christ's disciples or deceiving ourselves. 'Here was no cheap grace, no mere formalism.'[37] While the Tractarians were distrustful of any outward display of such sanctity the almost magnetic energy produced by so much passionate intensity held under control by a restraining simplicity of life was a source of powerful attraction. To many who gathered about them it made them appear to glow with an inner light. They seemed to make the unseen world real.

The revival of religious communities

Some of the Tractarians, and notably Pusey, worked for the revival of the religious life in the Church of England as one way of promoting holiness.[38] At the Reformation the Church of England made a great breach with antiquity, and with pre-Reformation Church life and practice, when it discarded monasticism. In the second decade of the nineteenth century the Poet Laureate, Robert Southey, asked why there were no Beguines or Sisters of Charity in the English Church, adding that in his opinion they were badly needed. The Oxford movement leaders determined to restore what they considered to be a lost heritage. They regarded religious communities as good in themselves, but also, and especially as a means of doing good works. The idea of the religious life had never completely died out since 1559, when the last

---

[37] Frederick H. Borsch, 'Ye shall be Holy: reflections on the spirituality of the Oxford Movement', in Geoffrey Rowell (Ed.), *Tradition Renewed*, pp.68, 69.
[39] See Peter F. Anson, *The Call of the Cloister* (London, 1955), Introduction, on which these comments are based.

of the old communities had been dissolved. As we have seen, in the seventeenth century there was the Little Gidding community, although this was not stricly monastic. In the eighteenth century, the monastic ideal remained alive, although but faintly. A number of writers deplored the lack of monastic institutions in the Church of England. These included Bishop Atterbury in 1723, William Law in 1740, George Berkeley in 1741, and Samuel Richardson in 1754; and there was a proposal by Sir William Cunninghame in 1727 for a scheme to found a religious community. There was also an awakened interest in Gothic architecture and the more romantic aspects of medievalism. This was stimulated by novels such as Horace Walpole's *The Castle of Otranto. A Gothic Story* (1764) and Thomas Percy's *Reliques of Ancient English Poetry* in 1765. Sir Walter Scott powerfully evoked the more picturesque features of pre-Reformation religion, largely through his longer poems such as *Marmion* (1808), and his novel, *The Monastery* (1820). The influx of countless Roman Catholic bishops, priests, monks, nuns and laymen driven from France by the Revolution of 1789 contributed to an increased awareness of Roman Catholicism.

The first step in restoring religious community life in England in the nineteenth century was taken by the Tractarians in 1841 when Marian Hughes, who attended St Mary's, Oxford, and who owed much to the teaching of Newman, took a vow of holy celibacy. Pusey's much loved eldest daughter, Lucy, resolved to devote herself to God in the same way, but died prematurely before she was fifteen, in 1844. A seed was also sown with the religious community which Newman established at Littlemore in 1842, and which lasted until he left the English Church in 1845. The community members were not bound by vows and it was not a religious order, but it paved the way for such orders in the future.

In 1844 a group of laymen, including William Gladstone, Lord John Manners, afterwards Duke of Rutland, and Lord Lyttelton, established a Sisterhood of Mercy at 17 Park Village West in the parish of Christ Church, Albany Street in London, with the approval of the Bishop of London, Dr Blomfield, and in memory of Robert Southey. In 1848 Bishop Phillpotts officially sanctioned the formation of The Church of England Sisterhood of Mercy in Devonport and Plymouth, and gave his blessing to Lydia Sellon and her friend Catherine Chambers as the first two members of the Society. Meanwhile other communities were being founded: the Community of St Thomas the Martyr was established in Oxford in 1847, and in 1848 the Sisterhood of St Mary the Virgin, Wantage was begun under the guidance of the vicar of the town, W.J. Butler.

Societies began to spring up in and around centres of High Church revival. In 1849 Marian Hughes founded the Community of the Holy and Undivided Trinity in Oxford; in 1851 the Community of All Saints was founded by the incumbent of Margaret Street Chapel, Upton Richards, and the following year the Community of St John the Baptist was established at Clewer by Harriett Mansell, inspired by the saintly and influential rector, Canon T.T. Carter, to provide help to the needy through a penitentiary, or house of mercy for the fallen. In all these foundations in London, Exeter and Oxford, the diocesan bishop had at least not been hostile, and was even well disposed towards the movement.This was not so in the case of the two communities which arose in the Diocese of Chichester – the Community of St Margaret at East Grinstead, founded by John Mason Neale in 1855 as a body of district nurses living under rule who would serve the needs of the area, and the Community of the Blessed Virgin Mary, founded in the same year by the vicar of St Paul's, Brighton – where the approval of the local Bishop was possibly secured by Bishop Samuel Wilberforce of Oxford.

During the last half of the century the number of communities multiplied. New communities were founded in 1856, 1857, 1858, 1861, 1865, two in 1866, one in 1867 and two in 1868, one each year in 1870, 1873, 1874 and 1877, two in 1879, and at least five in the last decade of the century. Thus, the total was perhaps in excess of thirty within seventy years of the start of the Oxford movement; a remarkable indication of its persistent vitality and ability to evoke a response of dedication and commitment.

Such a revival of an unfamiliar aspect of Church life, associated in the minds of many with Roman Catholicism and an alien pattern of religiosity, aroused extreme and militant opposition. In Devonport there were fierce verbal and written attacks on the sisterhood; Neale and the sisters of St Margaret's were mobbed at the funeral of a sister at Lewes, with Neale being knocked down, and the sisters hustled and insulted, so that they were with difficulty rescued from the mob. But in many cases the mouths of opponents were stopped, and the aggression assuaged by the manifest godliness, good works and usefulness of the sisters, for the sisterhoods were almost invariably established to serve the region in which they were located.

Communities for men emerged more slowly. It was not until 1866 that Richard Meux Benson, vicar of Cowley, Oxford, founded with two other priests the Society of St John the Evangelist, which was to become established in four continents and be a household name in the Church of England before Benson's death in 1915. In 1891 the Society of the Sacred Mission was begun by Father H.H. Kelly, moving to Kelham in 1903. Charles Gore founded the Community of the Resurrection in 1892, which moved to Mirfield in Yorkshire in 1898; it was a society which was to establish a fine reputation in many parts of the world throughout the first hundred years of its life. Other smaller, or less permanent, Orders were founded in the last years of the century; and guilds and societies included the Brotherhood of the Holy Trinity at Oxford (1844), initially a centre for studying ecclesiastical art and later a society for senior members of the University, the Guild of St Alban (1851), which did splendid service as a society of laymen, united on a strictly religious basis for prayer, study, and Church work of every sort, and the Sacrae Trinitatis Cantabrigiensis, which was very successful in uniting Churchmen, graduates and undergraduates at Cambridge in a union for prayer and worship. In the academic sphere there was also, as previously mentioned, the foundation of Pusey House in Oxford.

Frederick Denison Maurice (1805–72)

Religious communities gave expression to a High Church concern that the church should serve the society of its day and generation. And this was at the heart of the radical teaching of Frederick Denison Maurice. But he took the argument a stage or two further than some High Churchmen wished. 'Convinced that human beings, created in the image of the triune God and knit together in Christ, are members one of another, Maurice insisted that our life with God cannot be considered apart from our relations with our neighbours. Our family life, our politics, our economics are all sacred.It is impossible, he argued, to lead a Christian life apart from the divine society which God has ordained for the human race.'[39] Maurice confronted High Churchmen with the possibility of deepening their incarnational and sacramental theology, most importantly by joining it more explicitly to the doctrine of the Kingdom of God. Here was radical theology indeed, and the seed for a potentially more extreme radicalism in the future. 'It was this, more than anything else, which transformed what had been a conservative faith into a potentially revolutionary one.'[40] Maurice taught that the Kingdom of God was not a safe haven reserved for the faithful after death, but a present reality, destined to supplant the kingdoms of this world and to be enjoyed by the whole human race. The supreme task of the Church, therefore, is to proclaim this divine order against which all societies are to be judged. To Maurice true socialism was the inevitable result of a social Christianity.

At the time that Maurice made his startling pronouncements, the Evangelicals had largely lost their momentum in the promotion of social reform, and were

---

[39]. John Orens, 'Priesthood and Prophecy: the Development of Anglo-Catholic Socialism', in Kenneth Leech and Rowan Williams (Eds.), *Essays Catholic and Radical. A Jubilee Group Symposium for the 150th Anniversary of the beginning of the Oxford Movement 1833–1983* (London, 1983) p. 165. An essay to which this section on Maurice owes much.

[40]. John Orens, *op.cit.*, p.165.

becoming preoccupied with other issues. The Broad Churchmen had not developed either a social theology or a plan of social action. It was left to Christian Socialists and Anglo-Catholics to challenge the comfortable indifference of the Anglican establishment. Although Maurice found the Anglo-Catholic understanding of post-baptismal sin and belief in everlasting damnation repugnant, and Anglo-Catholics regarded Maurice as woolly-minded and even heretical, nonetheless, many of the ritualists and the slum priests, whom we are about to consider, found themselves echoing Christian Socialist beliefs, and acknowledging their indebtedness to Maurice.

11

Mission at Home

Slum Priests

Confronted with the religious indifference of the impoverished, unsophisticated working classes, the 'Anglo-Catholic slum priests' of the second half of the nineteenth century offered a religion with 'colour, movement, action, and, above all, simple rules for being a Christian. This was in contrast to the dreariness of an average Anglican service at the time, the centre of which was a long and often boring sermon – sometimes little more than an intellectualized interpretation of Christianity.'[1] Methodism had lost its initiative, energy and effectiveness and Anglo-Catholics in the second half of the century recognised a home missionary task which needed to be undertaken with dedication and determination; they were convinced that they

[1] W.S.F. Pickering, *Anglo-Catholicism. A study in religious ambiguity* (London, 1989), p.67. This is an important work on recent Anglo-Catholicism, to which this chapter is indebted. Works relevant to the themes in this chapter, not cited previously, include J. Bentley, *Ritualism and Politics in Victorian England: the Attempt to Legislate for Belief* (Oxford, 1978), T. Christensen, *Origin and History of Christian Socialism 1848–1854* (1962), L.E. Ellsworth, *Charles Lowder and the Ritualist Movement* (1982), Alan D. Gilbert, *The Making of Post-Christian Britain. A History of the Secularization of Modern Society* (1980), John H.S. Kent, *Holding the Fort: Studies in Victorian Revivalism* (1978), Michael Reynolds, *Martyr of Ritualism. Father Mackonochie of St. Alban's, Holborn* (London, 1965), G.W.E. Russell, *Arthur Stanton. A Memoir* (1917), Maria Trench, *Charles Lowder. A Biography* (1881), D. Voll, *Catholic Evangelicalism* (1962; ET 1963).

alone could give the Church of England inroads into urban working-class areas. The Anglo-Catholic slum priests of the period were fired by a great sense of mission and a deep concern for the well-being of those to whom they ministered. One of the earliest of these priests, James Skinner, spoke in the 1850s of building up men's souls.[2] Fr James Adderley (1861– 1942), a well-known mission priest, delighted in calling himself, and others like him, 'Gospel Catholics'[3], and, for instance, criticised a sermon of the Nonconformist theologian R.J. Campbell, saying, 'There isn't enough Gospel in this to save a cat!'[4] Fr Stanton, the great urban priest, whom we will consider more fully, wrote to an undergraduate who was hindered from making his confession, 'Nothing must ever take away our rest in the old Evangelical love and trust in Jesus'[5], and his biographer described him as a 'Bible-Christian'. Stanton's sermons generally, and more especially those delivered in the West London mission of 1885, centred strongly on the need for conversion in Evangelical terms. Late in his life, after much experience of human misery and with his own spiritual life greatly matured, he exhorted his congregation from his heart: 'Never be ashamed of the Blood of Christ. I know it is not the popular religion of the day...you are Blood-bought Christians...let us remember that our religion is the religion of a personal Saviour. It is not a system of ethics, it is not a scheme of philosophy, it is not a conclusion of science, but it is personal love to a personal living Saviour: that is our religion!'[6] Fr Dolling was regarded as a Romaniser, but was in many respects an Evangelical, and was very warmly disposed towards non-denominational Evangelicals. Fr Wiggett of the Society of St

[2] J. Embry, *The Catholic Movement and the Society of the Holy Cross* (London, 1931), p.xxxi, quoted in W.S.F. Pickering, *op.cit.*, p.67.

[3] T.P. Stevens, *Father Adderley* (London, 1943), p.27, quoted in W.S.F. Pickering, *op.cit.*, p.67.

[4] T.P. Stevens, *op.cit.*, p.23.

[5] G.W.E. Russell, *Arthur Stanton. A Memoir* (London, 1917), p.75, quoted in W.S.F. Pickering, *op.cit.*, p.67.

[6] E.F. Russell (Ed.), *Father Stanton's last Sermons in St. Alban's, Holborn* (1916), pp. 312, 313, quoted in Geoffrey Rowell, *The Vision Glorious*, p.138.

John the Evangelist, spoke of the need in the Church of England for Evangelicals to preach about the atonement. The Rt. Hon. G.W.E. Russell, friend and biographer of Stanton, tried to demonstrate in 1878 in a lecture to the English Church Union that Catholic theology was at heart Evangelical, and that Evangelical doctrine in 'so far as it is constructive and affirmative' was 'truly Catholic'.[7]

These examples are sufficient to show that doctrinally Anglican Catholics and Evangelicals had much in common, and certainly far more than either group had with the liberals of their day, or subsequently. The Anglican Catholics, unlike the Evangelicals, wanted to combine the proclamation of personal faith with an emphasis on the role of the priest, the sacraments and ritual, which were integral to their churchmanship, but both Anglo-Catholics and Evangelicals shared a seriousness about religious matters which sometimes united them; and they had two common enemies, religious apathy and liberalism. Unfortunately it was the differences, especially of priestly function and ritual or, more accurately, liturgical expression, which inflamed passions and produced conflict and confrontation when, perhaps with greater insight, spiritual discernment and tolerance, there could have been a measure of convergence in the face of a desperate need for dedicated and compassionate mission.

It was undoubtedly the Anglo-Catholic slum priests who were especially effective in making the gospel a living reality to people living in deprived urban areas where there was little folk religion or Christian understanding to help them in their mission task. In his study of religious influences in London at the turn of the century Charles Booth concluded that in parishes where the poor, as he defined them, were in the majority the 'High Church section is more successful than any other. They bring to their work a greater force of religious enthusiasm', and their 'evidently self-denying lives appeal...to the imagination of the people'. But even so, the result of these

---

[7.] G.W.E. Russell, *The Household of Faith. Portraits and Essays* (London, 1902), p.314, quoted in W.S.F. Pickering, *op.cit.*, p.68.

efforts, as measured by church attendance, was more questionable. Booth concluded that 'the churches themselves' were 'largely filled by a people from other districts and of higher class, attracted by the stir of religious life'.[8]

Pusey and church-building

Although the work of the slum priests was by far the most heroic Anglican Catholic attempt at home mission in the nineteenth century, it was not the first such effort. There is little evidence that the early Tractarians were seriously concerned about mission at home and abroad, but it did have a place in their thoughts, and Pusey was outstanding in his initiatives. As early as August 1832, he preached 'a sort of incidental protest against the sad neglect of our heathen countrymen in our great towns'. He also gave the impulse to a great church-building movement in London by an article he contributed to the *British Magazine* in November 1835:

> Those in authority ought to know that there were those who would gladly lay up treasure in heaven by parting with their treasure here; who would make sacrifices; who look with sickening hearts at the undisputed reign of Satan in portions of our metropolis, at the spiritual starvation of myriads, baptized into the same body with ourselves; who would gladly contribute their share, if they were but directed.[9]

Bishop Blomfield of London consulted Pusey about the Metropolitan Churches Fund formed in 1836, and Pusey himself contributed £5,000 anonymously, as well as giving

---

[8.] C. Booth, *Life and Labour of the People in London*, third series, *Religious Influences*, 7 (1902), pp.35–37, 46, 47, quoted in Geoffrey Rowell, *The Vision Glorious*, pp.139, 140.

[9.] See C.P.S. Clarke, *The Oxford Movement and After*, p.131, for comments and quotation.

£1,000 towards the building of Christ Church, Albany Street.

Pusey's concern to minister to the poor, religiously alienated masses, especially in the newly formed industrial towns, assumed a very practical, personally agonising and traumatic form in the funding and equipping of a new parish, St Saviour's, Leeds, with a church, school and clergy house.[10] Pusey had known the area for some time through his contacts with the High Church incumbent, Walter Farquhar Hook, of whom we will hear more very soon. The district had been a slag heap, created by the working of a coal mine. Through it flowed a branch of the river Aire, thick with mud, dye-grease and sewage. Mills bordered the gloomy stream, and over all was a thick pall of smoke. The inhabitants mostly worked long, hard hours in the mills, and lived packed together in narrow streets and alleys where the opportunity for public recreation was largely confined to the public houses, the streets and the dancing saloons. Drunkenness was rife, and immorality, even among the very young, was blatant and rampant.

Pusey donated well in excess of £6,000, and made noble personal efforts, in an attempt to provide a caring Christian ministry to those deprived, submerged people, and in doing so found himself in a sea of difficulties. There was trouble with the site on which it was proposed to build the church, for it was undermined and threatened to subside. The Bishop objected to the proposed dedication of the church to the Holy Cross; 'to the inscription over the west door; to a stone altar; to the west window; to the altar linen; to the plain wooden cross over the screen; to the inscription on the altar plate'.[11] Notwithstanding the aggravations and obstacles, the church was completed, and consecrated in October 1845. But more trouble followed. Tales were spread which aroused the passions of local Evangelicals against the church and against Hook in whose parish it was located. Hook became agitated, and he sent a number of somewhat bitter letters to Pusey. 'I think', he wrote in November 1846, 'that semi-popish colony in the heart of

---

[10.] The following description owes much to C.P.S. Clarke, *op.cit.*, pp.135f.

[11.] C.P.S. Clarke, *op.cit.*, p.136.

Leeds an affliction and a curse.'[12] As if to substantiate the accusations of Popery, in January 1847 three members of the staff seceded to Rome; and then the vicar resigned, and the only remaining curate was dismissed. For some months there was no resident priest, and when a new vicar was appointed he only stayed three months before he was elected Bishop of Brechin. Other problems ensued, including the secession of all the clergy except one in 1851 at the time of the Gorham judgement.

Pusey greatly regretted the secessions but did not panic or despair. He held fast to his belief in the need for such churches as St Saviour's as possibly the only way to win the religiously alienated masses for Christ and his Church. For many years before his death he had the satisfaction of seeing the work taking root, and was able to feel that his expenditure of money, the difficulties, responsibility, toil and prayer had not been wasted.

William James Early Bennett (1804–86)

One of the earliest High Church slum priests was W.J.E. Bennett, who, in his early life, had been an Evangelical, but became a convert to Tractarianism while serving a curacy. In 1840 he was appointed to take charge of the new parish of St Paul's, Knightsbridge, which was carved out of the parish of St George's, Hanover Square, and was consecrated in 1843. He introduced a type of service which was at that time novel. 'The prayers were intoned and the psalms chanted; the clergy and a surpliced choir walked to their places in procession; there were lights and flowers on the altar.'[13] By 1850 the generosity of the wealthy pew-holders of St Paul's enabled him to build a daughter church in a poor, neglected part of the parish lying nearer the river, which became the parish of St Barnabas', Pimlico. The church stood in the middle of a deplorable slum

---

[12.] Pusey House MSS, quoted in C.P.S. Clarke, *op.cit.*, p.137.

[13.] C.P.S. Clarke, *op.cit.*, p.142.

which had a sewer running through it, and housed a largely criminal population. He and his colleagues had endeared themselves to even the roughest inhabitants by their devoted service during the cholera epidemic of 1849, but he had become embroiled in controversy with Bishop Blomfield because of his use during the epidemic of a prayer for the dead.

After the Gorham judgement of 1850, the Bishop wrote to Bennett remonstrating about his adoption of the eastward position; the practice of his assistant priest standing at the altar steps facing east at a Celebration, instead of being at the south side facing north; the invocation at the beginning of the sermon; the use of the sign of the Cross, the use of flowers on the altar, and especially red flowers on a saints' day which he described as being 'worse than frivolous and to approach very nearly to the honours paid by the Church of Rome to deified sinners'; the use of an altar cross; and the way the colours of the frontal were changed according to the season. He did not make reference to the fact that St Barnabas' was the first church in London which gave equal facilities for worship to rich and poor. Bennett wrote a conciliatory reply, and relations were improving when Pope Pius IX issued a Bull establishing the Roman hierarchy in England to the accompaniment of a great outburst of anti-Roman frenzy. The Prime Minister, Lord John Russell, seeing his Government in danger, gained a measure of popularity by writing an Open Letter to the Bishop of Durham protesting at the Anglican Romanising practices. Inflamatory articles, comments and speeches ensued, and a mob invaded St Barnabas'. At a great meeting in the Free-masons' Tavern, Lord Shaftesbury declared, 'I would rather worship with Lydia on the banks of the river than with a hundred surpliced priests in the gorgeous temple of St. Barnabas.'[14]

The riots continued. The Bishop called on Bennett to give up the ceremonial to which objection had been taken, or resign. In March 1851, he resigned.

Bennett was succeeded as Vicar of St Paul's in 1851 by the Hon. Robert Liddell. A suit was set in motion by the

[14.] Quoted in C.P.S. Clarke, *op.cit.*, p.149.

churchwarden, Westerton, for the removal of the high altar and its cross, candlesticks, coloured altar-cloths, and the credence table. The Bishop of London's Consistory Court pronounced in favour of Westerton on all points except the candlesticks which were adjudged legal if used for giving light. Liddell lost an appeal to the Provincial Court presided over by the Dean of Arches, but on further appeal in 1857, the Judicial Committee of the Privy Council pronounced altar-frontals, the credence table, and the cross on the screen legal, and in other respects confirmed the decision of the lower courts. The candlesticks were not mentioned in the appeal. The judgement upheld the 'Ritualist' interpretation of the Ornaments Rubric, and supported the Anglo-Catholics in their contention that the use of the ornaments was legal, and that episcopal interference with such use was arbitrary and unjustified. This did much to encourage the development of ceremonial.

Ceremonial

Ceremonial had been of little concern to the early Tractarians. Despite their sacramental sense they were not ritualists. Pusey had professed to know little about it and deprecated 'seeking to restore the richer style of vestments used in Edward VI's reign', as likely to minister to vanity:

> It seems beginning at the wrong end for ministers to deck their own persons: our own plain dresses are more in keeping with the state of our Church which is one of humiliation: it does not seem in character to revive gorgeous or even in any degree handsome dresses in a day of reproach and rebuke and blasphemy: these are not holyday times.[15]

Unlike Pusey, Newman had two churches of his own, but he also attached little importance to 'externals', and called those

---

[15] Quoted in C.P.S. Clarke, *op.cit.*, p.154.

who were part of a 'strong movement in the aesthetic direction... improper Tractarians...and the gilt ginger-bread school'. J.R. Bloxam was the leader of those so designated by Newman, and was described, long afterwards by Lord Blachford, as 'the father and grandfather of all ritualists'.

W.G. Ward occupied a midway position between these two groups, and thought elaborate ceremonial was only necessary for the poor:

> In other cases but an accessory, though a most important one, becomes in these an absolute essential, for in what other way can religious truths be possibly impressed deeply upon those whose minds are worn down by unceasing anxiety and care, and whose bodies are exhausted with protracted toil.[16]

John Mason Neale (1818–66) and the *Ecclesiologist*

It was Cambridge rather than Oxford, and more especially John Mason Neale, who first treated ceremonial seriously, 'as an indispensable and important part of worship, instead of something to be apologized for and left to the weaker brethren'.[17] In 1839, together with other undergraduates, he founded the Cambridge Camden Society which, from 1841, published a magazine called the *Ecclesiologist*. In 1846 its name was changed to the Ecclesiological Society, and its headquarters were moved to London. Its declared concerns included 'the science of symbolism; the principle of church arrangement; Church music and all the decorative arts, which can be made subservient to religion'.[18]

The *Ecclesiologist* 'succeeded in stimulating an avid, informed and deepening interest in church architecture as the setting for traditional Catholic worship and thus stimulated the

---

[16.] Quotes from C.P.S. Clarke, *op.cit.*, pp.156, 157.
[17.] C.P.S. Clarke, *op.cit.*, p.158.
[18.] Quoted in C.P.S. Clarke, *op.cit.*, p.160.

liturgical and ceremonial revival of the Anglican Church of the later nineteenth century'.[19] Almost all the neo-Gothic churches of the latter half of the century were built under the impetus and inspiration of the Ecclesiological Society, and even the restoration of medieval churches was on lines they recommended. 'It is doubtful if there is a Gothic church in the country, new or old, which does not show their influence.'[20] But buildings were not intended as an end in themselves. The aim was not primarily architectural but ecclesiological – the revival of Catholic Churchmanship. 'Gothic architecture was not to be viewed simply aesthetically, as supplying an appropriate ornamentation for churches. It was itself the outworking of liturgical and theological principle, an architectural medium which proclaimed a theological message.'[21] To build a new church in strict accordance with ecclesiological principles was an affirmation of the difference between a sacramentally worshipping church and a meeting house or preaching conventicle. To restore a medieval church, 'clearing away box pews, and the three-decker pulpit, refurbishing the chancel and sanctuary, reinstating the font, and uncovering ancient sedilia, aumbries, and picinas, was to provide a sacramental expression of the church catholic and its worship'.[22]

Associated with architectural activity was the influence of the Ecclesiological Society on ritualism. It was concerned to cultivate a sense of mystery by making full use of symbolism. The members were convinced that awe and devotion could be encouraged and enhanced by a measure of ornateness in ritualism. The consuming interest of some Anglican Catholics in the late decades of the nineteenth century 'in vestments, incense, lighted tapers, chanting and intoning, the careful observance of fasts and festivals, geneflexions, crossings, candles, flowers and crosses on the communion-table, the reservation

[19] Horton Davies, *Worship and Theology in England from Newman to Martineau, 1850–1900* (Princeton, London and Oxford 1962), p.119.

[20] Horton Davies, *op.cit.*, p.120.

[21] Geoffrey Rowell, *The Vision Glorious*, p.101.

[22] Geoffrey Rowell, *The Vision Glorious*, p.101.

and adoration of the Eucharist, is partly to be accounted for by the work of the Ecclesiological Society'.[23]

J.M. Neale himself was an erudite hymnologist, liturgiologist and historian of the Eastern and Western Churches. He, like his fellow High Church ecclesiologists, was fully aware of the importance of architecture and church furnishing in encouraging Anglican Catholicism, and that Catholic doctrine could be most effectively taught through Catholic ceremonial. And he personally did much to promote higher ceremonial. In 1846 he became Warden of Sackville College, East Grinstead, a Caroline almshouse. He set up a chapel with a stone mensa arrayed in a green frontal, and he introduced hymns and a weekly Celebration. In 1850 he first wore a chasuble, a garment which had possibly been revived by Hawker of Morwenstow in 1840. Rioters were active against Neale and his innovations from 1848, and in 1851 they nearly destroyed the college by fire; it was a protest provoked by Neale's mild attempt at funeral service reform, when he used a wheeled bier and a purple pall with a plain cross upon it. Riots re-occurred in 1856.

Neale also maintained the Tractarian tradition in his outpouring of hymns. 'He first unlocked the doors of the Church's treasuries of sacred song, doors which had been closed for three centuries since the old Latin hymns had been disused, and by his exquisite translations he restored to English Churchmen a long-forgotten part of their heritage.'[24] His hymns included 'Jerusalem the Golden', 'For thee, O dear, dear country', and three or four more hymns which are based on the work of Bernard of Morlaix. 'Art thou weary, art thou languid?' and 'O happy band of pilgrims' although based on Greek originals, were in effect Neale's original work. He contributed to a number of excellent collections of hymns which resulted from the revival, and which 'caused something like a revolution in the Sunday worship of English parish churches'.[25] Ceremonial and hymnody were central to the home mission in the second phase of the movement.

[23] Horton Davies, *op. cit.*, p.120.
[24] S.L. Ollard, *A Short History of the Oxford Movement*, p. 206.
[25] S.L. Ollard, *op. cit.*, p.207.

Charles Lowder (1820–80)

One of the great figures in the Ritualistic and urban mission movement was Charles Lowder. He was the son of a banker. After graduating from Exeter College, Oxford, with Second Class Honours, he worked for some years as a country curate. He seriously considered overseas missionary work, but gave up the idea for family reasons, and dedicated himself to urban ministry in England. He joined the staff of St Barnabas', Pimlico, in 1851, just when it was rapidly becoming the most notorious of London's ritualistic churches, and when it was experiencing some of the worst and most brutal mob demonstrations. The time Lowder spent there heightened his appreciation of both the possibilities and the difficulties of a ministry among the very poor.

Inspired in 1855 by reading Abelly's life of St Vincent de Paul, the seventeenth-century pioneer of French town and country missions, Lowder was the principal founder of a small fraternal band of priests called the Society of the Holy Cross, which initially consisted of all the staff members of St Paul's and St Barnabas'. Its objects, as he wrote later, were:

> ...to deepen and strengthen the spiritual life of the clergy, to defend the faith of the Church, and then, among others, to carry on and aid mission work both at home and abroad. The members of the Society, meeting together as they did for prayer and conference, were deeply impressed with the evils existing in the Church, and saw also, in the remedies adopted by St Vincent de Paul, the hope of lessening them. They all felt that the ordinary parochial equipment of a rector and curate, or perhaps a solitary incumbent, provided for thousands of perishing souls, was most sadly inadequate; that in the presence of such utter destitution, it was simply childish to act as if the Church were recognized as the Mother of the people. She must assume a missionary character...[26]

[26.] Michael Reynolds, *op.cit.*, p.39.

The Society's notion of mission was not, as was the later widely held concept, a few days of special preaching in the parish targetted at non-church people, but the establishment of a permanent Christian missionary presence in areas where there was a mass alienation from the church of the resident population. And it was not long before they found such a battleground. Some members started work in the parish of St George's-in-the-East, in response to an invitation from the Rector, Bryan King. Hitherto the church had made little impact on the life of the local, formidable community. After various experiments a mission-house was found in an area near the river which had a population of about 6,000, grossly deprived and poor people. With a licence from the Bishop of London, a room in the house was opened for daily prayer and frequent preaching, and this gradually attracted a small congregation. A boys' choir was formed and classes were conducted for instruction in the Bible and preparation for Confirmation and Holy Communion. In 1856 a temporary 'iron church' was erected in the garden of the mission-house, and there, from the first, the eucharistic vestments were used. The work was greatly strengthened by the arrival in 1858 of a seasoned warrior, Alexander Mackonochie.

Opposition was fierce and embittered. From the early summer of 1859 there began what became known as the St George's riots. The disturbances were even more violent, and attracted even greater publicity, than those at St Barnabas', Pimlico, nine years earlier. As the disruption became more widely known, largely through press cover, more and more people came from far and near to reinforce the attacking mob, to join in the fun or just to watch the spectacle. They came as individuals, as groups and as parties sponsored by such bodies as the National Protestant Society and a kindred organisation, the Anti-Puseyite League. The interference with the services was a disgrace. The uproar was so great that it sometimes prevented the saying of the Litany or the conduct of worship. The Mission had been gravely compromised by the defection of two of its priests prior to the arrival of Mackonochie, and, in addition to the riots, had survived numerous other troubles. But Lowder and his fellow-workers persisted in their labours, and the work made splendid progress. Public interest and sympathy were especially aroused by the devoted service of Lowder and his staff during the East London cholera epidemic of 1866. It was in that same year that a move was made from the old iron chapel to a fine new church, built by subscription. Named St Peter's, London Docks, it became, under Lowder's incumbency, the centre of a new parish carved out of St George's-in-the-East and the adjoining parish of St Paul's, Shadwell.

There was a prospect of a similar development in another area, and one of Lowder's curates, a rich young man, had promised to build a church there. But this hope was abruptly extinguished, and the whole district concerned was lost to the mission in 1868, when suddenly, and without a word of warning, all three curates went over to Rome. It was a terrible blow.

When Lowder died in 1880, he had won the affection and respect of the East End population whom he had lovingly served for almost forty years. He had gained the honourable title of Father Lowder, and had been the means of bringing a great number of East Londoners to the Christian faith. His funeral in Wapping, as described by Mackonochie afterwards, was a testimony to the mutual love and high regard which had grown over the years between priest and people:

> It was most striking when compared with twenty-five years since, to see the patient crowd on each side lining the way, many in tears, some audibly praying for the rest of his soul, while a long, slow procession of surpliced clergy and weeping parishioners first met the body at Old Gravel Bridge, conducted it to the church, after service again escorted it to the bridge, and returned at the same slow processional pace to the church. Traffic, of course, was stopped, but all was most reverent and respectful. The scene at Chislehurst [where the internment took place] was equally striking, as we walked across the great common amid throngs of people and stood in the crowded churchyard. Clergy of all schools of thought came to show their respect for the man whom they were obliged to look up to, though they differed from him.[27]

[27.] Michael Reynolds, *op.cit.*, pp.240, 241.

Alexander Heriot Mackonochie (1825–87)

Alexander Heriot Mackonochie – Father Mackonochie, of St Alban's, Holborn – who gave this account 'is a key-figure in the history of the Church of England in the second half of the nineteenth century. It is possible to trace in his career three of the characteristic and dominating ecclesiastical themes of the period: the development of the Oxford Movement from Tractarianism to Ritualism; the impact which Ritualism made on the religious, and social, life of the urban working classes; and the whole problem, raised by the Ritual prosecutions, of what constitutes "lawful authority" in the English Church.'[28]

Mackonochie was born in 1825. His father, a Colonel in the Army, died in 1827, and he and his elder brother were brought up by their mother, their grandmother and unmarried sisters of their mother in a sober, disciplined, restrained and somewhat severe household. He entered Wadham College, Oxford, as a commoner in 1845, and by dint of sheer grind emerged with Second Class Honours. At Oxford he came increasingly under Tractarian influence, in a slow and unspectacular process. He received deacon's orders in 1849, and was appointed to the Wiltshire parish of Westbury-under-the-Plain. He was ordained priest in 1850, and in 1852 joined the staff of W.J. Butler, the Vicar of Wantage. There he had the rich experience of working with one of the most dynamic and innovative Anglican Catholic parish priests of the day, and as a fellow-curate he had the brilliant protégé and disciple of Pusey, Henry Parry Liddon. But, although he enjoyed the experience, and was not unconscious of its importance, he appears to have increasingly hankered after more arduous service under harsher conditions. After having his plans to go as a missionary to Newfoundland vetoed by Bishop Wilberforce, Mackonochie found his opportunity for self-giving service when he joined the St George's Mission in the East End of London.

By the 1850s there were perhaps a score of ritualistic churches, which included All Saints', Margaret Street, the successor to the pioneer Margaret Chapel; St Andrew's, Wells Street; St

---

[28.] Michael Reynolds, *op.cit.*, p.13.

Mary's, Crown Street, Soho, as well as St Paul's, Knightsbridge and St Barnabas', Pimlico. Mackonochie served under Lowder until 1862 when he was put in charge of the newly built church of St Alban's, Holborn. The church was constructed when Ecclesiology was in its heyday, by the favourite of the Camdenians, William Butterfield, and, typically for such architecture, it was grand, original and moving. To the condescending wonder of many observers, it was open to and attracted the poor. 'The bonnetless and the shoeless were in sufficient numbers, and as there were no pew-rents and no appropriations, they were enabled to feel that they had as good a right to their own church as anyone else.'[29]

Mackonochie became the leader of a closely knit clergy team. It was a hand picked, compact body of assault troops, whose commitment to service and gaiety had 'something of the proud, carefree quality of laughter under fire'. An early recruit, and foremost among the young warriors, was Arthur Stanton, 'the personification of the St Alban's tradition, with its elan, buoyancy, self-abandonment and devotion'.[30] Stanton remained at St Alban's for more than fifty years, until his death. By then he was one of the most famous priests and preachers in the country, and yet he was still an assistant curate, but content. And he could well have afforded a life of far greater ease for his father in his lifetime kept him well supplied, and on his death in 1863 left him not a great fortune but enough to make him independent. He also had on offer the congenial living of Tetbury in Gloucestershire. But he resolved to give his service to St Alban's, and from the start it was, by agreement, without pay.

From the consecration of the church until 1867 there was steady progress, with large and increasing congregations. The annual total of communicants rose from about 3,000 to more than 18,000. A powerful and elaborate parochial organisation was developed, which included guilds and associations for men and boys, women and girls; an infant nursery; a choir-school; parochial schools built at a cost of

[29] Michael Reynolds, *op. cit.*, p.92.
[30] Michael Reynolds, *op. cit.*, p.94.

£6,000 and educating 500 children; night-schools for boys and girls; and various other agencies ranging from a blanket-loan fund to a cricket club. In 1869 a group of Sisters from the Clewer Community began work in the parish under Mackonochie's direction.

During the 1860s, the ceremonial at St Alban's, although it was not more elaborate than at several other London churches, acquired greater notoriety, and with this came the usual violent demonstrations, and the prolonged, vicious and persistent personal attacks on Mackonochie himself, who became the victim of extended litigation. It was in the spring of 1867 that the notorious lawsuit of Martin v. Mackonochie began. Mackonochie was then forty-one and at the height of his powers: by the end of the affair he was fifty-seven, a broken old man, with only four more years to live. The legal action formed part of the first concerted Protestant offensive 'to put down Ritualism'. The onslaught failed. It broke Mackonochie, but not the things for which he stood.

The whole drawn out affair was hugely publicised at a national level, partly because ritualism was rapidly becoming a topic of animated debate in the Convocation of Canterbury and in Parliament, and partly because the battle over ritualism was being joined on a wide front, with two organisations, the English Church Union and the Church Association, both predominantly lay, as the main contestants. During the twelve years from 1868, the Church Association spent £40,000 on assisting in legal proceedings against ritualists, involving the prosecution of scores of priests. And Mackonochie was at the top of their list. The underlying aim of the Church Association was an attack, not on ritualism *per se*, but on the whole sacramental system which it represented, and in particular the doctrine of the Real Presence. By the late 1860s St Alban's had come to be regarded as the representative ritualistic church, and its incumbent as the representative ritualist. The charges against Mackonochie all concerned his manner of celebrating the Holy Communion. They were elevation of the sacrament; 'excessive kneeling' during the prayer of consecration; ceremonial use of incense; the mixed chalice; and altar lights.

Year after year the Church Association hounded him. At

times they appeared to be gaining the victory, but in the end the ritualism was not stopped, and little was achieved. Throughout the ordeal Mackonochie refused to retaliate either in speech, gesture or action against his persecutors; he appeared to retain an outward equanimity, despite his inward torture. He may, when it started, have had heart for a fight, but by 1878 he was becoming surfeited. Finally, when he was faced with the possibility of deprivation, he agreed to an exchange of livings with the incumbent of St Peter's, London Docks. It was an unhappy arrangement, and he speedily deteriorated in both physical and mental health. He became unequal to any sustained mental effort. He rarely preached after 1885, only occasionally heard confession, and would not trust himself to celebrate except on very special occasions. For him this was the supreme sacrifice. It was a sad end to such an heroic ministry. He went on holiday in Scotland. There he set out on a mountain walk, accompanied only by two dogs. Darkness descended, he did not return, and he was never seen alive again. He was found in the snow, guarded by the two dogs, but on his face there was a look of peace and joy, and not a trace of suffering, although there was evidence of a distressing struggle in the dark amid the rocks.

Hundreds of people lined the way, bare-headed and silent, as the hearse passed through Holborn; a great number came out of deep respect as he lay in the chapel preparatory to the day of the funeral; the church was packed for the Requiem and a large number were unable to gain admittance; the funeral procession was on a massive scale, with hundreds of clergy, scores of mourners and a huge crowd of people anxious to honour his memory, even including some who had shown scant sympathy for him during his lifetime. It was a fitting tribute to such a servant of God and friend of the people.

Such lives as these, which we have but briefly touched upon, must, through lack of space, stand to illustrate the dedication and fortitude of a small, distinguished band of self-giving Anglican Catholic slum priests. In addition to those already mentioned, they included George Rundle, Robert Dolling, C.C. Crafton, George Body, R.W. Enraght, J. Bell Cox, R.J.

Wilson, Arthur Tooth and others of equal distinction. Many of them were little regarded in their life times, and even despised, but they are worthy of honour in any account of the nineteenth-century church.

Christian Socialism

While the slum priests engaged in front line battle with the forces arrayed against them in a valiant effort to bring the gospel to deprived areas and deprived people, Christian Socialists attempted to construct a distinctly Christian theological social critique. In general, however, the societies they founded or supported were socialist in name but not in belief or intent. Stewart Headlam's Guild of St Matthew was to some extent an exception, for he had a grasp of socialist principles with his first hand knowledge of working class conditions and politics as a Fabian Socialist member of the London County Council from 1888 onwards. He was a High Churchman who advocated secular education, campaigned for freedom of thought, for the abolition of liquor licensing, for disestablishment, and for land tax reform. Like two other High Church members of the socialist movement in the Church of England, Percy Deamer and Conrad Noel, he spoke at 'Labour Churches' – the secular societies for working men which were closely associated with the emerging labour politics. He believed that society needed to be re-cast in order to provide for the redistribution of wealth, and this could only be achieved by the power of the state. There must be action by the state to effect a new order of social priorities. He believed that if anyone wanted to be a good Christian, he must be something very much like a good Socialist. All this was too strong meat for many other High Church 'socialists' who gave a much more muted, conformist definition of 'socialism'. Headlam founded the Guild of St Matthew in 1877 in Bethnal Green. It had a small membership of never more than four hundred, about a quarter of whom were priests; and none even of these was working class. Within it there were divisions and ideological conflicts, but it had influence, for instance in the debates of the

1888 Lambeth Conference. It reached its peak in the last decade of the century, but then declined, and was dissolved in 1909. 'It had earned the respect of most of the leading Fabians in England, and, whatever its eccentricities, it had at least familiarized some with the notion that systematic Socialism and formal Christianity were not irreconcilable.'[31]

Very different was the Christian Social Union (the CSU). It was established in 1889 by Henry Scott Holland, Charles Gore and Brooke Foss Westcott. Like the Guild of St Matthew, it was exclusively Anglican, but, unlike the Guild, it was rapidly and widely accepted with approval within the Church of England as an expression of the prevalent social-services idealism of the upper, or upper-middle class clergy who organised and sustained it. It was not a socialist body, but more a respectable forum for academic debate, with a rather vague notion of the brotherhood of man, based on the Fatherhood of God as the perceived key to the solving of social and class problems, and there was very little involvement in social action. In 1893 the Oxford branch compiled 'white lists' of firms whose wages were thought adequate (although they set an adequate wage at a very low level), and there was a boycott of sweated industry by a handfull of intellectuals, an action which was imitated elsewhere and attracted some public attention to the evil working conditions in some small trades. But most of what they advocated related to individual moral attitudes rather than collective social action. For almost all of its members, and the majority of Christian Socialists in the late nineteenth and early twentieth centuries, the socialism of Marx was not remotely acceptable, nor was any theory which implied a fundamental re-ordering of society. Few questioned the basic structure of society, nor was there much willingness to identify with working class movements such as the New Unionism and the early stirrings of working class party politics. 'Although many of its members called themselves socialists, or allowed themselves to be called socialists, the Union was not even formally committed to socialist doctrines.'[32] It never had any working-class person

---

[31.] E.R. Norman, *Church and Society in England, 1770–1970* (1976), p.180.
[32.] E.R. Norman, *op.cit.*, p.181.

among its large membership, which at one stage reached six thousand. It had little if any political influence, but it was immensely influential among the leadership of the Church, and helped to give the Church of England the lead in the espousal of social radicalism.

The Union made explicit some of the common assumptions of the Holy Party. 'Then, as later, there was usually a correlation between liberalism in theology and radical political idealism.'[33] But this radicalism was almost invariably interpreted as attempting to add a new moral dimension to already existing political parties. Thus, Canon Henry Parry Liddon reckoned himself a Christian Socialist and yet remained a supporter of Gladstone's Liberal Party whose economic ideas and whose doctrine of economic individualism made it the enemy of collectivism. Many High Churchmen at that time stressed that they were prepared to enunciate great political and social principles, but they were not prepared to undertake work for their immediate application and implementation: they shunned political involvement and social reformation. Nonetheless, Christian Socialism had its effect. By the first decade of the twentieth century 'there were very few Church leaders who did not adopt attitudes critical of industrial organisation and social order – attitudes expressed in language, and according to a frame of reference, which was clearly furnished by the sort of atmosphere nurtured by the CSU...It was unusual, after 1900, to find a bishop who did not regard the declaration of social principles a primary duty.'[34]

By the early years of the new century most Christian Socialists were far more collectivist in their views, with a definite belief in the rightful use of the State machinery to bring about a social and economic transformation, than the former generation had been. The founding of the Church Socialist League in 1906 reflected this and the possibilities which radical priests saw opening up as a result of the election of fifty-three Labour and Lib-Lab members to Parliament in

[33] E.R. Norman, *op.cit.*, p.181.
[34] E.R. Norman, *op.cit.*, pp.222, 225.

the General Election that year. There was a mood of boundless optimism. The High Church leaders and inspirers of the League were largely from Northern England, where Mirfield was a centre of particular importance and supplied such prominent Christian Socialists as Fr Paul Bull, Fr Samuel Healey and Fr Neville Figgis. The League was predominantly Anglo-Catholic and clerical, and it provided some serious political and economic analysis, as indicated by the inclusion of R.H. Tawney, Maurice Reckitt and A.J. Penty among its membership; and, in 1912, George Lansbury, later Leader of the Parliamentary Labour Party, became its President. At the forefront of the League were the Rev. Frederic Lewes Donaldson and the persistent and durable upper-class leader Conrad Le Despenser Roden Noel, who had served under Fr Dolling in Portsmouth and, from 1910, was incumbent of Thaxted, which he made the centre of Christian Socialism in England for the following thirty years. Although, as we will discover later, he was eccentric, addicted to such gestures as flying a red flag from the tower of his church, he was an enemy of the somewhat comfortable, armchair sort of liberal social reformism which was common among the CSU bishops. In its own distinctive way, his socialism had impressive qualities.

The dedication and sacrificial work of the Anglo-Catholics engaged in urban ministry, and the attempts by many sincere High Church Christian Socialists to construct a definitely Christian theological social critique did not, unfortunately, result in any fundamental Christian social impact, measured in terms of changes in government social policy, in terms of an amelioration of the social and economic condition of the mass of the submerged poor, or in terms of a turning to the Christian faith of the religiously indifferent working classes. 'It is interesting that the Church of England, which contained a much larger number of clergymen attracted to "Christian Socialist" ideas than any other denomination, was also the Church that most noticeably failed to attract a working-class membership. A few slum priests who were Socialists achieved working-class congregations for a time because they were sympathetic pastors, not because of their politics. Working-class men, like all Englishmen, did not expect their clergy to preach political opinions, and did not like it when they did so.'[35] The Baptist denomination, which was least concerned with a 'social gospel', actually grew in size at the end of the century.

The fault appears to have been not so much in the intention and activity of the clergy and laity who attempted to address the 'social question', or in any lack of sacrificial service, but rather in the social differences which separated the predominantly middle class Anglo-Catholics, with all their inherent social presuppositions and pre-dispositions, from the working classes who were, in most cases, geographically and socially living in different and alien worlds. Many 'forms of socialism and collectivism were unpopular because they were bourgeoise in origin'.[36] There was a widespread ignorance concerning the prevailing conditions in such areas as Bethnal Green, and an unfamiliarity with the social and cultural norms and values of the working class, and not infrequently hostility to such values and patterns of behaviour. Christian Socialists in general 'were unable to separate working-class values from the evil consequences of an appalling environment and economic hardship. Their simple instinct was to educate the working-classes into acceptance of their own cultural values. A chasm existed between styles of life which the Settlements did not bridge. They became little oases of upper-class life'.[37] The radical politics of many of the Christian Socialists was little related to the actual life situations of working class people.

[35] E.R. Norman, *op.cit.*, p.127.
[36] E.R. Norman, *op.cit.*, p.127.
[37] E.R. Norman, *op.cit.*, p.165.

12

Overseas Mission

Both Catholic Anglicans and Evangelicals in the last half of the nineteenth century were concerned about mission, and were engaged in mission at home and overseas; and both looked for conversions. But they differed in their modes of belief and action in undertaking mission. Raoul Allier, in his monumental work, *La Psychologie de la conversion chez les peuples non-civilises,* posited two types of approach to the conversion of preliterate peoples.[1] The object of mission and conversion is, he said, the same for both Catholic and Evangelical. But whereas the Evangelical missionary is often a lay person, usually sent by a society, who makes converts individually by his own preaching and contacts, then draws the converts together in a church, and administers baptism to those who are converted, the Catholic missionary is most often a priest, who erects a building, a chapel or church, and invites non-Christians in the neighbourhood to enter it with the hope that by their continuing presence in it they will gradually become Christians and, after instruction, will seek baptism and so will enter the Christian fold. In overseas missionary work the Anglican Catholics adopted the Catholic model, and also gave great importance to the missionary bishop who is sent forth by the Church, going before to organise the Church, rather than being sent only after the Church has been partially organised: bishops were

---

[1.] R. Allier, *La Psychologie de la conversion chez les peuples non-civilises,* 2 vols. (Paris, 1925), summarised in W.S.F. Pickering, *Anglo-Catholicism* (1989), p.68f, on which this present section is based.

seen as the *sin qua non* of the Church. 'From the emphasis on the bishop as possessing the fulness of Apostolic ministry, from whom all other ministry derived, there emerged the idea of the missionary bishop as the characteristic means whereby the mission of the Church should be forwarded. Episcopacy was not a desirable addition to already established churches, but the Apostolic foundation-stone.'[2]

Although the Tractarians became influential in the Society for Promoting Christian Knowledge (SPCK), which had been founded in 1698, and helped the Society for the Propagation of the Gospel (SPG), which had been founded in 1701, they were not as greatly concerned with overseas mission as the Anglo-Catholics later in the century. The Cowley Fathers made a significant contribution to missionary work abroad. The Community of St Denys in Warminster, Wiltshire, was founded in 1879, and a few of its sisters worked in South Africa. The Oxford Mission Brotherhood was started in Calcutta in order to work among high-caste Hindus, and a daughter order for women was started in 1902. In the 1890's, the Society of the Sacred Mission was established, and sent men and women to Korea and Africa. In addition, missionary colleges were created, including St Augustine's College, Canterbury, and St Boniface College, Warminster in 1869, both of which were Tractarian or Anglo-Catholic in ethos. But all these societies and enterprises were numerically small, made little impact upon the public imagination, and elicited little support. 'Beyond any shadow of doubt the greatest contribution to missionary work came with that unequivocally Anglo-Catholic society...the Universities' Mission to Central Africa.'[3]

The Universities' Mission to Central Africa

The UMCA originated with Dr Livingstone's famous appeal in the Senate House, Cambridge, on 4 December 1857. He had

[2] Geoffrey Rowell, *The Vision Glorious* (1983), p.160.
[3] W.S.F. Pickering, *op.cit.*, pp.86, 87.

stirred the nation with the portrayal of his adventures, and turned the thoughts of many to Central Africa. In his writings and speeches he made it clear that he regarded himself not so much as an explorer, but as a pioneer missionary. In unforgettable concluding words at the Cambridge gathering he challenged his audience: 'I go back to Africa to try to make an open path for commerce and Christianity. Do you carry on the work which I have begun. I leave it with you.'[4] The following year an association was formed, which took the name, The Oxford and Cambridge Mission to Central Africa, with the object of sending out at least six missionaries under a leader who should, if possible, be a bishop. The mission field would be in the region of the upper waters of the Zambesi, and the Mission was placed under the general oversight and care of the Bishop of Cape Town and Metropolitan of South Africa.

The committee worked and waited for a year, and finally Charles Frederick Mackenzie was chosen to be the leader of the proposed mission. He was a graduate of Gonville and Caius College, Cambridge, was second Wrangler, a Fellow of his college, and in 1859 was Archdeacon in Natal. It was almost a year before he was able to return to Africa, and in that time the Universities of Dublin and Durham had agreed to co-operate, so the association was re-named The Oxford, Cambridge, Dublin and Durham Mission to Central Africa. Before Mackenzie set sail it was arranged that he should be consecrated bishop by the South African bishops, in order that he and his party would be 'truly missionaries sent out on their mission by the Church'.[5]

So it was that a little band of seven set sail from Plymouth on board the SS *Cambrian,* prepared for a hard life. They included a carpenter and agricultural labourer as well as two priests, as they anticipated having to build their own homes and largely provide food for themselves. On 1 January 1861 Mackenzie was consecrated bishop: the first missionary bishop to be sent out by the Church in England for a thousand years.

[4.] Quoted in George Herbert Wilson, *The History of the Universities' Mission to Central Africa* (London, 1936), p.1. This is a work to which the present account of the UMCA is greatly indebted.

[5.] George Herbert Wilson, *op.cit.*, p.4.

Travelling up the Zambesi and its tributary the Shere, the missionaries, who had been augmented by some local volunteers, first settled in the territory of the most important chief in the district, Chibisa. The whole region had been plunged into turmoil by the slave raids and the cruelty of the slave trade. The expedition pressed on further into the interior accompanied by Dr Livingstone. They encountered a party of armed Yaos, a local tribe, with a train of eighty-four captive slaves, disarmed them, and freed the slaves. Those freed included men, women and children, so a new village was established at Magomero, which became the first headquarters of the Mission. They built their own houses and started to construct a church. The daily offices were said and an ordered routine of life was begun. But all around there was a continual state of war. There was famine and disease and the ever present threat of invasion and death. In an attempt to relieve the shortage of supplies, the Bishop, together with a local priest recruit, H.W. Barrup, set out to meet Livingstone who was on his way up the river. Then tragedy struck. One night the canoe in which they were travelling ran on to a sandbank and overturned and, although righted, their food was all soaked and they lost their medicine box, including all the quinine. As they waited for Livingstone on a mosquito-infested island, the Bishop fell ill of fever, and with no quinine he died on 31 January 1862. The party struggled back to Magomero with the sad news, and within three weeks Barrup too had died. In the next year or so they had to withdraw from Magomero, two more of the missionaries had died, and another was so desparately ill that he had to return to England. It was a dark hour for the Mission.

In 1863 a new Bishop, William George Tozer, was consecrated. He had to cope with a deplorable situation, with the temporary leader very ill and just waiting for Tozer in order to return to England, and all the missionaries showing signs of suffering. He decided to make a move to a healthier spot. First Morambala was chosen, and then removal from the Zambezi valley altogether to Zanzibar itself. In 1865 there was the first baptism of adults.

Though it was established in Zanzibar the Mission never lost sight of its original objective, the tribes in the neighbourhood of Lake Nyasa, and in 1867 a new attempt was made to penetrate the mainland, with a base being established at Magela, or, as it was later called, Msalabani. In 1872 a violent storm destroyed much of the Zambezi headquarters, and soon after that one of the most devoted of the gallant five missionaries, and a particular friend of the Bishop from their college days, died. It was a terrible blow to the Bishop on top of repeated trials, and more than he could bear with his failing health, so he returned to England and resigned his bishopric.

It was another severely testing time, but change was soon to come. In 1872 the Church of England for the first time observed a solemn day of intercession for missions, from which time can be traced a quickening of missionary zeal in the country. Then, in 1873, Sir Bartle Frere arrived in Zanzibar, sent on a mission by the British Government to try to persuade the Sultan to help in ending the slave trade. A treaty was signed, and it was agreed that the slave market at Zanzibar should be closed. It was purchased for the Mission, a thatched mud hut was built, and on the site of the whipping post, where abominable cruelties had been perpetrated for ages, the gospel was preached. A church was constructed which later became the Cathedral.

Bishop Tozer was replaced by his faithful friend and fellow worker Dr Edward Steere, a Doctor of Laws, and a very able, energetic, resolute and inspiring leader. His episcopate from 1874 to 1882 marks a great expansion in the work of the Mission. He called for volunteers who were to be paid a pittance and were asked to dedicate themselves to the Mission in lives of self-sacrifice. The response was immediate, and from that time onwards a stream of them carried the message of the Cross from the base at Zanzibar far and wide into East Africa. The Bishop was also architect, mason and overseer during the four years of building the Zanzibar church. It was first used on Christmas Day, 1877, when about two hundred joyful people assembled for Mattins, during which hymns were sung in Swahili and the Bishop preached to the congregation in their own tongue.

Gradually the mainland was evangelised. A station was established at Magela, a freed-slave village was started at Masasi and, in 1879, John Swedi became the first African in the UMCA to be admitted to Holy Orders, when he was ordained deacon. In the same year the first sixteen freed slaves to be baptised were admitted to their first communions.

But, with progress, there were further blows. In 1881 Bishop Steere died, and in 1882 the Angoni tribe made a terrible raid on Masasi, setting fire to the houses, looting, desecrating the church and killing seven people. Nonetheless, the missionaries carried on the work despite the tragedy and the threat by the Angoni to return again to slay all the Europeans they met and to take the heart of their leader as a charm to bring victory over the white men. Such courage and endurance was to have its reward, for the Mission was ready for a great advance in the next few years.

Before he had died, Bishop Steere had commissioned Dr W.P. Johnson to undertake what was to prove an historic expedition into the Yao hills, for it was the beginning of mission work around Lake Nyasa itself. Johnson was faced with the warlike Angoni, slaying, and plundering villages, but, with remarkable bravery, he boldly went out alone to meet them, won their trust and friendship, and set up missionary work in the area of chief Chityi in 1882.

After a long vacancy, Bishop Steere was succeeded in 1883 by Charles Alan Smythies. He reached Zanzibar in 1884 to be confronted by much encouraging work and progress. It was a time of promising development. He arranged for a theological department for the training of clergy to be started at the Kinngani school and training college for teachers. He also adopted the idea of a steamer for the Lake as a means of reaching the lakeside villagers, and rejoiced to see the vessel, named *Charles Janson,* put to effective use.

It goes beyond the scope of this book to tell of the growth of the Mission as new centres were established and the work was consolidated. Enough has been said to indicate that the history of the Mission enshrines many heroic tales of self-sacrifice, suffering and death; of persistence in the face of hardship, disappointment, despair and discouragement; of fortitude when confronted with war, unrest, hostility and the ravages of disease and natural disasters; of sheer hard, unremitting work and unstinting service; and of faith, hope and charity amid seeming failure, hopelessness and lovelessness. Many played their part without knowing what the end would be and how their small or great service contributed to a larger purpose which only hindsight could discern, and that but dimly. They sought for no reward, and they mostly found none. It was a noble saga, and the hearts of those pioneers would have been gladdened if they could have but glimpsed the future: the consecration of the first Bishop of Nyasaland in 1892; the arrival of Bishop Hine as the first Bishop of Northern Rhodesia in 1910; the consecration in 1926 of the first Bishop of Masasi; the many African bishops, priests and laymen who were to play such a distinguished part in the life of their homeland churches and in the wider councils of the Church; and the multitude of Christians who would come to faith and grow in grace because a former generation so cared that they went, and so loved that they gave themselves in the service of God, the Church and their fellow men.

This work in East Central Africa has been chronicled in some detail in order to show that High Church Anglicanism in the latter part of the nineteenth century had within it a passionate concern for world mission – a concern which was translated into outstanding and sacrificial service. Other examples may be cited. Suffice it to mention very briefly New Zealand as represented in the life and labours of George Augustus Selwyn, and Melanesia as represented by the missionary zeal of John Coleridge Patteson.

New Zealand and Melanesia

After British sovereignty over New Zealand was declared in 1840 the number of settlers greatly increased, and with this growth in the expatriate population came inter-racial mistrust, bitterness and war. In 1841 the Tractarian George Selwyn was made missionary Bishop of New Zealand, and over the next twenty-six years established himself as one of the most notable ecclesiastics of the century. Under his leadership the great majority of the Maori race made a profession of Christianity. It was also under the inspiration of Selwyn that New Zealand became the first of the new type of independent provinces within the Anglican Communion in 1857. What he did in New Zealand was of massive significance, and he made a further major contribution to mission in the Pacific with the establishment of the Melanesian Mission and the involvement of John Patteson in 1861 as the first Bishop of Melanesia.

Patteson was a man of great charm and Christian affection with a remarkable linguistic faculty which enabled him to master the many languages of his island world, and an intense humility. His strategy was to disturb the manners and customs of the people as little as possible in propagating the gospel. He hoped to achieve this by such methods as taking some of the more able boys from many islands and bringing them for training, first in New Zealand and later in Norfolk Island, so that they might later return to their home islands as teachers. On a fateful day in 1871 he landed alone and unsuspecting on the island of Nukapu in the Santa Cruz group, and was immediately set upon and killed, possibly in revenge for the kidnapping of some of the inhabitants by white men a few months earlier. His body was placed in a canoe to drift back to the ship. It was found that five wounds had been made in his breast, on which a palm branch tied in five knots had been placed: 'Christians could not but be reminded of the five wounds of another innocent Victim.'[6] In his death Patteson made more impact in England than he had done in his life, for the news of it made a profound impression and called forth a new wave of support for the work of the Church in the South Seas.

[6] Stephen Neill, *A History of Christian Missions* (Harmondsworth, 1964), p.352.

PART 5

1914 to 1945

13

Facing Two World Wars

The First World War

In the pre-First World War church there was virtually no anti–German sentiment. Germany was portrayed as a nation which was bound to England by both racial and dynastic ties; a nation which had given the lead in throwing off the papal yoke in the sixteenth century and shared with England almost four hundred years of Protestant history; and a nation which had produced some of Europe's finest artists, musicians, philosophers and men of letters. The Germans were held up as a people of the highest moral standards. The popular High Church Bishop of London, Winnington-Ingram, was to be in the forefront of those during the war who hurled torrents of abuse upon the German nation, but in 1908, as the London host to a group of German church people, he was effusive in his peroration:

> If you want to love Germans and Germany, go and live as I did in Germany. I will tell you some of the things that will make you love Germans and Germany. You will find there such kindly feelings toward England...I carried away first – and you would if you visited Germany – a sense of the genuine friendship of the people towards our country...I say, should we not love a nation like that? Why, it is akin to our own ! We are cousins, nay, we are brothers to the Germans, and therefore, as a nation, I

say, 'Wir alle lieben Deutschland und die Deutschen'.[1]

A benevolent attitude prevailed despite Germany's challenge to England's naval and industrial supremacy and its expansionist policies. Even in the immediate pre-war period, and indeed at the beginning of August 1914, such a view persisted. The High Churchman Henry Scott Holland had no qualms about taking governments to task when he thought them to be at fault, but in August 1914 he was adamant about non-intervention, and wrote to the papers to plead with all his soul for neutrality. When his advice was not heeded, 'with a violence uncharacteristic of this gentle, considerate scholar who enjoyed corresponding with children, he lashed out at the mass insanity that impelled rulers and subjects alike to cast civilization into the cauldron, all for the sake of a despicable little state like Serbia'.[2]

But the change in attitude was dramatic. Scott Holland was typical. By September he was writing to a friend that 'every day reveals the black blind horror of Prussianism. It is the very devil. It has to be fought: and killed. It is the last word in iniquity. I could not have believed that men could be so diabolical.' By the end of the year he saw war as not only a national duty, but as involving issues of ultimate right and wrong. 'We are eschatologists. God must win. We cannot have anything else.' Finally, by January 1915 he could portray the declaration of war as England's response to a summons from the Beyond a fleeting glimpse of the Infinite:

And under the sway of such a direct spiritual emergency we seemed for the moment to catch a sight of the eternal challenge which is the creative power behind all history – which is always there, always will be. Now it had blazed out, flung off all accretions and accumulations of time and chance, and we stood face to face with God, and we made our answer in His eyes. And we saw in an instant what He

---

[1.] Quoted in Albert Marrin, *The Last Crusade. The Church of England in the First World War* (Durham, North Carolina, 1974), pp.86, 87.

[2.] Albert Marrin, *op.cit.*, p.78.

wanted, and so we took our place within His purpose. 'Come up hither,' so the voice cried, 'and I will show you things that shall be.' And the world-drama was laid bare, and we saw the looms of God at work. We felt astir with the pressure and the tumult and the heat of those tremendous forces by which the energy of God is always driving our human story forward toward its great culmination.[3]

And Winnington-Ingram made an equally dramatic *volte-face*. As early as 6 September 1914 he preached a sermon to soldiers entitled 'The Holy War'. He began with stories of German brutality. After quoting the Kaiser, Treitschke, and Bernhardi from a recent issue of the *Daily Mail* and Rudyard Kipling's 'For All We Have and Are', and after a brief conventional confession of national and personal sins, he continued:

> But when we have said all that, this is an Holy War. We are on the side of Christianity against anti-Christ. We are on the side of the New Testament which respects the weak, and honours treaties, and dies for its friends, and looks upon war as a regrettable necessity...It is a Holy War, and to fight in a Holy War is an honour...Already I have seen a light in men's eyes which I have never seen before.

He reiterated this message in June 1915:

> I think the Church can best help the nation first of all by making it realise that it is engaged in a Holy War, and not be afraid of saying so. Christ died on Good Friday for Freedom, Honour, and Chivalry, and our boys are dying for the same things. Having once realised that everything worth having in the world is at stake, the nation will not hesitate to allow itself to be mobilised. You ask for my advice in a sentence as to what the Church is to do. I answer MOBILISE THE NATION FOR A HOLY WAR.[4]

[3.] Albert Marrin, *op.cit.*, p.79.
[4.] Alan Wilkinson, *The Church of England and the First World War* (London, 1978), p.253.

Lord Halifax, the influential Anglican Catholic lay leader, joined in what was to become a chorus of voices when, in November 1914, he issued one of the first proclamations of a Holy War. It was a view which was shared by the population as a whole, and by many Evangelical and Modernist Churchmen as well as High Churchmen. It did not totally preclude a sense of divine judgement on England as a nation. A few High Churchmen, and some others from different church traditions, saw the war in that way. The vicar of All Saints', Margaret Street, was vehement in asserting that in pre-war England 'the race was going from bad to worse; the worship of God was disappearing from our land. Hard, godless women were springing up in multitudes about us, increasing numbers of them refusing to bear children, and increasing numbers who had families were incapable of bringing their children to the feet of Christ...Well, the patience of God is exhausted, and the angel of death has appeared over the land, his sword in his hand.' [5]

But such self-examination, and self-condemnation, soon gave way to a concentration on the sins of Germany. Earlier impulses to credit her with at least some merits were suppressed. Winnington-Ingram reversed his former assessment, affirming that the war must not be called a punishment for England's sins, 'for if we had been more sinful, adding cowardice to our other faults, we might have avoided it altogether'.[6] Scott Holland asked several questions which many repeated throughout the course of the war. 'But why, in the name of God, have these peace-lovers allowed their rulers to be what they are ? Why have they tolerated the policy, the diplomacy, which has made Germany a byword in Europe ? Why have they allowed militarism to create another Germany which is the ironical confutation of the Germany which they portray to us?'[7] Scott Holland and a host of others replied explicitly or implicitly that the success of the warlords and of the war philosophers was explicable only if considered within the broader context of the failure of the German churches.

[5] Albert Marrin, *op.cit.*, p.83.

[6] Albert Marrin, *op.cit.*, p.90.

[7] Albert Marrin, *op.cit.*, p.109.

In September 1914 a group of eighty of the most renowned members of the German religious and academic communities, led by Adolf von Harnack, Adolf Deissmann, Ernest Dryander and Rudolf Eucken, issued an *Appeal to Evangelical Christians Abroad,* enthusiastically supporting their country's policies and defending 'the inner right of us and our Emperor to invoke the assistance of God'. They insisted that the Germans were fighting to save the West from Russian barbarism. Yet England, they asserted, while knowing this nevertheless deliberately misrepresented the issues and endeavoured through its worldwide propaganda network to point the finger of guilt to Germany alone. The *Appeal* claimed that Germany was fighting for its existence against a host of hostile powers. 'No scruple holds back our enemies, where in their opinion there is a prospect of seizing for themselves an economic advantage or an increase in power, a fragment of our motherland, our colonial possessions or our trade. We stand over against this raging of the peoples, fearless because of our trust in the holy and righteous God.'[8] It was disastrous to the *Appeal,* which was in any case unacceptable, that it was published in England within four days of the burning of Louvain and the massacres at Dinant and Tremonde, in which dozens of defenceless civilians were machine-gunned in reprisal for guerrilla activity. Far from being sympathetically received, the *Appeal* further inflamed public opinion. The reply, *To the Christian Scholars of Europe and America,* which was signed by leading High Churchmen, including Charles Gore, Henry Scott Holland and Walter Lock, examined the German contentions point by point, and refuted them in polite but firm and uncompromising language. As a final and most telling counter blow, the reply noted how Germany's actions spoke louder than all her paeans to Kultur and humanitarianism. In view of Louvain, 'will not the Christian scholars of other lands share our conviction that the contest in which our country is engaged is a contest on behalf of the supremest interests of Christian civilization?'[9]

---

8. Albert Marrin, *op.cit.*, pp.109, 110.
9. Albert Marrin, *op.cit.*, p.110.

As the war continued, as the full horror of it bore in on people more and more, and as the German 'atrocities' became known, the concept of a holy war took a firmer grip upon the population as a whole and hysteria mounted. There was an escalation in the proclamation of the war as a crusade, which not infrequently assumed an apocalyptic dimension. Opposition to this was weak, unorganised and late in developing; and it came almost entirely from High Churchmen. Outstanding among these was Bishop Gore. In the midst of a generally apathetic or hostile episcopate he denounced what he perceived as a shameful, unchristian upsurge of fanaticism. He was firmly convinced that no other course lay open to the country than to participate in the war; the ideals of German militarists had to be fought until they were smashed. But he warned against self-righteousness and prigishness. It was right to fight against the evil works of the devil in Flanders, but there was need to remember with sorrow and penitence that many evils remained to be destroyed at home. To Gore the Kingdom of God was more important than winning the war. In his visitation charge in the autumn of 1914 he anticipated the altruistic declaration of Nurse Cavell. He wrote: 'The thoughts and feelings which patriotism inspires legitimately fill our minds and imaginations. But this is not enough. I am sure that if we simply yield ourselves to these thoughts and feelings we shall fall disastrously short of what our Lord would have us think. The Bible is full of patriotic emotion; but even more conspicuously the Bible is full of a great warning against the sufficiency of patriotism, against the sufficiency of the thoughts natural to flesh and blood.'[10] He chided the enthusiasts for resorting to language historically associated with the Crusades, not the most glorious period in church history. Protests were also registered by the Rev. Walter Lock and Henry Scott Holland, both of whom maintained that, notwithstanding their crimes, the Germans remained children of God; and clergymen should remember their calling as His servants, and not go about as 'Mad Mullahs preaching a Jehad'.[11]

[10] G.L. Prestige, *The Life of Charles Gore* (1935), p.370.

[11] Albert Marrin, *op.cit.*, p.142.

To many of those who proclaimed the Holy War, conscientious objection was inconceivable, and was denounced as cowardice or worse. Again, it was Gore who took the lead in adopting a more moderate tone. He spoke in the House of Lords three times in successive years against the ill treatment of conscientious objectors. He did not agree with them, he found many of them among the most aggravating human beings with whom he ever had to deal, and he appreciated the immense difficulty in discerning aright between those with a genuine crisis of conscience, and a large number of others who, for a variety of reasons, were not genuine. Nonetheless, he was adamant that every effort should be made to ensure that a fair and just system of appraisal and treatment was adopted. Too many of the tribunals established had assumed that those trying to avoid military service were unpatriotic, and had thereby forfeited their rights under the law. This was reprehensible. It was, said Gore, inconsistent if the country claimed to champion freedom while at the same time it persecuted Quakers and others who rendered valuable service to society. He applauded the national repudiation of their ideas; but he thought that the country shamed itself by denying them the protection of the law.

From the outset of the war the question of whether the clergy should be combatants caused a lively and emotional debate. It was widely felt among bishops, clergy and the laity that ordination was a setting apart for a distinctive ministry, and was incompatible with military service. In this, as with so many other war-related issues, it was once again Bishop Gore who most clearly and explicitly expressed, and demonstrated in action, what was the typical Anglican Catholic view. He did everything he could to dissuade the clergy from enlisting as combatants, but encouraged the younger of them to volunteer as chaplains. Those who were responsible for large parishes were advised to remain where they were. If candidates for holy orders felt an overmastering call to enlist, he sent them off with his blessing. Those who did not sense a positive call of conscience, he encouraged to abide by their vocation, and to pursue their preparation for fulfilling it, even if they were derided as cowards. Most High Churchmen were of the opinion that service as a chaplain was a noble vocation. But there were few Anglican Catholic chaplains, especially in the early part of the war, and this was reckoned as the fault of one man – the Evangelical Chaplain-General, Bishop Taylor Smith.

Taylor Smith had a profound aversion to Anglican Catholics, making it almost impossible for them to obtain commissions and become chaplains. Eventually, a high-powered and vigorous campaign against this perceived discrimination was conducted by Lord Halifax and the *Church Times,* with a measure of success. Archbishop Davidson neatly circumvented Taylor Smith by appointing the widely known and well-liked Bishop L.H. Gwynne of the Sudan as Deputy Chaplain-General in charge of the chaplains in France, where most of them were serving.

Chaplains of all shades of churchmanship were faced by a common and overwhelming task, and they shared with all others in the Church of England an unprecedented and traumatic situation. During the course of the war England encountered a loss of life, and injury and suffering on a scale perhaps never before experienced in the history of the world. In four devastating years the country endured the agony of three quarters of a million dead and double that number wounded, many of them seriously. The Established Church was ill-prepared to cope with such excessive pain and bereavement.

In such circumstances the Anglican Catholics, together with the rest of the Church of England, could offer the consolation of the Christian message of the resurrection and the love of God, as well as the traditional reflections on, if not 'explanations' of, the 'causes' of suffering. But Anglican Catholics had something more to offer which the rest of the Church of England could not provide; prayers for the dead and the requiem mass. Anglican Catholic priests frequently displayed great spiritual qualities, and their response to the crisis of war, both at home and at the front, was widely appreciated and admired. As chaplains they showed great heroism and singleness of purpose, and in particular those who were members of the Community of the Resurrection, the Mirfield Fathers, appear to have given sterling service. They, and indeed the chaplains in general, became popular as padres, or fathers, and continued to be viewed as such after the war when they were in parishes. At home, the common practice of erecting street shrines, notably in the East End of London, to recall those who had died, was part of this widespread adoption of beliefs and practices which were more in harmony with Anglican Catholicism than with any other Church of England tradition.[12]

Although theological differences remained, the chaplains were less aware of them as they faced a common task in the front line. Catholics responded to dire spiritual need and became less rigid, and Evangelicals were more than usually ready to use ritual aids in worship. And there was one matter of national importance, involving a vital question of principle, on which Anglican Catholic and Evangelical leaders in general were remarkably at one; they stood firm against the general tide of public opinion in opposition to reprisals. The zeppelin and aeroplane raids by Germany on British towns, the shelling of coastal towns, and the menace of U-boats intensified public animosity and popular hysteria, and evoked a widespread demand for reprisals against German civilians. Despite their intense patriotism, and their commitment to the rightfulness of the country's holy war, a number of the most influential High Church and Evangelical leaders unambiguously condemned any retaliatory acts. Bishop Gore protested strongly when the British bombed German towns in 1917 in response to German raids: 'If we allow ourselves to be led by the Germans, the descent is easy and the end certain degradation.'[13] On a most moving occasion in the summer of 1917, at the burial of child victims of an air raid, Winnington-Ingram resolutely spoke out against the agitation for reprisals, despite his frequent bellicose utterances. He said that he did not believe that the mourners would want sixteen German children killed to avenge the dead British children. But he balanced this with a call for just counteraction: 'What all demanded was strong deterrent naval and military action...on the places from which these raiders came, and that the strongest punishment

---

[12.] Alan Wilkinson, *op.cit.*, ch.6.
[13.] Alan Wilkinson, *op.cit.*, p.101.

should be given to the perpetrators and designers of these raids.'[14]

In the midst of war church leaders, including Anglican Catholics, were not unmindful of the need to plan for peace. The Archbishops and many of the bishops, clergy and laity of the Church of England sought for such national preparation through the National Mission. Gore was doubtful about its timing, considering that a discouraged clergy and an unresponsive people were not ready for such an ambitious enterprise, but once it had been launched he threw himself with boundless energy into the promotion of the mission in his own diocese. Anglican Catholics were enthusiastic about the call both to individual conversion and national transformation, but many of them were anxious that there should first of all be a change of mind or re-conversion among Churchmen – what Gore called 'corporate repentance'. 'Certain things were obviously in need of amendment. Fresh beginnings were demanded of the Church as a teaching body and as a worshipping body. A stronger atmosphere of spiritual fellowship needed to be extended into the homes of the people. Corporate witness by the Church against great national vices must be intensified; and in particular the Church must play a far greater part in social reconstruction and the movement for "a better England" after the war.'[15]

The Second World War

In the 1930s Anglo-Catholics were remarkably ambivalent in their attitude to Germany, and even to Nazism, and this was part of a more widespread ambivalence in the Church, and indeed in society as a whole. They were probably influenced to some extent by the generally favourable attitude of Roman Catholicism to fascism, and by the extensive public support for appeasement. They were also to some degree influenced by

[14.] Alan Wilkinson, *op.cit.*, p.101.
[15.] G.L. Prestige, *op.cit.*, p.383.

the teaching of the Oxford Group movement. The leaders of that movement supported pro-Nazi 'German Christians', and the head of the movement, Frank Buchman, when he returned from an interview with leading Nazis, including Heinrich Himmler, in 1936, exclaimed: 'I thank heaven for a man like Adolf Hitler who built a front line of defence against the antichrist of Communism'.[16]

Fr Gabriel Hebert, the Kelham monk, approved of Barth's assault on liberalism. In his *Liturgy and Society* (1935) he condemned liberal theology as corrupting and persuaded many Anglicans to despise liberalism as individualistic. There appears to have been a connection between this and his qualified approval of Nazi corporatism. Although he went on to say that the object of worship in Germany was 'the magnified corporate ego of the nation rather than God, he commended 'experiment on communistic lines' and wrote of the 'success' of the 'great national movement' in Germany.[17]

Appeasement was personified for Anglo-Catholics in the High Church statesman Lord Halifax – Lord Privy Seal 1935–37, Lord President of the Council 1937–38, Foreign Secretary 1938–40 – whom they trusted, respected and even venerated. 'The Christian public thought him a humble and devout believer par excellence, genuinely striving to relate his Christianity to the conduct of foreign affairs. Surely, he was the one who, by his noble virtues and intuitive skill, would understand and moderate the wild men of Germany and Italy as he had promoted reconciliation (they believed) as Viceroy of India.'[18] In 1939, at the Canterbury Diocesan Conference, Lang commented that the reception given to a recent speech by Lord Halifax had been a tribute 'to the confidence of all parties in his spirit, his motives, his calmness, his steadiness of judgement'. People, Lang said, were deeply thankful that such a man should be Foreign Secretary at such a time. And there

---

[16.] Eberhard Bethge, *Dietrich Bonhoeffer* (London, 1977), pp.261, 282, 446, quoted in Alan Wilkinson, *Dissent or Conform? War, Peace and the English Churches 1900–1945* (London, 1986). p.143.

[17.] Alan Wilkinson, *Dissent or Conform?*, p.153.

[18.] Alan Wilkinson, *Dissent or Conform?*, p.187.

was thankfulness in many quarters that he took his Christian faith with him in dealing with the grave international affairs of the time. However, his background did not equip him to make accurate judgements about Hitler, Goering and others with whom he had discussions. He was out of his depth, and unable to fathom the wickedness of such men. His faith had taught him a certain detachment from the world. His biographer described his reaction to the Munich agreement:

> The belief in a Divine control over the affairs of the world led him to think that human beings could only move the course of events a little in certain directions, so that while prepared to do this, he was not ready to step in and stem the flood: and his profound belief in a future life made the disasters of this world seem by contrast transient and insubstantial. Thus armoured he could envisage human afflictions with an almost unearthly calm, and face war, when it came, with complete inner tranquillity... [19]

Lang's response to the Munich agreement was made very plain. He not only ignored a request from Dean Duncan-Jones, one of the only really well-informed priests in England on the state of Germany, that he should voice the conscience of England against what Duncan-Jones described as the 'most shameful betrayal in English history', but he was effusive in his praise for what had been done. Both on the radio and in the House of Lords he was at his most unctious in his oft-repeated expressions of gratitude at once to God and the Prime Minister. 'More than one member of Parliament said to me today as we all trooped into the lobby: "This is the hand of God".' For Chamberlain, he declared in the Lords, 'no praise could be too great'. [20]

The views of the appeasers set the tone among Anglo-Catholics, but they did not go unchallenged. No one was more fiercely opposed to the Mosleyites and the Munich agreement than the Anglo-Catholic Fr St John Groser, the East End

[19.] Alan Wilkinson, *Dissent or Conform?*, p.188.
[20.] Adrian Hastings, *A History of English Christianity 1920–1985* (1986), p.348.

socialist priest, who was a rebel against established authority in both church and state. His indignation at the Munich agreement is forthrightly expressed in a letter:

> Blackmail has succeeded. The threat of force has triumphed. ...That Mr. Chamberlain should talk of 'peace with honour' when he has surrendered to this blackmail, torn up Article 10 of the League Covenant without reference to Geneva, and sacrificed the Czechoslovaks in order, as he says, to prevent a world war, is bad enough; but that the Archbishop of Canterbury should say that this is the answer to our prayers...is beyond endurance.[21]

But he cried out largely in vain. His was not the attitude which prevailed.

It seems that there was never, either before or during the war, a wide-ranging, intense and passionate anti-Nazi, pro-British sentiment among Anglo-Catholics as a whole. 'In 1938, at least within the Church, both the right wing and the left, both the Establishment and the radicals, were appeasers. Only the odd man out questioned the wisdom of Mr. Chamberlain. For the clergy as a whole, peace, to be pursued by all means and at almost any cost, was the overriding preoccupation of the thirties, whether or not they subscribed formally to Pacifism.'[22]

A further reason for the lack of any significant Anglo-Catholic critique before or during the war was the absence of any dominant, powerful, charismatic figure who could and would proclaim a clear message. There was no one who, out of a full heart, set forth clear theological and moral principles, and commanded public attention.

Partly because of all these pre-war attitudes, the response of High Churchmen, and indeed of the Church of England in general, to the Second World War was remarkably muted as compared with the response to the First World War. Patriotism was as great, but there were not the same emotional appeals in an effort to promote a crusade, nor the same portrayal of the

---

[21.] Adrian Hastings, *op.cit.*, p.349.
[22.] Adrian Hastings, *op.cit.*, p.349.

issues in stark black and white terms which typified many Churchmen, including High Churchmen, less than thirty years before. Attitudes were more restrained, and the language used was decidedly less aggressive. But there was also less divisiveness. For instance, although the High Churchman Lang, as Archbishop of Canterbury, exhorted people to pray for victory, the appeal was issued in a very low key way, and he never attempted to rouse the nation. Indeed, there was far less comment of any kind on the war, or issues associated with it. The main exception was George Bell who spoke out with boldness, penetration and courage on a variety of matters raised by the war and, in the view of many, thereby forfeited any possibility of elevation to the archiepiscopate of Canterbury, for his opinions were often far from congenial to those in authority. He opposed any attempt by the Church to promote the idea of such an earthly war as a crusade; resisted any tendency by the Church to make the victory of the national cause the supreme concern; and encouraged links between Christians of all nations, including the warring countries. He distinguished between Germany and National Socialism, and while declaring that the allies could never make terms with the latter, held out the possibility of doing so with the former, under certain conditions. He attracted particular animosity by his fearless renunciation of the bombing of German cities.

High Churchmen as a whole were, in contrast to Bell, noticably silent. From articles and comments in the *Church Times* and other papers and journals it appears that the main source of anxiety for Anglo-Catholics during the war was the South India scheme. Fr Harry Williams remembered council flat tenants in Pimlico saying, as British bombers flew overhead to Germany, 'Poor wretches, I'm afraid that they're going to get it tonight.' He wondered who was the more Christian, these compassionate non-churchgoers or the devout Anglo-Catholic clergy agitating at that time with such hatred against church union in South India?[23]

---

[23] Alan Wilkinson, D*issent or Conform?* pp.278, 279.

It may not be too simplistic and strong to say that in what they taught and proclaimed, Anglo-Catholics, in common with the Church of England as a whole, with a few notable exceptions, erred by commission in the First World War and by omission in the Second.

14

Resurgence – The Congresses

To the younger generation of High Churchmen who survived the First World War, persecution for their distinctive beliefs and practices, episcopal opposition, mob violence, railing abuse in the press and every other manifestation of extreme hostility were unknown. They were entering a brave new world of hard won new opportunities, and they were bold, enthusiastic and visionary, hopeful of a bright future. They were inclined to look on the older High Churchmen much as Hurrell Froude and Newman had regarded the 'Zs', that is, with some measure of impatience and exasperation. They demanded action and a more adventurous approach than that of their fathers. They thought that the High Church wing of the Church had been on the defensive long enough, and that the hour for a fresh initiative had dawned. For a time there was tension between these somewhat triumphalist Anglo-Catholics and the long-established English Church Union headed by the aged Lord Halifax. It was one of Lord Halifax's last, and not least important, services to Anglican Catholicism that he managed to unite the two groups.

As soon as peace had been declared in 1918 there was a pronounced new tone and policy among Anglo-Catholics. They no longer acted as if they were a beleaguered minority in opposition, who needed to concentrate on apologetic. They demonstrated a renewed self-confidence and pride in what they stood for, and they launched an attack rather than resting content with defensive manoeuvres. This new found energy and assurance was manifested in a rather unpremeditated way in a series of congresses. Whether these are interpreted as exhibiting the new Anglo-Catholicism in the ascendant, or as being the climax of achievements over preceding decades, they were a clear indication of a movement which was at one of its high points. The congresses gave a focus for thirteen years of exultation to at least some of those war weary Anglo-Catholics, who could, with some justification, think that the moment of glory for their particular tradition had arrived.

The initial idea for the congresses came from the little known East End priest, the Rev. C.R. Deakin, vicar of Christ Church, South Hackney. The chief organiser and propagator of the project was the outstanding Marcus Atlay, vicar of St Matthew's, Westminster.

At the head of the programmes for the first, 1920, congress, there appeared a statement which applied to all the congresses: 'The purpose and aim of the Congress is the extension of the knowledge and practice of Catholic Faith at home and abroard, and by these means to bring men and women to a true realization of our Lord Jesus Christ as their personal Saviour and King.' 'It is the aim of the Congress', Atlay stated, as Chairman of the Executive Committee, 'to demonstrate to the world that the Catholic position is the true and real interpretation of what English religion is meant to be, and further to make it plain that English Catholics have no intention whatever of being driven to Rome or into schism; but they intend to claim, with no uncertain voice, their rightful heritage in the English Church.'[1]

The concern for evangelism was well attested in the handbook for one of the regional congresses established in the early 1920s, that at Bristol. After alluding to the achievement of the Tractarians in calling attention to the claims and privileges of the English Church, it went on:

> Now, however, another stage has been reached. The vast mass of the people has not been directly touched by the influence of any religious body. And in these days when congresses are the customary method of reaching the

---

[1] C.P.S. Clarke, *The Oxford Movement and After* (1932), p.287.

people it is fitting that Anglo-Catholics too should adopt such means. So it is that the aim of a congress is that of Evangelization. It is that first and foremost. It exists to bring men and women to a true realization of our Lord Jesus Christ as their personal Saviour and King.[2]

The enthusiastic response to the idea of holding congresses was far greater than the early organisers ever imagined possible. The numbers enrolled went up from one congress to another. According to the official reports there were thirteen thousand in 1920, fifteen thousand in 1923, twenty-one thousand in 1927, twenty-nine thousand in 1930 and seventy thousand in 1933. [3] The success of one congress after another was greeted by clerical and lay High Churchmen alike with jubilation. The largest public buildings in London had to be used to accommodate all the participants. In addition there were secondary congresses held in provincial cities in the months that followed some of the main congresses, addressed by some of the speakers from the central gatherings. There were also day conferences in some diocese; and a large number of special services, commemoration sermons and masses, as well as books published in 1933 at the time of the centenary of the Oxford movement.

From the outset there were three primary components of the congresses: worship and devotion; theological education, teaching, enlightenment and inspiration; and fellowship. Every congress opened with a great central act of worship, with hundreds of robed clergy and an enormous congregation – filling St Paul's Cathedral in 1923 and, in 1930 and 1933 occupying the White City Stadium because St Paul's was not large enough. At the concluding mass of the 1933 congress between forty-five and fifty thousand were said to be present. A subsequent commentator has caught something of the atmosphere of worship and praise at the 1920 congress:

[2] C.P.S. Clarke, *op.cit.*, p.288.
[3] See W.S.F. Pickering, *Anglo-Catholicism* (1989), p.56.

I think on the whole that perhaps the Thanksgiving Services were in some ways the most striking feature of the congress. I am told that by 7.30 on Friday evening the queue of people waiting to get into Southwark Cathedral stretched from the Cathedral gates right across London Bridge to the Monument. It is the first time, surely, at any rate since the Reformation, that London Bridge heard a great crowd singing to the honour of the Mother of our Lord, as the waiting multitude sang again and again, 'Hail Mary, Hail Mary, full of grace.' These are some of the things which passed practically unnoticed in the newspapers; but which we shall never forget.[4]

Some of the leaders and organisers of the congresses were unhappy with the very open and explicit Catholic character of the worship and devotions at the congresses, and favoured forms of worship which would be more acceptable to a wider range of Churchmen, and would at least not cause offence. There was particular concern about the Marian devotions as shown by the hymns sung to the Blessed Virgin Mary, and objections were expressed by Winnington-Ingram, who had been persuaded to be President of the 1923 congress. He declared such a focus of devotion to be contrary to the doctrine and practice of the Church of England. But the less cautious, less inhibited advocates of the more extreme forms of Catholic devotion won the day.

Each congress was addressed by about twenty theologians and church leaders, lay as well as clerical, mostly, but not exclusively, sympathetic to Anglo-Catholicism. For many of those attending, this provided teaching and inspiration of an order which they could experience nowhere else. The high calibre of instruction, exposition and exhortation was supremely demonstrated in the ministry of Bishop Frank Weston of Zanzibar at the 1923 congress, where he was both chairman and speaker. A measure of the impact of his personality and

---

[4] H.A. Wilson, *Received with Thanks* (London and Oxford, 1940), pp.88, 89, quoted in W.S.F. Pickering, *op. cit.*, p.51.

power of communication is given by the comments of Professor C.H. Turner of Oxford, an Anglo-Catholic layman, and Alec Vidler, a future dean of King's College, Cambridge, and in his early days an enthusiastic Anglo-Catholic. The former said, 'I think that the Bishop of Zanzibar was the greatest man I have ever met. I know he was the greatest orator I have ever heard'[5]; and Vidler said that Frank Weston 'moved and inspired me when he visited Cambridge more than any other speaker'[6]. Weston was an eminent, dynamic missionary bishop, a DD of Oxford, mentioned in despatches and awarded an OBE for his service in East Africa during the Great War, and he held great sway among all Anglo-Catholics. But any thought that he might be destined to be the leader of Anglo-Catholicism in England was dashed by his death in 1924.

The gathering together of so many like-minded Church people gave boundless opportunity for fellowship. There was a corporate sense of euphoria and increased hope, and a refreshing sense of participation in a revivified movement. But such exuberance as this was also accompanied by a feeling of sadness and incompleteness, for the movement remained unpopular among English bishops. It was tragic for all concerned that there were very few bishops, or indeed other ecclesiastical dignitaries, at the congresses, when it was reckoned by the participants that there could be no church without priests, and no priests without bishops. The bishops who did attend were largely from other countries.

'Perhaps the most important service the Congress movement rendered to the Anglo-Catholic Movement was to bring into the very forefront the need of missionary work not only in England but overseas.'[7] Partly because the Lambeth Conference was due to be held shortly after the 1920 congress, six out of the eight chairmen at the 1920 meetings were bishops from overseas and, as we have seen, Bishop Weston dominated the 1923 congress. Large sums were given or pledged at the congresses

[5] H.A. Wilson, *op.cit.*, p.121.

[6] A.R. Vidler, *Scenes from a Clerical Life* (London, 1977), p.31, quoted in W.S.F. Pickering, *op.cit.*, p.52.

[7] C.P.S. Clarke, *op.cit.*, p.289.

for the promotion and support of world mission, and evangelism at home and abroad was a persistent theme.

The five congresses engendered a sense of triumph, but it was perhaps inevitable that it could not be sustained at the high level of pitch and intensity set from the start. Such effervescent gatherings have their day and pass away. With hindsight, the magnificent high mass of the 1933 congress may be seen as a requiem for the exuberant, visionary type of Anglican Catholicism which the congresses represented.

Following the centenary year of the Oxford movement, the sixth Anglo-Catholic Congress was planned for 1940, to be the culmination of seven years evangelistic work in the parishes, and to coincide with the Lambeth Conference due for that year. The onset of war meant that both were postponed until 1948, and then they met under very much changed circumstances both for the nation, for the Church and for Anglican Catholicism.

15

Theological and Liturgical Issues

The two key theological works from within the Anglo-Catholic camp in the period 1914 to 1945 were *Essays Catholic and Critical* (1926) edited by Edward Gordon Selwyn, and Arthur Michael Ramsey, *The Gospel and the Catholic Church* (1936).

Essays Catholic and Critical

Essays Catholic and Critical was very consciously in the *Lux Mundi* tradition and was an attempt to do for theology, and more especially Anglican Catholic theology, what *Lux Mundi* had attempted to do almost forty years earlier. It aspired to being 'a fresh exposition and defence of the Catholic faith'. As with *Lux Mundi,* a group of mainly academics who had 'been brought into close touch with the vigorous currents and cross-currents of thought and feeling amid which Christianity has to render its own life and truth explicit', felt 'compelled, both for themselves and for others, to think out afresh the content and the grounds of their religion'.[1]

The essayists saw two main developments since the publication of *Lux Mundi* in 1889; a greater interest in the

---

[1.] E.G. Selwyn (Ed.), *Essays Catholic and Critical.* By Members of the Anglican Communion (London, Third ed., 1934), p.xxvii.

Works which help to provide a context for the matters discussed in this chapter, which have not previously been cited, include Horton Davies, *Worship and Theology in England: The Ecumenical Century: 1900–1965* (1965), and A.G. Hebert, *Liturgy and Society* (1935), together with works cited below.

supernatural element in religion and an expression of that in the context of Catholic unity and authority. This had taken place in the face of a disordered and impoverished Christendom. There was a need to respond afresh to the critical movement which, since *Lux Mundi,* was seen to have continued 'with unabated vigour to analyse and bring to light the origins and foundations of the Gospel'.[2] The authors were attempting 'to bring into synthesis the Catholic and the critical movements'.[3] By Catholic they meant 'everything in us that acknowledges and adores the one abiding, transcendent, and supremely given Reality, God; believes in Jesus Christ, as the unique revelation in true personal form of His mystery; and recognises His Spirit embodied in the Church as the authoritative and ever-living witness of His will, word, and work'. By critical they meant 'that divinely implanted gift of reason by which we measure, sift, examine, and judge whatever is proposed for our belief, whether it be a theological doctrine or a statement of historical fact, and so establish, deepen, and purify our understanding of the truth of the Gospel'. Both Catholic and critical were 'principles, habits, and tempers of the religious mind which only reach their maturity in combination'.[4] 'Liberal Catholicism' was the name given to such a combination, and the essayists as Liberal Catholics were aware of the difficulty, if not impossibility, of upholding reason and freedom while at the same time remaining faithful to tradition and authority. The exponents of such an approach laid themselves open to attack from the stalwarts of both camps. The conflict centred especially on the concept of authority.

The two essays on authority attracted considerable criticism at the time for being too vague. But this vagueness and unwillingness to give a more precise statement on what and where authority is, was subsequently defended by the editor as legitimate in view of Liberal Catholicism's reluctance to

[2] E.G. Selwyn (Ed.), *op.cit.,* p.xxvii.

[3] E.G. Selwyn (Ed.), *op.cit.,* p.v.

[4] E.G. Selwyn (Ed.), *op.cit.,* p.xxviii.

oversimplify what was a very complex matter. Liberal Catholics of the time, as reflected in these essays, were not prepared to propound a simple or single formula which identified authority as resting in an infallible Pope, an infallible Bible, or an infallible conscience. They found the source of authority 'in the Spirit of God, who revealed and still reveals the unsearchable riches of Christ'; and the seat of authority 'in the common mind of the Church', with its normative expression 'in the Scriptures, and especially in the revelations of the Apostles and those who knew our Lord personally', but also in the Church's creeds, its dogmatic formularies, its liturgical forms and phrases – in short, in whatever has nourished and borne fruit in the lives of the saints.

In summary, the essayists were united in seeking a reconciliation between religious faith and advancing secular knowledge. They claimed that they represented no transient phenomenon, but were continuing a long tradition which had every sign of appealing more widely than ever before. Their aim was not so much to criticise others as to create 'conditions in which mutual understanding between men of different allegiances may grow'. They wished to foster 'the sympathy by which different schools may be knit rather than frozen together'. In doing so, they considered that they were in harmony with what many considered the historic task of Anglican theology.

Although it had much in common with *Lux Mundi*, *Essays Catholic and Critical* differed from the former work in certain important ways. It was not, like *Lux Mundi*, a work of systematic theology, but rather a series of apologetics, and it was also less of a single coherent thesis. Some of the essays 'expound traditional doctrines with an eye upon the critical questions which have come to beset their presentation in the modern world', whereas some 'plunge the reader more deeply into the contemporary critical world'.[5]

Essays Catholic and Critical did not reflect the thoroughly Biblical approach which was in the process of revival in English theology, though Hoskyns' essay was a harbinger of it. In fact the book was to become somewhat dated, 'being later than the

---

[5.] Arthur Michael Ramsey, *From Gore to Temple* (London, 1960), p.103.

dogmatic theology of Gore and earlier than the return to the Biblical "theology of crisis".[6] Nonetheless, the writers of the essays, and others akin to them, did have considerable influence in the inter-war period. They reached out eirenically to the Liberal Evangelicals and their approach to theological and Church issues was mirrored in the *Report of the Archbishops' Commission on Doctrine in the Church of England,* and in the writings of William Temple and O.C. Quick.

The volume we have been considering greatly contributed theologically to Liberal Catholicism in the 1920s. In the 1930s there was a more general Anglican Catholic influence. 'The movement towards dogma, and scholasticism, towards the transcendental theology of the Word in the Bible, and away from the spirit of synthesis with the contemporary age, came in full flood. The categories of experience and piety, of evolution and apologetics, gave place to the categories of theology in its classic forms.'[7] But in the midst of this transformation, a future High Church Archbishop of Canterbury, and a theologian of note, Arthur Michael Ramsey, made a contribution to theological thinking in his book *The Gospel and the Catholic Church* (1936) which was to have a more enduring and stimulating influence than the volume we have just reviewed.

The Gospel and the Catholic Church

The underlying conviction of Ramsey's book was 'that the meaning of the Christian Church becomes most clear when it is studied in terms of the Death and Resurrection of Jesus Christ'.[8] Ramsey expounded this theme. If the Church's meaning was seen as lying in the fulfilment of the sufferings and resurrection of Christ, he asserted, then every part of its history is intelligible in these terms. 'The right interpretation of the Church's task, in this present as in every age, will begin

---

[6] Arthur Michael Ramsey, *op.cit.,* p.104.

[7] Arthur Michael Ramsey, *op.cit.,* pp.109, 110.

[8] Arthur Michael Ramsey, *The Gospel and the Catholic Church* (London, 1936), p.vi.

with the Biblical study of the Death and Resurrection of the Messiah, wherein the meaning of the Church is contained. The New Testament portrays the Church as more than the "extension of the Incarnation".' The disciples 'knew themselves to be the refounded Israel of God through being partakers in the Messiah's death'.[9] Catholic Anglicans needed to expound the meaning of the Catholic Church not in legalistic and institutional language, but in evangelical language as the expression of the Gospel of God. Thus, for instance, it needed to be asked what truth about the Gospel of God did the Episcopate, by its place in the one Body, declare.

The Church was set forth by Ramsey, not as a loose collection of believers in Jesus, but as a new nation with the solidarity of one race, brought to birth by a creative act of God, owing its existence to the death of Christ. 'Christianity therefore is never solitary. It is never true to say that separate persons are united to Christ, and then combine to form the Church; for to believe in Christ is to believe in One whose Body is a part of Himself and whose people are His own humanity, and to be joined to Christ is to be joined to Christ-in-His-Body; for "so is Christ" and Christ is not otherwise.'[10] This did not diminish individualism in Ramsey's view, but enhanced it. '"Individualism" therefore has no place in Christianity, and Christianity verily means its extinction. Yet through the death of "individualism" the individual finds himself; and through membership in the Body the single Christian is discovered in new ways and becomes aware that God loves him, in all his singleness, as if God had no one else to love.'[11]

The outward order of the Church was depicted by Ramsey as no indifferent matter, but rather of supreme importance, for it is related to the Church's inner meaning and to the Gospel of God itself. Every part of the Church's true order bears witness to the one universal family of God and points to the historic events of the Word-made-flesh:

[9] Arthur Michael Ramsey, *The Gospel and the Catholic Church*, p.6.

[10] Arthur Michael Ramsey, *The Gospel and the Catholic Church*, p.36.

[11] Arthur Michael Ramsey, *The Gospel and the Catholic Church*, p.38.

Baptism is into the death and resurrection of Christ, and into the one Body (Rom. 6.3, 1 Cor. 12.13); the Eucharist is likewise a sharing in Christ's death and a merging of the individual into the one Body (1 Cor. 11.26, 1 Cor. 10.17); and the Apostles are both a link with the historical Jesus and also the officers of the one *ecclesia* whereon every local community depends. Hence the whole structure of the Church tells of the Gospel; and not only by its graces and its virtues, but also by its mere organic shape it proclaims the truth. A Baptism, a Eucharistic service, an Apostle, in themselves tell us of our death and resurrection and of the Body which is one.[12]

Ramsey believed that there was no fundamental conflict between the Evangelical and the Catholic elements in the Church of England – they were utterly one. The one gospel of God inevitably included the Scriptures and the salvation of the individual; but as inevitably it included the order and the sacramental life of the Body of Christ, and the freedom of thought wherewith Christ has made us free. The two aspects of Anglicanism – Evangelical and Catholic – cannot really be separated. Anglicanism 'possesses a full Catholicity, only if it is faithful to the Gospel of God; and it is fully Evangelical in so far as it upholds the Church order wherein an important aspect of the Gospel is set forth'.[13] And Ramsey was clear and decisive in applying this to the daily life of the Church:

Translated into practice this means that the parish priest has a heavy responsibility; he must preach the Gospel and expound the Scriptures, and he must also proclaim the corporate life of the Church and the spiritual meaning of its order. In every parish the Prayer Book entitles the laity to hear the Gospel preached, and the Scriptures expounded, and also to receive the full sacramental teaching of the historic Church including the ministry of

[12.] Arthur Michael Ramsey, *The Gospel and the Catholic Church*, p.50.
[13.] Arthur Michael Ramsey, *The Gospel and the Catholic Church*, p.208.

Confession and Absolution for those who desire it. For the Anglican church is committed not to a vague position wherein the Evangelical and the Catholic views are alternatives, but to the scriptural faith wherein both elements are of one. It is her duty to train all her clergy in both these elements. Her Bishops are called to be not judicious holders of a balance between two or three schools, but, without any consciousness of party, to be the servants of the Gospel of God and of the universal Church.[14]

Ramsey had a deep and comprehensive theology of the Church, so that he was saddened but not downcast by the divisions within the Church universal. To him, the three branch theory held by earlier High Churchmen, and classically expressed in William Palmer's *Treatise on the Church of Christ*,[15] was unacceptable. It depicted the Church as one, yet represented by three great branches, Greek, Roman and Anglican. But to Ramsey such a claim to unity, with its acquiescence in schism, avoided the fact that Church order is maimed by disunity. The theory was an unconscious attempt to make the best of both unity and schism, and it obscured the relation between Church order and the Gospel. Ramsey stressed that the Church is 'the people of God, whose unity of race continues despite the scandal of outward division'.[16] In the search for this visible unity he believed that 'the Episcopate succeeded the Apostolate as the organ of unity and continuity'.[17] The restoration of one Episcopate was needed by all Christian people, in order that all might share in a Eucharist which is, both inwardly and outwardly, the act of the one Church of God. But in the meantime the broken Church in all its weakness is the body of Christ. 'Its order, its worship, its history, its problems of unity and disunity mean the Passion of Jesus.'[18] The life and death of the Messiah

---

[14.] Arthur Michael Ramsey, *The Gospel and the Catholic Church*, p.209.

[15.] William Palmer, *Treatise on the Church of Christ*, 2 vols. (London, 1818).

[16.] Arthur Michael Ramsey, *The Gospel and the Catholic Church*, p.223.

[17.] Arthur Michael Ramsey, *The Gospel and the Catholic Church*, p.223.

[18.] Arthur Michael Ramsey, *The Gospel and the Catholic Church*, p.224.

have their counterpart in his Body, the Church. But he rose again, as he said he would, and his people, the Church, share in the certain hope of the resurrection.

The contribution to the inter-war years theological thinking of the two books we have considered was vital, but it was just a part of a general greater Anglican Catholic engagement in theological issues. Biblical scholarship, and more especially the influence of Barth, was of course prominent. But side by side with that movement was a resurgence of the theology of the Church, the sacraments and the liturgy. In this period, 'the Church came to occupy in the minds of Protestants a position which had once been thought to be peculiar to Catholics'.[19] Indeed, these years have been described as 'the beginning of the high summer of Anglo-Catholic theology'.[20] It was the culmination of a process which had been maturing for decades and it found expression in the 1930s in both the universities and the religious orders.

Theological resources

Although Michael Ramsey was foremost in Anglican Catholic thinking, behind him were some established scholars like Lionel Thornton of Mirfield, A.G. Hebert of Kelham, Dom Gregory Dix of Nashdom Abbey and Kenneth Kirk, Bishop of Oxford, as well as brilliant young priests like Eric Mascall and Austin Farrer. The new school was not devoid of an anti-Protestant and anti-Nonconformist note, but it was a great deal less narrowly partisan than many earlier Anglo-Catholics had been. This was partly because it was increasingly biblical in character, partly because of the influence of F.D. Maurice and P.T. Forsyth and partly because of the growing together of the Anglo-Catholic with the Student Christian Movement thread

[19] G. Stephens Spinks, *Religion in Britain since 1900* (1952), p.169, quoted in Adrian Hastings, *A History of English Christianity 1920–1985* (London, 1986), p.298. Hastings is a book to which this whole section is much indebted.

[20] Adrian Hastings, *op.cit.*, p 298.

in Anglican life. There was a new openness among Anglican Catholic theologians. The Thomist strain became more explicit. Anglican Catholics were content to learn from Jacques Maritain or Père Clerissac. And throughout the inter-war years theological scholars representing a wide spectrum of theological and ecclesiastical traditions were prepared to associate with Anglican Catholics. Such men as E.G. Selwyn, for a time the Editor of *Theology*, A.E.J. Rawlinson, Sir Edwyn Hoskyns and E.J. Bicknell identified themselves in corporate endeavours with men of such long-standing reputation as Charles Gore, T.A. Lacy, Darwell Stone and Professor A.E. Taylor. Tensions undoubtedly existed as, for example, between Charles Gore and some of the younger men, for Gore was not prepared to make any move towards a 'symbolic' interpretation of the articles of the creed which dealt with questions of historical fact, but there was nevertheless a vitality in Anglican Catholic theological debate which could not be gainsaid. The Anglo-Catholics were beginning to find themselves at the centre of Anglican theology and life, providing both bishops and university professors, and this greater responsibility produced on the whole greater tolerance.

An important by-product of the overall vigour of Anglican Catholics in these years, and of their evident involvement in the theological thinking of their day, was their ability to attract men and women of superlative intellectual standing, as amply demonstrated with the conversion and enlistment into their ranks of the brilliant young American T.S. Eliot. His *Murder in the Cathedral*, written for the Canterbury Festival of 1935, was not only rightly acclaimed as a major literary and religious creation, but it made it clear that Anglo-Catholicism was able to inspire and animate the imagination of those engaged in the world of the arts.

Liturgical developments

From theological writings we turn quite naturally to the liturgical life of the Church; and it was a period of considerable liturgical activity and importance.

By the beginning of the twentieth century Anglo-Catholics as a whole were committed to at least the weekly, and not infrequently the daily, celebration of communion or mass, the eastward position and candles on the altar, and, in the case of over two thousand churches, vestments. Reservation of the sacrament was accepted, and it was further stressed by many Anglo-Catholics that if the consecrated bread was reserved for the sick, it must signify an enduring sacramental presence of Christ, justifying reverence and prayer before it.[21] All this was abhorrent to Evangelicals and provoked strong reaction. Litigation against 'Ritualists' was, by the turn of the century, replaced by demonstrations, protests and the interruption of services by John Kensit and his Wycliffe Preachers and other uncompromisingly 'Protestant' bodies, such as the Protestant Truth Society.

The situation was tense. There was a degree of anarchy in the Church of England as a number of non-Prayer Book services were widely introduced in the 1890s, the most controversial being the Veneration of the Cross, on Good Friday. In 1898 the bishops took steps to discourage such departures from the Prayer Book, but with little effect, and the 'Ritual Question' remained as a prominent public issue. Church Discipline Bills were introduced in 1899 and in each of the four years following, and finally, in 1904, a Royal Commission on Ecclesiastical Discipline was appointed. It was to 'inquire into the alleged prevalence of breaches or neglect of the Law relating to the conduct of Divine Service in the Church of England and to the ornaments and fittings of Churches; and to consider the existing powers and procedure applicable to such irregularities and to make such recommendations as may be deemed requisite for dealing with the aforesaid matters'.[22]

The Report was issued in 1906. It gave an authoritative picture of worship at the turn of the century, and summarised a mass of material with the remark:

[21.] These comments are based on Adrian Hastings, *op. cit.*, pp.77–80.

[22.] Quoted in G. J. Cuming, *A History of Anglican Liturgy* (1969), p. 210. A book to which this section owes much.

The law relating to the conduct of Divine Service and the ornaments of churches is, in our belief, nowhere exactly observed; and certain minor breaches of it are very generally prevalent. The law is also broken by many irregular practices which have attained lesser, and widely different, degrees of prevalence. Some of these are omissions, others err in the direction of excess.[23]

Finally, it enunciated two main conclusions:

First, the law of public worship in the Church of England is too narrow for the religious life of the present generation. It needlessly condemns much which a great section of Church people, including many of her most devoted members, value....Secondly, the machinery for discipline has broken down....It is important that the law should be reformed, that it should admit reasonable elasticity, and that the means of enforcing it should be improved; but, above all, it is necessary that it should be obeyed.

Most importantly, it recommended that:

Letters of Business should be issued to the Convocations with instructions: (a) to consider the preparation of a new rubric regulating the ornaments (that is to say, the vesture of the ministers of the Church, at the times of their ministrations) with a view to its enactment by Parliament; and (b) to frame, with a view to their enactment by Parliament, such modifications in the existing law relating to the conduct of Divine Service and to the ornaments and fittings of churches as may tend to secure the greater elasticity which a reasonable recognition of the comprehensiveness of the Church of England and of its present needs seems to demand.[24]

[23.] G.J. Cuming, *op.cit.*, p.211.
[24.] Quoted in G.J. Cuming, *op.cit.*, pp.211, 212.

'Letters of Business were duly issued, and the way was once more open for a revision of the Book of Common Prayer after the lapse of nearly 250 years.'[25]

Meanwhile, the steady rise of Anglican Catholicism had been accompanied by a great desire for 'enrichment' of the Prayer Book services, usually by borrowing from the Roman Missal. The publication of *The English Liturgy* in 1904 had successfully shown how this could be done without departing from the Anglican Communion. It was largely the work of Percy Dearmer and W.H. Frere, both of whom emphasised the continuity of the Church of England with the pre-Reformation Church. The Alcuin Club was founded in order to promote this approach to liturgiology and church furnishings, and produced some beautifully printed liturgical texts.

For a host of Anglican Catholics, the very centre of their lives lay in their devotion to the Christ of the mass. This is well depicted in the graphic portrayal by his biographer of Viscount Halifax, the leading lay Anglo-Catholic for many decades, and the President of the Church Union almost continuously for over fifty years after 1869:

> The picture rises up before me of many an early Mass in that rather dark, private chapel at Hickleton which he loved so well. I have always found that, however early I went to the chapel to say my preparation before Mass, there was always kneeling in the front row of seats on the right, and wrapped in the French cloak which he always wore, quite still, and almost invisible, the venerable figure of Lord Halifax...There was an intensity about him and the sense of entire recollection when he was praying...During Mass he made the responses quietly but audibly; he received the Holy Communion with deep devotion, and, returning to his prayer desk, knelt again and remained quite still. I have known him not to leave the Chapel for his frugal breakfast for two hours after he had received our Divine Lord.[26]

[25] G. J. Cuming, *op. cit.*, p.212.
[26] Quote in J.G. Lockhart, *Charles Lindley Viscount Halifax*, II (1936), pp. 337–338, quoted in Adrian Hastings *op. cit.*, p.84.

It was Cosmo Gordon Lang who 'catholicised' the Church of England probably more than anyone else, and largely without giving offence, in the period 1908 to 1942, when he was Archbishop of York until 1928 and then Archbishop of Canterbury. By 1908 he was publicly committed to advocating the legalisation of the 'Six Points' – eucharistic vestments, the lighting of candles upon the altar, the use of wafers in the place of common bread for Holy Communion, the eastward position of the celebrant, the ceremonial mixing of water with wine in the chalice and the use of incense. And these were the main outward symbols which, in the view of both Anglican Catholics and Evangelicals, distinguished the mass of the one from the communion of the other. Lang was the first archbishop since the Reformation to wear a mitre and to make the cope the normal liturgical dress for bishop and archbishop.[27]

Prayer Book revision

But as the twentieth century advanced Prayer Book revision replaced liturgy as the topic of preoccupation and conflict. The story of the attempted revision of the Book of Common Prayer, and of the double rejection of the proposed new book by the House of Commons in 1927 and 1928, has been often and well described.[28] Our focus must be upon the Anglican Catholic stance taken during the 1920s when the revision so preoccupied the Church of England as a whole and the bishops in particular.

Few Anglo-Catholics were enthusiastic for what was proposed. Lang thought the suggested changes in the Order of Holy Communion were too meagre to be of much use to the Church. He favoured the Liturgy of 1549, but 'when it became clear that there must be an alternative Liturgy, and that this could not be that of 1549', he fell into step.[29] Some Anglo-

[27.] See Adrian Hastings, *op.cit.*, p.198.

[28.] See especially G.K.A. Bell, *Randall Davidson. Archbishop of Canterbury*, 2 vols. (Oxford, 1935).

[29.] J.G. Lockhart, *Cosmo Gordon Lang* (London, 1949), p.300.

Catholics, led by Darwell Stone, argued for the rejection of the proposed new book because it did not go far enough. A considerable section even of comparatively moderate Anglo-Catholics were dissatisfied with the proposed alternative order of Holy Communion, which seemed to them to threaten Anglican traditions of eucharistic theology. They were also unhappy with the restriction of the reserved sacrament for the sick only, as they thought that such restriction unnecessarily excluded from the benefits of reservation all others who, for good reasons, might be prevented from communicating at the ordinary times of service. Charles Gore sympathised with such opinion, but he was astonished at the Catholic opposition to the Revised Book. 'He laid great stress on the enormous labour which had been spent on its production, and on the paramount need for regularising and controlling the growth of lawless habits in the conduct of divine worship. But he also regarded with approval the substance of the revision. "It represents on the whole an advance altogether beyond what I had dared to expect".'[30] He urged that a book which was 'presented after so many years' labour, and accompanied by such urgent appeals for loyal acceptance, should claim the support even of the half-hearted "as an act of loyalty to authority"'.[31]

At this crucial time, in the midst of an often somewhat heated debate, it was the archetypal Anglo-Catholic, Viscount Halifax, who inadvertently dealt a severe blow to the whole revision process. He fuelled pervasive anti-Roman fears as a consequence of the Conversations at Malines, of which he was a prime architect, and in which he played a leading part. Ever since the 1890s Halifax had been endeavouring to obtain Roman Catholic recognition of the validity of Anglican priestly orders with a view to his ultimate goal – which was no less than to unite the Church of England with the Roman Catholic communion. His attempt to achieve his purpose in the 1920s through conversations with the Abbé Portal and Cardinal Mercier was quite staggeringly audacious. The first conversations took place entirely unofficially in 1921, but the

[30] G.L. Prestige, *The Life of Charles Gore* (1935), p.505.
[31] G.L. Prestige, *op.cit.*, p.506.

three of them were subsequently successful in obtaining official authorization from both Rome and Canterbury. When the conversations resumed in 1923 the Church of England was represented by Halifax, Frere and Dean Armitage Robinson – all High Churchmen. The high point was in 1925 when there appeared to be some possibility that the true corporate existence of the Church of England as a Church might have been recognised by Rome. But the moment passed, circumstances and attitudes rapidly changed, and it became evident that Roman Catholicism was moving in a quite different direction. The conversations were abruptly terminated.

Nonetheless, even with the fears aroused by the Malines conversations and the strong opinions generated by an active Evangelical and Anglo-Catholic campaign against the Revised Book, there was an overwhelming vote in favour of revision in all Houses of the Church Assembly. The Bill for the revision of the Prayer Book was also passed by the Lords after a three day debate of high quality and fine tone. But then it was twice defeated in the Commons.

Lang, as Archbishop of Canterbury, had to lead the Church of England in the aftermarth of this devastating blow. It was a time of liturgical confusion and crisis both within the Church and in church-state relations. But Lang 'was neither the man to enforce the decision of parliament, nor to challenge it'.[32] The Church of England inevitably suffered from such a state of affairs, and in the late 1930s Anglican Catholics responded by changing their liturgical focus. *The Parish Communion,* edited by Fr Hebert, and published in 1937, helped to direct their enthusiasm less towards the mass and more towards the promotion of parish communions which could combine what was best in both Catholic and Protestant traditions. Such a change of emphasis also helped to remould Anglo-Catholicism for its re-appearance after the Second World War.

[32.] Adrian Hastings, *op.cit.*, p.207.

16

The Social Question

Up to the First World War, for all the stir they had made, and it was not inconsiderable, the Guild of St Matthew, the Christian Social Union and the Church Socialist League always remained small societies of committed enthusiasts. The Guild never numbered more than four hundred; the Union, despite its moderation, only reached a membership of 6,000 at its height in 1910; and the League at about the same time boasted 1,200 members.[1] Bearing in mind that this was a time when the number of practising church people was quite high and the interest in social issues was both widespread and intense, the figures seem almost microscopic. Not only were they minority organisations, but whether they were revolutionary or reformist in tone, they appeared to be eccentric to the essential purpose of the Church, 'involving at worst a grave distortion of religion and at best a more or less legitimate hobby for specialists'.[2] They suffered from what was at its best a somewhat chilling tolerance. They had little or no authorisation from official

---

[1] Maurice Reckitt, *Maurice to Temple: A Century of the Social Movement in the Church of England* (London, 1947), p.160. A book on which the following comments are largely based.

Other books which cover aspects of what is discussed in this chapter, or provide a background to the discussion, which have not previously been cited, and are not cited below, include Robert Graves and Alan Hodge, *The Long Weekend. A Social History of Great Britain 1918–1939* (London, 1940), G.L.H. Harvey (Ed.), *The Church and the Twentieth Century* (London, 1936), Roger Lloyd, *The Church of England 1900–1965* (London, 1966) and C.F.G. Masterman, *The Condition of England* (London, 1909).

[2] Maurice Reckitt, *op.cit.*, p.160.

sources for the message they proclaimed. They often allowed themselves to be driven into a posture of opposition to their ecclesiastical superiors, and this sometimes led them to be outlawed. It was an unhealthy state of affairs, but the 1916 National Mission of Repentance and Hope was a turning point in the development of the movement which these societies represented.

The National Mission and its consequences

The National Mission declared that the social order was a spiritual reality in which the grace of God was manifest, with purposes which require to be understood and laws which need to be obeyed. And since this was so, social righteousness could never be assumed to be an inevitable result of the consecrated intentions of individuals. As the sponsors of the mission asserted: 'All the citizens of a nation might be individually converted, yet public life be conducted on principles other than Christian.' In thus adopting a social perspective, and in acknowledging the need for the Church to be involved in social issues and to seek social righteousness, the National Mission offered an opportunity for the dedicated members of the Christian social movement to work constructively for social justice within the framework of Anglicanism. No one saw this more clearly than the man who by that time was the strongest influence in the Church Socialist League, Percy Widdrington. In April 1916 he wrote: 'The time for criticism is past. The day of action has come; it has been our misfortune to find ourselves in constant opposition to the authorities in the Church, and we have been out of sympathy with our fellow churchmen. We have been driven for our fellowship outside rather than inside the Church. We have almost become "aliens" to our mother's children. Such a state of things is to be deplored. It has been to some of us spiritually disastrous. Thank God the day of better things has come.'[3]

[3.] Quoted in Maurice Reckitt, *op.cit.*, p.161.

The Mission was followed by the setting up of five committees which reported in 1918. The last of the reports, on *Christianity and Industrial Problems*, appeared auspiciously in the month following the Armistice. It was an able and powerful statement, and exceptionally energetic efforts were made to propagate its conclusions. High Churchmen, or High Church sympathisers, were intimately involved in the Committee and in the writing of its Report. The Chairman was Bishop Taylor of Winchester, a leader of the CSU since its earliest days, and Bishop Gore and Bishop Kempthorne of Lichfield were amongst its members. Others included A.L. Smith, Master of Balliol and R.H. Tawney, who was credibly rumoured to have written a major part of the Report.

The Report became the charter of the Industrial Christian Fellowship, an organisation which had come into being as a timely fusion of an evangelistic agency (the Navvy Mission) which lacked a social message, and the socially minded CSU, which had never achieved any successful contact with the working class. 'The ICF, with its great open-air "Crusades", its missioners at the street corners and in the factories, and its educational work through correspondence class and study circle, manifested in the post-war years, more effectively than had ever been done before, the concern of the nation's Church at once for the spiritual and the social condition of the masses of the nation.'[4] And the new organisation obtained a greater degree of episcopal patronage than any such Christian body had so far enjoyed.

The death of Henry Scott Holland in March 1918 seemed to signal the end of the CSU and the need for a new initiative. The new men who came forward to meet the challenge and to serve in the ICF were for the most part those who had served overseas as chaplains with the citizen armies, and who, because of their sharing of the hardship and soul-searching experiences of ordinary people, gained an unusual insight into the physical, mental and spiritual needs of people whom they might not otherwise have known and understood so profoundly. Pre-

---

[4] Maurice Reckitt, *op.cit.*, p.166.

eminent among these was Geoffrey Studdert-Kennedy
('Woodbine Willie') who, it has been well said, 'was in the true
line of succession of Stanton, Dolling and Wainright'. They
were all remarkably selfless lovers of God and man, 'impetuous
and often it may be injudicious, but ready to burn their lives
away without hesitation if the truth that is in them can but be
spoken and the souls they yearn to rescue can but be reached
and restored'.[5] Archbishop Temple said of Studdert-Kennedy,
'the urging impulse was not in his thought but in his heart; it
was the passion of sympathy with the victims of our present
injustice'. To him the sacrament of the Eucharist was central
not only to his own personal life, but to the dream of a Christian
social order. His life was dedicated to making Christ known to
individuals and in the social order, and he died in the midst of
such service in 1929 at the age of forty-six.

The Kingdom of God and the quest of a Christian sociology

Percy Widdrington was concerned that the Church social
movement should be guided by a right theological
understanding. He believed that the post-war era, with its
reaction against immanentism in theology, with its growing
doubts about evolutionary collectivism which had been too
readily endorsed by too many Christian social thinkers, and
with its underlying political assumptions, demanded a Christian
re-appraisal. There was a need for 'a radical re-examination of
the title deeds of the Church's social movement'.[6] He was
convinced that the conception of the Kingdom of God provided
the necessary means of interpreting the social scene and
equipped the church with a social ideal. Once the Kingdom of
God is restored to its proper place as 'the regulative principle
of theology', he wrote excitedly, and once the Body of Christ
is 'aflame with the faith of the Kingdom', the Church 'will be
compelled to adopt towards our industrial system the same

5. Maurice Reckitt, *op.cit.*, p.164.
6. Maurice Reckitt, *op.cit.*, p.168.

attitude which our missionaries take towards the social order of heathendom. It will then challenge the Industrial World as it challenged the forces of Roman Imperialism in the days of the persecution.' The consequences will be awesome, Widdrington insisted: 'a Reformation in comparison to which the Reformation of the sixteenth century will seem a small thing'.[7] The concept of the Kingdom of God pointed backwards to the gospels themselves, and to medieval Christendom, where Widdrington perceived that amid all the social limitations of feudalism and the spiritual corruption of ecclesiasticism a conscious and not unsuccessful effort had been made to introduce a Christian interpretation of social life; and it pointed forward to the introduction of a Christian sociology. It was indicative of such thinking that the militant ex-members of the Church Socialist League in 1923 formed the League of the Kingdom of God.

The search for a Christian sociology resulted in two significant publications which appeared in the same month, November 1922. In *Is there a Catholic sociology?* Egerton Swann answered his own question with a resounding Yes. He proposed that the three pillars of the Church's own distinctive programme should be distributed property, the just price, and a guild organisation of industry. Such a programme did not take over ready-made opinions of either the Labour movement or Socialism, but cut across all existing cleavages, leaving the Church in a position of sovereign independence which might require it to defy alike the Labour movement and the plutocracy.

The other publication was more ambitious but arrived at similar conclusions. *The Return of Christendom* was the product of several years work by the group surrounding Widdrington, which had first been assembled at Coggeshall in Essex in 1920, and which had undertaken a comprehensive study of the ideals of medieval Christian society. It 'represented an elaborate, if not wholly satisfactory, exploration of the philosophical, theological and sociological foundations for a reformulation

---

[7] Quoted in John Orens, 'Priesthood and Prophecy: the Development of Anglo-Catholic Socialism', in Kenneth Leech and Rowan Williams (Eds.), *Essays Catholic and Radical* (London, 1983), p.171. An essay to which this section owes very much.

of Catholic social teaching'.[8] The group was Catholic in its inspiration, although its members were attached only somewhat loosely or not at all to the organised Anglo-Catholic movement which was promoting the Congresses and the energetic propaganda throughout the country. Anglo-Catholicism as a whole had not fully welcomed Headlam's fusion of Mauricean theology with Catholic sacramentalism, and had never been completely alive to the implications and the responsibilities of its heritage of social teaching, despite the heroic work of its slum priests. The challenging note struck by Bishop Weston at the 1923 Congress when he confronted his audience with the madness of worshipping Jesus in the sacrament while sweating Him in the bodies and souls of His children, and his call for appropriate works of mercy, did not go unheaded. Some among the leaders of the Congress turned for aid to Percy Widdrington and his newly constituted League of the Kingdom of God.

Widdrington and his friends were determined to overturn the existing social order, but they believed that to 'lose sight of the principles of Christian society in order to gain some political advantage was too high a price to pay'.[9] This approach is the root of their much-criticised medievalism, which was a pronounced feature in the work of both the League of the Kingdom of God and in that of the Christendom Group, the League's intellectual nucleus and eventual successor. They argued that whatever the failings of medieval society it was animated by a Christian vision. Justice, not profit, was regarded as the highest economic good. Production was intended to meet human needs, rather than men and women being treated as mere hands. Medieval society was a rich community of communities, not an homogeneous order governed by an omnipotent state. This idealised portrait of life in the Middle Ages was presented as a contrast and criticism of the present, and not as a clarion call to return to the past. There was, however, a faintly antiquarian air about much of the philosophy

---

[8.] Maurice Reckitt, *op.cit.*, p.169.
[9.] John Orens, *op.cit.*, p.172.

and work of the Christendom group, which was heightened by its neo-Thomist view of natural law and its consequent exaggerated confidence in the ability of theology to determine social policy.

Widdrington and his circle strove to preserve the theological heritage of the nineteenth-century Christian Socialist movement and to apply it to political, economic and social problems of their day. In doing so they offered direction to those Anglo-Catholics who were eager to do battle with capitalism, and yet were disenchanted with socialism. 'But the very refusal to take sides in the day-to-day political struggle between Left and Right kept the Christendom Group from exercising much influence outside the small world of Anglo-Catholic intellectuals',[10] although the Christian Sociology which they promoted, was later popularised, especially by Maurice Reckitt, and was received sympathetically by many Churchmen outside the ranks of the Anglican Catholics.

The Christian 'Sociology' as it developed in the 1920s and 1930s was not really sociology as it subsequently emerged as an academic discipline:

It was not, that is to say, a quantitative and comparative study of society and opinion. It was normative, propagandist, not descriptive: but it was a serious attempt to define distinctly Christian principles of society, derived from Christian doctrine, and not just an attempt to identify Christianity with secular social ideas. It rarely reached anything like that sort of goal, however, and most of the writings of the period which claimed the label 'Christian Sociology' turned out to be the sort of moralistic social criticism which had been produced in the Church for decades.[11]

The Christian Sociology of the period was normative in that it was chiefly concerned to identify which particular political structure most readily facilitated the ordering of social life for

[10.] John Orens, *op.cit.*, p.172.
[11.] E.R.Norman, *Church and Society, 1770-1970* (1976), p.320.

the common good. This was especially emphasised by V.A.
Demant, who also urged the Church to exercise its prophetic
role and, where necessary, to intervene in political affairs.

During the inter-war years many of the bishops perpetuated
the old Christian Social Union approach, but there was by then
no particular society or group to give expression or coherence
to that tradition. Christian sociology fulfilled this function to
some extent, but it was the remarkable ascendancy of William
Temple, especially after the Conference on Politics, Economics
and Citizenship (COPEC) in 1924, which was the chief source
of cohesion for mainline Church social radicalism.

The Catholic Crusade

For those ardent Anglo-Catholics and others who were impatient
with discussions of Christian Sociology, or the more
accommodating type of radicalism associated with William
Temple, an option was the Catholic Crusade, a group of
Anglican radicals gathered round Conrad Noel at Thaxted,
which was started in 1912 but was most active and effective in
the period 1918 to 1936. Noel was a remarkable and colourful
personality. He had been one of the young radicals in the Guild
of St Matthew who had rallied to the Church Socialist League
only to be disillusioned by what he regarded as its vague
theology and unimaginative politics. What he demanded was
revolution. Like Headlam, he delighted to shock middle class
churchgoers. He had a deep conviction that 'the Christian
Socialist movement, and the Church itself, had no future
unless they took part in the great struggle to overthrow
capitalism and usher in the Kingdom of God'.[12] Faced with the
grim years between the two World Wars, the Crusade set itself
'to explain and justify the new revolutionary socialism
manifested in the Russian Revolution of 1917'.[13] There was

[12.] John Orens, *op.cit.*, p.173.

[13.] Gresham Kirby, 'Kingdom Come: the Catholic Faith and Millennial Hopes',
in Kenneth Leech and Rowan Williams (Eds.), *op.cit.*, p.52. An essay to which the
present chapter is greatly indebted.

something deliberately outrageous both in the utterances and actions of Noel and in the determination of the Crusade 'to shatter the British Empire and all Empires to bits...to break up the present world and make a new in the power of the outlaw of Galilee'.[14]

Foremost in the purpose of the Crusade was the determination to do all in its power to help bring to pass the coming of the Kingdom of God on earth, the fulfilment of the biblical hope. In this, as had been the case in the past with many other Christian Socialist groups, it claimed to carry on and develop the tradition derived from F.D. Maurice. In the mid-nineteenth century, in response to Chartist demands, he had declared: 'To me, the Kingdom of Heaven is the great existing reality which is to renew the earth.'[15] It was asserted that the central belief of the Church of the first three centuries had been the coming of the Kingdom of God on earth, and that the contemporary Church should put that at the top of its agenda. Unlike Charles Gore and many others, both Widdrington and Noel argued against the view which regarded the Church itself as the Kingdom of God on earth, a lie on which, Widdrington said, medieval Catholicism was founded. The Kingdom of God was rather the whole sphere in which the reign of God is actualised. It was the world which was the scene of a 'divine order'.

The 1930s were marked by the virtual demise of the various forms of Anglican Catholic Socialism. In 1932 some of the keenest members of the Catholic Crusade were driven out because they did not take the 'party line'. Soon after this the Crusade began to be rent asunder over the Stalin-Trotsky argument, and in 1936 it was disbanded. Although the Order of the Church Militant perpetuated something of the same ethos, teaching and activity as the Crusade, it only continued until Noel's death in 1942, for by then the zest and momentum had been lost. In the early 1930s the League of the Kingdom

---

[14.] Reg Groves (Ed.), *The Catholic Crusade, 1918-1936* (London, 1970), p.9, quoted in John Orens, *op.cit.*, p.173.

[15.] Cited in M.B. Reckitt, *P.E.T. Widdrington: a study in vocation and versatility* (London, 1961), and quoted in Gresham Kirby, *op.cit.*, p.52.

of God ceased, and the Christendom Group did not survive the inter-war period.

Basil Jellicoe (1899–1935)

Before we leave our consideration of the social question in the turbulent inter-war years, when various charismatic figures sought to arouse the Church to meet its social obligations, mention should be made of a man described by William Temple as 'one of Christ's most precious gifts to the Church of our generation', Basil Jellicoe. 'As a young man of twenty-two in the sordid man made wilderness of Somers Town Jellicoe saw a vision of the Church summoned to "build old wastes and raise up the former desolations." "Over-crowding and poverty", he declared forthrightly, "are being used by the Devil to steal from the children of God the health and happiness which are their right; and so the Church must fight for these things, confident in the presence of the living God".'[16] And Jellicoe led by example. With confidence in the presence of God and in the justice of his cause, by faith he removed mountains of slum property, largely through the agency of the St Pancras Housing Association which he began in 1924. He had a burning passion for setting the world to rights in what he perceived as God's way. He attached himself to the group around Widdrington, and he inspired a host, including an influential band of Oxford undergraduates, by his actions, his leadership and his force of character, to join the Church's social movement. In 1935, at the age of only thirty-six, he died, having packed into a short life more than most men or women achieve in a long one, and having set his mark not only on his generation but upon the century in which he lived.

[16.] Quotations are from Maurice Reckitt, *op.cit.*, p.179, a book on which the comments on Jellicoe are based.

PART 6

1945 to 1993

17

Recovery Starts Within

In 1945 Anglican Catholics, as part of the national Church, were confronted not only with the aftermath of war but with a society in an advanced stage of secularisation.[1] 'At least until the 1880s, and (despite early symptoms of organisational decline), with little apparent diminution before the First World War, British religion retained an historical importance among the central insitutions of the society.'[2] Although the culture was probably in many ways growing more secular, however such a concept is defined, religion continued to play an important role in society, and figures relating to religious practice were, at least superficially, not too depressing in the nineteenth and early twentieth centuries. They compared unfavourably with what was revealed by the 1851 census, which itself had caused alarm at the time, but they were not bad enough to cause widespread consternation. Membership, attendance and other related statistics indicated that 'in all the major Churches organizational expansion continued to the eve of the First World War'.[3] From then onwards organisational

[1] For a discussion of the concept and process of secularisation see the works listed under note 4 of chapter 7.

Works not previously cited which are relevant to the issues covered in the present chapter include David L. Edwards, *Leaders of the Church of England 1828–1978* (1978), Jean A. Rees, *His Name was Tom. The Biography of Tom Rees* (1971), *Towards the Conversion of England* (1945).

[2] Alan D. Gilbert, *The Making of Post-Christian Britain. A History of the Secularization of Modern Society* (London, 1980), p.76.

[3] Alan D. Gilbert, *op.cit.*, p.76.

decline, which had its roots in the nineteenth century, although uneven, became definite. All the Churches lost substantial ground during the War. The decline was arrested to some extent in the 1920s when most Churches virtually held their own even taking into account the increase in population. But the 1930s saw a further deterioration as measured by indices of total membership and membership as a percentage of the total adult population. The Second World War exacerbated this trend. There was some minimal, short-lived upturn in the late 1940s and early 1950s, but there was an underlying drift downwards.

At the beginning of the period we are about to consider it was currently estimated that only 10% – 15% of the population were linked to some Christian church; that 25% or 30% were sufficiently interested to attend a place of worship upon special and great occasions; and that 45% – 50% were indifferent to religion though more or less well disposed towards it, while 10% – 20% were hostile.[4] In England the Easter Day communicants of the Church of England fell from just under 10% of the population aged over 15 years in the period just before 1939, to 6.5% in 1960, and 5% in 1968. Despite a greatly increased population in the country, the electoral roll of the Church of England dropped from 3,700,000 in 1930 to 2,700,000 in 1968. There were also ominous indicators of possible future woes in the statistics relating to Sunday schools. In 1939 there were 218 Church of England Sunday school children per 1,000 population aged three to fourteen years in England. By 1953 this figure was 177, and by 1960 it was 133. For the same three years the number of Sunday school teachers had likewise dropped from 127,000 to 98,000 and then to 85,000.[5]

In the aftermath of war Anglican Catholics faced a nation which was bent on reconstruction and restoration. There was a new political party in power, and expectations were high that a new world would be born out of the agony of war. 'Britain was

---

[4] B.G. Sandhurst, *How Heathen is Britain?* (1946).

[5] Bryan Wilson, *Religion in Secular Society. A Sociological Comment* (Harmondsworth, 1966), pp.28, 29.

straining forward to peace and a new social order, anxious that the disillusionment and lost opportunity which followed the First World War should not be repeated this time.'[6] At home, Anglican Catholics were soon to encounter in E.W. Barnes, *The Rise of Christianity* (1947), a voice within the Church which lauded modern science, and contrasted the orderly universe of science with the, by inference, disorderly and therefore unacceptable miraculous elements in the Gospels. In the wider world, proposals for the creation of the Church of South India were to cause the Anglican Catholics agony and division within their own ranks.

The problems, rapid changes and massive tasks to be accomplished at home and abroad demanded confidence, vision and energy of any Church group which was to be effective and make its mark in the difficult years ahead. The Anglican Catholics were not moribund. The buoyant and heady days of the inter-war Congresses and High Church social radicals were a thing of the past, but the Anglican Catholics still showed many signs of strength and vigour. In their ranks they had men of the calibre of Dom Gregory Dix, T.S. Eliot, the Rev. A.G. Hebert, the Rev. R.C. Mortimer (later Bishop of Exeter) and the Rev. A.M. Ramsey (later Archbishop of Canterbury). In 1945 Dom Gregory Dix published *The Shape of the Liturgy,* which did much to revive and popularise liturgical studies in the Church of England; in 1947 Anglican Catholics produced a Report, *Catholicity,* which showed that they were still theologically competent; in J.W.C. Wand and the London Mission of 1949 they demonstrated that they had a man with all the necessary gifts to serve London at a critical time, and with a commitment to evangelism which was in the best tradition of past High Church evangelists; and abroad their stand for justice and righteousness in South Africa, largely through the life and work of G.H. Clayton, Joost de Blank, Ambrose Reeves and Trevor Huddleston, was outstanding.

[6.] Adrian Hastings, *A History of English Christianity 1920–1985* (1986), p.403.

The Shape of the Liturgy

Dom Gregory Dix (1901–52) owed his incredible influence to his brilliance as a scholar, his unconventionality and good humour as a controversialist, and his most distinguished work, *The Shape of the Liturgy*. The book opened a new era in English liturgical studies. It was a study of the 'ritual pattern' of the Eucharist. Abandoning the search for an archetypal eucharistic prayer, Dix set out to show that underlying all the older liturgies is to be found 'a single normal or standard structure of the rite as a whole'.[7] He called this the 'shape' of the liturgy, and said that it is based on Christ's actions at the Last Supper.

> Our Lord (1) took bread; (2) 'gave thanks' over it; (3) broke it; (4) distributed it, saying certain words. Later He (5) took a cup; (6) 'gave thanks' over that; (7) handed it to His disciples, saying certain words. We are so accustomed to the liturgical shape of the eucharist as we know it that we do not instantly appreciate the fact that it is not based in practice on this 'seven-action' scheme, but on a somewhat drastic modification of it. With absolute unanimity the liturgical tradition reproduces these seven actions as four: (1) The offertory; bread and wine are 'taken' and placed on the table together. (2) The prayer; the president gives thanks to God over bread and wine together. (3) The fraction; the bread is broken. (4) the communion; the bread and wine are distributed together.[8]

The thesis was then worked out in great detail in his massive book, which reached an unexpectedly wide readership and made its influence felt with all the subsequent revisions for many years, during a period of considerable liturgical activity.

---

[7] Gregory Dix, *The Shape of the Liturgy* (1945), reprinted 1960, p.xi.
[8] Gregory Dix, *op.cit.*, p.48.

Catholicity

In November of the same year that Dix published this work, 1945, he was invited by the Archbishop of Canterbury, Geoffrey Fisher, 'to convene a group of Anglicans of the "Catholic" school of thought to examine the causes of the deadlock which occurs in discussions between Catholics and Protestants and to consider whether any synthesis between Catholicism and Protestantism is possible'.[9] The membership of the group ensured the high quality of what was included in the Report they produced. It consisted of the Rev. E.S. Abbott, Dean of King's College, London, and Canon of Lincoln, the Rev. H.J. Carpenter, Warden of Keble College, Oxford, and Canon Theologian of Leicester, the Rev. Dr V.A. Demant, Canon and Chancellor of St Paul's Cathedral, the Rev. Dom Gregory Dix, Monk of Nashdom Abbey, T.S. Eliot, the Rev. Dr A.M. Farrer, Fellow of Trinity College, Oxford, the Rev. F.W. Green, Canon and Vice-Dean of Norwich Cathedral, the Rev. Fr A.G. Hebert, of the Society of the Sacred Mission, the Rt. Rev. E.R. Morgan, Bishop of Southampton, the Rev. R.C. Mortimer, Regius Professor of Pastoral Theology in the University of Oxford, and Canon of Christ Church, the Rev. A.M. Ramsey, Van Mildert Professor of Divinity in the University of Durham, the Rev. A. Reeves, Rector of Liverpool, and Canon Diocesan of Liverpool, the Rev. C.H. Smyth, Fellow of Corpus Christi College, Cambridge, Canon of Westminster and Rector of St Margaret's and the Rev. Dr L.S. Thornton of the Community of the Resurrection. The group was chaired by Michael Ramsey. The Report it produced shows the state of Anglican Catholic theological thinking in the immediate post-war period, and is worthy of full consideration.

At the outset of the Report the authors made clear their distinctive view of the nature of the Church, and immediately Ramsey's insights are very much in evidence. They wrote:

---

[9] *Catholicity. A Study in the Conflict of Christian Traditions in the West, being a Report presented to His Grace the Archbishop of Canterbury* (London, 1947), Preface.

...it is a distortion of the apostolic doctrine to say that men are first united to Christ, through faith, within an invisible society of the truly faithful, and then find admission to the visible Church. The right order is not: Christ – faithful individuals – the Church; but: Christ – the Church – faithful individuals. It is Christ-in-His-Body who justifies men, and their justification is their deliverance into His Body. The visible Church is part of the Gospel: there is no Scriptural sanction for the view that the Gospel is something that is complete, without the Church, and that the Church is a further stage that follows after the acceptance of the gospel.[10]

'The "wholeness" of the visible Church manifests itself in its outward form.'[11] It embodies itself in the apostolate and in the apostolic succession, in baptism as the rite of initiation and in 'the central act of primitive Christian worship, the Eucharist'. 'Out of the complex of Christian life, lived and embodied in dogma, worship and institutions, proceeded the Scriptures of the New Testament, which presuppose and interpret the faith and "the Way" from within which they are written.'[12] The group emphasised that to abstract the New Testament writings from the setting, life and belief which produced them, that is to oppose 'Scripture' and 'Tradition', is wholly artificial and arbitrary. 'If theologians are not agreed from the outset in believing the Church to be a Divine fact prior to the individuals who compose its membership, in believing its outward order to be a part of its being, in affirming the unity of the faith, in recognising the authority of "Tradition" together with that of Scripture, then they have not reached agreement about the first principles of the unity they are seeking.'[13] This Tradition was seen as many-sided, encompassing various tensions, as between the eternal and the temporal, as between the Church's apartness from the world and its mission to engage with the

---

[10.] *Catholicity, op. cit.*, p.13.
[11.] *Catholicity, op. cit.*, p.13.
[12.] *Catholicity, op. cit.*, p.14.
[13.] *Catholicity, op. cit.*, p.15.

world and bring to it the Gospel of God, and as between the divine nature of the Church and the sinfulness of its members. But the main problem of re-union, the group declared, was the recovery of the 'wholeness' of Tradition.

This 'wholeness' was impaired in the early centuries of the Christian era by such ominous phenomena as Marcionism, Montanism, Novatianism and Donatism, and was severely broken by the schism of 1054, so that the Western tradition which split up in the sixteenth century was already a defective tradition. The separated Western tradition has in its turn broken down into orthodox Protestantism, Liberalism and post-Tridentine Catholicism, all of which are represented in the Church of England. The Church of England has a comprehensiveness which allows for Evangelicals, Anglo-Catholics and Liberals to find a home within its fellowship, and this comprehensiveness 'opens the way for the Church of England to be a school of synthesis over a wider field than any other Church in Christendom'.[14] The power in Anglican diversity for constructing such a synthesis comes, said the Report, from theologians who, recognising the limits laid down by Anglican formularies, were able to combine the appeal to Scripture and to sound learning with the appeal to ancient Tradition and, as a result, could escape from the blinkers of sixteenth century systems and controversies. The group regarded Richard Hooker as the first person to make a significant attempt to construct such a synthesis. Hooker's doctrine of the Church was coloured by the Calvinist idea of an invisible Church, but he 'broke away from Calvinist presuppositions in making the Incarnation the centre of his theology, in linking the Sacraments directly with the Incarnation, and in rejecting the tendency to draw a close circle around the inward and spiritual'.[15] Hooker was a pioneer, but was succeeded by the Caroline divines who went even further in the recovery of the fulness of Tradition.

Yet, despite its rich history, 'it remains true that the possibilities of synthesis within the Anglican ideal are still

[14.] *Catholicity, op.cit.*, p.45.
[15.] *Catholicity, op.cit.*, p.50.

largely unrealised'.[16] The various parties have 'jostled side by side, unreconciled and openly antagonistic'.[17] Sometimes it is mistakenly assumed that the truth lies in a middle position which avoids both extremes, and the result is an insipid centrality which misses both the Catholic and the Evangelical truth, and is no more comprehensive than either of them. Sometimes it is assumed that theological conflicts can be solved by piecing views together, whereas the true solution 'demands an exploration of Scripture, Tradition and learning that goes far behind the contemporary party views'.

The group saw strong forces of disintegration in the Church of England of their day. There were Anglican Catholics who practised an introverted and pietistic ecclesiasticism. There were those who in their eagerness to preach divine redemption ignored, as they claimed the recently published *Towards the Conversion of England* ignored, the doctrine of creation which is its groundwork. And there were other manifestations of what the group saw as distortions of the truth.

The authors of the Report especially lamented the fact that the close relationship of the Church of England to the state and the use of the Book of Common Prayer, which had both in the past safeguarded the unity of the Church of England, were ominously ceasing to fulfil that function. The course of events since the rejection of the Revised Prayer Book by the House of Commons in 1928 had shown that it was not the state connection which held the Church together or determined the limits of its teaching and worship. And, far more importantly, the Book of Common Prayer had, in recent history, failed to remain the bond of unity which it had once been. On the one hand the Catholic movement which had formerly been content with the Prayer Book as being patient of a Catholic interpretation, contained many who were seeking a richer devotional liturgy by supplementing the Prayer Book from other sources. On the other hand there were those who found satisfaction in the piety and theology represented by *Songs of Praise,* who were out of

---

[16.] *Catholicity, op.cit.,* p.51.
[17.] *Catholicity, op.cit.,* p.51.

sympathy with the Biblical patterns of truth set forth in the Morning and Evening Prayer, and who felt free to distort the structure of the services at will. The Prayer Book was still a means of acquainting countless Church people with the Anglican tradition, but it was no longer an effective authority for unity in worship and teaching. Nor, it was surmised, would any revised Prayer Book be likely to acquire any such authority unless it arose out of a common theological understanding.

The Report ended by considering what was the principle upon which the Anglican Communion was one and could remain one despite the tensions within her. It concluded that:

> It is by a principle of constancy in Scriptures, Creeds, Sacraments and Apostolic Succession, that the Anglican Communion, for all the diversity within it, remains one. If this principle may be called, at the lowest, the historical condition of our unity in the Anglican Communion, we believe it to be at the highest the precondition of the task of theological synthesis to which the Anglican Communion is, in the Divine Providence, called.[18]

If the Report, *Catholicity,* well expressed the essence of Anglican Catholic theological thinking in the post-war period, it was J.W.C. Wand who most clearly embodied Anglican Catholic theology in action, as well as in his writings. He was the recognised leader of the Anglican Catholics in England in the decade after the war.

John William Charles Wand (1885–1977)

Wand was widely and genuinely respected by all shades of Churchmanship, by civic and political leaders representative of the whole ideological spectrum, and also by 'the man in the street'. There 'was in his Anglican churchmanship something

---

[18.] *Catholicity, op.cit.,* p.56.

that was steady, firm and deep'.[19] Wand was so much the key High Church figure in the immediate post-war period, that we need to give full consideration to his life, beliefs and work. He saw himself as in the tradition of Laud, and there were indeed parallels in both the origins as well as the Churchmanship of the two.

John William Charles Wand was born on 25 January 1885. His father was a butcher and the close-knit family of parents, William and his two brothers, lived in a small house in Grantham where the butcher's shop was rented. His father was a consistent Conservative in politics, and both parents were active Christians, although his father, despite having been confirmed in the Church of England, had, because of personal inclination and musical taste, been drawn to a local Calvinist chapel, where he played the harmonium. His mother remained faithful to the parish church. John went to the chapel with his father.

At the age of twelve Wand won a scholarship to King Edward VI School at Grantham. There, he was attracted by a wider Christian teaching than he had so far encountered. He was facinated by the views of Charles Kingsley, and by the High Church emphasis upon the historical Church, the *Ecclesia Anglicana,* and the importance of the sacraments.

Wand went up to St Edmund Hall, Oxford, in 1904. At Oxford he was profoundly impressed by the preaching of Winnington-Ingram, Bishop of London, and within his college by the teaching of his Vice-Principal, S.L. Ollard, the historian of the Oxford movement. He graduated with a First, was made deacon in 1908 and priest in 1909. He served his curacy in a mixed but predominantly working class parish in Newcastle, where he was responsible for the mission church in a district of five thousand people. He was married in 1911 and moved to Lancaster Priory Church as curate. The church dominated the town, had very large congregations and a very considerable spiritual influence in the community. In 1914 he was appointed as a minor canon of Salisbury Cathedral. He taught at the theological college and preached frequently in parishes in and

---

[19.] John S. Peart-Binns, *Wand of London* (London and Oxford, 1987), p.vii. A book to which the present account of the life and work of Wand is greatly indebted.

around Salisbury. He then served as a chaplain in the Army, and like many chaplains found an easy rapport with the soldiers. From 1919 there followed six years experience as a parish priest, as vicar of St Mark's, Salisbury, where he 'combined an evangelical love for souls with firm Catholic teaching and a liking for ordered ritual',[20] in a ministry which was not spectacular, but which left a strong body of faithful people who valued the sacraments. In 1925 he was honoured as a parish priest in perhaps a unique way by being elected Fellow and Dean of Oriel College, Oxford.

'Wand was forty years old and in a hurry. There was much reading and writing to be done. And where better to do it than at Oriel College...?'[21] As Dean Wand was second in command to the head of the college, disciplinary officer, Chaplain to the college and theological tutor. His seriousness, single-mindedness of purpose and diligence was appreciated by members of the college, and his productivity was notable, especially in the writing of four books, of which perhaps the second, *A History of the Modern Church from 1500 to the present day* (1930), has best stood the test of time.

By 1933 he had a wide range of pastoral, administrative, teaching and writing experience behind him, and he was ready for higher office. In that year he was elected Archbishop of Brisbane and Metropolitan of the Province of Queensland. At the outset of his new and demanding ministry, he was devastated by the loss of his dearly loved, remarkably able, mature and dedicated Christian son Paul in a mountaineering accident. It left him desolate and with a wound from which he never recovered, but it also left him and his wife determined not to let their son down, but to live up to his high expectations, 'to be the kind of people he thought he knew', and do 'the work he expected us to do'.[22]

No attempt will be made to describe Wand's Australian Archiepiscopate in detail, as his main significance for us is his subsequent London ministry. In Australia he attempted, with

[20.] John S. Peart-Binns, *op.cit.*, p.35.
[21.] John S. Peart-Binns, *op.cit.*, p.44.
[22.] John S. Peart-Binns, *op.cit.*, p.67.

mixed success, to introduce a greater measure of discipline in Church life and improve diocesan organisation. He expanded the work of the Church by, for instance, building many new churches; improving the quality and provision of theological education; being adept at communication through the media; being assiduous in his diocesan duties; and being generally a strong leader who commanded respect and even awe. But he was not universally popular. His learning, his forthrightness and his views alienated and antagonised many. In 1943 he was appointed Bishop of Bath and Wells.

After a protest from the National Union of Protestants about his popishness, he was enthroned in November 1943. In a short period he managed to tighten the lax diocesan organisation, give the careworn and war-weary clergy a vision of new hope for the future, and help in giving greater unity to the diocese. But he was in the see for only a short time, for in June 1945 he accepted the bishopric of London. He was about to undertake his most telling work both in his new diocese and in the life of the nation.

Once again his appointment was the signal for a campaign and pamphlet war by the National Union of Protestants. At his consecration on 9 October 1945 'Wand was sixty and everything about him suggested sanctified toughness. He had a heavy frame which somehow reflected solid achievements, firm convictions and bold determination. He looked sufficient to tackle the formidable administrative, physical and evangelistic tasks of rejuvenating the blitz-torn Diocese of London.'[23] The two foci of his work were the chapel at Fulham Palace, because his life was rooted in prayer, in the daily Office and the celebration of the Eucharist, and the study where the plans of action were made.

Wand was quite clear that in order to make spiritual provision for the four and a half million and more Londoners wise and bold replanning was required for the whole diocese. Of the 701 churches, 624 were bomb damaged and 91 had been completely destroyed. The population also needed to recover from the

---

[23.] John S. Peart-Binns, *op.cit.*, p.131.

devastation of war. Demographic change had been accelerated by the war, with a huge migration of people from central London to the ever expanding suburbs. Church schools were in desperate need of modernisation, and in some cases reconstruction. There was also an urgent need for the consolidation and expansion of social and youth work, and a pressing need for more clergy. And high on the agenda for a missionary minded man like Wand was the making known of the goodness of God to the people of London after the traumatic ordeal of the war years. All this required the overhaul of existing machinery, the redistribution and reinforcement of resources, and much money. Wand promptly set about galvanising the diocese into action. He called upon the Church to seize its chance to assume moral leadership, and to proclaim afresh the Gospel in the heart of the nation.

His own personal life was disciplined and concentrated on the issues facing him; he was master of his time and methodical; he never postponed tasks any longer than absolutely necessary, and he unhesitatingly delegated work and responsibility where this seemed appropriate. In everything he was prayerfully centred on God.

The culmination of his early stategy and activity was the Mission to London of 1949. Under the motto and rallying phrase 'Recovery Starts Within' he enlisted thousands of helpers from the worst-bombed parts of the East End and the residential districts of Middlesex and elsewhere, from the cities of Westminster and London, from Paddington and Tottenham, and from all types of Churchmanship. Wand defined the Mission's targets:

There were to be three points of attack. We were to make our main endeavour that of winning the outsider, the person who hitherto had been either indifferent or mildly antagonistic to religion. As a by-product of this effort we hoped at the same time to stir up new interest in those who had lapsed...The third aim was more unusual. It was felt that in society as at present constituted under a Welfare State it was very important to show how Christianity applied not only to the individual, but also to the common life... We felt that if a Mission was to have a really good and lasting effect, it must show that Christianity had a message for every common concern of mankind.[24]

In May 1948 eight thousand Church people gathered in the Royal Albert Hall and committed themselves to prepare for the Mission one year later. 'It was no ordinary mass rally. There was an air of excitement and tautness. Little wonder, as those attending were about to be transformed into the Church's shock troops.'[25] By the turn of the year fifteen thousand were in preparation. Publicity was widely distributed, the media was kept alerted, missioners were commissioned. During the Mission itself meetings abounded. 'The Church was everywhere, in pub and club, factory, street and shop.'[26] Lectures were given simultaneously in St Paul's Cathedral, Westminster Abbey and Southwark Cathedral. 'All London seemed to be talking about God and many lives were being changed.'[27] Of course there was some dimming of the vision, and some falling away after the Mission was ended, but it was a major evangelistic effort, and a significant turning point; and it was masterminded by a man who was dubbed a Liberal Catholic!

The purpose of Wand, not only in the Mission to London but more generally, is cogently articulated by him in 1948:

We must make the whole environment in which we live capable of expressing the beauty and splendour of Almighty God. I believe that in the parishes where that effort is consciously made there is a beauty, a power, and a splendour that comes out from the Church, flowing from the altar, penetrating every home, and kindling a fire on every domestic hearth. The greatest gain we have made in the religious sphere in the last century has been

---

[24.] J.W.C. Wand (Ed.), *Recovery Starts Within. The Book of the Mission to London 1949* (London, 1950), p.150.

[25.] John S. Peart-Binns, *op.cit.*, p.149.

[26.] John S. Peart-Binns, *op.cit.*, p.152.

[27.] John S. Peart-Binns, *op.cit.*, p.152.

the renewed grasp of the sacramental principle and the endeavour to work it out in every detail of our daily lives. If we in these days can reinforce that lesson and adapt our teaching of it to the needs of our generation, then I believe we shall be able to give to the men and women of our day something which they very sorely need. We have the answer to our questions in the Gospel of the Kingdom. That is the Gospel we must preach, and today is our day of opportunity.[28]

Wand gloried in the Church of England which, he asserted, alone among all the Christian bodies in the world, tried to fuse both Catholic and Protestant together in a unity which comprehends both. It enshrines the great principle of non-papal Catholicism, for it has never forfeited or renounced its heritage in the saints and in the teaching of the undivided Church. It inherits from the undivided Church the Creeds which define its faith and the sacraments and prayers which provide the norm of its devotion. It accepts the threefold ministry and episcopal succession, the continuity of priestly office and of sacramental ministrations in direct descent from Christ and his Apostles. For Wand, the Reformation was not something of which to be ashamed; it was a removal of accretions and a cleansing of the deposit, providing controlled freedom and mystery in co-existence with catholicity and apostolicity.

Although Wand was devoted to serving London he was not parochial in outlook or commitment. He was Chairman of the Executive of the British Council of Churches and participated in the crucial discussions concerning the Church of South India. What he, as an inheritor of the Catholic tradition, meant by union, and that for which he longed, was the enjoyment of communion together of all those baptized into Christ; but, in keeping with the Catholic tradition, he held that this goal could not be achieved by leap-frogging over everything that lies in between.

By 1955 Wand was seventy and it was time to retire. In the

[28.] J.W.C. Wand, *Our Day of Opportunity* (London, 1948), quoted in John S. Peart-Binns, *op. cit.*, p.139.

following year he was granted what he had longed for in early days, for he was made a Canon of St Paul's. He attended services regularly and he wrote prolifically. In 1969 he resigned his Canonry and retired to Sussex. He died in 1977. Although he had not been a figure of the first rank historically, he was a Churchman of stature and significance in his own day and generation, and an important representative of the High Church tradition in the Church of England.

Overseas mission

The concern for mission shown by Wand was also central of the lives of a number of outstanding High Churchmen overseas. The post-war era was perhaps the time when a new type of missionary appeared: the person who assumed a more 'political' role and a greater social involvement than had previously been customary, and who was engaged in activities which were more clearly an integral part of the local indigenous church life. This was in contrast to the pioneers of the late nineteenth and early twentieth centuries, and the change was simply a consequence of changed circumstances. The new type of missionary did not exclude the pioneer, for there remained many unevangelised areas of the world, but it was a distinctive mid-twentieth century development.

South Africa offers a good illustration of the new missionary role and strategy, and it is of note that some of the leading actors in the South African drama of the post-Second World War years were High Churchmen. Notable among these were G.H. Clayton, Ambrose Reeves, Joost de Blank and Trevor Huddleston. We will take two of these to demonstrate the link between 'home' and overseas mission work in what was rapidly becoming a global village, and the way these new type of missionaries exercised their ministry in an overseas country.

Richard Ambrose Reeves (1899–1980)

Richard Ambrose Reeves was born on 6 December 1899.

Before going up to Cambridge his life among a variety of 'ordinary' people gave him a good grounding for his future ministry. His father was a pharmacist who became manager of a pharmacy in East Anglia. He attended the local Church of England school and then won a scholarship to Great Yarmouth Grammar School. When he was just seventeen, in 1917, he was enlisted into the Army. It was while he was undertaking military service that he felt the first stirring of desire to offer himself for the priesthood as a means whereby he could serve others. After the war he went to the Knutsford Test School in Cheshire which had been established by the two Archbishops as a place where ex-servicemen could further their education, and test their vocation to the ordained ministry. By now his calling was clear. He entered Sidney Sussex College, Cambridge, in 1921. During his time there his interest in post-war social reconstruction based on Christian principles, which had been growing for some years, was fostered by the writings and speeches of Charles Gore, William Temple and G.A. Studdert-Kennedy. He also became more politically aware.

After graduation, he went to Mirfield College, where the singleness of purpose of the Mirfield Fathers – to serve God and man – was absorbed by him and became an essential part of his own character. He was ordained, and then spent a year at the General Theological Seminary in New York. After marriage in 1931, he served as Rector of a Scottish Episcopal Church in Fife, then on the staff of the World Student Christian Federation, then as Vicar of the industrial parish of St James the Great, Haydock in the diocese of Liverpool, before doing a magnificent work of rebuilding, renewing and restructuring as Rector of Liverpool Parish Church from 1942 to 1949, in a parish ravaged by war, with its church damaged by enemy action. Not only did he inspire and lead the parish in its recovery, but he was in great demand as a speaker, preacher, chairman and committee member. He was also, as we have noted, one of the group of High Churchmen who produced the Report, *Catholicity,* in 1947. Whatever his other activities it was, however, his intervention in the Liverpool Dock Strike of 1945 which introduced him to the general public far beyond Liverpool. In this action he helped as a mediator to bring the strike to a reasonable conclusion. He had demonstrated in a number of ways that he was a man of God who was concerned to be intimately involved in public affairs, and the scope for this was immeasurably increased when he was enthroned in June 1949 as Bishop of Johannesburg.

Throughout his time in South Africa Reeves combined a number of interlocking roles. He was especially 'a disturbing prophetic presence' and 'an evangelist looking for ways to build up the Church into a real loving, caring, worshipping community'.[29] After an initial period of surveying the Diocese, he called together the Evangelistic Council, and embarked on a three-year evangelistic campaign. In 1951 there were Church Weeks to give to members of the Anglican Church a greater understanding of what their churchmanship meant, and to instil in them a greater sense of personal responsibility for spreading the Good News of the Gospel. They were a great success, and were followed in 1952 by Family Weeks, and a Family Life Exhibition. The third and final phase of the campaign took the form of Crusade Weeks in 1953 in which a team of missioners from various countries, all experienced in evangelistic work, headed up an evangelistic thrust reminiscent of the Mission to London.

Reeves achieved a worldwide reputation as a consequence of his forthright, sustained and heroic struggle for social justice and civil rights. He abhorred apartheid, and everything directly or indirectly connected with it. He regarded it, and the treatment of non-Whites in the name of apartheid, as unjust and un-Christian. He believed that the Church had a duty to speak out against the system, the philosophy which underlay it, and the actions it provoked. He appreciated the difficulty of ordering the life of a complex, multi-racial society. He was not a fanatical agitator or demonical antagonist, but a reconciler. He could not see common ground between what he regarded as a Christian understanding and the policy being adopted by Dr Malan and his government, but nevertheless searched for it. He concluded that it could not be found.

[29.] John S. Peart-Binns, *Ambrose Reeves* (London 1973), p.71, a book on which this section on Reeves is based.

In his crusade against apartheid Reeves was prepared to work in alliance with Marxists and Liberals and others with different ideological outlooks than his own. He vigorously opposed The Suppression of Communism Act, The Native Laws Amendment Bill and The Bantu Education Act, and in doing so he found himself in opposition not only to leaders of the state, but also to other members of the Episcopal Synod. He was first an irritant to the Government, then he became a declared enemy. He challenged the authorities not with emotional appeals but with facts. Facts about the severe discrimination which condemned the non-Whites to a much inferior education system than the Whites; facts which showed the appalling housing situation in the shanty towns; facts which made evident the depressed and depressing conditions endured by masses of non-Whites, and the effect in their daily lives of being treated as inately inferior to the Whites. He made the facts known abroad, and especially in England and the United States of America. He travelled, he spoke, he wrote articles, he contributed to a number of books and he enlightened visitors to South Africa. He intervened with appeals in court cases, and especially where the death sentence had been pronounced, and he was not infrequently successful. He acted promptly and effectively in the 1956 treason trials, and the Government was humiliatingly defeated. He chaired an organisation for co-ordinating some fourteen bodies, all opposed to apartheid, with the aim of concertedly resisting the Government on certain issues. It was 'probably the most important and potentially effective instrument of opposition to the Nationalist Government of its time', and Reeves was 'possibly the one man in South Africa capable of uniting all opposing factions to the Government's policies against the Government'.[30] He became the friend and trusted adviser of African leaders like Chief Albert Luthuli and Oliver Tambo. He counselled and assisted a multitude of individuals, and he encouraged African writers, artists and musicians. He was a force in the land.

The climax for Reeves came with the most tragic consequence of the pass laws – the massacre at Sharpville on 21 March 1960.

[30.] John S. Peart-Binns, *Ambrose Reeves, op.cit.*, p.202.

The pass laws were the most effective method employed by the Government for enforcing apartheid. A large unarmed crowd of mainly Africans, including a high proportion of women and children had, it appears, gathered for a variety of reasons including a protest against the pass laws. It seems that they were noisy but unaggressive. As the hours passed the increasing number of people was accompanied by larger and larger police reinforcements. The details of what happened, and what was the sequence of events was never made plain. It was stated that an order was given to 'Load five rounds', and that two policemen opened fire, to be followed by fifty others, using service revolvers, rifles and sten guns. But the devastating consequence was not in doubt. Sixty-nine people were killed, including 8 women and 10 children, and of the one hundred and eighty people wounded, 31 were women and 19 children. It all happened in a fateful forty seconds, during which time seven hundred and five rounds were fired. The event sent a shock wave around the world.

Reeves was not present at the time, but when informed he immediately sprang into action. He visited the wounded in hospital, comforted the bereaved, organised legal aid, helped in the organisation of a fund to provide food, clothing and money to assist the dependents of the wounded and killed, and fed the press with information. What he did was decisive. He had become the leading white radical figure in South Africa. It was in no small measure due to him that there was an official enquiry, and that there was more than one side presented to it. Sharpville was a crisis point for South Africa, and also in Reeves' career.

Well-informed African friends told him that he was on the list of those to be arrested by the Government under powers conferred by a declared State of Emergency. After consulting others, he made a decision which many held against him for the rest of his life – he resolved to leave the country. He travelled to England via Swaziland, determined that if he was to be silenced in South Africa, then he would speak elsewhere. And so he did. The world's Press gave him headline treatment, and he undertook a heavy schedule of speaking engagements.

The rest of his career was in many ways a somewhat sad

epilogue. In his absence he was invited by his diocese to resign, but he returned to Johannesburg to re-assert his authority. He was almost immediately deported – the first time that such action had been taken against an Anglican in South Africa. Again, the event attracted major publicity on a world scale. By taking such a step the Government had done what it had been anxious to avoid, and made him into a martyr. He returned to England, but no post was offered to him for almost two years, largely perhaps because his previous flight from his diocese had left the Church authorities in doubt about his suitability for otherwise appropriate work. Then, in May 1962 he accepted appointment as General Secretary of the Student Christian Movement. It was not a very satisfactory solution, and during his tenure of the post he aroused much opposition. After three years a meeting implied, if it did not actually pass, a vote of no confidence, and he resigned. He again left a sphere of work without further work to go to. In the same year he accepted appointment as Priest-in-Charge of the church of St Michael-in-Lewes, and was formally licensed to take charge in April 1966. It was a quiet and undramatic ending to a full, drama-filled, purposeful and dedicated Christian career.

Trevor Huddleston (b. 1913)

Trevor Huddleston was born in 1913. His father, Captain Sir Ernest Huddleston, served in the Indian Navy and became Director of the Royal Indian Marine.

He was educated at Lancing and Christ Church, Oxford, and then went for training to Wells Theological College. He was greatly influenced in his undergraduate days by the arrival of hunger-marchers in Oxford on their way to London during the depression, and was impressed by the Anglo-Catholic movements commitment to socialism. He was ordained in 1937, and served as a curate at St Mark's, Swindon, where he met, and immensely liked, the railwaymen of the area. This experience persuaded him to become a monk, and he joined the Community of the Resurrection in 1939 taking the three vows of poverty, chastity and obedience. In 1943 he was sent to

South Africa to be Priest-in-Charge of the Community's Mission in Sophiatown. In 1949 he was appointed Provincial of the Community in South Africa, and Superintendent of St Peter's School, which has been called 'the Black Eton of South Africa'.

He became a legend in South Africa, loved by the black people and feared and hated by many whites, especially those in authority. The black people called him 'Makhalipile', the dauntless one, after a bold warrior who had been adopted by another people when their leaders were lost or captured. What seems to have especially appealed to the Africans was his great sense of humour and joyous nature which had such affinity with the African character. In 1956, for reasons which are still unclear, he was recalled to England and appointed Master of Novices. Through his writings, most notably his book *Naught for Your Comfort,* and his frequent media communications, he became a household name. He used all the opportunities he could to promote support for those engaged in the struggle against apartheid in South Africa and the establishment of a just and equitable society. Underpinning his lifelong struggle was his theological view of man:

> I believe that, because God became Man, therefore human nature in itself has a dignity and a value which is infinite. I believe that this conception necessarily carries with it the idea that the State exists for the individual, not the individual for the State. Any doctrine based on racial or colour prejudice and enforced by the State is therefore an affront to human dignity and 'ipso facto' an insult to God himself. It is for this reason that I feel bound to oppose not only the policy of the present Government of the Union of South Africa but the legislation which flows from this policy.[31]

It was not in books that he learned to hate apartheid, but in his encounters with people. He found by experience that the entrenchment of racism was totally destructive of people,

---

[31.] Trevor Huddleston, *Naught for Your Comfort* (1956), p.16.

denying them the gifts they had. In Sophiatown Huddleston raised his hat to a black washerwoman. It was a revelation to her son Desmond Tutu, who happened to be watching, as he had never before seen a white man do such a thing, and there and then he decided on his vocation. And, in keeping with his personal motto, 'Act on impulse', Huddleston also provided the fourteen-year-old Hugh Masekela, who was to become a jazz musician of world renown, with his first trumpet.

Although he loved England dearly, he still perhaps yearned for the continent and country he left. In 1960 he went back to Africa as Bishop of Masasi in what became Tanzania, where he remained until 1968, when he became Bishop of Stepney. From 1978 to 1983 he was Bishop of Mauritius and Archbishop of the Indian Ocean. He then once more returned to England, but not to a life of retirement and ease, for, late in life, with his accustomed energy and enthusiasm, he undertook the daunting and demanding task of President of the Anti-Apartheid Movement, with its punishing round of meetings and letter-writing. Here indeed was a new-style, late twentieth century missionary.

18

A High Churchman at the Helm

By the time that Michael Ramsey became Archbishop of Canterbury in 1961 the secularisation to which we alluded in the last chapter was gaining pace and taking a firmer grip on society; and this was increasingly so during his archiepiscopate. 'Since 1960 declining membership, attendance, Sunday-school participation, baptisms, confirmations, and numbers of candidates offering themselves for the professional ministry have presented a consistent picture of massive crisis.'[1] In the 1960s Episcopalian Easter Day communicants fell by 24.5% in England. In 1957 Gallup found that 14% said they had been to church the previous Sunday, but this figure dropped to 12% in 1958 and 10% in 1963.[2] The number of people on the Church of England Electoral Roll had declined from 3,638,000 in 1925 to 3,423,000 in 1940, to 2,959,000 in 1950, 2,862,000 in 1960 and 2,692,000 in 1964. As a rate per 1,000 of the total population this represented 143 in 1925, 120 in 1940, 96 in 1950, 89 in 1960 and 81 in 1964.[3]

The work of the Church of England was hindered by a decline in the total number of parish clergy, and this had dire consequences for the ministry of the Church in rural and urban areas. The total number of Church of England clergy dropped from 15,488 in 1961 to 15,223 in 1971 and, drastically to 10,922 in 1981. The decline had been evident from the

---

[1] Alan D. Gilbert, *The Making of Post-Christian Britain*, p.77.
[2] Peter Brierley, *'Christian England'. What the English Church Census Reveals* (London, 1991), p.58.
[3] Bryan Wilson, *Religion in Secular Society*, p.29.

beginning of the century and by 1990 almost every rural area which by then comprised a rural deanery had lost approximately one clergyman every 15 years since 1900. And the situation was even worse in urban areas because, as the *Leslie Paul Report* made clear in 1964, a disproportionate number of the clergy worked in rural areas. Whereas there was one Anglican clergyman per thousand of the population in the countryside, in the towns and cities it was one per six thousand. The *Sheffield Report* ten years later introduced a formula which was an attempt to deploy the clergy in such a way that there would be a significant redistribution in favour of urban ministry. Nevertheless, despite this wholly commendable attempt to adjust its ministry, the Church was conscious that it faced a grave situation which was becoming worse.

In his sociological analysis published in 1964, Bryan Wilson commented:

> In general, there can be little doubt about the decline in church-going, church-membership, sustained religious commitment, and the general standing of the Church in society. It is evident that institutionally the Church remains favourably placed, and that its agencies are well entrenched in many respects. The conclave of the Church – the Anglican Church Assembly and Convocation – remain important forums of opinion, and their debates receive publicity and attention. In their representation in the House of Lords, reduced in significance as that assembly now is, the bishops have another vehicle for the expression of Anglican opinion through which to influence the social, political and moral life of the nation. But even these facilities have more the appearance of power than the reality of it...[4]

At the same time as this decline in institutional religion, the majority of the population professed to believe in God. For example, the Independent Television Authority's 1970 *Opinion Research Centre Survey of Popular Attitudes* found that 29% of

---

[4.] Bryan Wilson, *op.cit.*, p.39.

British people who disclaimed membership of any church or denomination still described themselves as 'very' or 'fairly' religious. Although a smaller proportion of the total population in lower socio-economic groups attended church, a higher proportion than in the middle socio-economic groups assented to certain basic assertions of Christian belief. To the statement 'Jesus Christ is the Son of God', 89% of the former category said 'True', compared with 79% of the latter; and to the statement 'People who believe in Jesus as the Son of God can expect salvation', the response was respectively 71% and 59%. All this indicates that then, as possibly for the next few decades, there was probably a widespread, ill-defined religious disposition among the total population which did not express itself in terms of church attendance.

Here indeed was a challenging situation for the Church of England, and more particularly for Archbishop Michael Ramsey. And as he was also for many years the foremost representative of the High Church tradition in the Church of England, and has been regarded subsequently by Catholic Anglicans as an example to be followed in his teaching and practice, we will consider his life and views in some detail. We will then proceed to an extended account and analysis of the most pressing issues with which he and other Anglican Catholics had to grapple, and we will conclude by reflecting on some of the theological, sociological and other factors which contributed to the further Anglican Catholic decline during these years.

Arthur Michael Ramsey (1904–88)

'No biographer, not even a Boswell, could write Michael Ramsey's life. It needs the mannerisms, the tone of voice, the unspoken humour which is not communicable.'[5] To capture something of his quality and character, and describe his main activities and achievements in the space of a few pages is hard

---

[5.] Dick Ladborough, quoted in Owen Chadwick, *Michael Ramsey. A Life* (Oxford, 1990), p.v. This is an excellent book on which we rely heavily in our description of the life and work of Michael Ramsey.

indeed, and does but little justice to such a complex and interesting character.

Ramsey was born in Cambridge on 14 November 1904 into a family which was alive with religious and Socialist belief and activity. His father was a Congregationalist minister. His mother was a child of the vicarage, but attended the Congregationalist church. During her short life she was a Socialist and a suffragette. Although she was not a violent demonstrator, she worked hard, was vociferous at meetings, campaigned for votes for women, and, after the First World War, was active in the co-operative movement and the Labour Party. Socialist thinkers and politicians were frequent visitors to the Ramsey home.

After various attempts to educate him locally, Michael was sent on a scholarship to Repton. During his early life he had considered himself somewhat backward, especially in comparison with his academically able brother, Frank, and other people thought him rather odd in his behaviour. At Repton, under the headmastership of Geoffrey Fisher, he was not good at sport, achieved a reputation for absent mindedness in the cricket outfield, quaintness of character and studiousness. That is, he continued to be regarded as odd. In his last years at the school he was happier, largely because he discovered a gift as a debater, and established a very considerable reputation in the school as a participant in the debating society. He 'won the right to be an oddity'.[6] He also developed an interest in Anglo-Catholicism. In 1922 he won the top classical scholarship to Magdalene College, Cambridge.

At University he soon made a name for himself in Union debates. In 1925 he became Secretary of the Union, in the same year vice-president, and in the following year president. Patrick Devlin, a contemporary at Cambridge, regarded Ramsey as the most effective speaker of his time. He used his powers of oratory in a sustained effort to resurrect the ailing Liberalism at Cambridge during a period when it was being widely conjectured that Liberalism was at an end, and that the future lay between the Conservatives and the Socialists. He was popular

[6.] Owen Chadwick, *op.cit.*, p.11.

with the Union and very impressive. On one occasion Asquith, having heard him speak, publicly prophesied that he would one day be the leader of the Liberal Party. In his second year at Cambridge he declined an offer to be Liberal candidate for the County of Cambridgeshire because of the need to concentrate on academic work, but he had decided that his career would be in politics.

Throughout his years at Magdalene he was seeking a spiritual home. An early interest in church architecture and brasses drove him out on exploratory tours of the countryside, and in so doing he discovered Anglo-Catholic churches which fascinated him with their noticeboards, chancel fittings and ornaments. 'He rode his bicycle like a pilgrim on the quest for a holy city.'[7] Anglo-Catholicism in Cambridge was strong, and in the nearby parish church of St Giles he found that for which he had been seeking, 'a sense of mystery, and awe, and of another world at once far and near'.[8] Gradually he began to place greater importance on the eternal verities than on political excitements. He was persuaded that more could be done for humanity by Churches than by political parties. The Churches touched upon a more profound level of engagement with the human predicament than even his most cherished Liberal Party. But he was still uncertain of his rightful place among various Christian traditions. He tried meetings of the Student Christian Movement and was bored. He tried CICCU, the evangelical Christian body in the University, and was repelled by the literalist approach to the Bible. In 1926 there was a mission at the University, and William Temple as the chief missioner convinced him that the quiet explanation of a Christian philosophy of life was the right way to expound Christianity in modern society.

In 1926 he abandoned the study of law and switched to theology, in which he obtained a first class degree. His new studies refined and consolidated his Anglo-Catholicism, and he opted to go to Cuddesdon to prepare for the ordained ministry. Barely two weeks after his arrival his mother was killed

---

[7.] Owen Chadwick, *op.cit.,* p.17.
[8.] Quoted in Owen Chadwick, *op.cit.,* p.22.

in a car crash in a car which his father was driving. The effect on Michael was devastating, and for many months he was under a psychiatrist. In 1928 he was ordained deacon, and he was appointed curate of St Nicholas, the parish church of Liverpool. The experience helped to ground him in the situations and life styles of ordinary people, but in 1930 it was with a sense of relief that he left the parish to take up an academic post as sub-warden of Lincoln Theological College. At Lincoln he lectured on biblical and doctrinal matters. He also wrote a book which was later published as *The Gospel and the Catholic Church*.

In 1936 he once again became a curate, this time at Boston in Lincolnshire. Then, in 1939, he moved back to Cambridge as vicar of St Benet's, but he remained there only a few months before he was appointed Professor of Divinity at Durham University and Canon of Durham Cathedral. Soon after this, his life was transformed and enriched by his marriage in 1942: it provided the companionship, support and mutual understanding which were to be so important in the rest of his life and career.

At Durham he taught and wrote. As we have previously noted, he was chairman and principal author of the report to the Archbishop of Canterbury on *Catholicism* (1947). He travelled – notably to Amsterdam in 1947 as a consultant at the first meeting of the World Council of Churches. Then, in 1950, he was appointed Regius Professor of Divinity at Cambridge. Two professorships in succession and now back in his beloved Cambridge, it seemed that he was settled in academic work for the remainder of his career. But soon he was faced with perhaps the hardest decision of his life, for in 1952 he was offered the bishopric of Durham: he accepted, and was consecrated on 29 September 1952.

As a bishop, Ramsey relished parish confirmations, the care and counselling of ordinands, the friendship of clergy and lay Church people which he took time to cultivate, and the pastoral and teaching aspects of his ministry. He was not good at consulting with the suffragan bishop or the archdeacons who expected to be consulted. And he later regretted that he had not moved about more among the wider community or

done all that he might have done about the miners and the
working men, although this was possibly too self-deprecating
for he was popular in the mining parishes. Throughout these
years he was manifestly growing in stature. He 'was already a
leader, not just in the diocese of Durham, but in the Church.
He had a big personality. What he said counted...The Catholic
minds in the Church rejoiced to have one of such influence,
and such prayerfulness, high in the counsels of their Church.'[9]

In 1956 he was translated to York, amid protest from John
Kensit, the secretary of the Protestant Truth Society. At York,
as at Durham, it was perhaps his pastoral concern which
elicited most appreciation. He continued to conduct retreats,
and the work dearest to his heart was the development of the
Retreat House at Wydale Hall near Scarborough. At the
Lambeth Conference in 1958 he was outstanding and confirmed
the opinion of many bishops that he should be their next
leader. He did not disguise his Anglo-Catholicism: he addressed
the Church Union, the organ of Anglo-Catholics, at their
eucharistic congress just before the Lambeth Conference, and
attended a memorial requiem for Lord Halifax. By his open
and continued encouragement of Anglo-Catholicism he
offended Geoffrey Fisher, the Archbishop of Canterbury, and
caused Fisher to doubt his suitability for Canterbury. Doubt he
might, but Ramsey was translated to Canterbury and enthroned
in June 1961. An avowed Anglo-Catholic was at the helm.

Ramsey was Archbishop for thirteen years, and it was a full,
varied and eventful archiepiscopate. In all that time he had
definite priorities, preferences and dislikes. He disliked, and
was bored by administration, except in vital matters like the
choice of bishops, or personal correspondence; and there was
plenty of the latter. There were about fifty letters a day, and
Ramsey tried to deal with those which required his individual
attention. 'The greater part of my time as a Christian pastor',
he said, 'is spent in helping ordinary people.'[10] His predecessor,
Fisher, had been a gifted administrator, and Ramsey's

9. Owen Chadwick, *op.cit.*, p.86.
10. Quoted in Owen Chadwick, *op.cit.*, p.114.

shortcomings, and especially his ineptness at man-management, made staff relations somewhat difficult.

Prominent among the moral issues which loomed large in Ramsey's time as Archbishop, and on which he was expected to pronounce or arrange for the Church to comment, were homosexuality, the re-marriage in Church of divorced people and the question of the grounds on which divorce was acceptable, abortion, euthanasia, capital punishment and race relations; and on all these he gave a lead which was well considered and, in some instances, as, for example, on the matter of race relations, unambiguous, fearless and uncompromising. He had not lost his earlier concern, and even passion, for social justice. He was still a Liberal politician at heart, and his yearning for a just and fair society led him to forthright condemnations of South African apartheid and the Rhodesian regime of Ian Smith, which provoked violent criticism from some politicians and civic leaders. Indeed, as a result of his pronouncements he was suddenly at the centre of what has been described as 'the windiest political storm endured by an Archbishop of Canterbury since the revolution of 1688'.[11] In retrospect Ramsey wondered how he survived 1965, when the storm was at its height, and thought that he had been helped by a kind of interior peace which he had learned at Cuddesdon.

Ramsey was an ecumenist by conviction and in practice. For example, he was not against women priests, but was against the Church doing something so unusual and fundamentally contentious and divisive without reference to other Churches. He wanted it to be an act of the whole Church. He valued the Catholic inheritance, and the link with Catholic Christendom in the East and the West, and hoped that the ordination of women would not be conceded until it was endorsed by the whole Church. He rejoiced in his spiritual affinity with such leaders as Athenagoras, the Ecumenical Patriarch of Constantinople. In 1956 he visited Moscow, and again experienced a spiritual empathy with Orthodox believers as he joined with them in worship, and he developed a close friendship

[11.] Owen Chadwick, *op.cit.*, p.205.

with Patriarch Alexei. The subsequent visit of Alexei to Lambeth in 1964 was the first such visit ever of a Patriarch of Moscow to Britain. It was a high point of harmony between Canterbury and Moscow. Ramsey greatly valued the Orthodox tradition, studied its classical documents, used its liturgies and respected its monastic ideals. He wanted members of the Anglican Church to appreciate the Orthodox way and thereby grow into a fuller understanding of Catholicity.

The Vatican Council and the new openness of the Roman Church to Protestants was welcomed by Ramsey. Geoffrey Fisher had visited the Vatican in an unofficial capacity; in 1966 Ramsey made an official visit. Demonstrators wearing black armbands marched across Lambeth Bridge to the gate of Lambeth Palace, and Dr Ian Paisley led a group of protestors in a much publicised demonstration at the airport. Ramsey met Pope Paul Vl in the Sistine chapel. His proposal for a joint commission of theologians was accepted and became what was subsequently called ARCIC. The Pope and the Archbishop worshipped together in the basilica of St Paul-without-the-walls, the place where, it was supposed, St Paul was buried. An agreed declaration was read, and at the end of the service Pope and Archbishop jointly said the blessing in Latin. They exchanged the kiss of peace and went forth, walking side by side amid a clapping and cheering crowd. When the Pope said goodbye, he gave Ramsey perhaps the most precious gift he was able to bestow, for he slipped off his episcopal ring and put it on Ramsey's palm, and Ramsey put it on his own fingure. 'No Pope could have said anything louder about that vexing sore over the validity of Anglican Orders. It spoke more loudly than any bull or encyclical.'[12] Ramsey wore it for the remainder of his life, and after his death his wife, Joan, gave it to Archbishop Runcie so that it should become the permanent property of the see of Canterbury. Not all was harmony between Rome and Canterbury, and there were not infrequent moments of crisis, tension and irritation, but a new era had been inaugurated in Anglican-Roman Catholic relations.

[12.] Owen Chadwick, *op. cit.*, p.322.

The Anglo-Catholic lover of Eastern Orthodoxy and friend of Roman Catholicism was also deeply committed to the concept of Anglican-Methodist unity. The failure of the scheme to unite the two churches has been portrayed as the big failure of his life, although it is difficult to see what he could have done to steer it through, or where he failed. Probably Ramsey had dedicated himself to the scheme because his understanding of Catholicity had changed with his wider experience of the world and of other Churches. It is apparent that the rejection of the scheme hurt him greatly. It was near to shattering his faith in the Church of England and his enthusiasm for it.

Ramsey was above all else a man of God, with all the sense of vulnerability of one who was sensitive to suffering in himself and in others, and all the humility of one who was deeply aware of his human frailty. In many respects he was a man who was in the world but not of the world, although he was profoundly in touch with the life of the world. He longed that righteousness and justice should prevail, yet his engagement with the affairs of the world was only achieved as a consequence of great self-control and personal discipline. He loved monks and nuns, and his ideal of religion was quietness and retirement. He loved silence and contemplation, but also loved the complementary pastoral activity of caring for others and service in the world. He loved Taizé as a religious community, full of young, questioning people, with Catholics and Protestants worshipping and praying together. He was convinced that the world was suffering from lack of silence and stillness. Prayer was not to him an isolated religious experience but part of a many-sided converse between the soul and its Maker; a part of the total experience of life in which the beauty of nature, the events of history, the stirrings of conscience and the inspired writings or utterances of men and women all had their part.

Ramsey retired in 1974, and died, 'peacefully, still cherished by Joan, still with his sense of glory, in the early hours of 23 April 1988'.[13]

[13.] Owen Chadwick, *op.cit.*, p.398.

Honest to God

It is ironic that it was during the years of Michael Ramsey's archiepiscopate of Canterbury that the Anglican Catholics exhibited signs of that crisis of identity which was to become acute in the succeeding two decades and more. It was partly that they, in common with the Church of England as a whole, had to cope with three major issues: a surge of liberalism within the Church, epitomised by the publication of John A.T. Robinson's *Honest to God* (1963); the consequences of the Second Vatican Council; and the debate and decisions concerning Anglican-Methodist unity. It was partly that many of the goals for which their forefathers had fought had been achieved: Catholic teaching on such matters as the spiritual conception of the Church, the centrality of the sacraments in the life of the Church and especially the importance of the Eucharist, liturgical reform and the development of religious orders. What was their rightful place within the Church of England at a time when there was so much flux? The Evangelicals were beginning to experience a marked increase in confidence and cohesion, which was to continue for the ensuing twenty years, until the end of our period, but this only helped to emphasise the decline of the Anglican Catholics.

'Whatever its other merits may be, Dr J A T Robinson's best-selling paper-back volume *Honest to God* has at any rate attracted attention to a movement in present-day theology which, while it has not perhaps the monopoly of enlightenment and constructive thought with which some of its more fervent exponents have credited it, may be more widespread than has been commonly recognised in English-speaking religious circles.'[14] Thus spake one Anglican Catholic, E.L. Mascall, two years after *Honest to God* had taken the unsuspecting general lay Christian public by storm in 1963. A process was seen by many churchmen to be taking place which Mascall described as 'the secularisation of Christianity', and *Honest to God* was perceived

---

[14] E.L. Mascall, *The Secularisation of Christianity: An Analysis and a Critique* (London, 1965), p.40.

as the most public and explicit declaration and evidence of this trend: the sudden emergence of radicalism at the heart of the Established Church. Even if, as was pointed out at the time, it was but expressing in a popular form what was commonplace among theologians, it was a shock to the uninitiated. Here was a questioning of the very fundamentals of the faith, or at least the traditional language in which such fundamentals were expounded; and here was an alarming new morality which seemed to endorse or give encouragement to the prevailing liberalism and libertinism of the age. In the face of such developments there was a quite widespread failure of nerve which 'stampeded many contemporary theologians into a total intellectual capitulation to their secular environment'.[15] Anglican Catholics were disturbed as much as any other churchmen, but they were fortunate in having two such competent theologians as Ramsey and Mascall to respond to *Honest to God* and all that it represented.

Michael Ramsey was a pastor at heart, and charged with pastoral responsibility of a high order as Archbishop of Canterbury, as well as being an eminent theologian. It was therefore very appropriate that his most widely read response to *Honest to God* took the form of a small pamphlet which had in mind people who had been perplexed by the ferment of ideas about God and religion.

'It is', said Ramsey, 'the putting of our own feeble little grasp of God, or our own individual picture of God himself which is the peril of "religion".' But he saw a greater peril still. Religion could mean 'a set of pious attitudes and practices within which we look for God, forgetting that God may sometimes be found less amongst them than amongst the things we call non-religious or secular'.[16]

Ramsey pointed out that some Christian thinkers, for instance Paul Tillich, had asked modern man not to look for God in religion at all, as had been the way in the past, but to look for God in the midst of the human relationships of everyday life in

---

[15.] E.L. Mascall, *op. cit.*, p.282.

[16.] Arthur Michael Ramsey, *Image Old and New* (London, 1963), pp.3, 4.

our secular existence, and he showed some sympathy for this view. He thought that there was validity in helping a man who is estranged from ordinary religious talk to find God by thinking in depth about himself and his own meaning. Indeed, Ramsey suggested that many who had tried to commend Christian belief in recent years had been saying such a thing in a similar way. Dietrich Bonhoeffer had, however, gone further and suggested that all religion was obsolete, and must go. It was part of man's immaturity and must be replaced by man's own discovery of purpose, love and ultimate reality in the depth of his being and in the concrete situations of human relationships. In *Honest to God,* the Bishop of Woolwich had asked that Christianity should be separated from religion, and he declared the prevailing and traditional image of God to be outmoded.

Ramsey asserted that even if the frame of a Christian's relation to God is to be set within the secular it will still be a relation to a Beyond. 'Call it deep down, but it always means a Beyondness...' And he asked if, despite any possible radical changes in terminology and presentation, religion will not remain with us: 'reverence, awe, dependence, adoration, and penitence'.[17]

On the matter of Christ's divinity, Ramsey said that he had 'never met either a "simple" Christian or a theologian who believed that God travelled through space to visit the planet'. The background of the orthodox doctrine was the contrast between Creator and creature and it was in that contrast that the imagery about 'coming down' was used. 'One who is divine, the Creator, by an act of divine humility took upon himself our creaturely human existence.'[18]

He was concerned that much in Robinson's treatment of the New Testament was left obscure, especially in relation to the atonement and the resurrection, which were demythologised.

He argued for the centrality in the Christian life of withdrawal, and while he acknowledged the dangers of worship and prayer becoming unrelated to the world and not being set within the

---

[17.] Arthur Michael Ramsey, *op.cit.*, p.7.
[18.] Arthur Michael Ramsey, *op.cit.*, p.9.

common life, he believed that the new way of thinking, which gave such a prominent place to engagement in and with the world, was liable to miss out on a whole dimension of truth – an inescapable strain of asceticism and renunciation was to be found both in the Gospels and in a long line of great exponents of the Christian way.

Although Ramsey expressed appreciation of the new approach to morals, for instance in its concern to avoid legalism, he stressed that Christ came to fulfil and not to abolish the law, and the teaching of Paul made it clear that love did not supersede the law but profoundly expressed its meaning.

Mascall set himself to make an analysis of the case for secularised Christianity, as propounded in *Honest to God,* and by Paul van Buren in *The Secular Meaning of the Gospel,* to offer a critique, and to state the approach which he thought should characterise the Christian theologian. He was categorical in his assertion that one 'of the most imperative duties with which the Christian theologian is confronted is that of relating the revealed datum of Christian truth, final, absolute and fundamentally permanent as he must by his Christian commitment believe it to be, to the essentially incomplete, relative and constantly changing intellectual framework of the world in which he lives'.[19] This is necessary in order that Christians themselves shall 'understand their faith as adequately as is possible and feel at home in it as contemporary men and women'; in order that the Church may 'commend its message to those who are outside it'; and in order 'that Christians shall be able to see the relevance of their faith to the problems of contemporary society'[20] and bring their particular Christian understanding to bear upon the solution of those problems.

Mascall viewed the new school of Protestant theology, represented in the work of its best known if not most coherent exponent, John Robinson, as being a reaction to the long dominant biblical school of Karl Barth. The biblical school had conceived the primary task of the Christian theologian as the

[19.] E.L. Mascall, *op.cit.,* p.1.
[20.] E.L. Mascall, *op.cit.,* p.4.

proclamation and exposition of the Bible in biblical terms, and it had generally considered that both the application of critical techniques to the examination of the bible and the expression of Christian truth in contemporary non-biblical idiom to be outside the proper concern of theologians as such. The new school in contrast took as its starting-point the outlook of contemporary secularised man, and demanded that the traditional faith of Christendom should be completely transformed in order to conform to it. Mascall considered that this was particularly deplorable at a time when Western civilisation was, at least in its outlook, radically irreligious. It was said by the new theology that contemporary man was so radically secularised that he simply could not accept supernatural Christianity; therefore we must completely de-supernaturalise Christianity in order to give him something he can accept. Such an approach, said Mascall, was utterly unacceptable. It discarded the essentially unchanging Gospel, and not least among its weaknesses was its entire undermining of the whole notion of Christian social theology. Because it entirely capitulated to the outlook of the contemporary world it had no criterion for passing judgement on it. The 'whole of the great tradition of social thought which was revived in our own Church by F.D. Maurice and which produced such great figures as Gore, Temple and Widdrington is deprived of all ground and justification.'[21]

Mascall saw behind this new secularisation of Christianity the programme of 'demythologising' inaugurated by Rudolf Bultmann. By reinterpreting the Christian message in terms of the existential philosophy of Heidegger, Bultmann claimed that it was possible to discard 'myth' in the New Testament, but retain kerygma, and thereby avoid the discredited approach of the by then old-fashioned Liberal Protestantism which had rejected both 'myth' and kerygma. Mascall did not repudiate this out of hand, but while showing an appreciation of what Bultmann was attempting, he dismissed 'demythologising' as an undesirable and unjustifiable manifestation of the new theological reductionism.

[21.] E.L. Mascall, *op.cit.*, p.8.

Mascall made a careful, systematic and sympathetic assessment of *Honest to God,* determined to do his best to be fair to its author and not to concentrate on accidental obscurities of style or infelicities of phrasing. He concluded that in his resolve to undertake a radical recasting of Christianity, 'in the process of which the most fundamental categories of our theology – of God, of the supernatural, and of religion itself – must go into the melting, Robinson was 'a very unclear thinker and that his heart is where his head ought to be'.[22] Mascall was outspoken in his criticism. 'One might be pardoned', he wrote, 'for supposing that Robinson had despaired of trying to convert the world to Christianity and had decided instead to convert Christianity to the world.'[23] But even in that basic objective Robinson seemed to Mascall to contradict himself, and to be muddled in his thinking. Robinson had failed to see 'the importance of discriminating between the essential Christian Gospel and the forms in which it may be expressed at any particular epoch, difficult as it may be to draw the line with absolute precision'.[24]

It was, Mascall affirmed, over simplistic and inaccurate for Robinson to assert that Christians naively believed in a 'three-decker universe'. The Christian belief in God as the absolute necessary Being, could validly be expressed analogically in such spatial terms, but this was supplemented by the equally analogical notion of God as being everywhere.

Mascall wanted to conclude his review of *Honest to God,* and of the whole new theology of which it was a sample, on a positive and challenging note. He wrote:

> What we are called to in this twentieth century is not the abandonment of the accumulated treasures of our Christian heritage, but their putting at the service of the contemporary world. This will involve us in tasks of interpretation which will tax us to the uttermost as we try to interpret Christian truth not only to Western

[22.] E.L. Mascall, *op.cit.*, p.109.
[23.] E.L. Mascall, *op.cit.*, p.109.
[24.] E.L. Mascall, *op.cit.*, p.110.

industrialised, secularised man, but also to the people of
the East and of Africa, with their own great heritages of
philosophic thought and religious practice. After this
long and, I fear, extremely tedious examination of Dr
Robinson's programme, I can only repeat, though in a
sense presumably different from that which he intended,
that, in its exclusive concern with one small section of our
community, it is not too radical but not nearly radical
enough. It does not get down to the roots.[25]

Despite the robust, confident and authoritative responses of
Ramsey and Mascall, the new liberal theology which started to
be expressed at this time in a particularly strident manner, and
in a 'popular' form, did have a corrosive effect in the ranks of
High Churchmen. It both undermined and unsettled many
Anglican Catholics, and also found a home in some quarters.
It was a disturbing phenomenon for churchmen who in any
case were struggling with their own problems of identity and
purpose, and were beginning to have a collective sense of
insecurity and uncertainty about their distinctive beliefs and
their special role and function within the Church of England.

Vatican II

The second major event of the Ramsey era with which Anglican
Catholics had to come to terms was the Second Vatican Council
and all that flowed from it. Ever since the Oxford movement,
many Anglican Catholics have had a sneaking or open regard
for Roman Catholicism, and major changes in the life of that
Church have been of significance to them. This was undoubtedly
so with the Second Vatican Council. It was a watershed in
modern Roman Catholic history. The Council was convened
in 1962 and over the next few years promulgated radical
reforms designed to bring the Roman Catholic Church up-to-
date. Its effect was dramatic and global. It created a great sense

---

[25.] E.L. Mascall, *op.cit,*, p.189.

of freedom and openness and introduced measures and ideals which were seemingly copied from traditional Protestant churches. It caused confusion among Anglican Catholics, and little short of panic and despair among Anglo-Papalists.

The changes in liturgical practice were especially devastating to those who had looked to the Roman Catholic Church as the bastion of traditionalism, conservatism and orthodoxy. The previous, apparently sacrosanct, practices and cults of the Counter-Reformation, which a large number of Anglican Catholics had so much admired and copied, now suddenly became out of fashion, even forbidden. There was an overnight reversal of attitude and policy: that which a moment before had been regarded as sacred and inviolate, was, without warning, profaned, derided and abandoned. The rigid structure of the Tridentine mass, which was universally recognised and respected, which was seen as an ideal by many Anglican Catholics, was suddenly swept away. It was replaced by a new, variable structure, new musical settings and accompaniments, and the use of the vernacular. What had hitherto been a solomn, awesome service, with a profound sense of mystery pervading it, had, with alarming rapidity, been permeated with Protestant ideas and customs, making it 'a simple and direct, homely and even folksey, gathering'.[26] Evening masses, in apparent imitation of the previously much despised Protestant evening communion services, were also introduced. The previous seemingly immovable liturgical fixed points were being discarded, and Anglican Catholics were placed in a dilemma: whether to follow the example being set, or to diverge from the church which had hitherto provided their model in order to retain their long established liturgical principles and practices. It helped in the creation of uncertainty and confusion, and aggravated an already serious identity crisis.

[26.] W.S.F. Pickering, *Anglo-Catholicism* (1989), p.203. A book to which this present section is greatly indebted.

Other changes introduced by the Council only aggravated this problem for Anglican Catholics. Protestants were no longer denounced as heretics, but treated as separated brethren with whom dialogue should be conducted. Rules over Friday fasting were relaxed. The theology of the Church was reviewed, and the escalation of Marian doctrines halted. Greater freedom was granted to enter into 'dialogue with the contemporary world'.

The *Alternative Service Book 1980*

It was all very bewildering, and it was made more so by changes, especially liturgical changes, within the Church of England itself, for the 1960s saw the beginning of a progressively accelerating process of liturgical experimentation, which reached a high point with the acceptance of the Alternative Service Book (ASB) of 1980. Such changes caused further divisions of opinion within Anglican Catholicism. Some saw them as in keeping with the decrees of Vatican II, and they delighted in the extent to which Catholic ideas and practices had been incorporated into the new service book. Other more cautious and conservative Anglican Catholics preferred the 1662 Prayer Book and shunned what they regarded as changes in the ASB which were too Protestant in tone; and anyhow there was the beauty of the 1662 language. Such liturgical changes, and the varied reaction to them, further undermined the Anglican Catholic awareness of a common purpose.

Anglican–Methodist unity

The third traumatic experience for Anglican Catholics, as for the Church of England in general, during the sixties and early seventies was the whole sad saga of the abortive Anglican-Methodist unity scheme. Official conversations between the Church of England and the Methodist Church commenced in 1956. In 1963, *Conversations between the Church of England and the Methodist Church: A Report,* was published. It proposed a scheme of reunion in two stages. At the heart of stage one was a service of reconciliation bringing with it full communion, with Anglicans and Methodists being able to receive the sacraments in one another's churches, and with priests and ministers being able to officiate in either Church. It was proposed that the Methodist Church would accept the validity of the historic episcopate and, in the future, the practice of episcopal ordination. There would be unresolved matters such as the Church of England relationship with the Establishment, the need to synchronise the two administrative systems, the future of patronage and the parson's freehold, the fusion of diocesan and district structures, the acceptance by Methodists of episcopal confirmation, and a number of other issues.

The *Report* was referred to the dioceses for discussion, but this was, in the opinion of many, done in a haphazard and unsatisfactory way, as was the assessment of diocesan opinion. In May 1965 the convocations of the provinces of Canterbury and York decided that there was sufficient approval from the dioceses to allow the Church of England to enter into negotiations with the Methodist Church. It soon became clear that there was a groundswell of discontent and opposition in both Churches, and this involved many Anglican Catholics and Anglican Evangelicals as well as Methodists, the Voice of Methodism, the Methodist Revival Fellowship, the Church Union and the Society of the Holy Cross. Some of those who were unhappy about the basis and trend of the official negotiations were convinced that unity should be fostered and should grow out of local church life rather than be negotiated from on high; and there was a fear that the negotiations which had been initiated would result in a scheme which would cause division and even the creation of yet another dissenting body.

In 1967 the Anglican-Methodist Unity Commission published an interim statement, *Towards Reconciliation*. It was so worded that it seemed to be deliberately imprecise, and to so encourage an openness and liberty of interpretation in what it stated, that it made a virtue of excessive ambiguity – especially in the matter of the service of reconciliation, which could or could not be regarded as re-ordination. Those who opposed this ambiguity were particularly indignant at what they considered as doctrinal imprecision. The service of reconciliation would require doctrinal agnosticism in those who were to participate in it with a clear conscience. Graham Leonard, the High Church Bishop of Willesden, was especially vehement in his denunciation of the service and of the whole approach which it symbolised. The opposition was made all the more poignant by the frequently voiced criticism of the scheme by the former Archbishop of Canterbury, Lord Fisher. Leonard issued a statement with which other Anglican Catholics such as E.L. Mascall and the Rev. A.H. Simmons (Master of the Society of the Holy Cross) would probably have concurred, in which his convictions were clear and his accusations were set forth in unequivocal language:

> The report is suspect in general and in particular with regard to the honesty of what it advocates. The proposals for reconciliation involve an intentional ambiguity which makes the prayers of the service of reconciliation irrelevant. Many of us cannot see how, with a clear conscience, we can take part in prayers to God which are deliberately disingenuous. This is not a matter of a fine point of theology – it is a matter of common honesty. We believe that true Christian unity can only be achieved with the help of the Holy Ghost, the Spirit of Truth, and that this is completely incompatible with any deliberately determined disingenuity.... The proposals, as they stand, present a device to escape reality and a formula to avoid clarity. Far from achieving true unity, they will cause further divisions.[27]

Anglican Catholics and Evangelicals were not alone in their opposition to the proposed scheme, but they spearheaded the attack. It was unfortunate for the Anglican Catholic opponents that the Anglican Catholic Archbishop of Canterbury, Michael Ramsey, was identified so strongly with the scheme, and lay such great store by its acceptance and implementation.

On 8 July 1969 the Methodist Conference approved the scheme by a majority of 76%. The Church of England had

---

[27.] John S. Peart-Binns, *Graham Leonard. Bishop of London* (London, 1988), p.64.

decided that it must itself have 75% approval. After a debate of high quality the joint convocations, voting by houses, in total voted 263 for and 116 against – a 69% vote in favour, but insufficient for approval. To some that appeared to be the end, but advantage was taken by the proponents of the scheme of the soon to be inaugurated General Synod – and it was clear that the scheme would be reintroduced for decision by the newly established body. In the event this was merely a prolonging and intensification of the agony.

Meanwhile, in 1970, three Evangelicals, Colin Buchanan, Michael Green and James Packer, and two Anglican Catholics, Graham Leonard and E.L. Mascall, published *Growing into Union*, which produced fast and furious reactions. The Anglican Catholic authors differed from the Evangelical contributors in their perceptions and reasons for opposing the scheme, but all of them shared a genuine desire to seek to be obedient to what they saw as God's truth in the situation facing them and the two churches; and in doing so they found much common ground. They advocated

> a one-stage procedure, the nub of the matter being expressed in this way: [we would recommend] the simple expedient of inaugurating a united Church in a piecemeal way territorially, leaving the existing denominations to exist alongside each other in every place where conscience, even untutored conscience, might so decree. This is the conclusion, novel in the history of English ecumenical discussion, to which we have come. This will do justice to the various principles on which we wish to build far better than any other procedure which has suggested itself to us. And it is a principle which, if novel in England, has some precedent in South India. As South India is the only existing union in which Anglicans have joined, we may well look cautiously in that direction for help.[28]

Their goal was a reintegrated English Church which would embrace diversity while at the same time being genuinely

[28] John S. Peart-Binns, *op.cit.*, pp.75, 76.

national and comprehensive within explicit limits set by biblical essentials.

Although the approach advocated commanded quite widespread support, there was fierce criticism of both the content and the style of the book. Many Anglican Catholics were as unhappy with the proposed method of dealing with non-episcopally ordained ministers as they were about the proposals for this in the official scheme. The implementation of what was suggested was seen as possibly leading to administrative, legal and financial chaos. More fundamentally, the entire 'piece by piece' approach was regarded by certain of its critics as theologically unsound, highly divisive, and productive of little more than a form of congregationalism. Strong objection was also taken to what was described as the 'arrogant, polemical and even abusive' tone of the work, and the fact that the authors, in the opinion of some, 'displayed such self-satisfaction with the rightness of their views'.[29]

The book caused a stir and much discussion, but rather than responding to the challenge it presented, the authorities went ahead as they had previously planned, bent on reintroducing their own scheme. The day for a final decision was 3 May 1972. The vote of 333 for and 173 against gave a somewhat reduced majority, compared with the previous vote, of 65.8% The scheme was dead. The response was relief rather than rejoicing among the opponents, and mingled sadness, despair, bitterness and resignation among its supporters. The whole episode had done little if anything to unite or strengthen the Anglican Catholics. Some, like the scholar bishop and moral theologian R.C. Mortimer of Exeter, intensely disappointed opponents of the scheme, and riled advocates of integrity like Leonard, by openly supporting ambiguity; others, such as Ramsey, were accused of disloyalty to the High Church tradition. Indeed, there was a quite severe difference of opinion between Leonard and Ramsey. Leonard respected Ramsey for his intellectual stature, but he did not admire or stand in awe of him as almost all the other bishops did. He thought that the author of *The*

[29] Paul A. Welsby, *A History of the Church of England 1945–1984* (Oxford, 1984), p.171.

Gospel and the Catholic Church was not the appropriate leader for the runaway Church of the 1960s, nor the right person to give the right lead in the Anglican-Methodist scheme for unity. His mind was too subtle. And in any case Leonard thought that Ramsey had changed his theological position, and was accepting, encouraging or even initiating a uniformly liberal Church policy on major moral and ethical issues during these years. Ramsey's handling of the Anglican-Methodist unity dscussions only reinforced Leonard's apprehension; and Leonard's strident opposition to the official scheme was deeply resented by Ramsey. It was a tragedy for Anglican Catholicism that during the years when it was beginning to struggle with an identity crisis its two foremost leaders were at such odds with each other. It was also perhaps ironic that such an intense and extended debate over the scheme for unity, and such momentous decisions on the question of unity, should have caused such anguish and such disunity, and should have contributed to a deterioration in the fortunes of an Anglican Catholicism which was already in a state of decline.

Charismatic renewal

Lastly, in this review of the years of Ramsey's archiepiscopate, it is pertinent to recall that his thirteen years at the helm coincided with the early period of the modern charismatic movement in England. Between 1962 and 1964 members of the Church of England became vaguely aware that something new and extraordinary was happening in parishes like St. Mark's Gillingham, St Mark's, Cheltenham and St Paul's, Beckenham, where there were reports of speaking in 'tongues'. In 1964 Michael Harper founded the Fountain Trust to assist Christians in all denominations who had been 'baptised in the Spirit'. During the next decade this movement of renewal grew and received an ever greater public profile.

For most of this time Anglican Catholics were generally indifferent or hostile to this unfamiliar phenomenon. In other parts of the Anglican Communion the response, as with the Church of the Redeemer in Houston, USA, was different, and local church life was transformed. 'It was the spread of the charismatic renewal among Roman Catholics that alerted Anglican Catholics in England to the movement.'[30] They were intrigued, for there was talk about Catholic Pentecostals, and 'Catholic' and 'Pentecostal' were regarded as almost contradictory terms. An Anglo-Catholic charismatic prayer meeting was organised in East London, and in 1973 the first of the Anglo-Catholic charismatic conferences was held at Walsingham. After a few years it had grown so large that it had to be transferred to High Leigh near Hoddesdon.

Ramsey was interested, and not dismissive. He considered what the movement said to the Churches. He wanted to be assured that those who saw the Spirit at work in exciting and ecstatic and emotional events, and in life-changing personal experiences, should also see the Spirit at work in the humdrum ways of ordinary life and in rational existence as well as emotional. 'Where exciting charismata are seen, there is the Spirit; but where hard work is done with cheerful and unexciting perseverance, where sorrow and pain are borne with quiet fortitude, where scholars pursue the truth with patience, where contemplatives serve us all by praying with a love beyond our own experience, here too is the Holy Spirit, here is the charismatic Christ.'[31]

---

[30] John Gunstone, *Pentecostal Anglicans* (1982), p.93.
[31] Owen Chadwick, *op.cit.*, p.217.

19

Divided and Besieged

In continuing the theme of 'secularisation' as providing the social context for a consideration of post-Second World War High Churchmanship, we are considerably helped by the English Church Census conducted by MARC Europe in 1989.[1] 'Without any question', George Carey, the newly appointed Archbishop of Canterbury, wrote in the Forword to 'Christian England', which was the published summary of the findings of the Census, 'the survey undertaken by MARC Europe is the most thorough and comprehensive ever done of English churchgoing. It is therefore a significant "map" of the Christian presence.'[2] The comments which follow are based on that most informative study.

The Census, together with information from a previous Census in 1979, quantified the decline in the total number of adult churchgoers, which embraced all Christian denominations, including the Roman Catholic Church. In 1975 there were 4,093,000, representing 11.3% of the total adult population of the country. By 1979 this had declined to 4,025,000, a 2% reduction compared with 1975, and representing 11.0% of the total adult population. In 1985 it was 3,755,000, a 7% reduction on 1979, representing 9.9% of the adult poulation. For 1989 the total was 3,700,000, a 1% decline since 1985, and representing 9.5% of the total adult population.[3]

[1] Peter Brierley, 'Christian England'. What the English Church Census Reveals (London, 1991).

[2] Peter Brierley, op.cit., p.9.

[3] Peter Brierley, op.cit., p.30.

The figures did not suggest a major falling away from faith. The decline was caused largely by deaths: there were, in the years covered, more people over 65 years of age in the churches as a whole in England than in the population as a whole (19% against 15%) and as they died they were not being fully replaced by younger people. One reason for this was the reduced birth rate, especially in the early 1980s.

For the Church of England the decline in adult churchgoing was from 1,302,000 in 1975 to 1,256,000 in 1979 (-4%), to 1,181,000 in 1985 (a further 6% reduction), to 1,143,900 in 1989 (-3% compared with 1985).[4] For children aged 14 years and under the decline was from 445,000 in 1975 to 415,000 in 1979 (-7%), to 367,300 in 1985 (-11%), to 348,000 in 1989 (-5%).[5] In 1985 71% of children attending Anglican churches were in Sunday school, but 4 years later this had dropped to 64%.

An analysis by location showed a considerable variation in the sizes of Anglican congregations. The average number of adult churchgoers per church were as follows: city centre 90, inner city 84, council estates 71, rural:commuter/dormitory 60 and other rural 34, with an overall average of 70.[6]

How did Anglican Catholics fare amid all this? Respondents were asked to categorise the churchmanship of their church, and we will take those Anglicans who identified with either of the two categories 'Catholic' or 'Anglo-Catholic' as covering Anglican Catholicism.

The Census revealed that of the 1,143,900 adult Anglican churchgoers in 1989 283,200 were Anglican Catholics as we have just defined them in the terms used by the Census. This represents 25% of all the adult churchgoers, and compares with 292,200 for all types of Evangelicals (26%), 118,400 Low Church (10%), 209,400 Broad Church (18%), 223,300 Liberals (20%) and 17,400 Others (1%).[7] The Census actually showed the number of Anglican Catholic churches to be greater than for

4. Peter Brierley, *op.cit.*, p.53.
5. Peter Brierley, *op.cit.*, p.85.
6. Peter Brierley, *op,cit.*, p.114.
7. Peter Brierley, *op.cit.*, pp.163, 165.

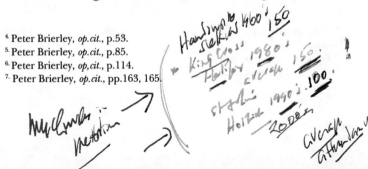

any other category of churchmanship (26% of the total). 18% of the churches were Evangelical, 13% Low, 23% Broad, 18% Liberal and 2% others.[8] Interesting also was the breakdown of the Anglican Catholic churches by area of location. 4.5% were found to be in city centres, 8.5% in inner cities, 8% on council estates, 22% in suburban/urban fringe areas, 11.5% in separate towns, 4% in other built-up areas, 17% in rural:commuter/ dormitory areas and 24.5% in other rural areas.[9] In another survey in 1985 of clergy in Urban Priority Areas, 38% declared themselves 'high church' compared with only 23% in non-UPA parishes, and this compared with 32% of the clergy who declared themselves 'low church/evangelical' and 28% who declared themselves 'middle of the road'.[10] On the showing of this sample survey, Anglican Catholics were more than playing their part in the difficult task of urban ministry.

The picture which emerges from this welter of statistics is of a Church which, taken as a whole, was loosing ground in terms of churchgoers and was not winning over the young and others in sufficient numbers to compensate for losses by death or to keep pace with increases in population. It was a church in which Anglican Catholics were declining in number, but in which they remained significant numerically. 1974 to 1993 was also a period during which there were many movements, trends and differences of opinion within Anglican Catholicism, so that by 1993 the Anglican Catholic scene was quite complex. But before we turn to a consideration of those matters we will first of all give some attention to the man who, more than any other, was a key figure in these turbulent years for Anglican Catholics, Graham Douglas Leonard.

Graham Leonard (b. 1921)

Leonard was born on 8 May 1921. He was educated at Monkton Coombe, where the earnest Evangelicalism of the school is said

---

[8.] Peter Brierley, *op.cit.*, p.169.

[9.] Peter Brierley, *op. cit.*, p.114.

[10.] *Faith in the City* (London, 1985), p.34.

to have touched his heart but not satisfied his mind.[11] He went up to Balliol College, Oxford, in 1940 where, for one term only, he was the college representative for the evangelical Oxford Inter-Collegiate Christian Union. But at that stage other influences became paramount. He found his Christian understanding, and indeed vision of God, enlarged and enriched, especially by the writings of Charles Gore, and by the powerful 'wholeness' of William Temple, who conducted a mission in Oxford in 1940. Leonard interrupted his University career by joining the Army, and remained, either in the Army or the Ministry of Supply to which he was seconded, until the end of the war. In 1943 he married Priscilla Swann, and by November 1945 he was ready for training for the priesthood, having become clear about his vocation.

After a period at Westcott House and serving in parishes in Cambridge, Huntingdonshire, and Essex, in 1952 he became the incumbent of St Mary the Virgin, Ardleigh, which had a High Church tradition. He never served in any of the more well-known Anglo-Catholic parishes, and never wished to do so. He described himself as a Prayer Book Catholic. In 1955 he became Director of Religious Education in the diocese of St Albans, and canon of St Albans. In 1958 he was appointed General Secretary of the National Society, a post in which he distinguished himself by his vigour, judiciousness and pastoral concern; qualities which were also very much to the fore during the succeeding period when he was Archdeacon of Hampstead from 1962 to 1964. He was also establishing a reputation as a man who 'thought theologically and acted sacramentally'.[12] This was a characteristic which he was to develop, and which was to be a hallmark of his future ministry, for he was concerned to be grounded in Scripture, Tradition, and a sense of history, and not to be overmuch swayed by the philosophy of any particular moment.

---

[11] John S. Peart-Binns, *Graham Leonard. Bishop of London* (London, 1988), p.4. A book which forms the basis of the present account of the life and work of Leonard.

[12] John S. Peart-Binns, *op.cit.*, p.35.

In 1964 he was appointed Suffragan Bishop of Willesden. In a sermon in 1970 he made plain his perception of the Church which he sought to build up:

> I look for men and women of faith, for priests and people who have the courage of their convictions, living in obedience to the truth as revealed in Christ. I look for priests who know themselves to be and live as stewards of the mysteries of God. I look for love – a love of real warmth and joy – in our relations within our common life together. I look for love which has for its motive not its usefulness to us or the comfort which it gives us but the desire to give honour to God. I look for parochial church councils and synods in which the members, as they deliberate, will be moved supremely by one desire that in all that is said and done God may be glorified. I look for priests and people, men and women, who honour and glorify God by faithfulness in taking their place Sunday by Sunday in the Christian assembly. I look for men and women who, in the Eucharist, obeying our Lord's command, show forth his death until He comes again, proclaim the glory of God and his love for mankind and are nourished in fellowship with him. I look for priests and people, men and women, who are concerned to honour and glorify God by expressing the relationship in continuing prayer – adoring, loving and interceding for those among whom they live and work. I look for those who are willing to leave things in God's hands not believing themselves to be indispensible and to give time in the adoration and contemplation of his eternal majesty and holiness for his sake.[13]

During the 1960s Leonard became increasingly prominent in the national life of the Church. Although he was generally loved and respected in his area and in the diocese, beyond that he increasingly attracted criticism and dislike. This was mainly

---

[13.] John S. Peart-Binns, *op.cit.*, pp.46, 47.

because of his firm conviction about the importance of the catholicity of the Church of England and the perils he saw ahead. As we noted in the previous chapter, he demonstrated his forthrightness, clarity of conviction and purpose, and his readiness to take an unpopular stand on controversial issues in his response to the Anglican-Methodist unity scheme. It was to be the first among several well-publicised confrontations with the Church of England and Anglican establishments.

In September 1973 Leonard was enthroned as Bishop of Truro. In 1976 he was appointed Chairman of the Board of Social Responsibility. In 1975 he was one of the elected delegates to the fifth assembly of the World Council of Churches. Throughout the 1970s he was also becoming established as the recognised leader of Anglican Catholicism, and he was in much demand as a lecturer, speaker and preacher in Great Britain and abroad.

A particularly onerous task, which was to remain a priority for him for the rest of his ministry, was his attempt to help revive the flagging Catholic movement in the Church of England. 'In the Church of the 1970s many parishes which would have called themselves Anglo-Catholic had turned in upon themselves, becoming shrines to a fading vision, which few people visited.'[14] An attempt was made in the midst of such a situation to put the Catholic movement back on the map; to engender Catholic renewal. This endeavour was spearheaded by the Church Union under the presidency of Eric Kemp, the Bishop of Chichester. The movement for renewal included all those elements which Leonard had insisted upon for many years: renewal of faith in God as creator and sustainer of the universe, in Jesus Christ and the Holy Spirit; faith in the Church, in the holy sacraments, and in God's gift of the apostolic ministry; renewal of hope and wholeness, with integration and completeness contrasting with what was partial, unbalanced and sectarian. There was concern that what were seen as narrow, pietistic and inadequate manifestations of

---

[14.] John S. Peart-Binns, *op.cit.*, p.144.

Christianity should be countered by the renewal of Catholic truth and life.

In September 1981 Leonard was enthroned as Bishop of London. He was to remain in the post until his retirement in 1991, and during that time he was to loom large in the affairs of the church national and international. Within the diocese his concern to care pastorally for the massive church and general population committed to his charge, his tenacious hold upon the great fundamentals of revealed faith, his generosity of spirit and courage in controversy endeared him to clergy and laity of all shades of churchmanship. But he constantly upset conventions and his bold, fearless and outspoken approach to matters of heated debate caused consternation in many quarters. One example will illustrate this.

In 1986 Tulsa, a small town in Oklahoma, USA, was almost unknown, certainly outside the United States; but it was soon to enter ecclesiastical history and to be involved in an affair which made it more than a footnote to the history of the Aglican communion in the latter part of the twentieth century. The Episcopal Church of the USA (ECUSA) suffered severely from internal division at that time, between those traditionalists who considered that it was failing to be loyal to the inherited truths and standards of the gospel, and those progressives who agitated for the ordination of women to the priesthood and episcopate, for changes in the liturgy and the introduction of 'inclusive' (not gender specific) language, and supported every liberal policy for a moral revolution.

In 1969 John C. Pasco moved to Tulsa to be priest in charge of a new congregation, St Michael's, and throughout the next ten years it grew as a traditionalist and conservative church. The Bishop of the diocese and his council decided that the church was not viable or acceptable with its distinctive churchmanship, and that it must discontinue in its existing form and move to a neighbouring town. This was resisted by the church which finally decided in November 1972 to lease, without diocesan permission, a warehouse in Tulsa and make it their church. In its new location, the church thrived, and in 1979 made a further move; it became a parish in 1981. Pasco continued to speak out against the reform of the Prayer Book, the ordination of women to the priesthood and the political stand of certain bishops. Tension grew between the church and the now new Bishop. In 1984 the Bishop reduced St Michael's to a mission, and its priest, wardens and vestry ceased to be recognised. The decision was endorsed unanimously by the diocesan convention. The congregation stood firm behind their rector. But St Michael's was isolated, and in its concern for episcopal support and oversight within the Anglican communion, so that it might maintain the traditional historic faith as the priest and congregation perceived it, and its expression in worship, it appealed to Leonard for assistance. In the meantime, in April 1986, Pasco was deposed as a priest by the Bishop. Leonard agreed, after long and careful consideration, that in his capacity as a bishop, as distinct from being Bishop of London, which may have implicated his successor, Pasco and his congregation could have fellowship with him within the fellowship of the One, Holy, Catholic and Apostolic Church; he would recognise the priesthood of Pasco, and the congregation of St Michael's as faithful Anglicans, and give them such spiritual and pastoral assistance as it was within his power to give.

It was a most controversial decision to take, and it created ripples throughout the Anglican communion. It further deteriorated the uneasy relationship which Leonard had with Archbishop Robert Runcie, who regarded Leonard's action as unwise, unwarranted, divisive and highly improper; and few people supported Leonard in public. The matter was debated in the House of Bishops, which voted by 47 to 1 with 2 abstentions against action such as that taken by Leonard, and invited the Archbishop of Canterbury to take any steps he thought appropriate to promote full understanding with the House of Bishops of ECUSA on this matter and on the pastoral issues involved.

The clarity of conviction and decisiveness of action which Leonard showed in the Tulsa affair was likewise demonstrated in his moral stance on some of the main questions of personal morality which confonted the Church, and in his declared, uncompromising, views on some of the public issues of his day.

He was convinced that the Church, and especially its leaders, had for decades failed to speak out fearlessly, declaring God's absolute, and to many unpalatable, standards, in opposition to the spirit of the age.

He was not a harsh rigorist, but he had a clear theological foundation for his ministry and life. He interpreted the post-Second World War history of the Christian Churches largely in terms of the affinity of such men and women of similar conviction. In 1987 he said:

> For a number of years I have been suggesting that within all Christian Churches, a fundamental realignment has been taking place, gaining momentum since the Second World War. It cuts across existing denominational divisions, as is often evident at ecumenical gatherings. I believe that in time it could acquire the dimensions of a second Reformation. To put it in very basic terms, it is a realignment between those, on the one hand, who believe that the Christian Gospel is revealed by God, is to be heard and received and that its purpose is to enable men and women to obey God in love, and through them for creation itself to be redeemed. On the other hand are those who believe that it can and should be modified and adapted to the cultural and intellectual attitudes and demands of successive generations, indeed, originates in them. To the former the scriptures are of unique authority as witnessing to the events of God in history which brought the Church into being, and as serving to speak of God's revelation to successive generations to enable them to discern how the truth of the Gospel is to be expressed in different times and cultures. The Creeds are accepted as serving a simple purpose by distilling the essential meaning of the biblical revelation. To the latter, however, as one scholar has contended, since both scripture and tradition have lost their authority, all decisions in Church matters must be made simply in the light of 'appropriateness' and 'expediency'. Significantly he gives no indication of the criteria by which 'appropriateness' and 'expediency' should be determined. In practice, they are determined

by the cultural outlook of the present day, the assumptions and prejudices of which are accepted without being brought under Christian judgement.[15]

Leonard represented conservative Anglican Catholicism. But throughout especially the last thirty or so years of his ministry there developed an increasingly powerful and vocal Anglican Liberal Catholicism, which was at odds with much of what he held dear. By the end of our period it was difficult to tell whether one of the two strands would attain the ascendency; whether they would discover an harmonious coexistence and even cooperation within a reinvigorated Anglican Catholicism; or whether, by their sniping at each other, and by their aggravation of internal Anglican Catholic divisions, they would only accelerate the decline of Anglican Catholicism as a whole.

Indeed, in the period 1971 to 1993 there were various movements and much internal activity within Anglican Catholicism. Some of the initiatives were addressed to the service of the community or the spread of the Christian message, some of them were turned inwards in the form of internicine strife.

The Jubilee Group

The Jubilee Group movement arose in the mid 1970s because of concern to renew the social conscience of Anglican Catholics. A number of Anglican Catholics were disturbed at what appeared to them to be a strong tendency in Anglican Catholicism towards a sickly pietism and a right-wing reactionary social and political alignment. They considered this to be a serious betrayal of the social tradition of Anglo-Catholicism, and they thought that it might spell the death of the movement. They were dubious about the possibility of reforming the existing organs of Anglo-Catholic opinion, and recognised that they were hardly likely to be transformed into organs of

[15.] John S. Peart-Binns, *op.cit.*, pp.249, 250.

revolutionary zeal. The Jubilee Group movement members regarded the prevailing Anglican Catholicism as far too inward-looking, preoccupied with such matters as liturgy and oblivious to changes and problems in a desperately needy world. Too many Anglican Catholics, they said, had made religion a substitute for life.

The appearance of the Jubilee Group antedated the emergence of the wider movement of Catholic Renewal in the Church of England. Although there was no official connection, the parallels were in some respects close, as an early leaflet of 1975 makes plain:

> The Group came into being as a result of a series of discussions on the current state of Catholicism in the Church of England. While there were, and are, some important differences between us, we found that we were united in (i) a commitment to the Catholic movement, and a strong sense of standing within the tradition of Catholic Orthodoxy; (ii) a sense of alarm and frustration at the present decayed and demoralised state of the movement; and (iii) a concern for the resurrection of the unity of contemplation and politics. In addition, within the wider framework of Christianity, we shared (iv) a concern at the woolly liberalism of much current social action in the church, and in particular at the state of the 'Christian Left' with its lack of clear theological thought.[16]

Although the Jubilee Group remained a tendency rather than an organisation, it had two main explicit concerns. The first was 'for Catholic orthodoxy and an insistence on the importance of revealed truth.'[17] It was critical of any reductionist trends in theology, but also struggled against the temptation to take refuge from hard theological questioning in the security of a traditionalism which was complacent and static. It called for a

---

[16] Kenneth Leech and Rowan Williams (Eds.), *Essays Catholic and Radical* (1983), Introduction, p.8. This is a volume to which the present work, and chapter, owes much.

[17] Kenneth Leech and Rowan Williams (Eds.), *op.cit.*, Introduction, p.8.

critical orthodoxy, a vigorous dialogue with tradition. The second concern was for the development of a theological critique of capitalism. There was a search for a revolutionary orthodoxy. Organisationally, Jubilee rejected centralization in favour of local groups and tried to integrate theory and praxis.

Two years after the appearance of Jubilee, in 1977, the Bishop of Chichester, Eric Kemp, called together a number of people concerned about the state of the Catholic movement in the Church of England. In the early days of the Catholic Renewal movement, which this gathering initiated, the stress was on the wholeness of the faith and the need for a social critique. Out of prolonged discussion of these matters came the Eastertide 1978 Loughborough Conference 'Proclaiming the Risen Christ'. About one thousand met together. The dominant note was one of mission, and teaching and worship were to the fore rather than intellectual debate. It was hoped that the Conference would help to bring about a renewal of social vision, but it did not happen. It partook somewhat of a one off event, lacking the force, impact and momentum of the Evangelical gatherings at Keele in 1967 and Nottingham in 1977. There was a sense of wholeness and a lack of fanaticism at the Conference, with the more extreme Anglican Catholics being quite quiescent, but in the years that followed there was a growing, rather unhealthy, retreat into preoccupation with matters of a mainly ecclesiastical nature without the counterbalancing involvement in the wider 'secular' world.

In 1983 there was an attempt to redress this balance with the publication of *Essays Catholic and Radical.* There was also some celebration of the one hundred and fiftieth anniversary of the beginning of the Oxford movement, including an open air Mass in the University Parks in Oxford and a Conference at Keble College, Oxford; and there was a second Loughborough Conference. But such activity, although it aroused some interest and produced some interesting comment, notably the Oxford Conference papers under the title *Tradition Renewed,* did not, to any marked extent, reinvigorate Anglican Catholicism as a whole, nor greatly enhance a sense of identity and 'mission'.

During the 1980s, there was a greater cleavage between the more traditional and conservative Anglican Catholics and the

Liberal Anglican Catholics, which was accentuated as the latter became more united and articulate. Some of the new Liberal Anglican Catholic theologians consciously followed in the tradition of *Lux Mundi*. This is well illustrated by the 1989 collection of essays by thirteen Oxford Liberal Catholic theologians in commemoration of *Lux Mundi*, entitled *The Religion of the Incarnation*. The authors, like their forebears a century before, were aware that they were confronting a ferment in Christian thinking which challenged the traditional shape of Apostolic belief and practice, and they restated the creed with which they approached the twenty-first century. Two tendencies in modern theology were seen as having especially caused confusion in the public mind since *Honest to God* (1963) and *The Myth of God Incarnate* (1977). The first was the responsible clarification of the church's language, which included distinguishing between doctrine, myth, and history. The second was 'the embarrassed elimination of mythical language that had been misunderstood in a literalistic way, and with it large tracts of the doctrinal tradition'. The first step (represented by Professor Wiles in *The Myth of God Incarnate*) was seen as always necessary, the second as 'a *faux pas* which most theologians nowadays are careful to avoid'.[18]

It was acknowledged by the writers of *The Religion of the Incarnation* that at a time when 'the prevailing winds were positivist, and religious language scarcely taken seriously, it was fatally easy for theologians to slip from analysis into reductionist interpretations of the religious tradition'.[19] Secular protestantism was thought to have surrendered much that was essential to the Christian religion. The authors chose the title of their work in order to revive Gore's focus on the Incarnation, which was a doctrine central to Christian faith, and one that most Anglicans had not abandoned. It was also a doctrine which was crucial in opposing the liberal protestant hostility to traditional Christological dogma.

[18.] Robert Morgan (Ed.), *The Religion of the Incarnation. Anglican Essays in Commemoration of Lux Mundi* (1989), p.xi.

[19.] Robert Morgan (Ed.), *op.cit.*, p.xi.

The essayists appreciated that the 'Anglican liberal catholic claim to pursue a middle way between the Enlightenment's theological rationalism which dissolves the creed, and a papal system which renders it brittle and burdensome (Matt. 23:4), is bound to look different today from a century ago'.[20] In their theological approach they had in common a concern to preserve something of both the liberal and the catholic traditions of Anglicanism. But the majority of them were more positive in their attitude towards the Reformation and the Enlightenment than most of their *Lux Mundi* predecessors, as they in their turn had been more positive about German theology than the Tractarians had been.

In the twenty years between the early 1970s and the early 1990s there were several issues on which the Anglican Catholic response was divided in a quite polarized way between the more extreme liberals and the traditionalists. And this was a self-perpetuating and reinforcing process, because the contrasting and frequently conflicting responses helped to draw attention to the differences of outlook of the two wings of Anglican Catholicism, and heightened and intensified thereby the divide. Three topics particularly aroused the emotions of Anglican Catholics, highlighted the tension between the two factions, and made public their discord: the whole debate about homosexuality, the question of the remarriage in church of divorced people, and, of course, the worldwide, highly contentious, divisive and well-publicised matter of the ordination of women to the priesthood and the episcopate.

Homosexuality

In the nineteenth century there were hints, or more than hints, that many High Churchmen who advocated and practised celibacy had homosexual tendencies. But as late as immediately before the Second World War homosexuality was a taboo subject, seldom, if ever, given a public hearing, other than in

---

[20] Robert Morgan (Ed.), *op.cit.*, p.xiv.

rare cases, such as the trial of Oscar Wilde, and especially taboo within the churches. With the general increase in permissiveness in society, and the greater openness and lack of restraint in the discussion of most issues, including sexual matters, homosexuality was more freely debated. The 1957 *Wolfenden Report* and the removal of legal sanctions against certain forms of homosexuality, made homosexuals more willing to identify themselves, often without any feelings of guilt or embarrassment, and their proclivities were more fully catered for by gay associations, gay pubs and gay clubs. They became a recognised sub-group which pressed its rights and demanded no discrimination on account of sexual orientation. And the whole situation was complicated and made more explicit and highly charged by the problem of AIDS.

During all this time the churches, and not least of all the Anglican Catholics, were quite seriously divided on the issue. There were sections of the Church, and most notably the Roman Catholic Church and Evangelical groups both within and outside the Church of England, which stood firm, and resolutely declared that all sexual acts outside heterosexual marriage were wrong and unacceptable. But some other groups, and especially those with a powerful liberal component, showed themselves in sympathy with the attacks on the traditional Christian sexual ethic. They were emboldened to take such a stand by the writings and pronouncements of leading churchmen like Bishop John Robinson, who, both by his book *Honest to God* and his extremely well publicised court statements in the *Lady Chatterley's Lover* case, gave credence to the popular belief that the church was less dogmatic and absolute in its moral teaching than it had formerly been.

Anglican Catholics found themselves caught up in an ever more painful and publicly damaging dilemma. As a group they did not follow the Roman Catholic example, which had so frequently been their wont in the past, and declare themselves unquestionably and unreservedly opposed to the practice of homosexuality. Some wished to do so, and some, with Graham Leonard at their head, did so, but others, mostly those identified as Liberal Catholics, did not. They spoke with a divided voice. What is more, Anglican Catholics themselves were suspected of harbouring homosexuals in their midst and of condoning the practice among their own members. In 1986 it was said that the 'homosexuality of many male members of the movement, both priests and laity, and of some female members also, is the movement's "open secret", widely recognized but little admitted'.[21] A Lesbian and Gay Christian Movement was established with thousands of members, including perhaps as many as one thousand clergy. Although of course not all these were Anglican, let alone Anglican Catholics, a number of the clergy to first declare themselves publicly as homosexuals were Anglican Catholics.

This whole ambiguity about the subject, and 'the long-standing association of Anglo-Catholics with homosexuality',[22] helped to undermine the self-confidence and integrity of Anglican Catholicism, and had an extremely damaging effect on their public image. It lowered their morale and weakened their influence, and it contributed to their decline.

The remarriage of divorcees

Still broadly within the area of sexual morality, and subject to similar social pressures arising out of greater permissiveness, was the question of the re-marriage of divorced persons in church. It was an issue which touched upon the whole Christian basis of marriage, the stability of the marriage relationship, the lifelong commitment of marriage and the distinctiveness, if any, in the Christian as compared to the non-Christian view of marriage.

By the early 1980s the issue had assumed considerable prominence in the internal Church of England debates. There had been a great increase in the level of divorces, even among clergy themselves. And the number of those who sincerely wanted to be remarried in church increased likewise. The apparent compromise of encouraging such re-marriage in a

---

[21.] F. Penhale, *Catholics in Crisis* (Oxford, 1986), p.148.

[22.] W.S.F. Pickering, *Anglo-Catholicism* (1989), p.193. A book to which this present section owes much.

Register Office, with a subsequent blessing in church was seen to be the worst of all worlds. Some Anglican Catholics were aghast that bishops were prepared to allow priests to perform the remarriage of divorced persons in church. The attempt to find some means of facilitating this, perhaps by the use of a specially appointed committee rather than the bishop personally, was a matter of considerable controversy. Again, there was severe division within Anglican Catholicism. The Anglican Catholic Liberals were prepared to consider re-marriage ceremonies, albeit with reluctance. But the more rigorous traditionalists strongly opposed the possibility. Thus Graham Leonard fought against any alteration in the Church's ruling :

> The problem is not divorce, for which it is possible to repent. The problem is remarriage which involves repudiation of the original vows. I do not see how the Church can endorse that, which in any case involves the Church in saying that there can be a limit to loving. I do regret that the Church of England has no mechanism for deciding whether a marriage is null and void *ab initio*. If I am convinced that an original marriage was null I find some way of indicating that the person can marry with a clear Christian conscience, but I have never approved of the use of the marriage service. The real problem in the Church of England over getting a proper nullity procedure is that some of us would want it on strict grounds of nullity whereas others want it on the basis that a marriage can 'die'. This idea I regard as incompatible with the Gospel which gives the pattern of love as being to the end.[23]

The ordination of women

Of the three topics we are considering clearly the most divisive was the question of the ordination of women. As the

[23] John S. Peart-Binns, *op.cit.*, p.247.

years passed the issue did not diminish in its power to drive a wedge even more firmly between the contending parties. It was important in its own right, but it was also highly charged symbolically for those Anglican Catholics who were becoming increasingly disillusioned with conservative Anglican Catholicism, and who finally decided to take steps to articulate an alternative approach.

The 1968 Lambeth Conference affirmed 'that the theological arguments as at present presented for and against the ordination of women to the priesthood are inconclusive'. By the time of the next Lambeth Conference ten years later, the Anglican Church of Canada, the Episcopal Church in the USA, the Church of the Province of New Zealand as well as the diocese of Hong Kong, had ordained women to the priesthood, or admitted women to the presbyterate.

The conservative Anglican Catholics who opposed the ordination of women were consistent and clear in their view, and it remained unchanged because they judged the issue by what they considered the unchanging yardsticks of biblical revelation and tradition. Again, Graham Leonard, in expressing the kernel of his own opinion, reflected the attitude of many Anglican Catholics:

> There are two basic reasons why I cannot accept that it is right to ordain women as priests and bishops, whose role is to represent Christ as head of his Church: First, I believe it undermines and questions the way in which God himself has taught us to speak of him and know him. I do not believe that it was by accident, but by God's deliberate choice that he chose to reveal himself in a patriarchal society and became man in Christ, as a male. The highest role ever given to any human being was given to a women, Mary, when she responded to God's call to be the mother of Christ. We cannot disregard these facts to suit our ideas today. Secondly, the Church of England claims to have continued the ordained ministry as given by God and received from the universal Church. I do not believe it has the right or power to alter it fundamentally without destroying that claim. In my judgement, the whole

approach (and the arguments) of those who press for the ordination of women questions and undermines the revealed nature of the Christian faith, as given by God, not devised by man.[24] *where does God reveal this?*

On another occasion, in a General Synod debate, Leonard declared: 'I do not appeal to Rome or Constantinople or Geneva as such, I appeal as Anglicans have always appealed, to scripture and tradition and reason, tested by scripture.'

In 1978 the General Synod rejected a motion 'to remove the barriers to the ordination of women to the priesthood and their consecration to the episcopate', and the following year a motion to enable women ordained abroad to exercise their priesthood in England in certain circumstances was defeated by the House of Clergy. The protagonists for the ordination of women were active, and indeed renewed their efforts with compaigning fervour. They were spearheaded by the Movement for the Ordination of Women, which numbered among its leaders the bishops of Southwark (Ronald Bowlby) and Manchester (Stanley Booth-Clibborn). Bishop John Austin Baker of Salisbury and Bishop Simon Phipps of Lincoln wrote pamphlets, and George Carey, Bishop of Bath and Wells and later Archbishop of Canterbury, wrote a booklet for MOW on *Women and Authority in the Church*. The moderator of MOW, and a woman of considerable influence in the cause of women's ordination, was Monica Furlong.

Anglican Catholics looked to Graham Leonard and Eric Kemp for leadership, but the Anglican Catholic movement was not able to mobilize itself effectively. This was partly because the Anglican Catholics were divided on the issue, as were the Evangelicals whom Leonard and others hoped to enlist in united opposition. As the debate continued, and as a vote by the General Synod in favour of the ordination of women appeared to be more and more inevitable, so Leonard declared unambiguously that it might entail schism, and the need for those who could not remain in communion with Canterbury to

[24.] John S. Peart-Binns, *op. cit.*, p.218.

find other ways of continuing in existence within the universal Church. In the *Daily Mail* of 19 February 1987 Leonard restated his position in brief: 'If the Church of England is split by the issue of ordained women, I will not be leading the division but responding to the inevitable consequences of a fundamental change which the Church has no right to make unilaterally.' It was calculated that as many as two thousand clergy would leave the Church of England. The conservative Anglican Catholics who opposed ordination asserted that it was not they who were the dissentients; it was those who wished to ordain women who were the innovators, while those who held fast to Scripture and tradition remained true Anglicans.

By the late 1980s Anglican Catholics were plagued by disagreement and discontent, and they were quite severely demoralised. One incident, or series of incidents, and one development amply illustrate this somewhat confused state of Anglican Catholicism.

Gareth Bennett (1929–87) and the *Crockford's Preface*

The suicide of Gareth Bennett in December 1987 attracted much national media attention. It was revealed that he was the author of the controversial 'anonymous' 1987/88 *Crockford's Preface* which had caused a mighty furore both within and without the Church of England because of its pungent criticism of the Church of England, and its strong personal attack on the leadership of the Primate, Robert Runcie. The affair turned the searchlight for a short time on the disillusionment of one prominent Anglo-Catholic, and thereby gave some insight into the sense of alienation and turmoil which was afflicting Anglo-Catholics as a whole. It helped to reinforce the portrait of Anglo-Catholics as a beleagured minority, and to make them more conscious of the malaise from which they were suffering.

Gareth Bennett was a distinguished Oxford don. He was actively involved in the local and national life of the Church of England. He was a governor of Pusey House, Oxford, a member of General Synod, where he was a respected speaker, on the Church of England Doctrine Commission, the Faith and

Order Advisory Group and the Board of Mission and Unity. For whatever combination of reasons, which may well have included a personal feeling of bitterness at having unfairly been excluded from high office in the Church of England as well as a cooler, detached historian's understanding and analysis, his *Crockford's Preface* was a powerfully expressed appraisal and condemnation of certain aspects of Church of England life from the perspective of a conservative Anglo-Catholic.

In the *Preface* Bennett bemoaned the undesirable, and indeed alarming changes in the Church of England in recent years. He especially deplored what he detected as a decline in the distinctive Anglican theological method. He compared what he regarded as the seventeenth century high point in Anglican theology, with the balance it gave to Scripture, tradition and reason; in which theological study was conducted in the context of the corporate life of the Church; and in which the end in mind was to deepen the spirituality and forward the mission of the Church; with the modern poverty of Anglican theology, in which there had been no eminent exponent of classical Anglican divinity since Michael Ramsey. Since Ramsey, the citadel had fallen to a younger generation of theologians who were uneasy at combining the role of theologian and churchman. Bennett observed a reluctance among such theologians to apply the teaching of Scripture or the patristic writers in order to prescribe modern doctrine or church practice. Professor D.E. Nineham in particular taught that 'first-century Christians had views about the universe, history and literary forms which we cannot share and which cannot be translated into our situation.'[25] Professor M.F. Wiles had 'questioned the relevance of the doctrinal formularies of the first four centuries for the modern Church.'[26] Such distancing of the modern Church from what had hitherto been regarded as its prescriptive sources clearly had serious consequences for Anglican ecclesiology. Bennett thought it was doubtful if these

[25] G.V. Bennett in Geoffrey Rowell (Ed.), *To the Church of England. Essays and Papers and The Preface to Crockford's Clerical Directory 1987/88* (Worthing, 1988), p.200.

[26] Geoffrey Rowell (Ed.), *To the Church of England*, p.200.

views, when explicitly stated, were acceptable to most Anglicans of his generation.

Among the unfortunate trends to which these theological tendencies had contributed, Bennett said, was an undermining of the authority of the Anglican Church as a worldwide corporate body, and a weakening of the unity and influence of the Anglican Communion. The Anglican Communion was in effect a loose association of independent churches, and without a strong, theologically based, acceptance of the imperative of a corporate mind on matters of theology and church practice, the centrifugal could well become greater than the centripetal forces.

Bennett discerned, and deeply regretted, a liberal ascendency among bishops and influential laity, especially in the Episcopal Church of the United States and in the Church of England. This unfortunate drift towards greater liberalisation in the leadership of the Church was facilitated by an apparent policy of passivity and indecision. And for this Bennett attrributed considerable blame to Robert Runcie, the Archbishop of Canterbury, whom he severely berated. According to Bennett, a liberal establishment had been created in the Church of England, much to the detriment of the Church. With the archiepiscopal partnership of Robert Runcie and John Habgood, the Archbishop of York and the leading Anglican Liberal, there had, according to Bennett, been a virtual exclusion of Anglo-Catholics from episcopal office and a serious under-representation of Evangelicals. Bennett thought that this discrimination was sometimes explained as a policy of appointing 'central' men, but he considered it 'a matter of legitimate doubt whether Liberals are so central to the life and spirituality of the Church of England or whether they are foremost in its mission'.[27]

In that mission, Bennett drew attention especially to the task facing the Church in rural and urban areas, and the place of black people in the life and witness of a church which needed

[27.] Geoffrey Rowell (Ed.), *To the Church of England*, p.221.

rescuing from its 'suburban captivity', so that it was once again 'a church for the English people'.[28]

In some respects the *Preface* was a sad commentary by an intelligent, sensitive man who was profoundly wounded by a sense of personal neglect.[29] But it was also a bold and incisive lament by an acute and observant traditional Anglo-Catholic who had a sincere love for the Church which he sought to serve, and a genuine concern to preserve apostolic doctrine and promote catholic values and mission in keeping with the best High Church tradition. And in this he was expressing the confusion and concern which typified a significant body of like-minded Churchmen at the time. But concern was not confined to the conservative Anglo-Catholics.

Affirming Catholicism

Throughout the late 1980s there were a substantial number of Anglican Catholics who were becoming more and more disgruntled with what they regarded as the over-negative, hidebound, inflexible theological and social outlook of traditional, mainstream Anglican Catholicism in the face of rapid theological and social change. And in 1990 some of them met together to discuss their concerns. The gathering at St Alban's, Holborn was entitled Affirming Catholicism. The speakers were Dom Edmund Flood OSB, Monk of Ealing, writer and broadcaster, the Rt. Rev. Richard Holloway, Bishop of Edinburgh, the Rev. David Hutt, Vicar of All Saints', Margaret Street, Dame Rachel Waterhouse and the Rev. Professor Rowan Williams, Lady Margaret Professor of Divinity, and Canon of Christ Church, Oxford.

From the evidence of letters received after the event and comments made during it, there was, said Richard Holloway, the same feeling expressed: 'it was just a relief to have done the thing at all, to have found some means of letting out some of

---

[28] Geoffrey Rowell (Ed.), *To the Church of England*, p.228.

[29] See William Oddie, *The Crockford's File. Gareth Bennett and the Death of the Anglican Mind* (London, 1989).

the pent-up tension and frustration, to have owned up to something in a public way, to have come out or shoved our heads above the parapet and found the view so bracing'.[30] It was acknowledged that this euphoria would have been felt no matter what had happened during the day; but what happened was of considerable importance to Anglican Catholicism.

In his retrospective assessment of the mood of the gathering, Richard Holloway drew attention to the note of caution, and the general sense that they wanted to take one step at a time and avoid becoming a party. They felt a responsibility to explore the way ahead. In the meantime they 'thanked God and took courage' (Acts of the Apostles, Ch.28 v.15). And this was one of the main thrusts in the telling opening address by Rowan Williams:

> I really hope that today will not mark the launching of a new 'party' – some kind of Catholic SDP, to use an analogy that sounds, just at the moment, suitably ill-omened...It's not much use fighting tribalism by inventing new tribes; and at present the Church of England is in an unusually tribal phase, when every group seems convinced that its vision of the truth is terminally at risk, and that everyone but them is making the running. Part of the trouble with this, of course, is that it fosters the delusion that unless we strain every nerve to preserve our vision, God's promise to be with the Church becomes void; as if God could do nothing unless we 'got it right' and defeated the opposition. If today's title is serious, we are supposed to be here to affirm something; which means helping each other towards confidence and gratitude and away from anxiety. The mentality of defending our heritage is understandable enough; but it regularly means that anxiety wins the day over celebration. And anxiety in large quantities is notoriously something that distorts judgement and clouds truthfulness.[31]

[30.] Richard Holloway in *Affirming Catholicism*. Papers given at the Day Conference at St. Alban's, Holborn on Saturday 9 June 1990, p.i.

[31.] Rowan Williams in *Affirming Catholicism, op.cit.,* p.1.

Williams strongly suggested that those gathered together wished to affirm tradition, but tradition in its proper and fullest sense, and tradition which was active:

> Listening to tradition is attending to all the resources a particular history has to offer you; and there are and should be times when such attention makes you look very critically at some of the things in that very same history. I've heard it said that one of the greatest triumphs of Catholic Christianity is its ability to train its own critics. And this means surely that Catholic tradition ought to be concerned with presenting a depth and range of resouces that will stop anyone from too easily believing that the Church at any one moment has got it all wrapped up, has fathomed the meaning of Jesus Christ. And this isn't polite agnosticism or do-it-yourself modernism – making up Christianity as you go along – but the fruit of trying to keep eyes and ears and heart open to the wholeness of what's being passed on to us – including the awkwardnesses, the half-hidden points of conflict, the half-muffled voices. Catholicism is supposed to have some connection with wholeness, yes ?[32]

Christian history is not a process of steady improvement, but rather of regularly taking two steps forward and one, two or even three steps back. Nonetheless, a few things seem to stick, and the Church did not retain its belief that marriage is inferior to celibacy, that absolute monarchy must be God's will or that slavery is an inevitable result of the Fall. Some things come to be seen as radically at odds with tradition – and upheavals in history help to force questions on the Church:

> So that if today there are Christians, trying to be faithful to the disciplines of prayer and sacrament, who are seriously asking what 'tradition' suggests about issues raised in contemporary culture, without expecting a quick and final answer, they're not to be written off as mindless

---

[32] Rowan Williams in *Affirming Catholicism, op.cit.,* p.2.

trendies. The Church has too often made a fool of itself when faced with new questions for anyone ('liberal' or 'conservative') to feel complacent. We should rather be asking how our thinking and reacting where such issues arise might take us further into the new world of Christ. And that at least blocks off the 'package deal' approach – either all technological modernity is good for you, or the Decline of the West is terminally upon us. A Catholic Christian prepared to raise the issue of the moral status of homosexuality is certainly not thereby committed to a bland acceptance of embryo research or abortion on demand; support for the ordination of women is not an endorsement of functional and managerial models of priesthood; serious engagement with our cultural and religious pluralism in Britain today doesn't entail settling down happily with a supposedly value-free secularism in public life; and so on.[33]

The true continuity of the gospel is sometimes promoted by apparent rupture and discontinuity. Disagreement should be welcomed for it is not so much a mutual threat as a mutual gift. We must listen to each other for in so doing we will be taken deeper into the life of the giving God:

Our Christian past is not a boxroom or a cupboard under the stairs or the bedroom of Prince Albert preserved by Queen Victoria exactly as the dear man left it. It is a room for living, a place to spend time learning and reflecting, a place whose inner geography changes subtly and naturally as we ourselves grow. 'Thou hast set my feet in a large room,' says the psalmist to God. I hope that sense will pervade what we say and do today and in the future, overcoming our own smugness and tribalism in the vision of a truth that, through its fleshly life, death and resurrection, has made us free and will not – in Augustine's great words – fall away when we wander from home.[34]

[33.] Rowan Williams in *Affirming Catholicism, op.cit.*, p.4.
[34.] Rowan Williams in *Affirming Catholicism, op.cit.*, p.6.

And this invitation to freedom in Christ and openness to choice was echoed by other speakers:

> As Anglo-Catholics our greatest joy should be to recognise that our liturgical and sacramental worship enables us to change and make choices in ways not possible for any unalterable fundamentalism, unless, of course, we make a similar strait-jacket for ouselves. It should enable us to set ourselves alongside the poor and struggling members of the human family as children of God's creation, not to separate ourselves from them. It brings to us the overwhelming message of the Incarnation, that we come to the supernatural through the natural. But because we have choices, we have to think our actions through. There can be no coasting home to God along someone else's railway lines. That wonderful diversity of gifts set out by Paul needs to be burnished, fashioned and utilised for God's service and for change in the context and beauty of the Catholic liturgy.[35]

Such freedom with responsibility was likewise stressed by David Hutt:

> For our mission to be successful we have to be fully in possession not only of our convictions but of our own freedom. The work begins here and it begins with ourselves. It cannot be otherwise. Unless we have a sense of our integrity as members of the Body, unless we are fully Incorporated – truly belonging – we cannot begin to address the controversial issues of our day. Elsewhere I have made a plea for a new forum, a new approach to the matters so closely involved with humanness and human sexuality. This plea must embrace a concern for the proper dignity of homosexuals, Christian or otherwise, of women in society and in the Church and here I make an especial claim for justice. Whatever my own conservatism

---

[35] Rachel Waterhouse in *Affirming Catholicism, op.cit.,* p.15.

I have to point out to those who subscribe to the movement involved with 'Cost of Conscience' that very many women have consciences too and that they pray, think and act in good conscience... Conscience is not the prerogative of any particular group or party! [36]

Affirming Catholicism has been freely and fully quoted because it well captures the essence and flavour of that wing of Anglo-Catholicism in the last decade of the twentieth century which saw itself as a true inheritor of the Anglican Catholic tradition, and its role as a true and faithful interpretor of that tradition. It also demonstrates the profound divisions within late twentieth century Anglican Catholicism. For on the one hand the Liberal Anglican Catholics were highly critical of the conservative Anglican Catholics, while on the other hand some of the conservatives were even of the opinion that certain of the liberals had discarded so much basic Christian doctrinal and moral teaching that it brought into question their right to be called Christian, let alone Catholic.

[36] David Hutt in *Affirming Catholicism, op.cit.*, p.22.

Epilogue

Few would claim that the second half of the twentieth century was among the most glorious or noteworthy periods in the history of Anglican Catholicism. Anglican Catholics had apparently lost their way. They had increasingly lost confidence. They had no clear perception of their purpose either within the Church or within society. They found themselves without a vision, and they did not need to be reminded that those without a vision perish.

'Today', said one Anglican Catholic as far back as 1968, 'Catholic Anglicans have lost their definition as a party, and though they are "of the Church" they have paid for their acceptance by being to some extent engulfed by the Church.'[1] Another observer, in the same year, commented that 'the movement has lost its momentum in the muds and eddies of post-war life and theology, and the call to "Catholic loyalties" no longer rallies an identifiable body of Anglican opinion that can speak with one voice. Older priests and laymen who remember former days say that a glory has departed from the Church of England.'[2] And this malaise was not healed with the passage of time. By the last decade of the century they were somewhat moribund and ineffectual, severely divided over key issues and on the defensive. And as they approached the twenty-first century they were confronted by yet another

---

[1.] John Wilkinson (Ed.), *Catholic Anglicans Today* (London, 1968), Preface, p.xi.
[2.] John Gunstone, 'Catholics in the Church of England', in John Wilkinson (Ed.), *op.cit.*, p.191.

367

crisis, for on 11 November 1992 the General Synod agreed that women could be ordained as priests in the Church of England. There were immediate expressions of disappointment and deep concern by a number of Anglican Catholics, and bodies such as Cost of Conscience, Women Against the Ordination of Women, the Church Union and the Association for the Apostolic Ministry discussed tactics, but there was no prompt declared corporate strategy in reaction to the decision.

It has been said of Dr Pusey that he 'had no wish to encourage party-spirit. He believed in the Catholic nature of the Church of England and it was this he was concerned to defend and make manifest.'[3] If this is an attitude to be applauded, what is the distinctive Catholic nature of the Church of England which Anglican Catholics are called upon to defend, and where lies their particular calling within a comprehensive Anglican Church?

There are those who would argue that the Anglican way is both Catholic and Evangelical. That Anglicans 'are called to be wholly Evangelical and wholly Catholic all the time. Not Catholic in order and Evangelical in doctrine, or some other half-and-half combination; and not symbiosis – Catholic and Evangelical living off each other; but wholly Evangelical and wholly Catholic in all that we are and do.'[4]

If this is so, the special contribution of Anglican Catholics is their sense of the corporateness and the importance in the economy of God of the Church, the distinctive role of its clergy and the centrality and significance of the sacraments, but all this and associated matters viewed and practiced with due regard for tradition, the exercise of reason and, supremely, under the overriding authority of Scripture. The most outstanding and authentic historical expressions of Anglican Catholicism have been informed and guided by a deep concern for the fundamental doctrinal truths of the Christian faith and

---

[3] Peter G. Cobb, 'Leader of the Anglo-Catholics?', in Perry Butler, *Pusey Rediscovered* (London, 1983), p.349.

[4] Peter Toon, 'Anglicanism in Popish Dress', in Geoffrey Rowell (Ed.), *Tradition Renewed*, p.173.

by a spirit of evangelism. The strength of Anglican Catholicism at its best lies in its ability to integrate profound liturgical, doctrinal and social beliefs and practices into a full and rounded life of Christian commitment within the context of the rich and secure fellowship and boundless resources of a well ordered and authoritative 'holy Catholic Church'.

A useful account though not very exciting!

Bibliography

The place of publication is London (or unknown) unless otherwise stated.

Abbey, Charles J. and Overton, John H., *The English Church in the Eighteenth Century*, 2 vols. (1878).

Addleshaw, G.W.O., *The High Church Tradition* (1941).

Allchin, A.M., *The Silent Rebellion: Anglican religious communities, 1845–1900* (1958).

Anglican - Roman Catholic International Commission, The Final Report (1982).

Anson, Peter F., *The Call of the Cloister. Religious Communities and Kindred Bodies in the Anglican Communion* (1955).

Arnold, T., 'The Oxford Malignants', *Edinburgh Review* 63 (1836), pp. 225-239.

Aveling, J.C.H., *The Handle and the Axe. The Catholic Recusants in England from Reformation to Emancipation* (1976).

Baker, W.J., 'The Attitudes of English Churchmen, 1800–1850, towards the Reformation' (Cambridge University Ph.D., 1966).

Battiscombe, Georgina, *John Keble:. A Study in Limitations* (1963).

Bebbington, D.W., *Evangelicalism. A History from the 1730s to the 1980s* (1989).

Bennett, G.V., *The Tory Crisis in Church and State 1688–1730. The career of Francis Atterbury Bishop of Rochester* (Oxford, 1975).

Bentley, J. *Ritualism and Politics in Victorian England: the Attempt to Legislate for Belief* (Oxford, 1978).

Bindoff, S.T., *Tudor England* (Harmondsworth, 1950).

Booth, C., *Life and Labour of the People in London,* third series, *Religious Influences* (1902).

Bossy, John, *The English Catholic Community 1570–1850* (1975).

Brilioth, Yngve, *The Anglican Revival: Studies in the Oxford Movement* (1925; repr. 1933).

371

Browning, W.R.F. (Ed.), *The Anglican Synthesis: Essays by Catholics and Evangelicals* (Derby, 1964).

Buchanan, C.O., Mascall, E.L., Packer, J.I., The Bishop of Willesden, *Growing Into Union: Proposals for Forming a United Church* (1970).

Burgon, J.W., *Lives of Twelve Good Men* (1891).

Butler, Perry (Ed.), *Pusey Rediscovered* (1983).

Carpenter, S.C., *Winnington-Ingram: The Biography of Arthur Foley Winnington-Ingram Bishop of London 1901–1939* (1948).

Carpenter, S.C., *Eighteenth Century Church and People* (1959).

Carpenter, S.C., *Church and People, 1789–1889: A History of the Church of England from William Wilberforce to 'Lux Mundi'* (1933).

Chadwick, Owen, (Ed.), *The Mind of the Oxford Movement* (1960).

Chadwick, Owen, *The Victorian Church*, 2 vols. (1966, 1970).

Chadwick, Owen, *Michael Ramsey. A Life* (Oxford, 1990).

Christensen, T., *Origin and History of Christian Socialism 1848–1854* (1962).

Church, R.W., *The Oxford Movement 1833–1845* (1891; 1892).

Churton, E., *Memoir of Joshua Watson*, 2 vols. (Oxford, 1861).

Clarke, C.P.S., *The Oxford Movement and After* (1932).

Clarke, W.K. Lowther, *Eighteenth Century Piety* (1944).

Clegg, H., 'Evangelicals and Tractarians. An investigation of the connecting links between the two movements in the Church of England in the earlier part of the last century and a consideration of how, and how far, these links came to be broken' (Bristol University M.A., 1965).

Cockshut, A.O.J. (Ed.), *Religious Controversies of the Nineteenth Century* (1966).

Coleridge, Sir J.T., *A Memoir of the Rev. John Keble M.A. Late vicar of Hursley* (Oxford and London, 1874).

Collinson, Patrick, *The Elizabethan Puritan Movement* (1967).

Collinson, Patrick, *Archbishop Grindal 1519–1583. The Struggle for a Reformed Church* (1979).

Collinson, Patrick, *The Religion of Protestants. The Church in English Society 1559–1625* (Oxford, 1982).

Conversations between the Church of England and the Methodist Church: A Report (1963).

Cornish, F. Warre, *The English Church in the Nineteenth Century*, 2 vols. (1910).

Craston, Colin (Chairman, Working Group), *The Charismatic Movement in the Church of England* (1981).

Cross, Claire, *Church and People 1450–1660. The Triumph of the Laity in the English Church* (1976).

Cross, F.L., *The Oxford Movement and the Seventeenth Century* (1933).

Crowther, M.A., *Church Embattled: Religious Controversy in Mid-Victorian England* (1970).

Davies, Horton, *Worship and Theology in England. From Watts and Wesley to Maurice ,1690–1850* (1961).

Davies, Horton, *Worship and Theology in England. From Newman to Martineau, 1850–1900* (1965).

Davies, Horton, *Worship and Theology in England: The Ecumenical Century: 1900–1965* (1965).

Davies, Julian, *The Caroline Captivity of the Church. Charles I and the Remoulding of Anglicanism 1625–1641* (Oxford, 1992).

Donovan, Marcus, *After the Tractarians* (1933).

Doran, Susan and Durston, Christopher, *Princes, Pastors and People. The Church and Religion in England 1529–1689* (1991).

Edwards, David L.(Ed.), *The Honest to God Debate* (1963).

Edwards, David L., *Leaders of the Church of England 1828–1978* (1978).

Edwards, David L., *Christian England,* 3 vols. (1981, 1983, 1984).

Elliott-Binns, L.E., *Religion in the Victorian Era* (1936).

Ellsworth, L.E., *Charles Lowder and the Ritualist Movement* (1982).

Every, George, *The High Church Party 1688–1718* (1956).

Faber, Geoffrey, *Oxford Apostles. A Character Study of the Oxford Movement* (Harmondsworth, 1954).

Fairbairn, A.M., *Catholicism, Anglican and Roman* (5th ed., 1903).

Fairweather, E.R. (Ed.), *The Oxford Movement* (New York and Oxford, 1964).

Flew, R. Newton and Davies, Rupert E. (Eds.), *The Catholicity of Protestantism* (1950).

Flindall, R.P. (Ed.), *The Church of England 1815–1948. A Documentary History* (1972).

Forrester, David, *Young Dr. Pusey. A Study in Development* (1989).

Frere, W.H., *The English Church in the Reigns of Elizabeth and James I (1558–1625)* (1904).

Gairdner, James, *A History of The English Church in the Sixteenth Century from the Accession of Henry VIII to the Death of Mary* (1903).

Gilbert, Alan D., *Religion and Society In industrial England: Church, Chapel and Social Change 1740–1914* (1976).

Gilbert, Alan D., *The Making of Post-Christian Britain. A History of the Secularization of Modern Society* (1980).

Gilley, Sheridan, *Newman and his Age* (1990).

Gladstone, William Ewart, *Letters on Church and Religion,* 2 vols. (1910).

Gore, Charles (Ed.), *Lux Mundi. A Series of Studies in the Religion of the Incarnation* (1889).

Green, V.H.H., *Religion at Oxford and Cambridge. A History c .1160 – 1960* (1964).

Greenfield, R.H., 'The Attitude of the Tractarians to the Roman Catholic Church 1833–1850'(Oxford University D. Phil., 1956).

Grisewood, H. (Ed.), *The Ideas of the Victorians* (1966).

Gunstone, John, *Pentecostal Anglicans* (1982).

Guy, John, *Tudor England* (Oxford and New York, 1988).

Halévy, E., *A History of the English People in the Nineteenth Century,* 6 vols. (1912 – ; ET ²1949–).

Haller, William, *Liberty and Reformation in the Puritan Revolution* (New York and London, 1955).

Hart, A. Tindal, *The Life and Times of John Sharp Archbishop of York* (1949).

Harvey, G.L.H.(Ed.), *The Church and the Twentieth Century* (1936).

Hastings, Adrian, *A History of English Christianity 1920–1985* (1986).

Hebert, A.G., *Liturgy and Society* (1935).

Hebert, A.G., *Fundamentalism and the Church of God* (1957).

Herring, George William, 'Tractarianism to Ritualism: A Study of some aspects of Tractarianism outside Oxford, from the time of Newman's conversion in 1845, until the first ritual commission in 1867' (Oxford University D. Phil., 1984).

Hill, Christopher, *The Century of Revolution 1603–1714* (1961; repr. 1978).

Hirst, Derek, *Authority and Conflict. England 1603–1658* (1986).

Hooker, Richard, *Treatise on the Laws of Ecclesiastical Polity,* 5 Books (1594, 1597).

Hutton, William Holden, *William Laud* (1895).

Hutton, William Holden, *The English Church from the Accession of Charles I to the Death of Anne (1625–1714)* (1903).

Ideas and Beliefs of the Victorians: An Historical Revaluation of the Victorian Age (1950).

Iremonger, F.A., *Men and Movements in the Church: A Series of Interviews* (1928).

Iremonger. F.A., *William Temple Archbishop of Canterbury: His Life and Letters* (1948).

Jasper, Ronald C.D., *George Bell: Bishop of Chichester* (Oxford, 1967).

Jay, Elizabeth (Ed.), *The Evangelical and Oxford Movements* (Cambridge, 1983).

Kent, John H.S., *Holding the Fort: Studies in Victorian Revivalism* (1978).

Kent, John H.S., *The End of the Line? The Development of Christian Theology in the Last Two Centuries* (1978).

Kent, John H.S., *The Unacceptable Face. The Modern Church in the Eyes of the Historian* (1987).

Ker, Ian, *John Henry Newman. A Biography* (Oxford, 1990).

Knappen, M.M., *Tudor Puritanism* (1939; repr. Gloucester, Mass, 1963).

Knox, E.A., *The Tractarian Movement 1833–1845* (1933).

Leech, Kenneth and Williams, Rowan (Eds.), *Essays Catholic and Radical* (1983).

Leslie, Shane, *The Oxford Movement* (1933).

Liddon, Henry Parry, *The Life of Edward Bouverie Pusey*, 4 vols. (1893).

Loades, David, *Revolution in Religion: The English Reformation 1530–1570* (Cardiff, 1992).

Lock, Walter, *John Keble. A Biography* (1893).

Lossky, Nicholas, *Lancelot Andrewes the Preacher (1555–1626). The Origins of the Mystical Theology of the Church of England* (Oxford, 1991).

MacCulloch, Diarmaid, *The Later Reformation in England 1547-1603* (1990).

MacMath, Fiona (Ed.), *The Faith of Samuel Johnson. An anthology of his spiritual and moral writings and conversations* (1990).

Marrin, Albert, *The Last Crusade. The Church of England in the First World War* (Durham, North Carolina, 1974).

Mascall, E.L., *The Secularisation of Christianity: An Analysis and a Critique* (1965).

Mather, F.C. 'High Churchmanship Reconsidered: Some Variations in Anglican Public Worship 1714–1830', *Journal of Ecclesiastical History* 36.2, April 1985, pp. 255-283.

Mather, J.C., *High Church Prophet. Bishop Samuel Horsley (1733–1806) and the Caroline Tradition in the later Georgian Church* (Oxford, 1992).

Maycock, A.L., *Nicholas Ferrar of Little Gidding* (1938).

McAdoo, H.R., *The Spirit of Anglicanism* (1965).

McGrath, Patrick, *Papists and Puritans under Elizabeth I* (1967).

More, Paul Elmer and Cross, Frank Leslie (Compilers and Eds.), *Anglicanism. The Thought and Practice of the Church of England Illustrated from the Religious Literature of the Seventeenth Century* (1935).

Morgan, E.R. (Ed.), *Essays, Catholic and Missionary* (1928).

Morgan, Robert (Ed.), *The Religion of the Incarnation. Anglican Essays in Commemoration of Lux Mundi* (Bristol, 1989).

Murray, Nancy, 'The Influence of the French Revolution on the Church of England and its Rivals, 1789–1802' (Oxford University D.Phil., 1975).

Neill, Stephen, *Anglicanism* (Harmondsworth, 1958).

Neill, Stephen, *A History of Christian Missions* (Harmondsworth, 1964).

Neill, Stephen, *The Interpretation of the New Testament 1861–1961* (Oxford, 1964).

Newman, John Henry, *Apologia Pro Vita Sua: Being a History of his Religious Opinions* (Everyman edition, 1912; repr. 1946).

Newsome, David, *The Parting of Friends: a study of the Wilberforces and Henry Manning* (1960).

Nockles, Peter, 'Continuity and Change in Anglican High Churchmanship 1792–1850' (Oxford University D. Phil., 1982).

Norman, E.R., *Church and Society in England, 1770–1970: a historical study* (1976).

Oddie, William, *The Crockford's File. Gareth Bennett and the Death of the Anglican Mind* (1989).

Ollard, S.L. *A Short History of the Oxford Movement* (1915; repr. 1933).

Ollard, S.L. and Mackay, H.F.B., *The Anglo-Catholic Revival. Some Persons and Principles* (1925).

Overton, John H., *Life in the English Church (1600–1714)* (1885).

Overton, John H., *The English Church in the Nineteenth Century 1800–1833* (1894).

Packer, J.I. (Ed.), *All in Each Place: Towards Reunion in England: Ten Anglican Essays with some Free Church Comments* (1965).

Packer, J.I., *Among God's Giants. The Puritan Vision of the Christian Life* (Eastbourne, 1991).

Packer, John W., *The Transformation of Anglicanism 1643–1660, with special reference to Henry Hammond* (Manchester, 1969).

Paget, Francis, *An Introduction to the Fifth Book of Hooker's Treatise of the Laws of Ecclesiastical Polity* (Oxford, 1899).

Park, J.A., *Memoir of the late William Stevens* (1859).

Peart-Binns, John S., *Ambrose Reeves* (1973).

Peart-Binns, John S., *Wand of London* (1987).

Peart-Binns, John S., *Graham Leonard. Bishop of London* (1988).

Plumptre, E.H., *The Life of Thomas Ken Bishop of Bath and Wells*, 2 vols. (1890).

Powicke, Maurice, *The Reformation in England* (1941).

Prestige, G.L., *The Life of Charles Gore. A Great Englishman* (1935).

Ramsey, Arthur Michael, *The Gospel and the Catholic Church* (1936).

Ramsey, Arthur Michael, *From Gore to Temple. The Development of Anglican Theology between Lux Mundi and the Second World War, 1889–1939* (1960).

Ramsey, Arthur Michael, *Image Old and New* (1963).

Reardon, Bernard M.G., *Religious Thought in the Victorian Age. A Survey from Coleridge to Gore* (1971).

Reckitt, Maurice, *Maurice to Temple: A Century of the Social Movement in the Church of England* (1947).

Rice, Hugh A.L., *Thomas Ken Bishop and Non-Juror* (1958).

Rigg, James H., *Oxford High Anglicanism and its Chief Leaders* (1895).

Robinson, John A.T., *Honest to God* (1963).

Rowell, Geoffrey, *The Vision Glorious. Themes and Personalities of the Catholic Revival in Anglicanism* (Oxford, 1983).

Rowell, Geoffrey (Ed.), *Tradition Renewed: the Oxford Movement Conference Papers* (1986).

Rowlands, John Henry Lewis, *Church, State and Society. The Attitudes of John Keble, Richard Hurrell Froude and John Henry Newman, 1827-1845* (Worthing, 1989).

Rupp, E.G., *Religion in England 1688–1791* (Oxford, 1986).

Russell, Conrad, *The Crisis of Parliaments. English History 1509–1660* (Oxford, 1971).

Russell, Conrad, *The Causes of the English Civil War* (Oxford, 1990).

Russell, G.W.E., *Arthur Stanton. A Memoir* (1917).

Sandhurst, B.G., *How Heathen is Britain?* (1946).

Selwyn, E.G. (Ed)., *Essays Catholic and Critical* (1926).

Semmel, Bernard, *The Methodist Revolution* (1973).

Sheridan, T.L., 'Newman and justification: A Study in the Development of a Theology' (Institut Catholique de Paris Th.D., 1965).

Smith, B.A., *Dean Church. The Anglican Response to Newman* (1958).

Smyth, C.H., *Cyril Foster Garbett: Archbishop of York* (1959).

Spurr, John, *The Restoration Church of England 1646–1689* (New Haven and London, 1991).

Stephen, James, *Essays in Ecclesiastical Biography* (1860).

Stephens, W.R.W., *The Life and Letters of Walter Farquhar Hook*, 2 vols. (1880).

Stevenson, G., *Edward Stuart Talbot, 1844–1934* (1936).

Stoughton, J., *Religion in England 1800–1850*, 2 vols. (1884).

Streeter, B.H. (Ed.), *Foundations: A Statement of Christian Belief in Terms of Modern Thought: By Seven Oxford Men* (1912).

Sykes, Norman, *Church and State in England in the Eighteenth Century* (Cambridge, 1934).

Symondson, A. (Ed.), *The Victorian Crisis of Faith* (1970).

Thompson, E.P., *The Making of the English Working Class* (Harmondsworth, 1968).

Towards the Conversion of England (1945).

Trench, Maria, *Charles Lowder. A Biography* (1881).

Trevor-Roper, H.R., *Archbishop Laud 1573–1645*, 2nd ed. (1965).

Trevor-Roper, H.R., *Catholics, Anglicans and Puritans. Seventeeth-century essays* (1987).

Troeltsch, E., *The Social Teaching of the Christian Churches* (1912; ET 1931).

Tulloch, John, *Movements of Religious Thought in Britain during the Nineteenth Century* (1885).

Tyerman, L., *The Oxford Methodists* (1873).

Varley, E.A., *The Last of the Prince Bishops. William Van Mildert and the High Church Movement of the early nineteenth century* (Cambridge, 1992).

Vidler, A.R. (Ed.), *Soundings* (Cambridge, 1962).

Voll, D., *Catholic Evangelicalism* (1962; ET 1963).

Walsh, Walter, *The Secret History of the Oxford Movement* (1898).

Walton, I., *Lives* (ed., Oxford, 1966).

Wand, J.W.C. (Ed.), *The Anglican Communion. A Survey* (1948).

Wand, J.W.C. (Ed.), *Recovery Starts Within. The Book of the Mission to London 1949* (1950).

Wand, J.W.C., *The High Church Schism. Four Lectures on the Non-Jurors* (1951).

Wand, J.W.C., *Changeful Page. The Autobiography of William Wand formerly Bishop of London* (1965).

Ward, Maisie, *Young Mr. Newman* (1948).

Ward, W.R., *Religion and Society in England 1790–1850* (1972).

Watts, Michael, *The Dissenters. From the Reformation to the French Revolution* (Oxford, 1978).

Waugh, E., *Brideshead Revisited* (1945).

Weber, Max, *The Protestant Ethic and the Spirit of Capitalism* (1904–05; ET 1930, 2nd ed., 1976).

Webster, A.B., *Joshua Watson: the Story of a Layman, 1771–1855* (1954).

Welsby, Paul A., *Lancelot Andrewes 1555–1626* (1964).

Welsby, Paul A., *A History of the Church of England 1945–1980* (Oxford, 1984).

Wickham-Legg, J., *English Church Life from the Restoration to the Tractarian Movement* (1914).

Wilkinson, Alan, *The Church of England and the First World War* (1978).

Wilkinson, Alan, *Dissent or Conform? War, Peace and the English Churches 1900–1945* (1986).

Wilkinson, John (Ed.), *Catholic Anglicans Today* (1968).

Willey, Basil, *Seventeenth Century Background* (1950).

Williams, N.P. and Harris C. (Eds.), *Northern Catholicism* (1933).

Williamson, James A., *The Tudor Age* (1979).

Wilson, Alan, 'The Authority of Church and Party among London Anglo-Catholics, 1880–1914, with special reference to the Church crisis, 1898–1904' (Oxford University D.Phil., 1988).

Wilson, George Herbert, *The History of the Universities' Mission to Central Africa* (1936).

Woods, Edward and MacNutt, Frederick B., *Theodore, Bishop of Winchester: Pastor, Prophet, Pilgrim: A Memoir of Frank Theodore Woods, D.D., 1874–1932* (1933).

Index of Authors

379

Index of Places

In general, pre-1972 County names are used. But for ease of reference, 'London' includes districts now in the Metropolis, though formerly in the Home Counties of Essex, Kent, Middlesex or Surrey.

Index of Persons

Unless otherwise indicated, tenure of last post mentioned lasted until death.

389

General Index

Dates when societies, journals, etc, were founded have been added.